Migration in Political Theory

Written by an international team of leading political and legal theory scholars whose writings have contributed to shaping the field, *Migration in Political Theory* presents seminal new work on the ethics of movement and membership.

The volume addresses challenging and under-researched themes on the subject of migration. It debates the question of whether we ought to recognize a human right to immigrate, and whether it might be legitimate to restrict emigration. The authors critically examine criteria for selecting would-be migrants, and for acquiring citizenship. They discuss tensions between the claims of immigrants and existing residents, and tackle questions of migrant worker exploitation and responsibility for refugees. The book illustrates the importance of drawing on the tools of political theory to clarify, criticize, and challenge the current terms of the migration debate.

Sarah Fine is a Senior Lecturer in Philosophy at King's College London. She was previously a Research Fellow at Corpus Christi College, Cambridge. She specialises in issues relating to migration and citizenship. Her forthcoming book, *Immigration and the Right to Exclude* (OUP), sets out to challenge the idea that the state has a moral right to exclude would-be immigrants. Her publications include 'Freedom of Association Is Not the Answer' in *Ethics*.

Lea Ypi is a Professor in Political Theory at the London School of Economics and Political Science and Adjunct Associate Professor of Philosophy at the Research School of Social Sciences, Australian National University. She is the author of *Global Justice and Avant-Garde Political Agency* (Oxford University Press 2012), *The Meaning of Partisanship*, (OUP 2016, with Jonathan White) and the co-editor of *Kant and Colonialism* (OUP 2014, with Katrin Flikschuh).

Migration in Political Theory

The Ethics of Movement and Membership

Edited by
Sarah Fine and Lea Ypi

OXFORD
UNIVERSITY PRESS

OXFORD
UNIVERSITY PRESS

Great Clarendon Street, Oxford, OX2 6DP,
United Kingdom

Oxford University Press is a department of the University of Oxford.
It furthers the University's objective of excellence in research, scholarship,
and education by publishing worldwide. Oxford is a registered trade mark of
Oxford University Press in the UK and in certain other countries

First Edition published in 2016
First published in paperback 2019

Published in the United States of America by Oxford University Press
198 Madison Avenue, New York, NY 10016, United States of America

British Library Cataloguing in Publication Data
Data available

Library of Congress Cataloging in Publication Data
Data available

ISBN 978–0–19–967660–6 (Hbk.)
ISBN 978–0–19–884308–5 (Pbk.)

For Doli Ypi, Lani Ypi, Doreen Samuels, and Elaine Charlton
With Love

Acknowledgments

A number of years ago, we met in Oxford to discuss the need for a new, major collection on the subject of migration in political theory, featuring leading scholars in the field. To that end, we planned a conference, "Migration in Legal and Political Theory: Remaining Challenges," which took place in Cambridge in October 2011. We would like to thank the Centre for Research in the Arts, Social Sciences, and Humanities (CRASSH) at the University of Cambridge, for its generous financial and administrative support of the conference. Special thanks to Helga Brandt at CRASSH for all her excellent work in helping to make the conference a great success. Thanks are also due to the London School of Economics and Political Science for its invaluable financial support.

The majority of the contributors to this book presented their papers at that conference, with later contributions from Sarah Song and Ayelet Shachar. Phillip Cole and Linda Bosniak gave excellent presentations at the conference, but did not contribute their papers to the book.

We thank the terrific contributors for their hard work and patience throughout the process. We would also like to extend our thanks to Dominic Byatt, Sarah Parker, Olivia Wells, and the rest of the team at Oxford University Press.

All of the papers in this book are original contributions published here for the first time, with the exception of Joseph Carens' chapter, parts of which appear in a similar form in his book, *The Ethics of Immigration* (Oxford University Press, 2013).

Finally, we would like to thank our dear families, especially Jonathan, Arbien, Duncan, Juliet, and Alice. The book is dedicated to Lea's mother, Doli, and brother, Lani, and to Sarah's mother, Doreen, and grandmother, Elaine.

Contents

Contents

Part III. Migration and Membership

List of Contributors

Arash Abizadeh, Associate Professor, Department of Political Science, McGill University

Joseph H. Carens, Professor of Political Science, University of Toronto

Sarah Fine, Lecturer in Philosophy, King's College London

Chandran Kukathas, Chair in Political Theory, London School of Economics and Political Science

David Miller, Official Fellow and Professor of Political Theory, Nuffield College, Oxford

Kieran Oberman, Chancellor's Fellow in Politics, University of Edinburgh

David Owen, Professor of Social and Political Philosophy, University of Southampton

Ayelet Shachar, Professor of Law and Political Science and Canada Research Chair in Citizenship and Multiculturalism, University of Toronto

Sarah Song, Professor of Law and Associate Professor of Political Science, University of California, Berkeley

Anna Stilz, Associate Professor of Politics, Princeton University

Christopher Heath Wellman, Chair and Professor of Philosophy, Washington University in St. Louis

Lea Ypi, Associate Professor in Political Theory, London School of Economics and Political Science

1

The Ethics of Movement and Membership

An Introduction

Sarah Fine and Lea Ypi

1.1 Migration and Political Theory

Suppose that you wish to move to the United Kingdom from another country. You are not currently a British citizen, you are not in British territory, and you hope to enter and settle via authorized channels. The first question is whether you will be granted leave to enter the UK. Your prospects of success will depend on a combination of factors about you, many of which are outside of your control. For example, which passports, if any, do you hold? Why are you leaving the country in which you are resident? What are your educational and professional qualifications? What are your occupational skills? Do you have family members in the UK? Then there is the question of whether you will be granted leave to remain in the UK. Again, this may depend on a combination of factors, including your current earnings, job prospects, how long you have been resident in the country, and your knowledge of "Language and Life in the UK."[1]

Some people, such as citizens of European Union member states, face almost no barriers to entering and settling lawfully in the UK. Others encounter a long, difficult, and costly process. Many, such as unskilled workers from outside the European Union, have little or no hope of obtaining the requisite authorization. The rules governing entry and settlement continue to change

---

[1] This is measured by a test. See the details here: <https://www.gov.uk/life-in-the-uk-test/overview>.

with successive governments, as they attempt to control immigration in line with their own commitments, promises, and priorities.

Beneath these practices lies a range of key assumptions informing much current political thinking about migration, as well as countless migration and naturalization policies. The core assumption is that states have various rights to control the movement of people across their borders, and the settlement of people in their territories. For the most part, there is a sense that states may act primarily in line with their own preferences, with just a few constraints. There certainly is nothing like an internationally recognized human right to immigrate (to accompany the existing human rights to freedom of movement within state borders, and to leave any country, and for citizens to return to their own state). It is assumed that citizenship comes with a selection of rights and privileges (as well as obligations), that states may and even should favor their own citizens (above resident noncitizens and noncitizens outside state borders) across a number of dimensions, and that states should have considerable discretion over their citizenship policies. Another crucial assumption is that states should be permitted to select between would-be immigrants on a range of grounds, such as on the basis of their occupational skills. Furthermore, it is assumed that we can distinguish between refugees and other migrants, and that this distinction is relevant for questions of admission, settlement, and membership.

This book sets out to highlight and scrutinize these central, prevalent assumptions about migration. Each of the chapters challenges some fundamental presuppositions about the ethics of movement and membership, and many of them call into question the very legitimacy of basic, near universal migration practices and policies. They shine a light on some of the dark corners of our political world, and illuminate the many inconsistencies and injustices of our existing institutions and practices. Despite significant points of disagreement among the authors, all of them highlight the urgent need to use the tools of political theory for clarifying, criticizing, and challenging the current terms of the migration debate.

1.2 Outline of the Book

The book is divided into three parts. The chapters in Part I address cores issues of entry and exit, exploring and disagreeing about the nature, justification, and scope of the right to freedom of movement. At present, it is widely believed that people should have the right to move freely within the borders of any state, and the right to emigrate from any state, but not that people should have the right to immigrate to any state. According to the conventional approach, then, there is an asymmetry between exit and entry.[2] This approach is exemplified in the Universal Declaration of Human Rights, Article 13 of which states that "(1) Everyone has the right to freedom of movement and residence within the borders of each state" and "(2) Everyone has the right to leave any country, including his own, and to return to his country."

Why not add the right to immigrate to that list? The first two chapters in the present volume engage explicitly with this question, and with each other, and come down on opposite sides of the debate. Kieran Oberman's chapter offers one of the most clearly articulated and robust arguments in defense of a moral human right to immigrate. Such a right, he contends, protects a set of essential interests. It is not absolute, as it may be restricted under a limited set of circumstances. Beyond that limited set of circumstances, though, Oberman argues that restrictions on immigration are unjust.

David Miller, by contrast, remains unconvinced. He introduces three key strategies that might be employed by advocates of a moral human right to immigrate: the direct strategy, the instrumental strategy, and the cantilever strategy. He examines each of these approaches and argues that they all fail in their different ways. The direct strategy does not identify interests that would ground a human right, while the instrumental arguments do not show that such a right is required in support of other already recognized human rights. Finally, the cantilever arguments, which seek to show that "it is inconsistent to recognize a domestic right of free movement while denying the corresponding international right," do not establish that the same considerations and conditions apply in the domestic and inter-national contexts.

The next two chapters continue with the theme of freedom of movement, turning our attention to the issue of emigration and the right to exit a state, which has only recently begun to attract attention in the political theory literature on migration. Is there a moral asymmetry between entry and exit, as current practice (which supports a human right to exit but no such right to enter) seems to indicate? If the idea of moral asymmetry between the two is troubling, perhaps symmetry ought to be sought by defending restrictions on emigration and the freedom to exit, rather than by defending a human right to enter and challenging the legitimacy of immigration restrictions.[3] In his chapter, Christopher Heath Wellman makes the case for the conventional view that there is indeed a moral asymmetry between immigration and

---

[2] See Phillip Cole, *Philosophies of Exclusion: Liberal Political Theory and Immigration*, pp. 43–4.
[3] See Lea Ypi, "Justice in Migration: A Closed Borders Utopia," *The Journal of Political Philosophy*, 16:4 (2008), 391–418.

emigration: he denies that there is anything like a right to immigrate, but supports a right to emigrate. However, in the course of his chapter, Wellman concedes that his argument leads to a "highly revisionist" conclusion regarding the right to *domestic* freedom of movement, namely that states might place severe restrictions on internal freedom of movement without violating human rights. Stilz's argument is revisionist too, but with respect to common views about the right to leave. She subjects the nature and scope of this right to careful analysis and contends that it might be justifiable for states to impose some regulations on the exit of citizens, where these regulations are justified with reference to the obligations of distributive justice between fellow citizens.

While Stilz's chapter pushes the unconventional line that obligations of justice between compatriots might be invoked in support of regulations on exit, Arash Abizadeh opens Part II with a challenge to the more conventional view that special obligations of justice between compatriots might be invoked in support of immigration restrictions. In this second part of the book, the chapters all take up the themes of equality and justice. Abizadeh grants the premise that special obligations are compatible with treating all people as equals, and that there may be special obligations between compatriots, but he challenges the notion that these special obligations serve to justify immigration restrictions. His argument proceeds from a distinction he draws between additive and prioritizing special obligations. He concludes that all the familiar arguments available for the justification of special obligations succeed at most in showing that compatriots have additional duties to each other, but fail to undermine the justice-based case for more open borders.

Core assumptions concerning the ideal of equality that are at the heart of Abizadeh's argument also play a central role in Sarah Fine's contribution to the volume. Her chapter develops a critique of arguments that defend the state's right to restrict immigration while denying the permissibility of discriminating between prospective immigrants on grounds of race or ethnicity. Focusing on racism and ethnic discrimination—a topic rarely discussed in the political theory debates on migration, despite its centrality in popular discourse—Fine illustrates the inconsistencies and challenges that arise for those who argue that some immigration restrictions are defensible whilst denying that such restrictions may be informed by racial or ethnic concerns. As she illustrates, a more careful historical analysis of the emergence of immigration restrictions shows how important colonialism, empire, racism, and ethnic discrimination have been in shaping both public attitudes and the institutional contours of the state's right to exclude. Therefore, she suggests, any attempt to disentangle the right to restrict immigration from considerations of ethnicity and race not only ought to acknowledge the gravity of the problem and offer prescriptions for how to avoid it, but also should be able to *diagnose* racism in immigration restrictions as a problem. This places issues of migration side by side with issues of rectification for historical injustice, a challenge that has not yet received sufficient consideration in the literature.

The distance between theoretical discussions of migration and the real world of immigration policy is also highlighted in Ayelet Shachar's pioneering chapter. Shachar draws attention to the ways in which states continue to differentiate between prospective entrants. While democratic states would deny that they discriminate between would-be immigrants on grounds of ethnicity and race, they make no secret of which immigrants are "wanted and welcome." From artists to academics, from elite athletes to IT innovators, the selection of immigrants by "merit" stands as a useful reminder of the tacit (or not so tacit) assumptions governing the criteria through which states seek to shape and police their civic and territorial borders. Measures designed to include the "best and brightest" and to exclude those who are unwanted raise important questions of fairness, both for the receiving and sending countries, and with respect to the treatments of migrants themselves. These practices also force us to confront challenging questions about the future of democratic equality, in a context that seems to reflect "a vision of an ideal citizen who is creative and contributory, who has been able to maximize her talent and turn herself into a 'net benefit'" for the country.

Problems of fairness are also central to Lea Ypi's chapter. Like Shachar, Ypi focuses on the phenomenon of labor migration, but she expands the scope of the analysis to examine the migration of low-skilled workers, and in particular the ethics of temporary workers' programs. Her chapter explores the charge of exploitation that is often leveled at such policies. She examines three different accounts of what is exploitative about guestworker programs: a domination theory, a sufficientarian theory, and an egalitarian theory. Identifying difficulties with all three theories, she suggests an alternative framework for analyzing the exploitation of guestworkers, where the issue of justice in migration is set in the context of wider debates concerning the exploitation of workers in general. Her contribution, like Shachar's, is an invitation to analyze dilemmas of labor migration against the background of wider global economic patterns and the constraints these place on the democratic ideals of equality.

Issues concerning equality and justice also inform the contributions in Part III, which all focus on the ethics of membership. Here, once again, the authors interrogate conventional assumptions and widespread practices, and argue in favor of some decidedly revisionist conclusions. Joseph H. Carens defends the practice of assigning citizenship at birth, against recent popular liberal critiques of these practices. Whereas others have rejected birthright citizenship because of the perceived tension between this way of assigning citizenship and liberal democratic ideals, Carens argues that the real problem is not birthright citizenship itself, but rather that people are not at liberty to change their citizenship by migrating and acquiring membership elsewhere. In fact, properly understood, liberal democratic ideals require states to grant citizenship at birth, not just to children of citizens but also to the children of settled immigrants.

In making this argument, Carens acknowledges the importance of the relationship between civic membership and territorial presence, an issue that is explored in more detail in Sarah Song's innovative contribution to the volume. Song's chapter seeks to explore the significance of territorial presence by examining the three different approaches to this issue—those which focus on principles of affiliation, fair play, and coercion—and considering how these account for the obligations between different categories of territorial insiders. In contrast to Carens' argument about the connection between citizenship status and territorial presence, Song maintains that there is a clear case for disaggregating the rights and obligations of different insiders.

Questions of territorial presence are particularly pressing in the case of refugees. Refugees raise distinctive, urgent ethical dilemmas regarding norms of admission and criteria for acquiring membership rights. These issues form the focus for the final two chapters of the book. David Owen and Chandran Kukathas both concentrate on the question of who is a refugee, on the limitations of the current international refugee regime, and on the distribution of responsibilities for refugees. But whereas Owen offers novel proposals for improving the international response and clearly defining political responsibilities with respect to refugees, Kukathas calls into question the very distinction between refugees and other migrants. This challenge, for Kukathas, is part of a more radical critique of migration restrictions and border controls. Therefore, while Owen recognizes some minimal conditions of legitimacy in the international order of states and suggests that responsibilities for refugees should be seen as a mechanism of legitimacy repair, Kukathas argues that the international regime itself is responsible for worsening the plight of people fleeing desperate conditions: it increases obstacles on their road to membership and merely serves the interests of powerful states.

These chapters represent a significant contribution to the emerging field of the ethics of movement and membership, at a time when migration questions have acquired such political weight and urgency. Of course, there are numerous topics and questions of great importance and interest that we have not been able to cover in any length, but the hope is that the essays in this volume will generate further debate on a wider range of migration-related subjects. For example, the debates here about migration and human rights, and about the future of democratic citizenship in the context of exclusionary migration policies, lay the foundations for a detailed examination of the democratic and human rights implications of the practices of detention and deportation.[4] The discussion of exploitative and discriminatory migration policies should prompt us to think more about issues related to sex and gender (such as the ways in which different migration policies serve to disadvantage women, in particular).[5] The discussion of migration restrictions and obligations of social justice may help us to think more about questions related to cultural diversity and social cohesion.[6] And the discussion about the refugees regime and the definition of a refugee should aid further analysis of the increasingly pressing issue of ecological "refugees."[7] So this is just part of the conversation and there is much work to be done. This volume is an invitation to think carefully, critically, and creatively about one of the defining issues of our century.

References

Anderson, Bridget, Matthew J. Gibney, and Emanuela Paoletti, "Citizenship, Deportation and the Boundaries of Belonging," *Citizenship Studies* 15:5 (2011), 547–63.

Cole, Phillip, *Philosophies of Exclusion: Liberal Political Theory and Immigration* (Edinburgh: Edinburgh University Press, 2000).

de Shalit, Avner, "Climate Change Refugees, Compensation, and Rectification," *The Monist* 94:3 (2011), 310–28.

Nawyn, Stephanie J., "Gender and Migration: Integrating Feminist Theory into Migration Studies," *Sociology Compass* 4:9 (2010), 749–65.

Silverman, Stephanie, "Detaining Immigrants and Asylum Seekers: A Normative Introduction," *Critical Review of Social and Political Philosophy* 17:5 (2014), 600–17.

van Parijs, Philippe (ed.) *Cultural Diversity versus Economic Solidarity* (De Boeck, 2004).

Ypi, Lea, "Justice in Migration: A Closed Borders Utopia," *The Journal of Political Philosophy* 16:4 (2008), 391–418.

[4] On theorizing detention and deportation, see Stephanie Silverman, "Detaining Immigrants and Asylum Seekers: A Normative Introduction," *Critical Review of Social and Political Philosophy* 17:5 (2014), 600–17, and Bridget Anderson, Matthew J. Gibney, and Emanuela Paoletti, "Citizenship, Deportation and the Boundaries of Belonging," *Citizenship Studies* 15:5 (2011), 547–63.

[5] For further discussion of gender in the context of migration research, see Stephanie J. Nawyn, "Gender and Migration: Integrating Feminist Theory into Migration Studies," *Sociology Compass* 4:9 (2010), 749–65.

[6] On this topic, see Philippe van Parijs (ed.), *Cultural Diversity versus Economic Solidarity* (Brussels: De Boeck, 2004).

[7] See Avner de Shalit, "Climate Change Refugees, Compensation, and Rectification," *The Monist* 94:3 (2011), 310–28.

Part I
Entry and Exit

2

Is There a Human Right to Immigrate?

David Miller

Is there a human right to immigrate? The importance of this question may need no underlining, but just to spell it out briefly: all states in today's world proclaim their right to control their borders, deciding who should be admitted and who should not. Moreover, in many cases this right is coercively enforced, through the familiar apparatus of border control, and the harsh measures that await would-be immigrants if they fail to satisfy the legal requirements for entry. If there were indeed a human right to immigrate, all of this would be unacceptable. States would have to open their borders to all comers unless they could show that there were specific individuals whose admission posed a threat to the human rights of others. So the question I have posed, if answered in the affirmative, would have very radical practical implications. But that is no reason not to explore it. Human rights can make heavy moral demands on us.[1] The fact that acknowledging this right would oblige us to abandon policies that may also serve important ends—if we think that immigration controls are necessary for social cohesion, or preservation of the national culture, or other values—would not be sufficient. We would at the very least have to show that these ends are so essential to human welfare that they can justify overriding a human right. But the issue does not arise unless it can be demonstrated that there is a genuine human right to immigrate. How might this be done?

If we tried to answer our question by consulting any of the standard human rights documents, the answer we would get would be an immediate No. A human right to immigrate means, I assume, a universal right to cross the borders of any state and remain within them for as long as one chooses. As

---

[1] This is true of human rights that have already gained widespread recognition, such as the right to subsistence.

I have just pointed out, to accept such a right would deprive every state of one of the powers it currently prizes, namely the right to decide whom to admit to its territory and on what terms.[2] Not surprisingly, therefore, since the main documents in which human rights are encoded have been drawn up and agreed to by states, or their representatives, this particular right is notable by its absence. The *Universal Declaration of Human Rights* of 1948 asserts, in Article 13, that:

(1) Everyone has the right to freedom of movement and residence within the borders of each State.

(2) Everyone has the right to leave any country, including his own, and to return to his country.

The failure of Article 13 to mention any right to *enter* is mitigated slightly, but only slightly, by Article 14, which states that:

(1) Everyone has the right to seek and to enjoy in other countries asylum from persecution.[3]

The rather lengthier *International Covenant on Civil and Political Rights* of 1966 sets out, in Article 12, essentially the same rights as in Article 13 of the Declaration, only pausing to draw them more narrowly by adding a list of grounds ("national security, public order (*ordre public*), public health or morals or the rights and freedoms of others") on which they may be restricted. The *European Convention for the Protection of Human Rights and Fundamental Freedoms* of 1950 makes no mention of the issue of migration in either direction (though a Protocol added in 1952 closely follows the wording of the *International Covenant*).[4]

This of course does not settle the matter, since it is widely recognized that these formal documents may well not capture all and only those provisions that deserve to be counted as human rights. If we consider the main philosophical treatments of the idea of human rights, however, the purported right to immigrate is rarely discussed. It does not feature, for example, in James Nickel's *Making Sense of Human Rights*, or in the third chapter ("Human Rights") of Allen Buchanan's *Justice, Legitimacy and Self-Determination*.[5] James

---

[2] States may in certain instances decide to relinquish this right, as the European states that have signed up to the Schengen agreement have done. But note that even here the relinquishing is only partial since the EU as a whole imposes tough controls on immigration from outside its boundaries.

[3] Ian Brownlie and Guy S. Goodwin-Gill (eds.), *Basic Documents on Human Rights*, 5th edn (Oxford: Oxford University Press, 2006), p. 26.

[4] Brownlie and Goodwin-Gill, *Basic Documents on Human Rights*, pp. 362, 612–16, 625.

[5] James Nickel, *Making Sense of Human Rights*, 2nd edn (Oxford: Blackwell, 2007); Allen Buchanan, *Justice, Legitimacy and Self-Determination: Moral Foundations for International Law* (Oxford: Oxford University Press, 2004). Buchanan does however mention immigration when discussing "the place of distributive justice in international law." He argues that the struggle for distributive justice often takes place in areas whose connection to standard conceptions of human

Griffin discusses the right to freedom of movement and residence in *On Human Rights*, but only to argue that even in domestic settings there is no such unlimited right.[6] We are more likely to find the right to immigrate defended as part of a more general argument in favor of open borders, and it is in fact tentatively asserted, although only in passing, in at least two of Joseph Carens' articles on immigration.[7] Something closer to a defense can be found in Michael Dummett's *On Immigration and Refugees*, though Dummett draws back from claiming that there is a strong right to immigrate.[8] He does so on the grounds that a genuine, obligation-imposing right must be unconditional, whereas he acknowledges two grounds on which states may justifiably set limits to immigration, one being their people's risk of being "submerged" by immigrants from a different culture, the other being population density. Dummett therefore argues that the right to immigrate can only be a right in the "weaker, conditional sense," amounting to a presumption that one should be allowed to enter unless the receiving state can give specific grounds for refusing entry.[9] However, nearly all accounts of rights are conditional in this sense, since they concede that catastrophic circumstances may arise in which even basic human rights can justifiably be set aside. I think, therefore, that we may count Dummett as a supporter of the human right to immigrate as normally understood.

An open borders view does not of course need to base itself on the proposition that there is a human right to immigrate. It can be defended in other terms—for example, by showing that borders must be open if equality of opportunity is to be realized at global level, or by showing that states lack the authority to exclude immigrants. Nevertheless, given the force of human rights arguments in contemporary political culture, the right in question, if it could be established, would provide the strongest available grounds for removing immigration restrictions. Kieran Oberman's contribution to this volume, which sets out explicitly to defend a human right to immigrate, is therefore a welcome development. Nevertheless I remain skeptical, and will try to show in what follows where Oberman's and other arguments go astray.

rights is unclear or at least indirect, and mentions "the right to immigrate to states that offer greater economic opportunities" as one such area (p. 194).

[6] James Griffin, *On Human Rights* (Oxford: Oxford University Press, 2008), pp. 195–6.

[7] Joseph H. Carens, "Migration and Morality: a liberal egalitarian perspective" in Brian Barry and Robert E. Goodin (eds.), *Free Movement: Ethical Issues in the Transnational Migration of People and of Money* (Hemel Hempstead: Harvester Wheatsheaf, 1992), pp. 27–8; Joseph H. Carens, "A Reply to Meilaender: Reconsidering Open Borders," *International Migration Review* 33 (1999), 1082–97 at 1093–6. Carens defends the right more openly in Joseph H. Carens, *The Ethics of Immigration* (Oxford: Oxford University Press, 2013), ch. 11.

[8] Michael Dummett, *On Immigration and Refugees* (London: Routledge, 2001), ch. 3.

[9] Dummett, *On Immigration and Refugees*, p. 57.

2.1 Clarifying the Human Right to Immigrate

It is important first to clarify what a human right to immigrate would mean. It is to be understood as a universal right held against all states not to prevent those who wish to settle on their territory from doing so. In the background there must be a conception of the rights that someone has as a matter of course merely by virtue of being a resident in the territory in question. This is needed to block the possibility that a state might impose no barriers to entry as such, but immediately consign all the immigrants who arrived to rat-infested dungeons. Clearly this would not count as recognizing a right to immigrate. On the other hand, it is not expected, even by those who favor open borders, that states must immediately extend full citizenship rights to immigrants.[10] The question then is how far immigrants may be burdened, relative to citizens, without violating their proposed human right to immigrate. One way to answer this question is to say that the right to immigrate is fulfilled so long as the *other* human rights of the immigrants are protected in the society they enter. This would rule out the rat-infested dungeons, but leave it somewhat flexible as to how far immigrants are given political rights, extensive rights to welfare, and so forth. Setting the bar fairly low here is intended to be a friendly gesture to those who want to defend the human right to immigrate, since it reduces the justificatory burden they have to bear.

Also friendly is my conception of the right to immigrate as a right not to be prevented from entering, and not as a right to be assisted in traveling to the immigrant's new homeland. In today's world, clearly, a major obstacle to migrating, for many people, is the financial cost of doing so. The arguments used to defend a human right to immigrate (which we will come to shortly) might then seem to entail that receiving states should take positive action to defray these costs. Against this, it could be argued that the burden of assisting migration needs to be shared on some equitable basis between all states, whether or not they are attractive to migrants. To avoid getting into the complexities here, I will interpret the would-be immigrant's human right simply as a right not to be prevented from entering, again making some tacit assumptions about what the "normal" costs of migrating would be.[11]

At the same time, however, the human right to immigrate must be understood to mean the right to migrate to *any* state, not just to one or a few states. It would not be satisfied by a system in which every human being was entered into a lottery whose results gave them the right to move to one country other

[10] See, for example, Joseph H. Carens, "The Rights of Irregular Migrants," *Ethics and International Affairs* 22 (2008), 163–86.

[11] This is to avoid the possibility that a state might claim to recognize a human right to immigrate by granting residence only to those who were willing to pay a very high fee, or by forcing airlines and shipping companies to charge potential immigrants extravagant fares, etc.

than their own, or even by a system that allowed each person to nominate the particular state they would ideally like to join. This underlines the point that the right to immigrate cannot be derived straightforwardly from the right of exit, included as we saw in the UN Declaration. The right to leave one's present country of residence can be satisfied so long as there is at least one other place that one is not prevented from entering. Of course it can be argued that the reasons underlying the right to leave can also be used to justify a universal right to immigrate.[12] Whether that argument holds remains to be seen. The analytical point is that the right to leave one particular state does not entail the right to enter any state of one's choosing. Further work needs to be done to justify the latter right.

With these clarificatory remarks concluded, let me now ask how one might set about justifying a human right to immigrate. As I have observed, this cannot be done by appeal to current international law insofar as it is embodied in the major human rights documents. Instead the justification has to appeal to whatever one takes to ground human rights generally. Before examining these grounds in greater detail, however, it is worth distinguishing three justificatory *strategies* that may be used when one seeks to add a new human right to the established list. This is important, because it is not always clear which strategy is being employed by advocates of a human right to immigrate.

First, there is the *direct* strategy. Here the argument moves directly from the grounding feature to the right. Suppose one thinks, as a general matter, that human rights are justified by showing that they serve basic human interests (perhaps picked out in a certain way). Then the justification offered in support of a human right to immigrate will be that such a right is necessary to advance the interests in question. The right will stand alongside and be justified in the same way as existing rights to bodily integrity, freedom of speech, subsistence, and so forth. Second, there is the *instrumental* strategy. Here the right is justified by showing that its recognition is instrumental to *other* human rights that have already found a place on the canonical list. Unless this new right is recognized, the argument goes, these other rights will not be properly realized, or will be insecure. Thus an instrumental argument for a human right to democracy does not try to show that democratic rights serve their bearers' interests directly, but that they are essential to guarantee other rights such as freedom of speech and subsistence.[13] Third, there is what might be called the

---

[12] This argument is made in Phillip Cole, *Philosophies of Exclusion: Liberal Political Theory and Immigration* (Edinburgh: Edinburgh University Press, 2000), ch. 3. See also Ann Dummett, "The Transnational Migration of People Seen from within a Natural Law Perspective" in Barry and Goodin (eds.), *Free Movement*, pp. 169–80. For further discussion of the right to leave, see the chapters by Anna Stilz and Christopher Heath Wellman in this volume.

[13] For a good example of such an argument, see Thomas Christiano, "An Instrumental Argument for a Human Right to Democracy," *Philosophy and Public Affairs* 39 (2011), 142–76.

cantilever strategy. This involves showing that the new right is a logical extension of human rights that are already recognized. The argument is that there is something irrational or arbitrary about recognizing A as a human right, but not recognizing B. In the case we are examining, arguments which claim that it is arbitrary to assert a right to free movement *within* state boundaries without also asserting a right to free movement *across* them (and hence rights to emigrate and immigrate) will qualify as instances of the cantilever strategy. (It remains a distinct strategy provided "arbitrariness" is not cashed out in terms of the same grounds applying in both domains, in which case it reduces to the direct strategy.) A cantilever argument proper will avoid delving into the grounds on which the right is claimed, and instead focus on the alleged absurdity of recognizing A as a right without at the same time recognizing B.

Of the three strategies for identifying human rights I have distinguished, the direct strategy seems most compelling. The instrumental strategy suffers from the weakness that it rests on an empirical claim about what is necessary for the protection of human rights other than the one at issue; such claims are often contestable. The cantilever strategy faces the difficulty that the assertions it makes about irrationality or arbitrariness may be challenged by those who think the supposed analogy between right A and right B is spurious, or that recognizing B would have (harmful) consequences that recognizing A does not have. Let us begin, therefore, with the direct strategy.

2.2 Direct and Instrumental Justificatory Strategies

How might a direct argument for the human right to immigrate be constructed? It would have to meet three conditions. First, it would need to show that the grounds on which the right is being claimed are sufficiently strong. Suppose, as suggested earlier, that the grounding will take the form of showing that the right is needed to protect certain human interests. We can leave it as an open question for present purposes how these interests are to be understood— whether they are interpreted as "human needs" or "conditions for human agency" or "conditions for human dignity," and so on. All that matters is that the interests should be ones that all human beings share and that they carry enough moral weight to support human rights.[14] Second, it would need to

---

[14] This condition rules out grounding human rights on a strong form of autonomy, which otherwise might be used to justify an expansive right to free movement. Autonomy in this sense, which goes beyond the requirements for human *agency*, is highly esteemed by liberals, but cannot plausibly be represented as an interest shared by all human beings. For further elaboration of this point, see my critical discussion of James Griffin's view in "Personhood versus Human Needs as Grounds for Human Rights" in Roger Crisp (ed.), *Griffin on Human Rights* (Oxford: Oxford University Press, 2014), pp. 152–69.

show that the right was feasible, in the sense that the obligations that would be created by recognizing it were ones that it was possible for other human beings to discharge. How this feasibility condition is to be understood is again something that needs to be left open,[15] since there can be different views about how "realist" or "utopian" our account of human rights should be, but it would not make sense, for instance, to claim that there is a human right to a life entirely free from illness simply on the grounds that people would have an interest in enjoying this. Third, the grounding argument must show that recognizing the candidate right would not interfere with other rights that have already been recognized, or if it would, that the relevant human interests are best served by admitting the new right and retrenching upon others. This, then, is a compatibility requirement. We know that the exercise of some rights we might think of as human rights can impact on others, either by imposing costs or by imposing obligations. An unlimited right of free speech may infringe rights to privacy—so we must either limit the former right by disqualifying speech that consists in revealing information about people that they have a strong interest in remaining private, or we must weaken the right to privacy so that speech does not count as infringing it. Or, another case, we might rule out a very expansive right to education or medical care on the grounds that this would impose excessive obligations on those who would have to provide the necessary resources.[16]

The reason for imposing such a compatibility requirement is that we want to avoid trading human rights off against each other if we possibly can. We cannot avoid all such trade-offs, because unusual circumstances may arise where we have to make a choice between infringing right A and infringing right B.[17] But we want the circumstances to be unusual, otherwise there is a danger that the special mandatory quality of human rights will be dissipated. The idea was invented mainly in order to set strict limits to what states can do to their own populations without attracting moral censure and international condemnation. For this purpose to be achieved, the human rights that we include on our list must serve as trumps in relation to the other policy goals that states may have, such as economic growth or promoting the national

---

[15] For a good discussion of the concept of feasibility in general, see Pablo Gilabert and Holly Lawford-Smith, "Political Feasibility: A Conceptual Exploration," *Political Studies* 60 (2012), 809–25; also Pablo Gilabert, "Feasibility and Socialism," *Journal of Political Philosophy* 19 (2011), 52–63.

[16] I have explored this compatibility requirement more fully in *National Responsibility and Global Justice* (Oxford: Oxford University Press, 2007), ch. 7, and in "Grounding Human Rights," *Critical Review of International Social and Political Philosophy* 15 (2012), 407–27.

[17] It is also true that there can legitimately be some variation when human rights are given precise specification in national constitutions or other instruments. Where exactly the boundaries of a right such as freedom of religion should be set is a matter for deliberation in each society. Nevertheless the process of specification should ensure that as far as possible the resulting rights do not collide with one another.

culture. But it will also be self-defeating if human rights are constantly having to be set against one another, because this will give states too much freedom to justify rights-infringing policies by appeal to what are claimed to be competing human rights.[18]

If we apply these three justificatory requirements—sufficiently strong grounds, feasibility, and compatibility—to the right to immigrate, the feasibility requirement seems least problematic. This is particularly so since I have defined the right to immigrate as a right not to be prevented from entering, and not as a right to be assisted. The main reason for thinking that it would be infeasible to recognize this as a human right is that states, and perhaps their populations, would oppose it; but this is not a relevant reason when we are considering human rights. It would certainly be possible for states to abandon border controls and open their territories to all comers. Perhaps one can envisage scenarios in which, say, everyone attempted to move to Lichtenstein, and this was physically impossible, but these can be set aside as the kind of exceptional circumstance under which virtually any human right might have to be curtailed.

Compatibility seems likely to be a greater problem, but first let us see whether the grounding condition can be met. As I noted earlier, there are different views about what can ground human rights, so it may be that the right to migrate will qualify on some of these but not others. What the various grounding theories have in common, however, is that they are trying to identify some feature of human beings that is vitally important to them. The general form of these theories is that X qualifies as a human right because if people are not granted X, something of great significance to them is likely to be lost—they will not be able to live in a way that it is morally essential for humans to live. So it is worth asking why migration might have this kind of importance in human life.

On the face of it, it seems unlikely that it could have. We can distinguish two aspects of migration. First there is the very act of moving across a border; then there is the resulting change of environment—one moves into a society whose physical features, economy, legal system, culture, and so on are to a greater or lesser extent different from those of the society one has left. Let us consider these in turn. How important could it be just to move across a border? There are certainly ways of life—nomadic ones—in which movement as such is

---

[18] Note that the argument I make here is distinct from the argument typically offered by libertarians in defence of the claim that genuine rights can never conflict—they must all be compossible. This libertarian argument, which has the effect of allowing only negative rights to count as such, relies upon the thesis that every right entails a strictly correlative duty. The argument I offer, in contrast, does not depend upon the correlativity thesis, which I reject, but upon the pragmatic claim that human rights can only play the role that they are meant to play in political argument if their content is such as to make conflicts between them relatively rare.

valued. It is also possible that a border might run across the traditional pathway that is followed by those who embrace such a way of life. Members of the Sami people of northern Scandinavia, for example, have to cross the borders between Norway, Sweden, and Russia as they follow the annual migration route of their reindeer herds. This would give those involved a contingent reason to demand a right to cross the border in question, but the very contingency of the case—the fact that it appeals to a culturally specific way of life—shows that a universal human right to immigrate could not be justified on this basis.

The second aspect seems much more promising. Most people who move across borders do so because of features of their new place of residence that were not available in the old. Many of these migrations, however, will best be understood in terms of personal preferences rather than vital interests. Rather than there being some essential interest that could not be satisfied in the original country of residence, the reason for moving is that the new country offers an opportunity not available before (which might take the form of satisfying an essential interest in a preferred way—for example moving to a better job).

For some people, on the other hand, migration may well be only the way to satisfy an essential interest even at minimal level: this is especially likely in cases where the migration is from a very poor country to a much richer one in which adequate food, medical care, and so on are available. Does this provide the basis for a human right to migrate? Notice that the argument in this form has become instrumental in character. It is not claimed that the migration in and of itself is necessary if the essential interests in question are to be fulfilled. The claim is rather that, given the prevailing circumstances, the only way in which rights that are already agreed to be genuine human rights—to food and medical care—can be realized is by recognizing an additional right, the right to migrate, whose exercise will allow those primary rights to be fulfilled. As such, it is vulnerable to the observation that there are other ways in which the primary rights can be secured—adequate food and medical care might become available in the original country, through aid in the short term and economic development in the longer term. Given these alternatives, to establish migration as a human right one would first have to apply the compatibility test, asking which way of realizing the primary rights involved least interference with the other rights of those who would bear the corresponding obligations (to admit migrants and to supply development aid respectively).

If the argument for a human right to migrate is to be more than merely instrumental, it needs to prove that there are essential interests that cannot be fulfilled *except* by establishing such a right. Oberman tries to show this by claiming that we have a basic interest in being "free to access the full range of existing life options," and he uses several examples to show how these life options may not be accessible in the state in which a person currently lives. These include: falling in love with a person who resides in another country; wanting to practice a religion that does not have adherents in the place where one lives; and having political aims that require travel abroad for research or to engage in political discussion.[19] (To make these examples watertight, we need to assume that there is some reason why such interests cannot be satisfied without migration—some reason why the loved one cannot move, etc.—but let's grant that this condition is met.)

Notice, however, two things about these examples. One is that they depend upon the subjectively strong interests of particular persons, not on the essential interests of human beings as such. Or rather, to put the point more exactly, interests that may in themselves be universal here take a form that is specific to one person. We all share a basic interest in having the opportunity to form a long-term loving relationship with another human being, but only I, perhaps, have an interest in forming such a relationship with Amélie specifically. Clearly the conditions that are required to realize the aggregate set of such specific interests are much more demanding than those needed to realize the shared general interest. Can a human right be such as to fulfill these demanding conditions? Consider by way of analogy the human right to food, and consider the position of someone in whom that basic interest takes the form of a passion for top-quality raw fish. Are we to say that the human right to food must be understood in such a way as to include the conditions that will make it possible for this person to obtain high-class sushi? Suppose highly restrictive legislation to preserve fish stocks is introduced, pushing the price of raw fish beyond the person's means. Has his human right to food been violated?

The answer to these rhetorical questions is, I assume, obvious. The human right to food is the right to have access to an adequate quantity of nourishing food, regardless of any preferences the right-holder may have for particular types of food. It can be satisfied by many different combinations of foodstuffs. The right is based on generic interests, not specific ones. So in what way are the rights that are generated by our interests in being able to form loving relationships, or to practice a religion, different? There is clearly one relevant difference here: potential partners and religions are not substitutable in the way that foodstuffs are. I may prefer bluefin tuna to hake, but that is just a strong preference, whereas if I cannot cohabit with Amélie or participate in Sutrayāna practices in Tibet, that is an absolute loss—there is no alternative that is merely a less good version of the same thing. The interest that we have is an interest in being able to form a relationship with the particular person

---

[19] Kieran Oberman, "Immigration as a Human Right," this volume.

whom we love, or to participate in the religion whose tenets we have come to believe. Such interests are not satisfied merely by the state providing us with an approved list of marriage partners or state-sanctioned religions. The rights we have to form relationships or practice religion demand more than that. Notice, however, that while they prohibit the state from deliberately imposing obstacles that would prevent us from exercising these rights, they do not require states to take positive steps to make the corresponding opportunities available.[20] Suppose that a small religious sect holds its weekly services in London. A potential adherent who is dependent on a low-wage job in Glasgow may find it impossible to attend. Unfortunate though this is, it is not a violation of the human right to freedom of religion. A person so placed has to search for another way to pursue her underlying interest in faith.

It is also worth noting here that the specific interests that are being cited in defense of a human right to migrate are interests that require the cooperation of others to fulfill, so they are anyway vulnerable to refusal on the part of these others. Amélie may decline to have me, and the Tibetan monastery whose teaching path I wish to follow may be unwilling to take me in. We would be inclined to say that they have the right to refuse. But would we say that so confidently if it were really the case that human beings were so made that they could not live minimally decent lives unless they were able to form relationships with just one identifiable other, or to engage in one specific religion? If human beings were like that, in general, wouldn't we say that there was an obligation to associate with them when they regarded this as essential unless doing so came at such high cost that the associate's own decent life was put at risk?

It might be said in reply here that there is a big difference between my hoped-for relationship with Amélie being blocked by Amélie's contrary inclinations, or in the other case by the preference of Tibetan monks not to have to cope with an ignorant Westerner, and these relationships being prevented by the border controls of a state. There is indeed a difference, but I think it resides in the fact that whereas the mere wishes of Amélie or the monks are sufficient by themselves to exclude me, the state cannot prevent me from immigrating on a mere whim—it must have solid grounds for refusing me entry. Which grounds should count is a matter to be addressed later. For the moment, the conclusion that I wish to draw is that the direct human rights argument cannot justify a right to migrate. So long as the state in which I reside provides

---

[20] Just how far a state must go by way of providing opportunities in order to protect the right to freedom of religion is a difficult and disputed question. I have addressed some aspects of the question, with respect to liberal states, in "Liberalism, Equal Opportunities and Cultural Commitments" in Paul Kelly (ed.), *Multiculturalism Reconsidered* (Cambridge: Polity Press, 2002), pp. 45–61, reprinted in David Miller, *Justice for Earthlings: Essays in Political Philosophy* (Cambridge: Cambridge University Press, 2013), pp. 93–114.

a range of opportunities that is adequate to meet my generic human interests, the fact that I may also have specific interests that cannot be satisfied unless I reside in another country gives me only a reason, not a full-blown right, to move there.

But what if the range of opportunities available to me where I am currently living is *not* adequate? Here we encounter the instrumental argument in favor of the right to migrate. For many people, clearly, moving across borders may provide the only chance they have of living a minimally decent life. By acknowledging the right to migrate, we bring it about that one obstacle at least to fulfilling other human rights, such as the right to subsistence and the right to freedom of conscience, is removed. But this argument, although valid, is limited in a number of ways. First, it holds only as long as we assume that the other human rights that provide the conditions for a minimally decent life *cannot* be secured without migration—that is, we rule out the possibility of transforming conditions in the originating society so that decency is achieved. Second, we have to be alive to the possibility that migration may provide the route to a decent life for some people while making conditions worse still for those left behind. This is a difficult empirical issue that essentially revolves around the question of whether the so-called brain drain effect is real and, if it is, whether it is adequately compensated for by remittances and other benefits flowing back to the originating country as a result of migration.[21] Third, the instrumental argument cannot be used to justify migration between societies all of whom already provide their members with an adequate range of opportunities, and in the case of those that don't, it justifies only a more limited right to move to *some* society that does provide that range. So a world in which Canada, say, opened its doors to everyone who wanted to move from societies that because of poverty and/or political repression failed the decency test, but in which everywhere else kept them shut, would satisfy the instrumental argument without recognizing a human right to migrate as I have defined it.

In reply to this it might be said that other human rights cannot be properly guaranteed without an unrestricted right to migrate. Relying on the willingness of Canada to take in all of those suffering from the effects of global poverty is not good enough. Clearly my example is not intended to be realistic, but a system of managed migration in which receiving states cooperated to issue immigration permits, valid only for specified countries, to those

---

[21] For analysis and evidence, see Devesh Kapur and John McHale, *Give Us Your Best and Brightest: The Global Hunt for Talent and its Impact on the Developing World* (Washington, DC: Center for Global Development, 2005); R. Faini, "Migration, Remittances and Growth" in George J. Borjas and Jeff Crisp (eds.), *Poverty, International Migration and Asylum* (Basingstoke: Palgrave Macmillan, 2005). For a critical discussion of appeals to the brain drain phenomenon in debates about immigration, see Kieran Oberman, "Can Brain Drain Justify Immigration Restrictions?," *Ethics* 123:3 (2013), 427–55. See also Ayelet Shachar's chapter and Anna Stilz's chapter in this volume.

who qualified for them on human rights grounds might be. Because migration flows would be controlled under such a system, it could plausibly be argued that it would do a better job than a free-for-all in ensuring that people who currently lacked the opportunity for a decent life were provided one—for example, migrants could be directed to the societies with the biggest labor shortages.[22]

2.3 The Cantilever Strategy

So much for the instrumental strategy for justifying the human right to immigrate. We are left with what I have called the cantilever strategy, which tries to show that, given the human rights we already recognize, it is inconsistent not to recognize this one. The most likely version of this strategy begins with domestic freedom of movement, which as we saw was a right included in the original UN Declaration.[23] As the cantilever argument is often expressed, since we would regard it as an unacceptable breach of human rights if a federal union like the U.S. or Australia were to prevent people from moving across the boundaries from one constituent state to another (say from Washington to Oregon), why is it acceptable to prevent them moving across the national boundary that separates, say, Washington State from British Columbia?[24]

To evaluate this, it is worth examining why domestic freedom of movement can qualify as a human right. Note to begin with that the right involved is actually quite limited in scope, in the sense that there are many laws concerning property, traffic regulation, and so forth that significantly reduce the portion of domestic space over which a randomly chosen person is free to move.[25] Moreover it is taken for granted, in the official Declarations and elsewhere, that further reductions can be justified on grounds of public

---

[22] Might there then be a human right to have such a managed migration system in place? No, because there are a number of different ways in which the human rights of people currently living in very poor or oppressive societies might be safeguarded, and even if it could be shown that such a system was likely to be the most effective of these, one cannot claim a human right to everything that is most conducive to the human rights one already has. I discuss this issue in greater detail in "Border Regimes and Human Rights," *Law and Ethics of Human Rights* 7:1 (2013), 1–23.

[23] Here is Carens deploying the cantilever strategy: "If it is so important for people to have the right to move freely within a state, is it not equally important for them to have the right to move across state borders? Every reason why one might want to move within a state may also be a reason for moving between states.... The radical disjuncture that treats freedom of movement within the state as a moral imperative and freedom of movement across state borders as merely a matter of political discretion makes no sense from a perspective that takes seriously the freedom and equality of all individuals" (Carens, "Migration and Morality," pp. 27–8), cf. Carens, *The Ethics of Immigration*, p. 239.

[24] A different way of resisting the cantilever strategy is developed in Michael Blake, "Immigration" in R. G. Frey and Christopher Heath Wellman (eds.), *A Companion to Applied Ethics* (Oxford: Blackwell, 2003), pp. 228–9.

[25] See on this Nickel, *Making Sense of Human Rights*, p. 134.

order, health, and so forth. On the other hand, for reasons of efficiency, it is obviously beneficial if people are allowed to move domestically in search of work, affordable housing, and the like, so states have little incentive to use coercive measures to reduce the scope of freedom of movement still further under normal circumstances. Moreover they have policy instruments available that allow them to affect the incentives that people might have for moving. Negatively, a predominantly national system of taxation and welfare provision means that there is not much incentive to move in order to reduce one's tax burden or obtain a higher standard of healthcare, for instance. Positively, states can create employment opportunities to counteract migration pressures by siting government offices and other public services in areas that are in danger of losing jobs. They control both ends of the migration route, so to speak, so they can influence the relative desirability of living at either end.

In the light of this, one might wonder why the right to domestic freedom of movement ever comes under threat, and why therefore it should be necessary to include it in the Declarations and Covenants. The answer, I think, is that for political reasons a state may wish to target a particular group of people by restricting their movement. Under the apartheid regime in South Africa, geographical separation of blacks and whites was used to prevent racial mixing, give whites an advantage in the labor market, and provide blacks with much poorer quality social services. Further back in history, Jewish ghettos were created within European cities that not only enforced religious segregation but also exposed the confined group to economic exploitation and social stigmatization.[26] Discrimination of this kind is likely to harm the essential interests of the targeted group and put others of their human rights at risk. Restrictions on movement may also be placed on political dissenters, to prevent them associating with like-minded others and spreading their message more widely. In this case it is rights of political assembly and free speech that are put in jeopardy. To prevent such policies being enacted, we need a human right to free movement. It gets its value not just from the inherent value of being able to move around in physical space, which by itself might only justify a right of quite limited scope, but from the way it helps support other rights such as those I have just mentioned. Its main purpose is to prevent restrictions of movement being detrimentally placed on some people that are not placed on others.

Suppose now we look at international freedom of movement through the same set of spectacles. Although it may be argued that the economic and other benefits of free movement accrue here much as they do in the domestic case, fewer instruments are available to states to manage the potential flows of

---

[26] See, for example, the account of the Venetian ghettos in Richard Sennett, *Flesh and Stone: The Body and the City in Western Civilization* (London: Penguin, 2002), ch. 7.

people without enforcing border controls. They are able to make their own societies more or less attractive for incoming people to join to some extent, though that extent is limited, at least in democratic societies, by legal norms that require the equal treatment of all residents, and (justifiable) pressures to admit immigrants to full citizenship status in a fairly short space of time. They cannot control what goes on in the places from which the immigrants are coming. Since tax and welfare regimes vary considerably, there may be strong incentives to move even for people whose essential interests are not being harmed by staying where they are. One can of course imagine favorable circumstances in which relatively few people wished to migrate and/or similar numbers of people wished to move in and out of each particular state, and then there would be little cost to states in recognizing a human right to immigrate. But if the right is to be justified, it has to be robust even under unfavorable circumstances. "Unfavorable circumstances" in this sense prevail in much of the world today.

So far I have suggested that states can have legitimate grounds for opposing an international right to free movement that they do not have in the domestic case. The other side of the coin is that restrictions on international movement, unlike restrictions on domestic movement, are not targeted at specific groups with the aim of disadvantaging them in ways that put their human rights at risk. The immigration policies pursued by states are of course discriminatory in that they typically privilege particular categories of immigrants, and in some instances do so on indefensible grounds (as in the case of the infamous "White Australia" policy). But even in the worst cases the excluded groups are not made vulnerable in the way that targeted insiders are. Responsibility for protecting their human rights rests primarily with the states that they are seeking to leave, and in some cases the rights they already enjoy may be as valuable as the rights they would gain if they were permitted to enter.

Consider political rights, for example. I argued above that the right of domestic free movement may be essential to support the right to associate politically with others and communicate one's views to a wide audience. Someone who is prevented from immigrating to society S cannot exercise these rights vis-à-vis the citizens of S, but so long as human rights are recognized in her home society she can do so vis-à-vis her fellow citizens. Do political rights include the right to associate and communicate with *anyone*? Oberman asserts that they do: "political life is not fully free if people are prevented from meeting, organizing, and protesting as they wish," which he takes to include engaging in these activities anywhere in the world as may be felt necessary.[27] If we lived under a world government, that might be true.

---

[27] Oberman, "Immigration as a Human Right," this volume.

But since we do not, there is a crucial difference between interacting with fellow-citizens, with whom together we are responsible for controlling the massive apparatus of the modern state, and interacting with people elsewhere with whom one may share aims and interests.[28] As usual, the issue here is not what is most desirable: it may be desirable that, as Oberman suggests, he can for instance travel to and stay in Sierra Leone in order to investigate the effects of British government policies in that country. The issue is what can be claimed as a human right. If I am correct in saying that the right to freedom of movement qualifies as a human right in part because of the way in which it supports other rights such as freedom of speech and assembly, then we need to settle how far these latter rights extend before we can decide how widely or narrowly the human right to free movement should be construed. Once we understand how political rights connect to essential human interests, we will not be inclined to interpret them so widely.

I have been pointing to disanalogies between domestic and international free movement in order to resist the cantilevering strategy used to support a human right to immigrate. By way of conclusion, let us briefly contemplate the nightmare scenario as presented by defenders of that right, in which Washington State does indeed control its border with Oregon in the same way as it does with BC.[29] That would undoubtedly be a huge inconvenience to all those who had become used to crossing that border freely, and for example had arranged to live in one state and work in the other. But that is an effect of the *status quo ante* being one of free movement, which we should therefore discount for purposes of evaluating the arrangement itself. Why would we be disturbed by the border closing once people had adjusted to it? If my analysis above is correct, we would be concerned that the closure was being used for discriminatory purposes (for example, to prevent Mexican immigrants who had made it as far as Oregon from moving farther north). We would be worried if, say, presidential candidates were being prevented by the border controls from addressing public meetings in Washington State. There might be other grounds for concern. But if, for example, these restrictions were simply used to limit the number of tourists taking vacations in the state, how concerned would we be? We assert the right of domestic free movement in its standard form because of an entirely reasonable fear that states may otherwise be tempted to impose restrictions on movement unjustifiably, violating other

---

[28] See here Michael Blake and Mathias Risse, "Immigration and the Original Ownership of the Earth," *Notre Dame Journal of Law, Ethics and Public Policy* 23 (2009), 133–65 at 147–8.

[29] Griffin contemplates another hypothetical case in which restrictions on domestic freedom of movement do not appear to amount to a human rights violation in *On Human Rights*, pp. 195–6. In his example, Brazil requires new immigrants to settle in the interior of the country rather than in Rio. See also Wellman's discussion of internal freedom of movement, and his distinction between a human right and a liberal right, in his contribution to this volume.

rights in the process, not because we think that we have an essential interest in being able to move just anywhere, even within national boundaries.

2.4 Reasons to Control Immigration

I have argued, against the cantilever strategy, that the oft-cited analogy between the domestic right of free movement and the putative corresponding international right does not hold. On the one hand, states have policy instruments at their disposal that they can use to control internal migration non-coercively that they do not possess in the international case. On the other hand, allowing states to *prevent* (rather than merely discourage) people from moving internally would give them a weapon with which to oppress minority groups or dissident individuals—and again there is no international equivalent to this.[30] Still, to complete the argument against a human right to immigrate, I need to show that states do indeed have good reason to control inward movement across their borders, so that granting such a right would potentially have significant costs. Let me draw attention to three considerations that, depending on the case, may provide such a reason.

1) Overall numbers. Unless counterbalanced by emigration, immigration will obviously increase the number of people within the state's jurisdiction. This will matter most immediately when the state has explicitly adopted a population policy that aims to cap that number, in the extreme case by making it illegal for a family to raise more than a specified number of children. Even in the absence of such a policy, however, the state is likely to have set targets for employment, for house-building, for the supply of health services, and so forth—perhaps in the future for overall levels of greenhouse gas emissions—which are dependent on the total number of people who fall under its jurisdiction. The point here is not that its interest will always be to hold this number below a fixed ceiling; clearly states have often wanted to encourage immigration for economic and other reasons. The interest is rather in being able to control the number—to increase, diminish, or maintain it as other policy goals require.

2) Cultural shifts. Whereas migration within a modern state will only change the prevailing culture in marginal ways, immigration from outside may change it more radically, and the receiving state and its citizens may have

---

[30] It is possible to imagine a number of states colluding to oppress an unpopular minority group, and using immigration controls to do so, but I cannot think of any real examples of this phenomenon. The expulsion of Roma by a number of European countries at different historical moments—most recently by France in 2009–10—has been suggested as a relevant case, but it is really a different phenomenon: it does not involve coordinated action between states, while on the other hand the ethical issues raised by expulsion are different from those raised by refusing entry.

an interest in preventing this. This may be because they do not want to see existing cultural divisions in the society deepening further, or just because they are attached to their inherited culture. Since this claim about the significance of culture is often misunderstood and/or dismissed out of hand, it is worth elaborating a little more fully.

First, it is often pointed out that existing liberal democracies are all to a greater or lesser extent multicultural, and immigration does nothing to alter that fact.[31] Even if a majority of citizens hanker after a culturally homogenous society, that particular horse has bolted so far away as to be irretrievable. But although complete cultural homogeneity is unachievable even if it was believed to be desirable, this does not exclude some degree of cultural convergence among people living in multicultural societies—convergence, for example, in language use, in political values, and in norms of socially acceptable behavior. Such convergence can be valued both for instrumental reasons—it allows people to interact with less friction, it helps to generate trust, which in turn supports active democracy, and so forth—and also intrinsically: people simply feel more at home when they live in a cultural milieu that they recognize as their own. Bringing the necessary cultural integration about, however, takes time and is not costless; in general it will be easier to achieve when the rate of immigration is steady and relatively low, so that integration mechanisms—language classes for new immigrants, and so forth—can be put in place.

Second, it is often said, correctly, that societal cultures are always in flux, and that preventing immigration in order to "freeze" a culture at a particular moment of time is therefore absurd. But from the point of view of the people whose culture it is, it makes a difference whether the sources of change are internal or external. Sometimes, of course, people may welcome the introduction of new elements of culture from the outside, but this is different from having changes forced upon you by external factors that you cannot control. The point I am making here is not about the *actual* effects of immigration over the last couple of generations, but about possible effects of institutionalizing an unlimited right to immigrate. Even authors who are favorably disposed towards open-borders policies, such as Dummett and Carens, recognize the normative relevance of claims about culture.[32] Dummett, for example, acknowledges that all nations have the right not to be "submerged"

---

[31] This criticism has been made not only by open borders advocates but by some of those who regard immigration controls as justified, including Michael Blake in "Immigration," pp. 232–4 and Ryan Pevnick, *Immigration and the Constraints of Justice* (Cambridge: Cambridge University Press, 2011), ch. 6, both of whom also contend that invoking culture as a ground for restrictions risks demeaning current citizens who do not form part of the majority culture.

[32] See Dummett, *On Immigration and Refugees*, esp. pp. 15–21; Carens, "Migration and Morality," pp. 36–40.

by invading cultures, and spends some pages explaining the importance to people of having a native land whose culture is such that they can feel it to be uniquely theirs. This, as was noted earlier, explains why for Dummett there cannot be an unqualified right to migrate. But while complete submergence is unlikely to occur for the reasons that he gives, citizens may still have an interest in resisting externally generated cultural change, and retaining control over immigration is one of the levers that allows them to do this.

3) The composition of the citizen body.[33] If we assume that immigrants will in due course be able to apply for full citizenship rights, then their admission will change not just the size, but to a greater or lesser extent the political complexion, of the citizen body. (Again there is a contrast with internal migration, whose political effects are only localized.[34]) This will matter most in democratic systems that are evenly balanced between, say, rival ethnic or religious groups. Even if one thinks that the membership of any demos is ultimately an arbitrary matter,[35] an established demos may still have the right to determine its own future membership, so long as it does so in a way that is consistent with recognition of the basic rights of those who will be affected by its decisions.[36] This seems to be an essential part of what it means to be self-determining: if a democratic body is entitled to take decisions on policies whose impact will be felt in decades to come, it is also entitled to resist changes in its own composition that might have the effect of reversing these policies (it cannot of course guarantee that the policies will not be changed, since successors may have different ideas, but it can legitimately try to make this less likely to happen).

2.5 Conclusion

In this chapter, I have been asking whether there is a human right to immigrate that would make the border restrictions that we see everywhere in the world today morally problematic. I have concluded that there is no such right.

[33] This aspect is also stressed in Christopher Heath Wellman, "Immigration and Freedom of Association," *Ethics* 119 (2008), 109–41, esp. 114–16 and in Christopher Heath Wellman and Phillip Cole, *Debating the Ethics of Immigration: Is There a Right to Exclude?* (Oxford: Oxford University Press, 2011), pp. 38–41.

[34] This is not *strictly* true, if national elections are held in local constituencies. It would be possible to invent a case in which movements of voters between constituencies determined the outcome of a closely fought election. But the point is that if the overall composition of the electorate remains the same, then the political impact of internal migration will only be marginal.

[35] As I do not: see David Miller, "Democracy's Domain," *Philosophy and Public Affairs* 37 (2009), 203–28, for thoughts about the principles that should guide the creation or alteration of a demos.

[36] The qualifying clause is needed to block the possibility that a citizen body might decide to change its composition by expelling a subset of its members, or denying admission to the offspring of existing members as they reached voting age.

At the same time, existing border regimes do raise serious human rights issues, some of which I have discussed in detail elsewhere.[37] These have primarily to do with the way that immigrants, and especially refugees, are treated when they approach the state asking to be let in. A number of procedural safeguards must be put in place to ensure that human rights are not violated, either directly by the receiving state, or indirectly by sending immigrants to places where their rights are forfeit. There are also human rights questions to be asked about the criteria used to select immigrants who do not qualify as asylum seekers, although the answers to these are less obvious. So my view is not that human rights have no place in discussions of immigration policy— quite the reverse. But these discussions get off on the wrong foot if they assume, openly or tacitly, that there is a general right to free movement that all border controls violate. By making that assumption, we rule out the very idea of a just immigration policy (other than a free-for-all), since a necessary condition of such a policy is that it should be human rights compliant. If the argument offered here is correct, no such assumption should be made.[38]

References

Blake, Michael, "Immigration" in R. G. Frey and Christopher Heath Wellman (eds.), *A Companion to Applied Ethics* (Oxford: Blackwell, 2003).

Blake, Michael and Mathias Risse, "Immigration and the Original Ownership of the Earth," *Notre Dame Journal of Law, Ethics and Public Policy* 23 (2009), 133–65.

Brownlie, Ian and Guy S. Goodwin-Gill (eds.), *Basic Documents on Human Rights*, 5th edition (Oxford: Oxford University Press, 2006).

Buchanan, Allen, *Justice, Legitimacy and Self-Determination: Moral Foundations for International Law* (Oxford: Oxford University Press, 2004).

Carens, Joseph H. "Migration and Morality: a liberal egalitarian perspective" in Brian Barry and Robert E. Goodin (eds.), *Free Movement: Ethical Issues in the Transnational Migration of People and of Money* (Hemel Hempstead: Harvester Wheatsheaf, 1992), pp. 25–47.

Carens, Joseph H. "A Reply to Meilaender: Reconsidering Open Borders," *International Migration Review* 33 (1999), 1082–97.

Carens, Joseph H. "The Rights of Irregular Migrants," *Ethics and International Affairs* 22 (2008), 163–86.

Carens, Joseph H, *The Ethics of Immigration* (Oxford: Oxford University Press, 2013).

---

[37] See Miller, "Border Regimes and Human Rights."

[38] This chapter was written for the conference on "Migration in Legal and Political Theory: Remaining Challenges," University of Cambridge, 28–9 October 2011. It was also presented to the COMPAS Fall 2011 conference, Ohio State University, 20–1 October 2011 and to the Department of Politics, Stockholm University on 3 November 2011. I am very grateful for the suggestions made at these meetings, especially by my commentator at Cambridge Zofia Stemplowska, and for incisive written comments by Sarah Fine, Margaret Moore, and Lea Ypi which have helped to improve the original version.

Christiano, Thomas, "An Instrumental Argument for a Human Right to Democracy," *Philosophy and Public Affairs* 39 (2011), 142–76.

Cole, Phillip, *Philosophies of Exclusion: Liberal Political Theory and Immigration* (Edinburgh: Edinburgh University Press, 2000).

Dummett, Ann, "The Transnational Migration of People Seen from within a Natural Law Perspective" in Barry and Goodin (eds.), *Free Movement: Ethical Issues in the Transnational Migration of People and of Money* (Hemel Hempstead: Harvester Wheatsheaf, 1992), pp. 169–80.

Dummett, Michael, *On Immigration and Refugees* (London: Routledge, 2001).

Faini, Riccardo, "Migration, Remittances and Growth" in George J. Borjas and Jeff Crisp (eds.), *Poverty, International Migration and Asylum* (Basingstoke: Palgrave Macmillan, 2005), pp. 171–87.

Gilabert, Pablo, "Feasibility and Socialism," *Journal of Political Philosophy* 19 (2011), 52–63.

Gilabert, Pablo and Holly Lawford-Smith, "Political Feasibility: A Conceptual Exploration," *Political Studies* 60 (2012), 809–25.

Griffin, James, *On Human Rights* (Oxford: Oxford University Press, 2008).

Kapur, Devesh and John McHale, *Give Us Your Best and Brightest: The Global Hunt for Talent and its Impact on the Developing World* (Washington, DC: Center for Global Development, 2005).

Miller, David, "Liberalism, Equal Opportunities and Cultural Commitments" in Paul Kelly (ed.), *Multiculturalism Reconsidered* (Cambridge: Polity Press, 2002), pp. 45–61, reprinted in David Miller, *Justice for Earthlings: Essays in Political Philosophy* (Cambridge: Cambridge University Press, 2013), pp. 93–114.

Miller, David, *National Responsibility and Global Justice* (Oxford: Oxford University Press, 2007).

Miller, David, "Democracy's Domain," *Philosophy and Public Affairs* 37 (2009), 203–28.

Miller, David, "Grounding Human Rights," *Critical Review of International Social and Political Philosophy* 15 (2012), 407–27.

Miller, David, "Border Regimes and Human Rights," *Law and Ethics of Human Rights* 7:1 (2013), 1–23.

Miller, David, "Personhood versus Human Needs as Grounds for Human Rights" in Roger Crisp (ed.), *Griffin on Human Rights* (Oxford: Oxford University Press, 2014), pp. 152–69.

Nickel, James, *Making Sense of Human Rights*, 2nd edn (Oxford: Blackwell, 2007).

Oberman, Kieran, "Can Brain Drain Justify Immigration Restrictions?," *Ethics* 123:3 (2013), 427–55.

Pevnick, Ryan, *Immigration and the Constraints of Justice* (Cambridge: Cambridge University Press, 2011).

Sennett, Richard, *Flesh and Stone: The Body and the City in Western Civilization* (London: Penguin, 2002).

Wellman, Christopher Heath, "Immigration and Freedom of Association," *Ethics* 119 (2008), 109–41.

Wellman, Christopher Heath and Phillip Cole, *Debating the Ethics of Immigration: Is There a Right to Exclude?* (Oxford: Oxford University Press, 2011).

3

Immigration as a Human Right

Kieran Oberman

Immigration restrictions curtail freedom. They prevent people from going where they want to go, seeing whom they wish to see and taking jobs they wish to take. When repressive states enact such restrictions internally, they face condemnation by the international community. Yet the legitimacy of immigration restrictions, which are enforced by almost all states, is commonly taken for granted.

This chapter argues that people have a human right to immigrate to other states. People have essential interests in being able to make important personal decisions and engage in politics without state restrictions on the personal and political options available to them. It is these interests that other human rights, such as the human rights to internal freedom of movement, freedom of association, and freedom of occupational choice, protect. Commitment to these already recognized human rights thus requires commitment to the human right to immigrate, for without this further right the underlying interests are not sufficiently protected.[1]

---

[1] While a number of authors have suggested that immigration restrictions are morally inconsistent with conventional human rights, the idea of a human right to immigrate has not been sufficiently developed or defended. This chapter addresses that shortfall in the literature, offering an account of what the right does (and does not) entail and the fundamental interests underlying it. For these related arguments see Steven Burr, "Immigration and the First Amendment," *California Law Review* 73 (1985), 1889–1928; Joseph H. Carens, *The Ethics of Immigration* (Oxford: Oxford University Press, 2013), pp. 225–87; Phillip Cole, *Philosophies of Exclusion* (Edinburgh: Edinburgh University Press, 2000); Robert E. Goodin, "If People Were Money..." in Brian Barry and Robert E. Goodin (eds.), *Free Movement: Ethical Issues in the Transnational Migration of People and of Money* (University Park, PA: Pennsylvania State University Press, 1992), pp. 6–22; Ann Dummett, "The Transnational Migration of People Seen From within a Natural Law Tradition" in Brian Barry and Robert E. Goodin (eds.), *Free Movement: Ethical Issues in the Transnational Migration of People and of Money* (University Park, PA: Pennsylvania State University Press, 1992), pp. 169–80; Hillel Steiner, "Hard Borders, Compensation, and Classical Liberalism" in David Miller and Sohail H. Hashimi (eds.), *Boundaries, Autonomy and Justice: Diverse Ethical Views* (Princeton, NJ: Princeton University Press, 2001), pp. 79–88.

Does this mean immigration restrictions are always unjust? On the view of human rights adopted here, human rights are not absolute. Restrictions might be justified in extreme circumstances in which immigration threatens severe social costs that cannot otherwise be prevented. Outside these circumstances, however, immigration restrictions are unjust. The idea of a human right to immigrate is not then a demand for open borders.[2] Rather it is a demand that basic liberties (to move, associate, speak, worship, work, and marry) be awarded the same level of protection when people seek to exercise them across borders as when people seek to exercise them within borders. Immigration restrictions deserve no special exemption from the purview of human freedom rights.[3]

Section 3.1 defines the idea of a human right to immigrate that the chapter defends. Section 3.2 introduces the core argument for this right, identifying the two main interests at stake. Section 3.3 develops the argument by explaining why people are entitled to access options that lie beyond a supposedly "adequate" range, accessible within their own state. Section 3.4 addresses two arguments for exclusion, from distributive justice and culture. Section 3.5 considers the objection that, in our current world, immigration restrictions are almost always necessary to prevent severe costs. Section 3.6 concludes.

3.1 What is the Human Right to Immigrate?

Before presenting my argument for a human right to immigrate, let me first define the right that I shall defend. It has four important features. First, it is a moral, rather than a legal, human right. Moral human rights set out what people are morally entitled to. Legal human rights are those recognized

---

[2] The open borders slogan is adopted by Joseph H. Carens, "Aliens and Citizens: The Case for Open Borders," *Review of Politics* 49 (1987), 250–73 although even Carens does not defend the absolutist stance that the slogan suggests. Carens has since described his position as supporting "open borders as an ideal" (Joseph H. Carens, "The Philosopher and the Policy Maker: Two Perspectives on the Ethics of Immigration with Special Attention to the Problem of Restricting Asylum" in Kay Hailbronner, David A. Martin, and Hiroshi Motomura (eds.), *Immigration Admissions: The Search for Workable Policies in Germany and the United States* (Providence, RI and Oxford: Berghahn, 1997), pp. 3–50 at p. 7. But if "open borders" is too strong a description of the non-absolutist, pro-free-movement position, "open borders as an ideal" is too weak. Something can be an ideal without entailing stringent duties upon anyone to bring that ideal about. For these reasons I think the language of human rights is preferable to that of "open borders."

[3] This freedom argument for a human right to immigrate can be distinguished from a poverty argument that regards immigration as a means to address global poverty. I have addressed the poverty argument elsewhere; see Kieran Oberman, "Immigration, Global Poverty and the Right to Stay," *Political Studies* 59 (2011), 253–68; Kieran Oberman, "Poverty and Immigration Policy," *American Political Science Review* 109 (2015), 239–51.

in law.[4] No current legal human rights document includes a human right to immigrate. There may be a case for enacting such a right into law, but that case is not made here.

Second, I shall assume an interest account of moral human rights according to which these rights "are grounded in universal interests significant enough to generate duties on the part of others."[5] To prove that there is a moral human right to immigrate I must therefore defend two claims. First, the "interest claim" holds that people have significant interests in being free to immigrate. Trivial interests cannot ground human rights. In Sections 3.2 and 3.3, I show that the interests people have in the freedom to immigrate are not only significant, but are, in fact, the same interests that ground already recognized human freedom rights. Second, the "duty claim" holds that the interests people have in the freedom to immigrate generate duties on the part of others to respect this freedom. Sections 3.4 and 3.5 defend this claim. The duties generated include, most obviously, the duty upon recipient states not to prevent people from entering or residing within their territory. However, further duties may also be generated, such as the duty to create the conditions under which the freedom to immigrate can be exercised without the infliction of severe social costs; this is an idea I explore in Section 3.5.

Third, as I have already indicated, the human right to immigrate is a non-absolute right. In this sense, it is exactly like other human rights. Sometimes, for the sake of competing moral values, a human right can justifiably be curtailed. As James Griffin has put it, human rights are "resistant to trade-offs but not too resistant."[6] If the costs of immigration are particularly severe, restrictions might be justified. I shall return to this point in Section 3.4.

Fourth, the human right to immigrate is a right people have to enter and reside in foreign states for as long as they like. It thus includes the right to visit a foreign state for a short period of time, as well as the right to permanently reside there. However, the right does not in itself entail a right to citizenship in the state in which one resides. While a strong argument can be made for awarding citizenship to long-term residents, it is a further argument to the one made here.

---

[4] For the difference between moral and legal rights see Thomas Pogge, "Severe Poverty as a Human Rights Violation" in Thomas Pogge (ed.), *Freedom from Poverty as a Human Right: Who Owes what to the Very Poor?* (Cambridge: Cambridge University Press, 2007), pp. 11–54 at p. 13.

[5] John Tasioulas, "The Moral Reality of Human Rights" in Thomas Pogge (ed.), *Freedom from Poverty as a Human Right: Who Owes what to the Very Poor?* (Cambridge: Cambridge University Press, 2007), pp. 75–101 at p. 77.

[6] James Griffin, *On Human Rights* (Oxford: Oxford University Press, 2008), p. 77.

3.2 The Underlying Interests

The human right to immigrate is grounded on interests that already recognized human freedom rights protect. By "human freedom rights" I mean the sorts of rights to basic freedoms that are found in international human rights documents. The Universal Declaration of Human Rights (1948),[7] for instance, lists rights to internal freedom of movement (Article 13.1), freedom of religion (Article 18), freedom of expression (Article 19), freedom of association (Article 20), freedom of occupational choice (Article 23.1), and the freedom to marry (Article 16). The first of these rights is, in a sense, the one most closely related to the human right to immigrate. Article 13.1 holds that "[e]veryone has the right to freedom of movement and residence within the borders of each state." The right protects people against the internal application of the sort of restrictions that immigration restrictions represent: restrictions on where people live, work, and travel. Such internal restrictions were enforced in Soviet Russia and apartheid South Africa and are still enforced in a number of repressive states today.

Let me first explain how the human right to immigrate follows from the human right to internal freedom of movement, before making the same point in regards to the other human freedom rights listed. Underlying the human right to internal freedom of movement are two interests: one personal, the other political. The personal interest is the interest people have in being free to access the full range of existing life options when they make important personal decisions. By "life options" I mean those options that give our lives meaning and purpose: friends, family, civic associations, expressive opportunities, religions, jobs, and marriage partners. If one's internal freedom of movement is subject to a non-trivial degree of restriction, then the range of life options one can access will also be constrained. If the state bans you from entering a region of a country, you are excluded from accessing almost all the life options that exist within it: you cannot visit friends or family, attend a religious or educational institution, express your ideas at a meeting or cultural event, seek employment, or pursue a love affair, anywhere within that region.

While the human right to internal freedom of movement protects our interest in being free to access the full range of existing life options, the protection it provides is insufficient since there are many life options that exist beyond the borders of the state in which we reside. As Joseph Carens notes:

> Every reason why one might want to move within a state may also be a reason for moving between states. One might want a job; one might fall in love with someone from another country; one might belong to a religion that has few

---

[7] Henceforth UDHR.

adherents in one's native state and many in another; one might wish to pursue cultural opportunities that are only available in another land.[8]

If human rights are to fully protect our freedom to access the full range of life options, then we must have a human right to immigrate to other states.

Let us turn to the political interest underlying the human right to free movement. People have an essential interest in enjoying a free and effective political process. Free movement is essential for free political activity since one cannot organize in support of a cause by (say) attending a demonstration if one is prevented from getting there. Moreover, since free movement is a condition for free association—one needs to move in order to meet people—it is also vital for everything that free association makes possible, including political dialogue, conflict resolution, and the free exchange of ideas.[9] Finally, free movement is necessary for the collection of reliable information regarding political affairs, for unless you can go to the affected areas or have someone you trust go for you, you cannot find out what is happening there.

These points support the human right to internal freedom of movement, but they equally support a right to immigrate. This is true even if we assume the traditional view that people have no rights to political participation abroad. In order to make informed and effective contributions to the political process in one's own country, one must have the freedom to talk to, learn from, and cooperate with people living elsewhere. In a world in which so many problems are international problems and the effects of government policies are felt globally, it is crucial for democracy that citizens of different countries are permitted to interact. It is by interacting that people can gain firsthand experience of the effect of their own government's policies on people living in foreign countries. It is by interacting that people can find out about ideas, policies, and approaches that may be working (or not working) abroad and deserve to be tried (or avoided) at home. And it is through interaction that people can effectively fight for those common causes, such as action on climate change, international financial regulation, and international conflict resolution, that require a transnational solution. The power of governments and corporations transcend borders; ordinary people must not be trapped behind them. Closed borders constrain political activity, restrict the free exchange of ideas, and prevent people from acquiring important information with which they can hold their governments to account.[10]

---

[8] Carens, Joseph H., " Migration and Morality: A Liberal Egalitarian Perspective" in Brian Barry and Robert E. Goodin (eds.), *Free Movement: Ethical Issues in the Transnational Migration of People and Money* (University Park, PA: Pennsylvania State University Press, 1992), pp. 27– 8.

[9] Of course, with modern forms of communication, *some* political and associative activity can take place without movement. Nevertheless, without freedom of movement, political and associative activity is profoundly constrained and thus not *free*. I expand on this point below.

[10] The US Supreme Court made this point in its rejection of emigration restrictions: "America is, of course, sovereign; but sovereignty is woven in an international web that makes her one of the family of nations. The ties with all the continents are close—commercially as well as culturally. Our

Note that to protect these interests in personal and political freedom, people must have the right to reside in a foreign state for as long as they like; a right to visit is not sufficient. A time restriction on a person's stay restricts the range of options available to them in much the same way as an entry restriction does. This point is clear in the case of long-term life projects, such as romantic relationships and employment opportunities, which often require more time than temporary visas allow. But the point also stands in the case of short-term activities such as visiting friends or attending a political meeting. Temporary visas allow us to engage in such activities, but only as long as their validation periods last. As soon as the validation period ends, the activities are once again prohibited. If I wish to meet a friend or attend a meeting on Tuesday but face deportation on Monday, then I am denied these options just as surely as I would have been had I been refused entry in the first place. Visas allowing people to stay in a country for a temporary period are no more acceptable than their domestic equivalent: permits allowing people to stay in an area of a country for a temporary period. Both violate underlying interests in personal and political freedom.

A similar point can be made regarding telecommunications. It is certainly true that the internet and other technology can help us pursue our personal and political projects across distances. Nevertheless, such technology cannot replace direct human contact. Humans, being as the creatures they are, have a special need for face-to-face communication. A romantic relationship or friendship conducted over Skype is no substitute for the real thing. A society in which people are kept under house arrest, but enjoy excellent broadband, is not a free society. When people are permitted to interact in person, and not just virtually, they inevitably meet different people, say different things, initiate a different set of projects, and, more generally, experience a different quality and intensity in their interactions. Restrictions on direct human contact are thus profound incursions upon personal and political liberty, even in the internet age.

There is one final point of analogy to be drawn between the human right to immigrate and the right to internal freedom of movement, which is that the latter, as well as the former, protects the freedom to access options available in foreign states. To see this, recall that Article 13.1 of the UDHR requires that everyone be granted "freedom of movement and residence within the borders of *each* state" (emphasis added). In a clarifying document, the UN Human Rights Committee has emphasized that the right is one that "[e]veryone

concerns are planetary, beyond sunrises and sunsets. Citizenship implicates us in those problems and perplexities, as well as in domestic ones. We cannot exercise and enjoy citizenship in world perspective without the right to travel abroad..." (*Aptheker vs. Secretary of State*, 378 U.S. 500 (1964), pp. 519–21). Also see *Kent vs. Dulles*, 457 U.S. 116 (1958), pp. 126–7.

lawfully within a State enjoys."[11] Thus the human right to internal freedom of movement, conventionally defined, applies to foreigners as well as citizens. As soon as foreigners pass passport control, they are entitled to go as they please. There is good reason why the right is defined in this way: people have essential interests, both personal and political, in being able to access life options available in foreign states. People should be left free to associate with friends, visit religious institutions, pursue love affairs, and attend conferences within the territory of foreign states, as well as their own. But if people have essential interests in being able to access life options available in foreign states, then they have a right to immigrate to those states. One cannot access options available within a state if one is denied access to its territory.

I have shown that the interests that ground the human right to internal freedom of movement also ground a human right to immigrate. Let me add that the latter right can equally be derived from the other human freedom rights I have referred to: rights to freedom of expression, association, religion, occupational choice, and the right to marry. Immigration restrictions place a bar between citizens and excluded foreigners. They interfere with the freedom of both to decide for themselves with whom they communicate, associate, worship, work, study, or marry. They cut people off from careers they may wish to pursue, religions they may wish to practice, ideas they may wish to explore, and people with whom they may wish to pursue relationships. Immigration restrictions act, in other words, precisely like those internal restrictions on individual liberty that conventional human freedom rights protect us from. Our set of human freedom rights is thus incomplete without the human right to immigrate.[12]

3.3 The Inadequacy of an "Adequate" Range

Having sketched the argument for a human right to immigrate let me defend one important aspect of it: the claim that conventional human freedom rights are grounded upon an interest people have in accessing the *full* range of existing life options. Against this claim it could be argued that a smaller range of life options is sufficient to satisfy the essential interests that human rights serve. We might imagine a range large enough to award us a decent choice of occupations, associations, religions, and so forth but nevertheless far smaller than the total number of options the world has to offer. If such a range

---

[11] Human Rights Committee, "General Comment No. 27: Freedom of Movement (Article 12)," CCPR/C/21/Rev.1 (1999), para 1.
[12] For the argument that immigration restrictions violate freedom of association see Steiner, "Hard Borders." For a similar argument regarding freedom of speech see Burr, "Immigration."

of options is sufficient, then the argument for a human right to immigrate collapses. States could offer this smaller range internally and no one would have an essential interest in entering a foreign state to access additional options.[13]

Let us call this view of human freedom rights the "adequate range view." The first point that needs to be made regarding this view is that it cannot support conventional human freedom rights. The human right to internal freedom of movement, for instance, is defined by the UDHR as the "right to freedom of movement and residence within the borders of each state."[14] A proponent of the adequate range view must deny that people have this human right. If the human right to freedom of movement only entitled people to an "adequate" range of options, then those living in a state with a larger than "adequate" range would lack a human right to freedom of movement across the whole territory of their state. If Belgium offers an "adequate" range of options and the US offers many times more options than Belgium, then the US offers a range of options many times larger than an "adequate" range. On the adequate range view, the US could divide its territory up into hundreds of Belgium-sized chunks, placing guards and razor wire at the borders of each one, without violating the human right to freedom of movement.

Next, consider the other human freedom rights I have mentioned . If people only have a human right to the freedom to access an "adequate" range of options, then states could radically curtail the freedoms they protect without violating our human rights. Judaism could be banned, without any violation of the human right to freedom of religion, as long as an "adequate" range of religions went unrepressed. The government could burn books in the town square without any violation of the right to freedom of expression, as long as there was an "adequate" range of books left on the shelves. Public meetings could be shut down and social clubs closed without any violation of the human right to freedom of association, as long as an "adequate" range of meetings and clubs remained open.[15]

---

[13] David Miller, *National Responsibility and Global Justice* (Oxford: Oxford University Press, 2007), pp. 205–8; Ryan Pevnick, *Immigration and the Constraints of Justice* (Cambridge: Cambridge University Press, 2011), pp. 84–5.

[14] "The right to move freely relates to the whole territory of a State, including all parts of federal States" (Human Rights Committee, 1999, Human Rights Committee, "General Comment No. 27," para. 5).

[15] Could anyone really believe that such acts do not constitute a violation of human freedom rights? In *National Responsibility*, 207, n.6, Miller suggests just this, arguing that while in liberal countries people may demand a "free choice of occupation, the right to practise any religion they choose, etc.," in non-liberal countries rights "do not extend as far." In his contribution to this volume, Miller seems to have revised his view, at least in relation to the human right to internal freedom of movement. Miller now contends that people do have a human right to freedom of movement across the entire territory of a state, but that this is only because it is necessary to

Still, it is worth asking what precisely is wrong with the adequate range view? What essential interest do people have in accessing options beyond an "adequate" range? In answering these questions it is helpful to draw a distinction between two ways people relate to options. First, there are the options that each of us has chosen or has in some way become attached to: our family, our career, our religion etc. Second, there are all the other options that we are not attached to but could, at least potentially, be interested in pursuing, either now or in the future. Let us term the former "attachments" and the latter "possibilities."

It is relatively straightforward to see that people can have essential interests in accessing attachments that lie beyond an "adequate" range. Consider for instance, the example of someone who believes in a religion that is not represented in her own state and wishes to go abroad in order to practice it. What is a proponent of the adequate range view to say to this person? "It is sad that you cannot practice your religion here but there are other religions you could choose. Why not pick one of them instead?" For a religious believer, other religions are not genuine alternatives since they lack the primary quality the believer finds in her own religion: the quality of being the true religion. Or consider those separated from friends and family. There may be a range of other people with whom they could form relationships, but they cannot be expected to view these others as adequate alternatives to those they love.

Now while I think it clear that people have essential interests in accessing attachments, David Miller's contribution to this volume nevertheless contests that claim so it is worth pausing here to consider his objections. There are two. The first contends that the interests people have in accessing attachments, such as their religion or the people they love, are merely "subjectively strong interests of particular persons" not "the essential interests of human beings as such." Only the latter, Miller suggests, can ground human rights. Miller's second objection notes that when people seek to associate with other

---

prevent "restrictions of movement being detrimentally placed on some people that are not placed on others." I find this new argument as unconvincing as the "adequate" range argument. It is unconvincing for a number of reasons, but let me here confine myself to one central point. Any law can be discriminatorily applied. Laws against drugs, incitement, libel, sexual misconduct, or anything else can be (and have been) discriminatorily applied against one part of the population, leaving others free to do as they please. To solve this problem, we need not get rid of the laws. We can instead insist upon their universal application. This is as true of laws restricting freedom of movement as much as any other. Non-discrimination cannot then ground the human right to internal freedom of movement. All it can ground is a human right not to have one's freedom of movement restricted on a discriminatory basis—a right that is compatible with any level of restriction, including the blanket denial of free movement to all. If then we still wish to insist that internal freedom of movement be universally granted, not universally denied, it is because we recognize that the human right to internal freedom of movement is grounded on other values besides non-discrimination.

individuals (fellow religious believers, love interests, etc.) those other individuals are entitled to refuse to associate with them. From this, Miller concludes that the interest people have in associating with particular people cannot be an essential one. An essential interest could not be so easily waved aside.

Each of these objections involves a mistake. The first confuses universal interests with claims to generic objects. It is true that human rights are grounded on universal interests. It is false that universal interests can only ground claims to generic objects. People are entitled to be with the particular people they love and practice the particular religion they believe in because being with the people one loves and acting in accordance with one's fundamental beliefs are interests that all human beings share. Since the objects of one's affections and the prescripts of one's conscience are relative to the person, objects of a generic variety cannot fulfill these interests. As Miller himself concedes, "potential partners and religions are not substitutable in the way that foodstuffs are." The same principle applies in the case of other human rights. Consider the human right to healthcare. The right is grounded on a universal interest in leading a healthy life but what any individual needs to be healthy depends upon the person. When a diabetic complains against being prescribed AIDS medication and when an AIDS patient complains against being prescribed insulin, they cannot be dismissed as being fussy. In the case of healthcare, a generic solution is no solution. Likewise in the case of love, religion, and other attachments.

The second objection rests on a misconception of why people have rights to refuse to associate with others. Rights of refusal are not merely compatible with human freedom rights, they are a consequence of them. People are entitled to choose whom they marry, which religions (if any) they join, and with whom they spend their time. If people are forced into associations, they are denied these choices. The fact that people have rights of refusal is not then a sign that the freedom to choose with whom one associates is of little moral importance. On the contrary, it shows how vital it is. Miller is then quite wrong to suggest that the rights of individuals to refuse association are analogous to state restrictions on individual freedom, as if the two differed only by degree. In fact, rights of refusal and state restrictions are of opposing kinds. When individuals invoke rights of refusal, they *make* choices over whom they associate with. When states restrict individual freedom by blocking interactions between consenting adults, they *deny* people choices.[16] In choosing

---

[16] Note that there may be nothing wrong with states preventing nonconsensual interactions by (say) instituting anti-harassment laws. In such cases, the state is merely giving force to individual choice.

to refuse to associate with someone, an individual *exercises* her human freedom rights. In imposing unjustified restrictions that prevent consenting adults from associating, states *violate* these rights.[17]

I have said enough regarding attachments. What about possibilities? Possibilities, recall, are options to which we are not attached but which we may be interested in pursuing either now or in the future. That our human freedom rights protect our freedom to access possibilities, as well as attachments, is clear, for otherwise we could not explain the extensive scope of human freedom rights which permit us, amongst other things, to join and establish new civic associations, meet new people and make new friends, learn about and convert to new religions, and attend meetings on subjects we know little about. But why are our human freedom rights this extensive?[18]

There are at least three points to consider here. First, people have an essential interest in conscience, a value which involves more than simply acting in accordance with one's ethical beliefs but also searching for answers to "ultimate questions": "questions of life and death, the meaning of life, life's ethical foundation and so forth."[19] Because people have this interest they have an interest in the conditions of freedom that make conscience possible. As Martha Nussbaum has argued:

> From the respect we have for the person's conscience, the faculty of inquiring and searching, it follows that we ought to respect the space required by any activity that has the general shape of searching for the ultimate meaning of life, except when that search violates the rights of others.[20]

---

[17] Miller is right to think that immigration restrictions can sometimes be justified and also right to think that immigration restrictions require justification. However, in denying that people have a human right to immigrate, he sets the bar of justification much too low. Immigration restrictions can only be justified when they are necessary to prevent severe costs. See Section 3.4 below.

[18] Anna Stilz, in her contribution to this volume, seems to deny that people have rights to pursue possibilities. She distinguishes between the importance of being able to travel to a country to be with the person one loves, pursue one's career, or practice one's religion and the option of marrying someone from a country (North Korea in her example) whom one has not yet met. While the former freedoms are "basic liberties," the denial of the latter, according to Stilz, involves "no wrong" at all. Stilz is right to think that the freedom to maintain attachments is a basic liberty but mistaken to trivialize the freedom to pursue possibilities. Were the US government to ban her, a US citizen, from marrying American-Koreans, converting to Mormonism, or becoming an engineer, I think she and many others would think it a profound wrong, even if she takes little interest in these options at present. Stilz's failure to take immigration restrictions as seriously may stem from her tendency, exhibited in her choice of language, to skim over the fact that immigration restrictions are government imposed and not some natural occurrence. When I complain against being excluded or deported from a country, I am not complaining against "the context of choice I was born into," but against a foreign government that has coercively prevented me from living my life as I choose.

[19] Martha Craven Nussbaum, *Liberty of Conscience: In Defense of America's Tradition of Religious Equality* (New York: Basic Books, 2008), p. 168.

[20] Nussbaum, *Liberty of Conscience*, p. 168.

When a state removes certain life options from us, it narrows and distorts our search for answers to questions of ultimate meaning. Indeed, it may do worse than that: it may rob us of the truth. For who is to say that the religions and philosophical doctrines that state restrictions prevent us from accessing are not the true ones or contain an element of the truth?[21] Notice moreover that even if, at present, we are not interested in a particular option this does not mean that we will not be interested in the future. People can become deeply committed to ideas or ways of life that, twenty years previous, they dismissed as nonsense. Finally, note that even in regards to options that we are never interested in, the fact that they remain accessible to us can sharpen our understanding and commitment to options that we do pursue.[22] In short, conscience requires freedom: freedom not merely to pursue those options to which we are already attached, but also to question and explore options that lie beyond our immediate horizon. In practice, this means that we must be permitted to associate freely, to learn from others and express ourselves to others as we choose, to experiment with different ways of living, to study different ethical and religious traditions, and, by extension, to travel or settle where conscience—this faculty for searching and inquiring—takes us. Restrictions on freedom of association, expression, religion, or movement are thus restrictions on conscience whether they are imposed within states or at the borders.

Second, besides our interest in conscience, we have an essential interest in not having others, and in particular states, determine our options when we make basic personal decisions.[23] We have an essential interest, in other words, in what Joseph Raz has called "independence": a condition of autonomy that is violated if others subject us to their will by coercively narrowing the options available to us.[24] As Raz stresses, coercion infringes independence, and thus autonomy, even if it leaves those subjected to it with an "adequate" range of options.[25] Our interest in our independence is an interest we have in being

---

[21] John Stuart Mill, On Liberty, in John Stuart Mill (ed.), On Liberty and Other Essays (Oxford: Oxford University Press, 1998), pp. 1–128 at pp. 22–40.

[22] Mill, "On Liberty," pp. 40–51.

[23] Something like this sentiment is captured in the US Supreme Court's decision in Kent vs. Dulles, p. 126: "Travel abroad, like travel within the country...may be as close to the heart of the individual as the choice of what he eats, or wears, or reads. Freedom of movement is basic in our scheme of values."

[24] Joseph Raz, The Morality of Freedom (Oxford: Clarendon Press, 1986), pp. 377–8.

[25] Raz, The Morality of Freedom, p. 377. For a careful exposition of the claim that immigration restrictions are coercive and as such infringe autonomy, see Arash Abizadeh, "Democratic Theory and Border Coercion: No Right to Unilaterally Control Your Own Borders," Political Theory 36 (2008), 37–65 at pp. 57–60. For subsequent debate, see David Miller, "Why Immigration Controls Are Not Coercive: A Reply to Arash Abizadeh," Political Theory 38 (2010), 111–20; Arash Abizadeh, "Democratic Legitimacy and State Coercion: A Reply to David Miller," Political Theory 38 (2010), 121–30.

awarded certain standing by others, which involves the recognition that it is us, not them, who should get to determine the course of our lives.[26] From this perspective, a key purpose of human freedom rights can be seen as dividing off, from the host of issues over which states rightfully yield authority, a subset of matters, basic in each person's life, that the individual should be allowed to determine for herself. These matters include where she lives, with whom she lives, who her friends are, which religion she practices, which associations she joins, what work she does, and how she spends her free time. When states interfere in these matters, without strong justification, they deny us the recognition we are owed as autonomous persons. Unjustified restrictions, both internal and at the border, trespass on the personal domain.

Finally, we should not forget the political interest underlying conventional human freedom rights. This interest cannot be properly protected simply by awarding people an "adequate" range of life options or allowing people to access those options to which they are already attached. If governments are to be held to account regarding all geographical areas their policies affect, then people need to be able to access all these areas. The freedom to move around a locality or to access existing attachments is not sufficient to investigate the effects of government policies elsewhere. Moreover, the freedom to pursue possibilities includes the freedoms to explore new ideas and to change one's mind regarding political affairs; freedoms which are crucial to the maintenance of a free society. Governments must then grant people the liberty to meet, organize, and protest as they wish. When political activity is constrained, the opinions formed and decisions taken bear the mark of state coercion. If democratic decisions are to represent the genuine view of the electorate, rather than the view the electorate arrive at when subjected to state coercion, people must be awarded full political liberty.

To sum up: this section has shown that people do have essential interests in accessing options that lie beyond an "adequate" range. They have essential interests in accessing options to which they are already attached (such as religions and loved ones) and interests in conscience, independence, and political liberty that can only be satisfied if states refrain from interfering in their life choices. We should not then reject the conventional view of human freedom rights as protecting the freedom to access the full range of available life options. However, if we accept this conventional view, then we must accept that people have an essential interest in being free to immigrate to other states, for otherwise the range of life options they can access is greatly constrained.

---

[26] Raz, *The Morality of Freedom*, p. 378.

3.4 Objections from Culture and Distributive Justice

Someone might accept the above argument and yet insist that the interests identified cannot ground a human right to immigrate because states have a right to exclude foreigners if they so wish. This objector would, in effect, accept the interest claim (that people have fundamental interests in the freedom to immigrate) but deny the duty claim (that states must respect the freedom to immigrate).

There are many different arguments that have been given for why states have a right to exclude foreigners. Since I do not have space to address them all, let me pick out two that are particularly prominent: arguments from distributive justice and culture.[27] In replying to these arguments, I hope to offer the reader a model for how we might reply to all arguments of this sort: arguments, that is, which seek to justify the right to exclude on the basis of the supposed cost that immigration would otherwise impose in relation to some important value. The argument from distributive justice holds that exclusion can be justified to avoid deepening distributive injustice. Unrestricted immigration, it has been claimed, would drive down the wages of the poorest and destroy the social cohesion that sustains support for redistributive policies.[28] The argument from culture holds that exclusion can be justified to preserve a host state's culture. Without immigration restrictions, it is contended, host state cultures would be radically altered, if not entirely superseded, by immigrant cultures.[29]

The first point to note regarding these arguments is that they rely on empirical premises that are open to empirical contestation. It is far from clear, for instance, that immigration does drive down the wages of the poorest

---

[27] Another argument that is, perhaps, even more forceful, is that immigration produces brain drain that harms the global poor. I have addressed this argument in Kieran Oberman, "Can Brain Drain Justify Immigration Restrictions?," *Ethics* 123 (2013), 427–55.

[28] George J. Borjas, *Heaven's Door: Immigration Policy and the American Economy* (Princeton, NJ: Princeton University Press, 1999); Matthew J. Gibney, *The Ethics and Politics of Asylum: Liberal Democracy and the Response to Refugees* (Cambridge: Cambridge University Press, 2004), pp. 71–5; David Goodhart, "Too diverse?," *Prospect Magazine* (2004), 30–7; John Isbister, "A Liberal Argument for Border Controls: Reply to Carens," *International Migration Review* 34 (2000), 629–35; Stephen Macedo, "The Moral Dilemma of U.S. Immigration Policy: Open Borders Versus Social Justice?" in Carol M. Swain (ed.), *Debating Immigration* (Cambridge: Cambridge University Press, 2007), pp. 63–81; James Woodward, "Commentary: Liberalism and Migration" in Brian Barry and Robert E. Goodin (eds.), *Free Movement: Ethical Issues in the Transnational Migration of People and of Money* (University Park, PA: Pennsylvania State University Press, 1992), pp. 59–84.

[29] Carens, "Migration and Morality," pp. 36–40; Will Kymlicka, *Multicultural Citizenship: A Liberal Theory of Minority Rights* (Oxford: Oxford University Press, 1995), p. 93; David Miller, "Immigration: The Case for Limits" in Andrew I. Cohen and Christopher Heath Wellman (eds.), *Contemporary Debates in Applied Ethics* (Oxford: Blackwell, 2005), pp. 193–206 at pp. 199–201; Michael Walzer, *Spheres of Justice: A Defense of Pluralism and Equality* (New York: Basic Books, 1983), p. 39; see also Samuel P. Huntington, *Who Are We? The Challenges to America's National Identity* (New York: Simon and Schuster, 2004).

citizens. A prominent study on the effects of the large influx of Cuban immigrants to Miami, following the Mariel boatlift, found it had virtually no impact on wages or employment in the city.[30] Other studies have arrived at similar results.[31] Nor is it clear that immigration saps support for the welfare state. Canada stands as an example of a country that has sustained both high rates of immigration and high levels of social spending.[32] Europe too may offer a story of how immigration and welfare can be combined.[33] Even the assumption, underlying most arguments of this kind, that lifting immigration restrictions would result in a flood of new arrivals, requires closer analysis; a point I shall return to in Section 3.5.

It is not the empirical premises of these arguments that I wish to focus on, however, but the normative conclusion that the supposed costs justify restrictions. That conclusion is too quick. Even when costs occur, it may nevertheless be morally incumbent upon a state to permit immigration.

In fact, I will argue, social costs can only justify restrictions under two conditions: (1) the costs are particularly severe, and (2) there is no acceptable alternative means to address them. Since social costs can only justify immigration restrictions in this restricted range of circumstances, arguments for distributive justice and culture offer no objection to the idea of a non-absolute human right to immigrate.

The logic underlying this approach is that when we trade off the freedom to immigrate against other values we must award it the same weight as other basic freedoms when they face similar trade-offs. We should award the freedom to immigrate the same weight as freedom of movement, association, expression, religion, and occupational and marital choice, since, as we have seen, the same underlying interests are at stake.

That we award these other freedoms significant weight is clear from the fact that we recognize these freedoms as human rights. In certain cases, these freedoms may justifiably be restricted in order to avoid social costs, but such cases arise only when the threatened costs are particularly severe and there is no acceptable alternative means to avoid them. So, for instance, in the case of freedom of expression, it might be permissible to ban a political protest if it threatens to result in rioting but not to avoid some more minor cost, such as

---

[30] David Card, "The Impact of the Mariel Boatlift on the Miami Labor Market," *Industrial and Labor Relations Review* 43 (1989), 245–57.

[31] Rachel M. Friedberg and Jennifer Hunt, "The Impact of Immigrants on Host Country Wages, Employment and Growth," *The Journal of Economic Perspectives* 9 (1995), 23–44; Marco Manacorda, Alan Manning, and Jonathan Wadsworth, "The Impact of Immigration on the Structure of Wages: Theory and Evidence from Britain," *CEPR Discussion Paper* DP7888 (2010).

[32] Keith G. Banting, "Is There a Progressive's Dilemma in Canada? Immigration, Multiculturalism and the Welfare State," *Canadian Journal of Political Science* 43 (2010), 797–820.

[33] Marcus M. L. Crepaz, *Trust Beyond Borders: Immigration, the Welfare State and Identity in the Mordern State* (Ann Arbor, MI: University of Michigan Press, 2008).

temporary traffic disruption or offense to opponent groups. Nor would it be permissible to ban the protest if there was an acceptable alternative means to avoid the riot, such as increased policing.

If we award the freedom to immigrate the same weight as these other freedoms, then the same two conditions must apply. If we apply these conditions, however, then a number of justifications for exclusion fail, either because the supposed costs they refer to are not sufficiently severe or because there are alternative means by which the costs may be addressed. Let me develop each of these points in turn.

To see why many of the supposed costs of immigration do not provide sufficient reason to exclude, take the example of distributive justice. Some of the theorists that make the distributive justice argument suggest that exclusion can be justified not only when immigration threatens to deprive poor citizens of basic goods such as food and shelter but also when it threatens to harm the interests of those citizens who are merely poor relative to their richer compatriots.[34] In other words, these theorists claim exclusion can be justified not only for the sake of minimal sufficiency but also distributive equality.

This point is important, for while exclusion might be justified if immigration threatens to push citizens below some minimal sufficiency threshold, it cannot be justified in order to better realize more ambitious distributive ideals. If we consider comparable trade-offs between distributive justice and other important freedoms, we find that we are unwilling to make any incursions into these freedoms for the sake of further gains in distributive justice once people's basic needs have been fulfilled. Right-wing literature may undermine support for the liberal conception of distributive justice, but this provides no justification for banning its publication. Freedom of marital choice allows wealthy people to marry each other if they so choose (and they often do choose), frustrating one means by which poor people can better themselves, but this provides no justification for interfering in people's choice of who they marry.[35] Freedom of occupational choice allows talented people to threaten to refuse to do socially productive labor unless they earn higher than average wages, yet even G. A. Cohen, who has done much to raise this issue as a source of distributive injustice, argues that we should pay the talented more rather than infringe on their freedom of occupational choice.[36] Finally, freedom of movement within a state can undermine distributive justice by overwhelming local welfare programs with new applicants, but barring extreme cases when

---

[34] Isbister, "A Liberal Argument," p. 363; Woodward, "Commentary."

[35] Christopher H. Wellman, "Immigration and Freedom of Association," *Ethics* 119 (2008), 109–41 at p. 26.

[36] G. A. Cohen, *Rescuing Justice and Equality* (Cambridge, MA: Harvard University Press, 2008), pp. 181–222.

basic needs are under threat, distributive justice cannot justify internal restrictions.[37]

Next consider the argument from culture. Once again, we need to distinguish here between different levels of impact. If immigration were to threaten to destroy a state's culture or a crucial element of its culture, such as its language, then restrictions might be justified. Indeed, restrictions seem equally justified at the domestic level when minority cultures come under threat. Thus, there is a strong case to think native communities in North America can exclude outsiders given the vulnerability of their cultures. Sometimes, however, theorists making a culture-based argument go further, arguing that exclusion can be justified simply to prevent a culture from undergoing an important change. For instance, Carens has suggested that Japan might be permitted to exclude to prevent it from becoming a multicultural state.[38] To restrict immigration merely to avoid a cultural shift of this sort would be an unacceptable restriction on the freedom to immigrate.

Again, it is useful to consider analogous trade-offs with related freedoms. Take freedom of expression. By expressing themselves freely and absorbing new ideas, people produce profound cultural shifts. Think of the changes in social attitudes towards sex or the place of women in society that has occurred in the last fifty years. Or consider how cultures have been transformed by innovations in art, music, and entertainment. Such changes have been a shock to many and there have been some who have wanted to use the power of the state to stop these changes from occurring. Yet states cannot restrict free expression to prevent profound cultural shifts of this sort. People have a right to freedom of expression and this right cannot be overridden so easily.

Indeed, note that it is because immigrants tend to exercise their rights to freedom of expression that they are capable of producing profound effects upon a host state's culture. Were immigrants to keep publicly silent, expressing themselves freely only behind closed doors, their impact would be much diminished. It is because immigrants play their music in public, establish restaurants, open shops, set up radio stations, produce newspapers, and, above all, interact with the citizens of the host state that they tend to have a large cultural impact. The truth is that immigration restrictions are only as effective as they are in preventing shifts in culture because they allow states to do indirectly what human rights law prevents them from doing directly, namely, deny people opportunities for free expression.

Finally, consider the right to freedom of movement within a state. Western states tend to be culturally diverse, but there are areas within even the most

---

[37] Joseph H. Carens, "Immigration and the Welfare State" in Amy Gutmann (ed.), *Democracy and the Welfare State* (Princeton, NJ: Princeton University Press, 1988), pp. 207–30.
[38] Carens, "Migration and Morality," p. 37.

diverse states in which the population is as homogenous as Japan's. Think, for instance, of those rural areas in the U.S. or Canada where immigrants rarely venture. Sometimes, in boom times, such areas become attractive to immigrant populations in a way they were not before. An influx occurs, and the area begins to assume a multicultural character. While locals continue to practice their own way of life, they must rub shoulders with people who do not. Sometimes local people, upset by these changes, will demand that their authorities take action to prevent more immigrants moving in. Nevertheless, in such cases, restrictions on internal freedom of movement cannot be justified. The human right to internal freedom of movement, which all, including immigrants, are legally entitled to enjoy, must be respected even when local areas are subject to profound cultural shifts of this sort. A desire to maintain cultural homogeneity cannot justify internal migration restrictions, so why think that it can justify immigration restrictions?

So far we have been considering cases in which immigration necessarily threatens a cost to some other value. I have argued that even when a trade-off is unavoidable we should permit immigration except when the costs of doing so are particularly severe. My second point, however, is that often a trade-off is avoidable, for there are steps a state can take to avoid the costs in question without restricting immigration. The second condition for justified exclusion is thus often unfulfilled. Consider distributive justice. When immigration threatens to overload welfare programs, or lower wages for poor workers, the state has more than two options: doing nothing and excluding foreigners. Another option would be to raise taxes, either on richer citizens or the migrants themselves (or both) and use the money raised to fund the welfare programs and boost the incomes of the poorest citizens. Indeed if, as many economists argue, increased migration has efficiency gains, then it might be possible to fund these measures using revenue that would not otherwise be raised.[39] Immigration could, in this sense, pay for itself.[40]

Similarly if immigration threatens a state's culture, the state can adopt other means to protect it, by, for instance, encouraging immigrants to integrate into the host state's culture. How much integration a state can demand and what measures it can take in this regard are both controversial matters, but I think it is acceptable for a state to expect resident foreigners to learn the native

---

[39] Borjas, *Heaven's Door*, p. 87; Gabriel J. Felbermayr, Sanne Hiller, and Davide Sala, "Does Immigration Boost Per Capita Income?," *Economics Letters* 107 (2010), 177–9.

[40] Howard F. Chang, "The Disadvantages of Immigration Restriction as a Policy to Improve Income Distribution," *SMU Law Review* 61 (2008), 23–46 at pp. 31–3. It might be objected that, in a democracy, the government may be unable to raise taxes because of resistance from voters. But all this shows is that voters are capable of acting unjustly. The fact that a decision is made democratically does not relieve voters of the moral responsibility to make a just decision, quite the reverse.

language and encourage them to do so by refusing to provide translation for non-essential services, especially if at the same time it provides subsidized language classes.[41]

Finally, one policy that states can adopt in order to limit any cost that immigration imposes is encouraging foreigners to stay in their home state voluntarily by creating greater economic opportunities for them there: a point I shall return to in Section 3.5. To conclude this section: the freedom to immigrate must be given the same weight, when traded off against other values, as related freedoms which are already recognized as human rights. For this reason, exclusion can only be justified when the costs of admitting foreigners are particularly severe and there is no acceptable alternative means to avoid these costs. Because of these conditions, exclusion cannot be justified as easily as other theorists have claimed. The right that states have to exclude is a narrow one and is, as such, compatible with a non-absolute human right to immigrate.

3.5 The Objection from Scarcity

In this section, I wish to consider one further objection to the idea of a human right to immigrate. The objection holds that even if we accept only a narrow set of justifications for exclusion, as I have argued we should, rich states would still be justified in excluding a large proportion of the world's population from their territory. If immigration restrictions were lifted, it might be argued, vast numbers of would want to migrate, far more than rich states can accommodate. Human rights are supposed to entail duties. If a human right to immigrate would entail no duty upon rich states to admit most people that wish to enter, how can it be a genuine right?

The first point to make regarding this objection is that it is not clear how many people would move if they were free to do so. Admittedly there is evidence suggesting large numbers would move. A survey carried out in Mexico by Robert Suro of the Pew Hispanic Center found that four in ten Mexicans said they would migrate to the U.S. if given the opportunity to do so.[42] Sometimes when immigration restrictions are lifted, large numbers move. The UK Home Office estimates that 600,000 people entered the UK from the European accession states between May 2004 and June 2006.[43] On the other hand, people do not always move when they have an incentive to do

[41] Kymlicka, *Multicultural Citizenship*, pp. 95–100; David Miller, *On Nationality* (Oxford: Clarendon Press, 1995), p. 385.
[42] Robert Suro, *Attitudes Towards Immigrants and Immigration Policy: Surveys Among Latinos in the US and Mexico* (Washington, DC: Pew Hispanic Center, 2005), p. 13.
[43] BBC News, " 'Nearly 600,000' New EU Migrants," August 22, 2006.

so. Migration within the EU has historically been low despite sizeable wage inequalities between states.[44] Moreover, even when large numbers do migrate, they might return soon after, as many of those that came to the UK after accession have since done.[45]

Let us suppose, however, that the empirical premise is true: only a small proportion of those that would want to move could actually be accommodated. Even then the objection fails. The idea of human right to immigrate would remain meaningful since the right entails other duties besides the duty to admit, and these other duties could be fulfilled even when the duty to admit could not. As Jeremy Waldron notes, it is a mistake to think that rights correspond to duties in a one-to-one fashion.[46] Rather, rights generate a series of duties, including "background duties" that help to secure the right. David Miller, who supports this view, expresses it as follows: "in cases where because of scarcity we cannot meet our direct obligation to protect A's right, we can still act on background duties that make it more likely that that right will be fulfilled in time."[47] Thus if there is a shortage of medical resources (say), we may have no duty, at the present moment, to attend to everyone's needs, but we may still have duties to raise production of medical resources, train more doctors, or launch an inquiry into the state of health services. In this way, an "individual's right does not simply disappear from view once it has been traded off against the rights of others" but "remains in the picture and must be taken seriously as residual source of other duties and obligations."[48]

In the case of the right to immigrate, the relevant background duties are duties to implement policies that reduce the costs of lifting immigration restrictions. Perhaps the most important policy of this sort is the creation of greater opportunities in poor states. If poor states made much-needed reforms, such as tackling corruption, and if rich states provided fairer terms of trade, cancelled debts, and gave more (and better targeted) foreign aid, then over time, migratory pressure might be reduced to levels at which it would be safe for rich states to completely open their borders. In making this claim, I draw no simple equation between poverty and migration. The empirical evidence points to a "hump-shaped" relationship: better-off poor states produce *more* migrants than the poorest states. Were more done to tackle poverty, then, in the short term at least, migratory pressure might actually increase. Nevertheless,

---

[44] Robert J. Flanagan, "European Wage Equalization Since the Treaty of Rome" in Lloyd Ulman, Barry Eichengreen, and William T. Dickens (eds.), *Labor and an Integrated Europe* (Washington, DC: The Brookings Institute, 1993), pp. 167–87.

[45] Naomi Pollard, Maria Latorre, and Dhananjayan Sriskandarajah, *Floodgates or Turnstiles?: Post-EU Enlargement Migration Flows to (and from) the UK* (London: Institute for Public Policy Research, 2008), p. 5.

[46] Jeremy Waldron, "Rights in Conflict," *Ethics* 99 (1989), 503–19.

[47] Miller, *National Responsibility*, p. 194.

[48] Waldron, "Rights in Conflict," p. 512.

in the longer term, development should reduce migratory pressure.[49] The European Union provides evidence of this. As I noted, the history of free movement within the EU has, on the whole, been a history of low migration despite the persistence of sizeable wage inequalities between member states. Two factors help to explain this. First, poorer member states such as Spain and Ireland experienced sizeable development.[50] This development came partly because the EU has done more than simply lift immigration restrictions. It has also offered its members aid and free trade.[51] Second, quite simply, people generally seem reluctant to migrate. As Joseph Carens notes when he considers the EU case:

> Some people love novelty and adventure, but most people are not keen to leave home, family and friends and to move to a place where they don't speak the language and don't know their way about. Most consider doing this only when they think they have a lot to gain.[52]

In this section, I have argued that the right to immigrate entails background duties to create the circumstances under which exclusion is unnecessary. This relates closely to the point made in the previous section that states have a duty to avoid conflicts between the freedom to immigrate and other values. There I argued that *before* states trade off the freedom to immigrate for other values they have a duty to seek alternative means to address the problem. Here I am arguing that even *after* a state has traded off the freedom to immigrate for other values it still has a duty to undertake policies that, in time, will make such a trade-off unnecessary.

3.6 Conclusion

This chapter has shown that people have a human right to immigrate based on their interest in making important personal decisions and engaging in politics, free from state restrictions on the range of options available to them. While states may have a contingent right to exclude when the costs

---

[49] Rogers Brubaker, "International Migration: A Challenge for Humanity," *International Migration Review* 25 (1991), 946–57 at p. 949; Timothy J. Hatton and Jeffrey G. Williamson, "What Fundamentals Drive World Migration?" in George J. Borjas and Jeff Crisp (eds.), *Poverty, International Migration and Asylum* (London: Palgrave Macmillan, 2005), pp. 15–38 at p. 18.

[50] Flanagan, "European Wage Equalization," p. 184.

[51] Richard E. Baldwin and Charles Wyplosz, *The Economics of European Integration*, 2nd edn (London: McGraw-Hill, 2006), pp. 166–9; Antoni Castells and Marta Espasa, "Do Structural Actions Contribute to Reduced Regional Disparities in the European Union?" in Bernard Funck and Lodovico Pizzati (eds.), *European Integration, Regional Policy, and Growth* (Washington, DC: World Bank, 2003), pp. 167–77.

[52] Joseph H. Carens, "Open Borders and the Claims of Community," *APSA Annual Meeting Paper* (2010), 13.

of immigration are particularly severe, such a right is compatible with the idea of a human right to immigrate.

While immigration restrictions might be justified if necessary to avoid severe costs, outside these special circumstances they constitute a violation of our human rights. Since even the most progressive states restrict immigration and since it is implausible that all the restrictions they impose are necessary to avoid severe costs, we must conclude that even the most progressive states violate the human right to immigrate. The fact that the human right to immigrate is so frequently violated should not, however, make us any more tolerant of its violation. When states prevent us from going where we want to go, associating with whom we wish, or speaking our minds to those who care to hear our thoughts, the appropriate reaction is one of indignation. It does not matter whether states prevent us from doing these things by fining us, imprisoning us, deporting us, or denying us entry: indignation is the appropriate response since states have no right to interfere in our lives in these ways. Once we recognize and condemn unjustified immigration restrictions as the human rights violations they constitute, we take the first step in the long process of achieving their removal.[53]

References

Abizadeh, Arash, "Democratic Theory and Border Coercion: No Right to Unilaterally Control Your Own Borders," *Political Theory* 36:1 (2008), 37–65.

Abizadeh, Arash, "Democratic Legitimacy and State Coercion: A Reply to David Miller," *Political Theory* 38:1 (2010), 121–30.

Baldwin, Richard E. and Charles Wyplosz, *The Economics of European Integration* 2nd edn. (London: McGraw-Hill, 2006).

Banting, Keith G., "Is There a Progressive's Dilemma in Canada? Immigration, Multiculturalism and the Welfare State," *Canadian Journal of Political Science* 43:4 (2010), 797–820.

BBC News, "'Nearly 600,000' New EU Migrants," August 22, 2006.

Borjas, George J., *Heaven's Door: Immigration Policy and the American Economy* (Princeton, NJ: Princeton University Press, 1999).

Brubaker, Rogers, "International Migration: A Challenge for Humanity," *International Migration Review* 25:4 (1991), 946–57.

Burr, Steven, "Immigration and the First Amendment," *California Law Review* 73:6 (1985), 1889–928.

Card, David, "The Impact of the Mariel Boatlift on the Miami Labor Market," *Industrial and Labor Relations Review* 43:2 (1989), 245–57.

[53] Versions of this chapter have been presented to audiences in Oxford, Berlin, Keele, and Stanford. I am extremely grateful for the comments I received. Special thanks are owed to Danial Butt, Eamonn Callan, Simon Caney, Joseph Carens, Sarah Fine, Matthew Gibney, David Miller, Tiziana Torresi, Leif Wenar, and Lea Ypi.

Carens, Joseph H., "Aliens and Citizens: The Case for Open Borders," *Review of Politics* 49:2 (1987), 250–73.

Carens, Joseph H., "Immigration and the Welfare State" in Amy Gutmann (ed.), *Democracy and the Welfare State* (Princeton, NJ: Princeton University Press, 1988), pp. 207–30.

Carens, Joseph H., "Migration and Morality: A Liberal Egalitarian Perspective" in Brian Barry and Robert E. Goodin (eds.), *Free Movement: Ethical Issues in the Transnational Migration of People and Money* (University Park, PA: Pennsylvania State University Press, 1992), pp. 25–47.

Carens, Joseph H., "The Philosopher and the Policy Maker: Two Perspectives on the Ethics of Immigration with Special Attention to the Problem of Restricting Asylum" in Kay Hailbronner, David A. Martin, and Hiroshi Motomura (eds.), *Immigration Admissions: The Search for Workable Policies in Germany and the United States* (Providence, RI and Oxford: Berghahn, 1997), pp. 3–50.

Carens, Joseph H., "Open Borders and the Claims of Community," *APSA Annual Meeting Paper*, 2010.

Castells, Antoni and Marta Espasa, "Do Structural Actions Contribute to Reduced Regional Disparities in the European Union?" in Bernard Funck and Lodovico Pizzati (eds.), *European Integration, Regional Policy, and Growth* (Washington, DC: World Bank, 2003), pp. 167–77.

Chang, Howard F., "The Disadvantages of Immigration Restriction as a Policy to Improve Income Distribution," *SMU Law Review* 61 (2008), 23–46.

Cohen, G. A., *Rescuing Justice and Equality* (Cambridge, MA: Harvard University Press, 2008).

Cole, Phillip, *Philosophies of Exclusion* (Edinburgh: Edinburgh University Press, 2000).

Crepaz, Marcus M. L., *Trust Beyond Borders: Immigration, the Welfare State and Identity in the Mordern State* (Ann Arbor: University of Michigan Press, 2008).

Dummett, Ann, "The Transnational Migration of People Seen from within a Natural Law Tradition" in Brian Barry and Robert E. Goodin (eds.), *Free Movement: Ethical Issues in the Transnational Migration of People and of Money* (University Park, PA: Pennsylvania State University Press, 1992), pp. 169–80.

Felbermayr, Gabriel J., Sanne Hiller, and Davide Sala, "Does Immigration Boost Per Capita Income?," *Economics Letters* 107 (2010), 177–9.

Flanagan, Robert J., "European Wage Equalization since the Treaty of Rome" in Lloyd Ulman, Barry Eichengreen, and William T. Dickens (eds.), *Labor and an Integrated Europe* (Washington, DC: The Brookings Institute, 1993), pp. 167–87.

Friedberg, Rachel M. and Jennifer Hunt, "The Impact of Immigrants on Host Country Wages, Employment and Growth," *The Journal of Economic Perspectives* 9:2 (1995), 23–44.

Gibney, Matthew J., *The Ethics and Politics of Asylum: Liberal Democracy and the Response to Refugees* (Cambridge: Cambridge University Press, 2004).

Goodhart, David, "Too Diverse?" *Prospect Magazine* 95 (2004): 30–7.

Goodin, Robert E. "If People Were Money...." in Brian Barry and Robert E. Goodin (eds.), *Free Movement: Ethical Issues in the Transnational Migration of People and of Money* (University Park, PA: Pennsylvania State University Press, 1992), pp. 6–22.

Griffin, James, *On Human Rights* (Oxford: Oxford University Press, 2008).

Hatton, Timothy J. and Jeffrey G. Williamson, "What Fundamentals Drive World Migration?" in George J. Borjas and Jeff Crisp (eds.), *Poverty, International Migration and Asylum* (London: Palgrave Macmillan, 2005), pp. 15–38.

Human Rights Committee, "General Comment No. 27: Freedom of Movement (Article 12)," CCPR/C/21/Rev.1 (November 2, 1999).

Huntington, Samuel P., *Who Are We? The Challenges to America's National Identity* (New York: Simon and Schuster, 2004).

Isbister, John, "A Liberal Argument for Border Controls: Reply to Carens," *International Migration Review* 34 (2000), 629–35.

Kymlicka, Will, *Multicultural Citizenship: A Liberal Theory of Minority Rights* (Oxford: Oxford University Press, 1995).

Macedo, Stephen, "The Moral Dilemma of U.S. Immigration Policy: Open Borders Versus Social Justice?" in Carol M. Swain (ed.), *Debating Immigration* (Cambridge: Cambridge University Press, 2007), pp. 63–81.

Manacorda, Marco, Alan Manning, and Jonathan Wadsworth, "The Impact of Immigration on the Structure of Wages: Theory and Evidence from Britain," *CEPR Discussion Paper* DP7888 (2010).

Mill, John Stuart, "On Liberty" in John Stuart Mill (ed.), *On Liberty and Other Essays* (Oxford: Oxford University Press, 1998), pp. 1–128.

Miller, David, *On Nationality*. Oxford Political Theory (Oxford: Clarendon Press, 1995).

Miller, David, "Immigration: The Case for Limits" in Andrew I. Cohen and Christopher Heath Wellman (eds.), *Contemporary Debates in Applied Ethics* (Oxford: Blackwell, 2005), pp. 193–206.

Miller, David, *National Responsibility and Global Justice*. Oxford Political Theory. (Oxford: Oxford University Press, 2007).

Miller, David, "Why Immigration Controls Are Not Coercive: A Reply to Arash Abizadeh," *Political Theory* 38:1 (2010), 111–20.

Nussbaum, Martha Craven, *Liberty of Conscience: In Defense of America's Tradition of Religious Equality* (New York: Basic Books, 2008).

Oberman, Kieran, "Immigration, Global Poverty and the Right to Stay," *Political Studies* 59:2 (2011), 253–68.

Oberman, Kieran, "Can Brain Drain Justify Immigration Restrictions?," *Ethics* 123 (2013), 427–55.

Pogge, Thomas, "Severe Poverty as a Human Rights Violation" in Thomas Pogge (ed.), *Freedom from Poverty as a Human Right: Who Owes What to the Very Poor?* (Cambridge: Cambridge University Press, 2007), pp. 11–54.

Pollard, Naomi, Maria Latorre, and Dhananjayan Sriskandarajah, *Floodgates or Turnstiles?: Post-EU Enlargement Migration Flows to (and from) the UK* (London: Institute for Public Policy Research, 2008).

Raz, Joseph, *The Morality of Freedom* (Oxford: Clarendon Press, 1986).

Rodrik, Dani, "Final Remarks" in Tito Boeri, Gordon Hanson, and Barry McCormick (eds.), *Immigration Policy and the Welfare System* (Oxford: Oxford University Press, 2002), pp. 314–17.

Steiner, Hillel, "Hard Borders, Compensation, and Classical Liberalism" in David Miller and Sohail H. Hashimi (eds.), *Boundaries, Autonomy and Justice: Diverse Ethical Views* (Princeton, NJ: Pinceton University Press, 2001), pp. 79–88.

Suro, Robert, *Attitudes Towards Immigrants and Immigration Policy: Surveys among Latinos in the US and Mexico* (Washington, DC: Pew Hispanic Center, 2005).

Tasioulas, John, "The Moral Reality of Human Rights" in Thomas Pogge (ed.), *Freedom from Poverty as a Human Right: Who Owes What to the Very Poor?* (Cambridge: Cambridge University Press, 2007), pp. 75–101.

Waldron, Jeremy, "Rights in Conflict," *Ethics* 99:3 (1989), 503–19.

Walzer, Michael, *Spheres of Justice: A Defense of Pluralism and Equality* (New York: Basic Books, 1983).

Wellman, Christopher H., "Immigration and Freedom of Association," *Ethics* 119 (2008), 109–41.

Winters, Alan L., Terry L. Walmsley, Zen Kun Wang, and Roman Grynberg, "Liberalising Temporary Movement of Natural Persons: An Agenda for the Development Round," *The World Economy* 26:8 (2003), 1137–61.

Woodward, James, "Commentary: Liberalism and Migration" in Brian Barry and Robert E. Goodin (eds.), *Free Movement: Ethical Issues in the Transnational Migration of People and of Money* (University Park: Pennsylvania State University Press, 1992), pp. 59–84.

4

Is There an Unqualified Right to Leave?

Anna Stilz

Article 13 of the Universal Declaration of Human Rights states: "everyone has the right to leave any country, including his own, and to return to his country." Article 15 adds: "no one shall be arbitrarily deprived of his nationality nor denied the right to change his nationality."[1] The right to leave is considered to be a very weighty human right. Preventing a person from departing a territory, it seems, treats him as property of the state, a means to purposes that are not his own. Early modern mercantilist states viewed people (especially skilled workers) as resources of state power, and sought to curtail their emigration in this way.[2] Closer to our own time, Eastern Bloc countries—such as the Soviet Union and GDR—denied their citizens the right to leave, inter alia, on the grounds that free movement would create a "brain drain."[3] In part because of these historical examples, it has become a "liberal orthodoxy" that free exit should not be restricted.

While it is commonly believed that individuals do have a moral right to leave their country, the shape and scope of this right is not especially clear.[4] Can citizens justifiably be regulated in the act of leaving their state? Is it wrong to impose terms or conditions on their departure? Let me define a "regulation" as any law that places a cost on leaving compared to a situation in which no such law exists. A requirement of taxation at the moment of exit, taxation on income earned abroad, or the compulsory discharge of civil service obligations

---

[1] See <http://www.un.org/en/documents/udhr>.

[2] Alan Dowty, *Closed Borders: The Contemporary Assault on Freedom of Movement* (New Haven, CT: Yale University Press, 1987), pp. 26–31.

[3] Dowty, *Closed Borders*, pp. 114–27.

[4] Ryan Pevnick, *Immigration and the Constraints of Justice* (Cambridge: Cambridge University Press, 2011), pp. 96–8, has a nice discussion of this problem.

prior to leaving, all count as "regulations" in this sense.[5] While these requirements do not prohibit exit, they do make it more costly.

To get clear on whether exit can justifiably be regulated, I briefly outline
three interpretations of the grounds for exit rights. The first sees the right as
based on the claim to travel, the second on the claim to relocation, and the
third on the claim to renounce one's civic obligations (the right may also rest
on some combination of these claims).[6] I use the term "claim" to refer to a
strong individual interest that is weighty enough to justify a right in a range of
potential cases. I refer to a "claim," rather than a "right," however, to recognize the fact that sometimes this interest may be defeated by countervailing
considerations, and therefore may not always rise to the level of a right. I argue
that there are indeed strong claims to travel and relocate, and that these play a
significant role in grounding the right of exit. But I believe there is no claim to
unconditionally renounce one's civic obligations. This fact should affect our
interpretation of the exit right's scope. If my argument is correct, then certain
conditions on exit—those designed to enforce distributive obligations to
compatriots, without impeding travel or relocation—can be justified.

I want to be clear at the outset that I am not arguing that it is permissible for
states to *coercively prohibit* residents from leaving their territories. As I show in
Section 4.2, there are fundamental self-development interests that tell in favor
of people being allowed to leave. But the fact that self-development interests
play an important role in exit does not mean that no terms can be imposed on
departure. For consider the following analogy: people also have important
self-development interests in the freedom to choose their occupation. But still
we accept that certain terms can fairly be imposed on this choice. If I choose to
be an investment banker, it is acceptable for the state to require higher tax
contributions from me than if I were a fireman, making it more costly for me
to pursue this choice. If I decide to become a doctor, the state may impose
quotas for admission to medical school or limit the number of physician
licenses it grants, making it more difficult for me to accomplish my goal. In
adopting these policies, the state does not infringe my right to occupational
freedom: it simply regulates my exercise of it. The key claim of this chapter is
that we should think of the right to exit in a similar way—as a right whose
exercise can fairly be regulated within a legitimate scheme of law—not as an
"absolute" or "natural" right against the state.

---

[5] Gillian Brock argues for compulsory service requirements for high-skilled immigrants in
Gillian Brock and Michael Blake, *Debating Brain Drain: May Countries Restrict Emigration?* (Oxford:
Oxford University Press, 2015).

[6] For distinctions similar to those I develop here, see Frederick G. Whelan, "Citizenship and the
Right to Leave," *The American Political Science Review* 75 (1981), 636–53.

4.1 Three Interpretations of the Right to Exit

There are various interpretations of the grounds for exit rights. On one view, the right to leave is grounded in a claim to *travel* freely abroad.[7] The idea is that one ought not to be prevented by the state from moving across borders in order to access associates, institutions, and experiences that are important for one's self-development. Travel can be a means to pursuing many of our autonomy interests: one may wish to make a pilgrimage to a religious site; to visit family and friends abroad; to access educational opportunities; or simply to see the great wonders of the world.

On a second view, the right to leave is grounded in a claim to *relocate*: to move across borders, not just temporarily, but with the intention of residing for an indefinite time. Individuals have interests in economic opportunity, in family reunification, or simply in seeking out a society more congenial to their lifestyles, any of which might lead them to uproot themselves and move their place of residence. Sometimes the country where an individual is born fails to provide him sufficient opportunities, or is not suited to his aspirations.[8] If the right to leave is grounded in a claim to relocate, citizens have a strong interest in not being prevented by their own state from taking up extended (and possibly permanent) residence on another state's territory to pursue opportunities located there.

On a third interpretation, the right to exit is grounded in a claim to renounce one's citizenship obligations. On this view, the right to leave is linked to a claim to be released at will from binding allegiance to one's country and fellow-citizens.[9] Only if the option of renouncing citizenship is open can we say that citizens have consented to membership and are obliged to comply with their state's laws. If they instead signal their intention to exit, citizens have a strong interest in immunity from coercion to enforce their civic obligations, including distributive obligations to fellow-citizens. This *expatriation* view presents an ideal of the states system as a set of voluntary (or at least quasi-voluntary) associations, formed of individuals who freely assume and can freely renounce their civic ties.[10]

---

[7] Whelan highlights the interest in travel in "Citizenship and the Right to Leave," p. 638. Many of Kieran Oberman's examples in his contribution to this volume also support a travel claim.

[8] Joseph Carens has emphasized this argument. See Carens, "Aliens and Citizens: The Case for Open Borders," *Review of Politics* 49 (1987), p. 258: "One might fall in love with a citizen from another land, one might belong to a religion which has few followers in one's native land and many in another, one might seek cultural opportunities that are only available in another society." See also Oberman's contribution to this volume.

[9] Cf. Dowty, *Closed Borders*, p. 4, who suggests that emigration is grounded in a right of personal self-determination, which gives one "the right to remain party to one's social contract or to seek another"; Whelan, "Citizenship and the Right to Leave," p. 638, argues that a right to leave "seems to go at least part way towards making citizenship and its obligations entirely voluntaristic."

[10] In practice, of course, many expatriates voluntarily retain citizenship ties with their home countries. But the key feature of this expatriation view, as I am defining it, is that citizenship

I argue that the right to leave is not grounded on the claim to unconditionally renounce one's civic obligations, since there is no such claim. Instead, I believe there are important liberal reasons *not* to allow individuals to exercise discretion over their civic obligations, when those obligations are imposed on them by a legitimate state.[11] But I also hold that the freedoms to travel and relocate are highly valuable for personal autonomy, and polities that prohibit exit tend to be tyrannical. I therefore argue that we should recognize broad liberties of travel and relocation *without* extending these to the renunciation of civic obligations. A legitimate state would be within its rights to tax and regulate those who seek residence or citizenship elsewhere. But such a state should still permit its citizens to travel—and even to permanently relocate—to other countries, though it may enforce their citizenship obligations at the point of exit or during their stay abroad.

Before elaborating further, let me highlight one important caveat. It might be thought that if the right to leave is indeed rooted in a claim to travel or to relocate, then this has implications for the right of entry. For one's effective—and not just formal—ability to travel/relocate depends on receiving permission from a receiving state to enter its territory. Some thinkers have argued that the right to leave must be paired with a right to enter.[12] If their argument is correct, then by emphasizing our interests in travel and relocation when it comes to exit rights, it may seem that I am arguing for a right to immigrate as well.

It is not clear that this "pairing" view is correct, however. As Miller and Wellman note in their contributions to this volume, many other important rights (such as the right to marry, to associate with others, or to freedom of occupation) are conditional on finding willing partners for their exercise. Rights are made conditional in this way when potential partners have important interests (e.g., in choice or privacy) that are best protected by requiring their consent to the relationship. If citizens of receiving states have analogously important interests (in self-determination, in protection of their culture or their system of public welfare, or in control over their territory), then the claim to travel or relocate on the part of prospective migrants may only ground a conditional right to enter. Since this chapter primarily concerns the right to leave, I take no stand here about whether there are duties to allow

responsibilities are a matter of personal choice. Individuals have the right to renounce such responsibilities.

[11] Lea Ypi, in "Justice in Migration: A Closed Borders Utopia," *Journal of Political Philosophy* 16 (2008), 391–418, also argues that the right to emigrate should be qualified. But while she argues that justice in emigration may require preventing exit, I resist this conclusion.

[12] Phillip Cole claims that arguments for rights to exit or to control entry are all *symmetrical*—that is, if they imply that exit should be allowed, then entry should be allowed as well. See Phillip Cole, *Philosophies of Exclusion: Liberal Political Theory and Immigration* (Edinburgh: Edinburgh University Press, 2000).

entry on the part of receiving states. But I do wish to emphasize that even if claims to travel or relocate can only generate a conditional right to enter, they can still play an important role in justifying the right to leave. Your effective ability to travel or relocate depends on your own state allowing you to exit its territory, even if it also requires you to have a place to go.

4.2 Claims to Travel or Relocate

Why might we think that individuals have a claim to travel or relocate abroad? One could defend this idea by postulating a natural right of "free movement over the face of the earth," construed as "an aspect of natural liberty in general."[13] As Joseph Carens puts it, "the right to go where you want to go is itself an important freedom. It is precisely this freedom, and all that this freedom makes possible, that is taken away by imprisonment."[14] Hobbes defined freedom, in this negative sense, as the absence of "externall Impediments of motion," such as walls, chains, barriers, or other constraints.[15]

But this is not a convincing basis on which to defend a claim to travel or relocate, since it is not obvious there is any general "right to liberty" of the kind it presupposes. There are two reasons for being skeptical of such a right. First, one important purpose of a system of rights is to coordinate our uses of the spatial world, which involves limiting our free movement to a significant degree. It can't plausibly be said that such a system of rights makes us *less* free than we would be in its absence, since it is only once we have rules about property, uses of public space, and so on that we can freely pursue our projects.[16] Some limits on movement are necessary for us to enjoy autonomous lives in the first place.[17]

[13] Whelan, "Citizenship and the Right to Leave," p. 640; Dowty, *Closed Borders*, p. 12. See also Ann Dummett, "The Transnational Migration of People Seen from within a Natural Law Perspective" in Brian Barry and Robert Goodin (eds.), *Free Movement: Ethical Issues in the Transnational Migration of People and of Money* (University Park, PA: Pennsylvania State University Press, 1992), pp. 169–80.

[14] Joseph H. Carens, "Migration and Morality: A Liberal Egalitarian Perspective" in Brian Barry and Robert Goodin (eds.), *Free Movement: Ethical Issues in the Transnational Migration of People and Money* (University Park, PA: Pennsylvania State University Press, 1992), pp. 25–47.

[15] Thomas Hobbes, *Leviathan*, ed. Richard Tuck (Cambridge: Cambridge University Press, 1991), ch. 21, p. 147.

[16] Onora O'Neill, "The Most Extensive Liberty," *Proceedings of the Aristotelian Society* 80 (1979), 45–59.

[17] Carens acknowledges that although free movement is "an important liberty in itself," some restrictions on it can be justified. But it seems to me that the permissibility of such restrictions—including trivial ones necessary to promote, e.g., the flow of traffic—calls into question a view of free movement as a deontic natural liberty that normally trumps competing considerations. The importance of free movement may instead be mostly a matter of how it supports other basic liberties necessary to ensure self-development and equal citizenship. Carens relies on several arguments to support international free movement, however, some of which are closer to this last position.

A second problem is that not every coercive restriction on movement seems pernicious. A prohibition on jaywalking, or on driving the wrong way down a one-way street, restricts my movement, as does a prohibition on my entering my house of worship.[18] For the partisan of a general right to liberty, both restrictions would be equally bad, since it is the same good—negative freedom—that is taken away. But that seems wrong. The latter prohibition is of greater concern, and not because it takes away *more liberty*, in some quantitative sense of more opportunities to move or space within which to roam. We care, not just about the number of restrictions on movement, but also about the *quality* of the reasons for engaging in movement. A mere "rational basis" for restriction, rooted in relatively trivial public order considerations, is a good enough reason for restricting the flow of traffic. But trivial public order considerations are not sufficient to permanently prevent me from entering my house of worship. The freedom to practice my religion or to attend a political assembly are *basic liberties*, as the freedom to cross the street where I like, and to drive where I want, are not.[19] So if the argument for travel or relocation depends on a general right to be unrestrained in moving my body as I choose, it is not very plausible. Some kinds of movement are unimportant and can be restricted for extremely trivial reasons, while other kinds of movement are more fundamental.

But claims to travel or relocate need not be argued for on the basis of a general right to free movement. Instead, as Kieran Oberman notes in his chapter, such claims are better justified because they are instrumental to protecting the interests at stake in other basic liberties.[20] Travel and relocation are often part of, or necessary to, the exercise of rights we already recognize as justified.

To defend this view, of course, we need an account of what makes for a basic liberty. What is the difference between a non-basic liberty that can be restricted for trivial reasons and a basic liberty that cannot? There is more than one way of grounding this distinction, but let me here adapt Rawls' view. For Rawls, a basic liberty is "an essential social condition for the adequate development and full exercise of the two powers of moral personality" that political citizens possess.[21] These two moral powers are the capacity to form,

---

[18] Ronald Dworkin, "What Rights Do We Have?" in *Taking Rights Seriously* (Cambridge, MA: Harvard University Press, 1978), pp. 268–9; Charles Taylor, "What's Wrong with Negative Liberty?" in *Philosophy and the Human Sciences 2* (Cambridge: Cambridge University Press, 1985), pp. 217–19.

[19] David Miller draws a similar distinction between *basic* freedoms and *bare* freedoms in "Immigration: The Case for Limits" in Andrew Cohen and Christopher Wellman (eds.), *Contemporary Debates in Applied Ethics* (Malden, MA: Blackwell, 2004).

[20] Some of Carens' arguments for global free movement also appeal to the idea that free movement is instrumental to other basic liberties. See Carens, "Aliens and Citizens," pp. 258–9.

[21] John Rawls, *Political Liberalism* (New York: Columbia University Press, 1993), pp. 291–324.

revise, and pursue a conception of the good, and to access sufficient means for pursuing one's determinate conception thereof (*personal autonomy*); and the capacity for a sense of justice in applying principles of justice to the basic structure of society (*sense of justice*). Basic liberties like freedom of conscience and freedom of association are important because they facilitate the exercise of personal autonomy, while liberties like the right to vote and the right of free speech are justified because they facilitate the exercise of a sense of justice. Rawls further clarifies the *significance* of a basic liberty: "a liberty is more or less significant depending on whether it is more or less essentially involved in, or is a more or less necessary institutional means to protect, the full and informed and effective exercise of the moral powers."[22] The more a particular claim can be argued to be an essential institutional means to protect one of the two moral powers, the weightier that claim of right will be.

Where does a claim to travel or relocate abroad stand? Is it plausibly connected to the two moral powers, and if so, is it *significant?* It seems to me that travel or relocation abroad can often be an important institutional means to protect the very same personal autonomy interests that ground our domestic basic liberties. There are two ways to argue that freedom to move across borders is instrumental to other rights.

The first approach notes that the right to move abroad helps protect other basic liberties because it allows us to seek out alternative institutions when our rights are threatened by our own state. In addition to having their fundamental freedoms violated, religious minorities or political dissidents (such as Baha'is in Iran) have often been banned from leaving their country. This helps to intensify political persecution, making it more totalizing and effective. Allowing free exit thus may have useful effects in incentivizing the protection of rights domestically. If governments know that dissidents can leave the territory and organize political opposition abroad, they have greater incentive to engage in political compromise rather than repression.

A second, more controversial, argument notes that travel or relocation can be a means of pursuing the very interests that ground our domestic basic liberties. This is especially the case when options fundamental to my conception of the good are located outside my own country. Many of the examples Carens appeals to implicate personal autonomy interests in this way. For example, travel abroad to join loved ones or family members may be an important guarantee for my interest in marriage and family relationships. Or consider a case where I need to travel abroad in order to practice my religion—to make a special pilgrimage, or simply to find other adherents with whom to practice (suppose I am a Mormon stranded in Japan). Here too cross-border

---

[22] Rawls, *Political Liberalism*, p. 335.

movement could be an institutional condition for pursuing my conception of the good. Or suppose it is my aspiration to become an aeronautical engineer, but I live in Sierra Leone and the only suitable degree programs are in the U.S. and Europe. Again, it seems that the ability to travel could be a precondition for my exercise of occupational choice. If this is right, then our moral powers can be importantly implicated in the ability to move across borders, at least in some cases, in a way that has significant weight.[23]

David Miller has criticized this argument, holding that:

> what a person can legitimately demand access to is an *adequate* range of options to choose between—a reasonable choice of occupation, religion, cultural activities, marriage partners, and so forth. Adequacy here is defined in terms of generic human interests rather than in terms of the interests of any one person in particular—so, for example, a would-be opera singer living in a society which provides for various forms of musical expression, but not for opera, can have an adequate range of options in this area even though the option she most prefers is not available. So long as they adhere to the standards of decency sketched above, all contemporary states are able to provide an adequate range internally.[24]

I agree with Miller that no wrong is necessarily done to a person if she grows up in a society where not every valuable option is available, as long as the options at her disposal safeguard certain generic human interests. The fact that my choice of marriage partners here in the U.S. does not run to North Koreans does not mean that I don't have a perfectly adequate choice of partners. Though the context of choice I was born into no doubt influenced my options and thus my eventual marriage, that is no wrong to me. While I chose my husband from a less-than-global range of options, my choice was not less authentic because of that fact. My context of choice does not *impede* my pursuit of a conception of the good, though it does *shape* my choice of a conception.[25]

Unlike Miller, however, I think that sometimes states are not capable of providing an adequate range of options internally. This is especially true,

---

[23] Carens, "Migration and Morality"; Kieran Oberman, "Immigration as a Human Right," this volume.

[24] David Miller, "Immigration: The Case for Limits," p. 196.

[25] In his contribution to this volume, Oberman criticizes me for overlooking the importance of access to *possibilities*, "options that we are not attached to but could, at least potentially, be interested in pursuing, either now or in the future." Unlike Oberman, I do not believe that personal autonomy requires access to every possible option. To be autonomous, we do need access to some untried possibilities, but that range need not include every existing option. To hold otherwise is to come close to postulating a general right to liberty, by arguing that one fails to be autonomous if one faces *any* restrictions on one's ability to access possibilities. But that is unpersuasive: I am not less autonomous because I chose an academic career in a context where the option of being a sumo wrestler was unavailable to me. I had a wide range of career options, which is what matters. Beyond the need for an adequate range of possibilities, particular options become relevant only when they figure centrally in a person's conception of the good.

I believe, when (a) people are *already committed* to a particular conception of the good that comprehensively structures their life, and (b) a proposed border restriction would deprive them of access to an option that is fundamental to their pursuit of that conception, in a way that makes it very difficult for them to adjust. In the case of the right to leave, restrictions on exit will often prevent people from accessing options central to their conception of the good, but that aren't available (or aren't fully available) in the country where they now live. Restricting people from accessing options *they are already pursuing* seems much worse than simply placing them in a context where they are more likely to embrace some options than others. Suppose I went abroad on a school trip, met a North Korean, and fell in love with him. It seems much worse to deny me the ability to marry and live with this North Korean than it did to restrict my opportunities to meet and fall in love with North Koreans in the first place. For at this point my relationship with him may comprehensively structure my life.

In these cases, internal protection of basic liberties may not be adequate to fulfill the autonomy interests that ground these liberties. It is not sufficient to cut someone off from her husband, while pointing out that she can still access a range of marriage partners on this side of the border; or to cut her off from associates who practice her religion, while protesting that there is still a wide variety of other religions available to her in the area to which her movement is now restricted. The interests at stake cannot be pursued when one is prevented from accessing options that are central to one's conception of the good, and to which one lacks adequate alternatives.

In his contribution to this volume, Miller objects that the interests grounding a right must be generic interests, not interests that are highly specific to a particular person. But I believe the interests cited are suitably generic. The interests in marriage and family life, in practicing one's religion, in pursuing an education or accepting a job are the same interests that ground domestic basic liberties. It is true that only some particular people will need to move across borders in order to fulfill these interests. Many people will marry, raise a family, practice their religion, and work without ever leaving their home country. But the fact that only a minority will utilize a protection does not mean that the protection is grounded in an idiosyncratic interest. Many other human rights—such as the right to a fair trial, or the right to asylum—are similarly utilized by only a minority of people. I hope to live my entire life without exercising my right to a fair trial. Still, this right protects a generic interest that I share with many others, even if I never avail myself of it. So Miller's objection here seems unsuccessful.

To sum up, then, whether or not our personal autonomy interests are strong enough to ground a general right to *enter* every other country in the world, I believe they do play an important role in justifying the right to *leave*. Moving abroad is often instrumental to protecting the very interests that ground our domestic basic liberties, as in cases where these liberties are violated by our government, or where options fundamental to our conception of the good are located outside our home country. Our claims to travel and relocate thus seem quite strong.

In grounding a human right to leave, however, we must assess the migrants' interests in relocation against possible countervailing considerations. If recognizing a right to exit would carry significant costs, then this might tell in favor of limitations on it. There are two ways costs can matter in justifying a right.[26] First, if the costs of protecting a particular claim are prohibitive, or if the new claim would undercut other recognized rights, we might rethink whether the claim counts as a human right at all. Second, if exit rights seem to threaten significant costs, we might also consider whether it is possible to tailor the scope of the right more narrowly, in a way that protects the interests in travel and relocation while avoiding such costs. Indeed, I believe that emigration often does carry significant costs. But in Section 4.3, I argue that such costs can be mitigated if we uncouple the right to leave from the right to renounce one's civic obligations.

4.3 No Right to Renounce Civic Obligations

One might argue against recognizing a human right to leave on the basis that mass emigration, especially by the skilled and talented, can have highly negative effects on sending societies.[27] Let me outline three such effects.

First, there is the so-called "brain drain" effect that often deprives less-affluent societies of much-needed skilled workers. This is a particular concern in many African countries that are losing healthcare personnel at alarming rates, at the same time as they face a growing AIDS crisis. A recent study concludes that there are more Ethiopian, Kenyan, and Sierra Leonean doctors in Europe and North America than in their home countries. By 2001, half the teaching staff of the University of Ghana had left the country, leaving the institution unable to educate new doctors.[28] Not surprisingly, regions with the worst healthcare indicators tend to be those with a large percentage of their healthcare professionals working abroad. In 2000, the skilled emigration rate

[26] For a useful discussion of this issue, see James Nickel, *Making Sense of Human Rights*, 2nd Edition (Oxford: Blackwell, 2007), pp. 82–7.

[27] Phillip Cole highlights the argument that mass emigration can be just as detrimental to societies as mass immigration can. See Cole, *Philosophies of Exclusion*, p. 47.

[28] Mohamed El-Khawas, "Brain Drain: putting Africa between a rock and a hard place," *Mediterranean Quarterly* 15 (2004), 37–56. Lucas Stancyk reflects on the implications of these facts for occupational choice in "Productive Justice," *Philosophy and Public Affairs* 40 (2012), 144–64.

was 41 percent for the Caribbean region, 27 percent for Western Africa, 19 percent for Eastern Africa, 25 percent for Central America, and 36 percent for Central Africa.[29] The "brain drain" is not confined to the very poorest countries: more affluent countries like Poland or Argentina also find their talented citizens drawn to the economic opportunities in places like the U.S.

Second, sending countries have often invested lots of government money into training these professionals, to staff institutions and improve health, educational, and development outcomes for their native population. It costs governments $10,000–15,000/year to train a student, and it can cost $40,000 to educate a physician. Many African students are trained abroad, with governments paying to send them to the best universities. But 35 percent of African students sent abroad for training do not return, leaving their compatriots not only lacking the services they might have provided, but also stuck footing the bill for their education.[30] One might think emigrants' remittances are sufficient to repay this public investment. But remittances are purely discretionary, and tend to be paid to an emigrant's family, not to the fellow-citizens who financed his education. Further, even if they provide income, remittances do nothing to compensate for other impacts on the sending communities: the loss of human capital and erosion of economic opportunity domestically.[31]

Third, when high-skilled workers have a credible "exit option," this allows them to bargain for less progressive taxation and a more favorable "fiscal deal" in their home society, as a condition of not leaving. Ayelet Shachar's contribution to this volume details how rich countries compete for talent, offering lucrative packages to recruit professionals from poorer places, especially in the areas of healthcare, science, engineering, and academic research. As Devesh Kapur and John McHale emphasize in their recent study, the highly skilled have a much lower propensity to migrate in countries with high income inequality, like Brazil, because their lack of liability to redistributive obligations affords them a standard of living equal to what they might gain by moving to a richer society. But societies with more progressive tax rates— like India—have a much harder time retaining their skilled workers. Free movement for skilled workers, then, may generate a "race to the bottom," as receiving countries compete for talent by offering the highly skilled attractive income packages and sending societies enact regressive tax systems in order to retain talent, thereby exacerbating inequality. Kapur and McHale present evidence that average top marginal tax rates in developing countries have

[29] Devesh Kapur and John McHale, *Give Us Your Best and Brightest* (Washington, DC: Center for Global Development, 2006), pp. 306–7.
[30] El-Khawas, "Brain Drain," pp. 40–6.
[31] For a good discussion of the benefits and drawbacks of remittances, see Kapur and McHale, *Give Us Your Best and Brightest*, ch. 8.

fallen from 56 percent in the mid-1980s to 34 percent in 2001, at the same time as developed countries have begun to recruit high-skilled migrants.

These negative effects on sending societies seem troubling, and if we take them seriously, they might tell in favor of limiting the right to exit. Arguably, however, many of these bad effects could be prevented, while still allowing for relatively broad liberties of travel and relocation. The production of these effects depends upon the fact that in relocating, individuals divest themselves of any distributive obligations to former compatriots. They are no longer obliged, in most cases, to pay back the fees invested in their education, to help finance their government's search for replacement doctors or teachers, or to contribute to redistributive programs that support the less well-off in their home society. But why should emigrants be able to renounce their civic obligations in this way?

The voluntary renunciation of civic obligations is often defended with reference to the idea that a state's legitimacy is grounded in the consent of its members. In the classical, Lockean version of this argument, continued residence in the state's territory is taken to be a signal of tacit consent to that state.[32] Only if citizens have the ability to renounce their civic obligations, by leaving the territory, can we say they are truly bound when they decide to stay. This implies that our civic obligations—including our distributive obligations to fellow-citizens—bind us only insofar as we voluntarily accept them, and also that we might choose *not* to accept them. Robert Nozick makes this connection explicit:

> May a person emigrate from a nation that has institutionalized some end-state or patterned distributional principle?... [I]f emigration from the country were allowed, anyone could choose to move to another country that did not have compulsory social provision but otherwise was (as much as possible) identical. In such a case, the person's *only* motive for leaving would be to avoid participating in the compulsory scheme of social provision ... What rationale yields the result that the person be permitted to emigrate, yet forbidden to stay, and opt out of the compulsory scheme of social provision?[33]

Nozick believes that our commitment to emigration shows that distributive schemes can bind their subjects only if subjects have consented to those schemes. I argue, conversely, that the fact that non-consenting individuals should *not* be able to opt out of distributive schemes while on the territory actually demonstrates that we should qualify our commitment to emigration.

---

[32] See Locke's discussion of tacit consent in John Locke, *Second Treatise of Government* (Indianapolis, IN: Hackett, 1980), pp. 116–22. Locke also argues that those who have made "express declaration" of consent are perpetually obliged to the commonwealth and may not leave. But relatively few inhabitants of modern states (apart from some naturalized citizens) meet this standard.

[33] Robert Nozick, *Anarchy, State and Utopia* (New York: Basic Books, 1974), p. 173.

If distributive schemes of social justice can bind individuals without their consent, then they ought to bind those individuals whether they seek to exit the state's territory or not. If this is correct, then a legitimate state can enforce distributive obligations even against those citizens who decide to relocate.

I want to stress here that by emphasizing that emigrants have duties of distributive justice to their poorer compatriots, I am not denying that citizens of receiving societies have distributive duties to these people as well. A wide range of theorists have argued for duties of assistance with global scope, and nothing in what I say here is meant to undercut duties of this type. Indeed, my remarks may point to an additional category of *remedial duties* of international assistance: if the inhabitants of rich societies reap the rewards of other societies' investments, then they may be required, not just to assist burdened societies, but also to compensate them for the costs of training the skilled workers from whom they now benefit.[34]

Even once these other international duties are factored in, however, there is still room to ask about the obligations of emigrants themselves. For one thing, many theories hold that co-citizenship is an important factor in triggering a "more demanding" set of distributive obligations to compatriots.[35] If one accepts this type of theory, one might wonder whether someone can "escape" these obligations at will. Are emigration decisions simply outside justice's domain? Consider the following case:

> *Elite Escape:* Suppose the Cayman Islands publicizes a lucrative offer to the talented global "one percent," as measured by their performance on an intelligence test: "move here to work and you will never be taxed to support a less-talented compatriot again." Could the global elite renounce their existing distributive obligations, by moving to the Caymans *en masse?*

To argue against *Elite Escape*, we must refer to a theory of political obligation that holds that citizens have civic duties they are not able to voluntarily renounce. We might appeal to the *benefit* theory, perhaps stressing the fact that many sending countries spend large sums of money training their skilled workers. When a cooperative venture produces shared benefits, the recipients of those benefits have a duty to reciprocate, by bearing the burdens required to support the joint enterprise.[36] This duty is owed to the other participants in

---

[34] Gillian Brock makes a similar point in *Debating Brain Drain.*

[35] See, for example, Michael Blake, "Distributive Justice, State Coercion, and Autonomy," *Philosophy and Public Affairs* 30 (2002), 257–96; Andrea Sangiovanni, "Global Justice, Reciprocity, and the State," *Philosophy and Public Affairs* 35 (2007), 3–39; David Miller, *National Responsibility and Global Justice* (Oxford: Oxford University Press, 2007).

[36] For a prominent defense of this theory, see George Klosko, *The Principle of Fairness and Political Obligation* (Oxford: Rowman and Littlefield, 1992); *Political Obligations* (Oxford: Oxford University Press, 2005).

the cooperative venture, since it is the sacrifices of these participants that have created the benefits recipients enjoyed.

The benefit theory, however, is subject to a well-known objection, which points out that many benefits provided by the state—such as national defense or the rule of law—have not been voluntarily accepted. When benefits have been involuntarily received, an obligation to reciprocate them seems much less plausible. Nozick uses the example of a PA system to illustrate the point: suppose the people in your neighborhood create a public address system, and every day they take turns playing music. One day your turn comes and the neighbors demand you spend the afternoon manning the system. Though you may benefit from hearing the music, it does not seem that you are obliged to spend a day on the radio if you didn't sign up and don't wish to partici- pate.[37] You may not value these benefits enough to accept the burdens associated with their production. Various attempts to circumvent this "vol- untary acceptance" objection have been made, but I remain doubtful that they succeed.[38] After all, even where I am offered an *indispensable* benefit— say, an expensive operation that would prevent me from being bound to a wheelchair—it still seems that I would be within my rights to refuse it, on grounds that I would rather not foot the bill.

The "voluntary acceptance" objection is somewhat less potent in the case of skilled emigrants, however. Skilled workers have often willingly accepted their attractive educational packages. Take the case of a surgeon trained at state expense. Her fellow-citizens cooperated to provide her with an educational benefit, which she voluntarily accepted, and in so doing, she acquired an obligation to reciprocate that benefit. She was not forced to accept a free medical education from the state. Once she enters this bargain, she has a responsibility to pay back the special benefits she received, by providing care for the fellow-citizens who financed her education. If she reneges on her commitment, then she can be held responsible for making up the losses caused, either by paying back the educational and monetary benefits she received, by paying an exit tax to contribute to a search for her replacement, or by performing a term of compulsory service in an underserved area.[39]

Still, I don't want to rest my argument on the benefit theory alone. I do think it plays an important role in emigration, and that it can justify obligations on

---

[37] Nozick, *Anarchy, State, and Utopia*, pp. 93–5.

[38] Klosko argues that there is a category of "presumptive benefits" that are indispensable for an acceptable life. In the case of *these* benefits, we are obliged to reciprocate whether we would consent or not.

[39] One might worry that these arguments imply that government-funded medical students who stay in their home country but choose to become artists or gardeners, must also perform a term of compulsory service and/or repay the cost of their education. I accept this implication, and do not regard it as objectionable. Many scholarship programs—such as the U.S. National Health Service Corps or ROTC—already impose similar requirements on those who opt out.

the talented to reciprocate the publicly funded education they receive. But it will not always apply, especially in cases where skilled emigrants have financed their own training. Arguments that emigrants owe reciprocation for public goods like national defense or roads are less plausible, since they had no opportunity to refuse these goods. More controversially, I believe that even where the skilled and talented did *not* take any public money, and did not receive any special benefits beyond those provided to all citizens, they may still have distributive obligations to their poorer compatriots, and these duties may bind them even when they decide to leave the country. My reasoning for this conclusion appeals to a different theory of political obligation: *the natural duty theory.*[40]

I believe that many civic duties to compatriots derive from a more fundamental natural duty of justice that is binding on all human beings as such. Simply as rational agents, we have a duty to establish state institutions and to comply with their laws and policies, when these institutions are reasonably just and legitimate. This is an unconditional duty that is binding on us independently of any special relationships we may have, or any voluntary transactions we have engaged in. Along these lines, John Rawls has argued that we have a natural duty of justice that

> requires us to support and comply with just institutions that exist and apply to us. It also constrains us to further just arrangements not yet established, at least when this can be done without too much cost to ourselves. Thus if the basic structure of society is just, or as just as it is reasonable to expect in the circumstances, everyone has a natural duty to do his part in the existing scheme.[41]

A natural duty theory holds that no binding act of consent or acceptance is necessary in order for a citizen to have a duty to do his part in upholding a distributive scheme, if that scheme is imposed on him by a reasonably just state.

To see why justice requires a state that can specify and impose distributive duties on us, consider briefly the case of property rights.[42] Each individual has an important interest in a "fair share" of property, and a natural moral duty to respect the "fair shares" of others. But how do we know which particular things he and others have a right to possess? Here it seems essential to refer to a set of institutional background rules and the legitimate expectations they create. Partly the problem is one of coordination: even if each person has a basic interest in the goods necessary for a decent life, that does not by itself determine any answer as to how to structure many other issues, including

---

[40] We need not adopt one single theory of political obligation: both fairness theory and natural duty theory may explain our civic obligations in some contexts.

[41] John Rawls, *A Theory of Justice* (Cambridge, MA: Harvard University Press, 1999), p. 99.

[42] I have defended this (largely Kantian) natural duty theory at much greater length in Anna Stilz, *Liberal Loyalty: Freedom, Obligation, and the State* (Princeton, NJ: Princeton University Press, 2009).

property in the means of production, rights to transfer (subject to tax? at what level?), or rights to inherit. Partly the problem is one of moral disagreement: often individuals will not share a fully common understanding of what their "fair shares" are, so each person's good-faith attempt to respect others' property rights may not lead him to respect the claims these others take themselves to have. Individuals would be unable to resolve these problems without granting authoritative institutions a significant role in defining their property rights and the duties associated with them. According to the natural duty theory, these individuals are therefore obliged to participate in a legitimate state that can define and enforce a fair scheme of property law in their behalf. By setting up a uniform scheme of rules to define our property rights and the duties associated with them, the state overcomes problems of coordination, disagreement, and conflict among its constituents.

For this reason, our natural duty to treat others justly—by respecting their "fair share" of property—is an *institutionally mediated duty*. Only a legitimate state can give our property rights determinate and publicly knowable contours, and only the state has the proper standing to enforce such claims against other people. Principles of distributive justice—such as Rawls' difference principle—will guide legislators in designing this scheme of law. Our distributive duties to others are discharged through compliance with a fair scheme of taxation, measures regulating property, tort, contract, inheritance and copyright, and the regulations applied to the market. Citizens' "fair shares" are defined by the overall workings of these background institutions.

The argument for why there is no right to unconditionally renounce our civic obligations builds on the point that our distributive duties are conventional artifacts of a legitimate system of law. The terms under which individuals may divest themselves of distributive obligations to fellow-citizens are properly subject to whatever considerations of distributive justice apply to property law in general. Just as individuals may be fairly subject to taxation and regulation in their everyday choices, whether they consented to their state's legal system or not, so too they may be subject to taxation and regulation when they seek to exit the state's territory, if such measures are necessary to ensure distributive justice for others. On this view, citizens have no fundamental right to unqualified exit; their only claim is that the terms of departure ought to be regulated to preserve a fair distribution. In this vein, a notable feature of Rawls' argument for the difference principle is that it represents "an agreement to regard the distribution of natural talents as in some respects a common asset and to share in the greater social and economic benefits made possible by the complementarities of this distribution."[43] The naturally

---

[43] Rawls, *A Theory of Justice*, p. 87.

talented are not to gain—even through emigration—solely in a way that reflects the fact they are more gifted, but in ways that benefit the less well-off. Just as a legal system regulating property does not have to overcome the prima facie objection that individuals are naturally entitled to their pre-tax income, I believe that a legal system regulating migration does not have to overcome the prima facie objection that individuals are naturally entitled to leave on whatever terms they wish.

A common objection to the natural duty theory is that it cannot explain a person's special bond to his own particular state and his compatriots: it merely establishes the need for state authority in general.[44] While this objection may raise other difficulties for the theory, I don't think it creates any special problems for regulating emigration. The natural duty theory tells us that to do justice to others, we must comply with the tax, property, and contract laws of the territorial jurisdiction in which we live. We need not have robust ties to this particular state, beyond residence on its territory, to give it a right to enforce distributive duties against us, even when we seek to emigrate. Of course, as I discuss in more detail below, we may eventually wish to change our citizenship, and our home state should provide us legal channels for making this choice. But like other choices, the renunciation of citizenship may permissibly be encumbered with distributive duties. To be properly subject to these duties, we need have no more than a jurisdictional tie with the state we are seeking to leave.

I should emphasize that on the natural duty theory, not every existing state will be capable of imposing binding distributive duties on its subjects. The state must meet certain legitimacy conditions in order to qualify as a proper interpreter of our natural duty of justice. To be legitimate, a state need not be fully just, but it must give at least minimal consideration to each subject, by protecting his basic human rights. This includes his rights to life, liberty, and personal security; due process rights; rights against slavery and torture; and rights to freedom of conscience and free association. Such a legitimacy condition reflects our intuition that a scheme must provide the essentials of justice in order for subjects to be expected to do their part in upholding it.

Of course, many states today fail to protect basic human rights—including Zimbabwe, Iran, Sudan, China, Chad, and North Korea, to name a few. My argument for enforcing distributive duties against emigrants does not apply to these states. Where a state fails to be minimally legitimate, I believe citizens may use a range of "exit options" to ensure their rights are protected—including emigration, but also revolution or secession. While my argument fails to justify exit taxation in some of the worst brain drain cases, for example, in many

---

[44] See A. John Simmons, *Moral Principles and Political Obligations* (Princeton, NJ: Princeton University Press, 1979).

African states, this does not render it irrelevant. There are many countries vulnerable to brain drain in which these human rights conditions are met today—for example, India, Mexico, the Philippines, Poland, Peru, and Brazil. A case for exit taxation in these countries is not trivial: the Philippines, India, and Peru are currently among the largest senders of skilled emigrants to the U.S.[45]

As I argued above, a legitimate state should also guarantee its subjects' right to leave. But a "right of exit" is not the same thing as a "right of exit without conditions." Consider once more the analogy to freedom of occupation. Any just property scheme will also allow for the basic liberty of occupational choice. But that does not mean that individuals have a complaint of justice when their lucrative occupational choices are taxed at higher rates than if they had chosen a less high-paying career. In choosing to work as a surgeon rather than a gardener, I know I will be subject to higher taxes, but I still have a choice. Nor is my freedom of occupation infringed when a state sets quotas on university admission, or requires a license or career-long continuing education in order for me to practice a profession. These regulations are justified by important public purposes, and while they do make some choices more costly or difficult, they do not eliminate occupational freedom. But notice that we can say the very same thing about high-skilled emigrants. When an Indian chooses to work as a software engineer in the U.S., rather than in India, she may know she will face taxes she would not have to pay if she stayed home, but that fact does not undermine her choice. Lots of lucrative choices permissibly have burdens attached to them.

For these reasons, I see no objection to a legitimate state requiring emigrants to pay an exit tax, or subjecting them to taxation on income earned abroad, where these contributions are essential to sustaining a just distributive scheme for their compatriots. It is important that taxation not be so onerous as to effectively *force* an individual to work at an occupation he loathes, in order to pay his taxes; so too terms of emigration should not be so burdensome as to effectively force a citizen to remain for the rest of his life in a country he hates, because he cannot afford to leave. But as long as the taxes are set at reasonable levels, I see no reason to object.

Indeed, in dire cases where tax incentives alone are not sufficient to allow a country to staff its national health system, say, it may even be permissible for states to impose a term of compulsory service on emigrant doctors prior to leaving.[46] As long as length of the service term is limited—say, to one year—and the individual has reasonable options other than migrating—that is, to stay

---

[45] For statistics, see Kapur and McHale, *Give Us Your Best and Brightest*, p. 17.
[46] Both Gillian Brock and Lucas Stancyk have argued for this. See Brock, *Debating Brain Drain* and Stancyk, "Productive Justice."

home, or to work in a less lucrative occupation—then, in extreme circumstances, I think such measures may be acceptable.

Again, I should emphasize that these arguments apply only to legitimate states that protect the basic rights outlined above, not to states that fail to reach the threshold of legitimacy, as many current states do. And imposing distributive regulations on emigration assumes a background in which the right of exit is protected as a basic liberty, much as freedom of occupation is protected. Citizens must have the effective choice to leave the state's territory to travel or reside abroad, though they may be properly subject to tax burdens in doing so.

4.4 Thoughts on Institutionalization and an Objection

There are two ways we might institutionalize the scheme advocated here. First, citizens might be taxed extraterritorially on income earned while working abroad. While most countries tax only their residents, the U.S. taxes citizens on their worldwide income, including foreign-earned income. One implication of my argument, then, is that all states should engage in worldwide taxation. A common objection to this idea is that less-developed countries lack the infrastructure to effectively tax their citizens residing abroad. Computer technology is making it cheaper to collect the required information, however, and private firms often have the infrastructure to collect tax information, so this objection may be surmountable. Another worry is that taxing income earned abroad might represent an objectionable extraterritorial extension of state jurisdiction. But governments already regulate the foreign activities of persons subject to their jurisdiction: for example, the U.S. prohibits its persons from bribing foreign officials or engaging in drug trafficking abroad. So the proposal does not involve extraterritorial jurisdiction beyond what states already claim.

A second possibility is that receiving societies may collect the taxes on behalf of sending countries. This mechanism was proposed in the late 1970s as the Bhagwati tax. Bhagwati's initial idea was to have receiving societies collect a surtax on the income of emigrants and hand it over to sending countries.[47] Special tax treaties between countries could provide the legal backing for this mechanism. Since many emigrants wish to return eventually to their country of origin, a surtax may be a reasonable price to pay in order to retain their citizenship privileges. I believe, however, that there are important

---

[47] Jadish Bhagwati, *Taxing the Brain Drain* (Amsterdam: North-Holland Publishing, 1979). See also Mihir Desai, Devesh Kapur, and John McHale, "Sharing the Spoils: Taxing International Human Capital Flows," *International Tax and Public Finance* 11 (2004), 663–93.

reasons to avoid institutionalizing my proposal by imposing a lump sum tax at the moment of departure. If set too high, this tax might effectively prohibit people from leaving, and it could be illicitly used by governments to sanction prospective emigrants. It also privileges those who have access to capital now over those who may only have a stream of expected future earnings. It is more desirable to impose a progressive tax that can be amortized on earnings abroad over time.

We should further consider how these proposed regulations would interact with our current citizenship practices. Many children born abroad receive the citizenship of the country where they are born (Country A) as well as citizenship in their parents' country of origin (Country B). The worry here is that people with multiple citizenships may be unduly burdened with too many distributive obligations. To which country does this child have distributive duties, on my view? The natural duty theory holds that a person has distributive obligations to compatriots in his country of permanent residence. If another country also grants him citizenship rights, then my view would extend him the discretion—at the age of majority—to decide whether to accept or renounce that additional status without liability. If he does accept an additional citizenship status, then he may be subject to additional distributive obligations.

Finally, it is also important that emigrants have the option to change their country of citizenship eventually. Most receiving societies impose waiting periods (often five to ten years) during which one must reside in the country prior to applying for citizenship. On my proposal, sending societies might engage in taxation of their citizens' income earned abroad during this "transition" period. If the emigrant then wishes to naturalize, he may be subject to a one-time "tax event" at the point of renouncing citizenship. The idea here would be to structure something like a divorce settlement. This could be a lump sum "severance payment," or, more plausibly, an arrangement for gradually decreasing contributions over time. Just as people cannot dissolve a marriage without discharging their obligations, so too—on my view—people should not be able to dissolve their civic bonds without discharging their duties.

To conclude, I wish to consider an obvious moral objection. Under my scheme, citizens will remain morally connected to their compatriots simply because they happen to have been born in their country of origin, and they may be subject to onerous taxes if they wish to dissolve these ties. But isn't this arbitrary? Consider a scenario involving three equally talented surgeons working in the U.S. One was born in Alabama, and owes a relatively light tax burden due to the U.S.'s weak system of social provision. One was born in Sweden, and owes a much higher tax burden—or a costly expatriation tax—because his country has robust social provisions. And the last one was born in

Bolivia: he owes more just because his compatriots are needier. How can this be fair?

There are two possible responses to the moral arbitrariness objection, one less and one more concessive. A less concessive response holds that though there is indeed an inequality of burdens here, this inequality is not morally arbitrary, because it protects important values that we have reason to care about, like democratic self-determination. The surgeons' situation reflects economic inequalities that will exist in any system that allows for different societies to make different economic choices. For example, Israel's per capita GNP is currently about half that of Denmark's. If self-determination is a value, then Denmark's citizens do not have any duty to rectify this imbalance by sending their money to Israel: these countries' current level of wealth partly reflects their democratic decisions. We already accept that countries may make economic choices—like the acquisition of massive public debts—that differentially impact their future citizens' tax burdens, and the argument from self-determination simply extends this view. While I am sympathetic to this response, a full defense of it would need to explain the moral importance of self-determination. I will not attempt to do that here.

A more concessive response would hold that even if self-determination is not valuable enough to justify international economic inequalities, still these differential burdens on emigrants can be *provisionally* warranted. On a cosmopolitan view, economic policy ought eventually to be constrained by a global institution that can enforce egalitarian justice transnationally. But that ideal is not presently feasible, since we lack the necessary global institutions. The concessive response holds that regulations on emigration are a non-ideal response to the realities of the present states system, and that the cosmopolitan ought to endorse emigration regulations, while that system lasts. Why should the cosmopolitan endorse provisional emigration taxation? Unlike the libertarian, the cosmopolitan holds that the choices of talented individuals can permissibly be limited for the sake of improving the welfare of the least well-off. Of course, the cosmopolitan also calls for dramatic reforms in how distributive duties are enacted and enforced: he holds that they should extend to all humans, not just fellow-citizens. But the cosmopolitan's distributive goals will not be furthered by enabling the world's most talented individuals to renounce their obligations to the global poor, by clustering together in the world's richest countries. For that reason, exit taxation is a policy measure that can be least provisionally justified on cosmopolitan grounds, until a world distributive scheme becomes feasible.

To sum up, then, I have argued that individuals have strong interests in travel and relocation that tell in favor of recognizing a right to leave one's country. But I have also held that there is no claim to unconditionally renounce distributive obligations to one's compatriots. Instead, I believe we should uncouple the right to leave from the right to renounce one's civic obligations. Regulations on exit that are designed to enforce distributive obligations to compatriots, without impeding relocation, can be at least provisionally morally justified.[48]

References

Bhagwati, Jadish, *Taxing the Brain Drain* (Amsterdam: North-Holland Publishing, 1979).

Blake, Michael, "Distributive Justice, State Coercion, and Autonomy," *Philosophy and Public Affairs* 30 (2002), 257–96.

Brock, Gillian and Michael Blake, *Debating Brain Drain: May Countries Restrict Emigration?* (Oxford: Oxford University Press, 2015).

Carens, Joseph H., "Aliens and Citizens: The Case for Open Borders," *Review of Politics* 49 (1987), 251–73.

Carens, Joseph H., "Migration and Morality: A Liberal Egalitarian Perspective" in Brian Barry and Robert Goodin (eds.), *Free Movement: Ethical Issues in the Transnational Migration of People and Money* (University Park, PA: Pennsylvania State University Press, 1992), pp. 25–47.

Cole, Phillip, *Philosophies of Exclusion: Liberal Political Theory and Immigration* (Edinburgh: Edinburgh University Press, 2000).

Desai, Mihir, Devesh Kapur, and John McHale, "Sharing the Spoils: Taxing International Human Capital Flows," *International Tax and Public Finance* 11 (2004), 663–93.

Dowty, Alan, *Closed Borders: The Contemporary Assault on Freedom of Movement* (New Haven, CT: Yale University Press, 1987).

Dummett, Ann, "Natural Law and Transnational Migration" in Brian Barry and Robert Goodin (eds.), *Free Movement: Ethical Issues in the Transnational Migration of People and of Money* (University Park, PA: Pennsylvania State University Press, 1992).

Dworkin, Ronald, *Taking Rights Seriously* (Cambridge, MA: Harvard University Press, 1978).

El-Khawas, Mohamed, "Brain Drain: putting Africa between a rock and a hard place," *Mediterranean Quarterly* 15 (2004), 37–56.

Hobbes, Thomas, *Leviathan*, ed. Richard Tuck (Cambridge: Cambridge University Press, 1991).

Kapur, Devesh and John McHale, *Give Us Your Best and Brightest* (Washington, DC: Center for Global Development, 2006).

Klosko, George, *The Principle of Fairness and Political Obligation* (Oxford: Rowman and Littlefield, 1992).

Klosko, George, *Political Obligations* (Oxford: Oxford University Press, 2005).

Locke, John, *Second Treatise of Government* (Indianapolis, IN: Hackett, 1980).

---

[48] I am very grateful to Sarah Fine and Lea Ypi for written comments which helped to greatly improve the penultimate version of this chapter.

Miller, David, "Immigration: The Case for Limits" in Andrew Cohen and Christopher Wellman (eds.), *Contemporary Debates in Applied Ethics* (Malden, MA: Blackwell, 2004).

Miller, David, *National Responsibility and Global Justice* (Oxford: Oxford University Press, 2007).

Nickel, James, *Making Sense of Human Rights*, 2nd Edition (Oxford: Blackwell, 2007).

Nozick, Robert, *Anarchy, State and Utopia* (New York: Basic Books, 1974).

O'Neill, Onora, "The Most Extensive Liberty," *Proceedings of the Aristotelian Society* 80 (1979), 45–59.

Pevnick, Ryan, *Immigration and the Constraints of Justice* (Cambridge: Cambridge University Press, 2011).

Rawls, John, *Political Liberalism* (New York: Columbia University Press, 1993).

Rawls, John, *A Theory of Justice* (Cambridge, MA: Harvard University Press, 1999).

Sangiovanni, Andrea, "Global Justice, Reciprocity, and the State," *Philosophy and Public Affairs* 35 (2007), 3–39.

Simmons, A. John, *Moral Principles and Political Obligations* (Princeton, NJ: Princeton University Press, 1979).

Stancyk, Lucas, "Productive Justice," *Philosophy and Public Affairs* 40 (2012), 144–64.

Stilz, Anna, *Liberal Loyalty: Freedom, Obligation, and the State* (Princeton, NJ: Princeton University Press, 2009).

Taylor, Charles, "What's Wrong with Negative Liberty?" in *Philosophy and the Human Sciences* 2 (Cambridge: Cambridge University Press, 1985).

Whelan, Frederick G., "Citizenship and the Right to Leave," *The American Political Science Review* 75 (1981), 636–53.

Ypi, Lea, "Justice in Migration: A Closed Borders Utopia," *Journal of Political Philosophy* 16 (2008), 391–418.

5

Freedom of Movement and the Rights to Enter and Exit

Christopher Heath Wellman

Virtually no one doubts that there is a right, even a human right, to freedom of movement. Questions abound, however, regarding this right's scope. Some presume that the right of free movement entitles one to roam anywhere in the world, and therefore no country may permissibly stop people from either entering or exiting its territory. Of course, this construal of an individual's rights flies in the face of international law, which requires states to allow their citizens to leave but gives countries broad discretion to determine who may enter.[1] In other words, international law generally sides with the state when it comes to immigration but sides with the individual on the question of emigration. If one begins with a presumption in favor of individual liberty (as I believe we should), then it is incumbent upon those who would defend international law to supply a positive argument in defense of this asymmetric stance on the rights to enter and exit. I attempt to provide such a defense here.

I divide this chapter into three sections. First I invoke freedom of association to provide a preliminary defense of international law's asymmetric position regarding the rights to enter and exit. I do so by showing how freedom of association supports both (1) a legitimate state's right to restrict immigration and (2) an individual's right to emigrate. Next I consider three arguments which are designed to show that I have underestimated the importance of freedom of movement. And finally, I address the argument that states may permissibly limit emigration just as broadly as they restrict immigration.

---

[1] For instance, Article 13 of the Universal Declaration of Human Rights states that "Everyone has the right to freedom of movement and residence within the borders of each state" and "Everyone has the right to leave any country, including his own, and to return to his country." But no article of any core human rights document says anything even remotely like "Everyone has the right to enter any country."

5.1 In Defense of the Asymmetric View

While few contest the existence of a right to freedom of movement, no one supposes that it is perfectly general and absolute. No one thinks that your right to free movement makes it permissible for you to enter another's home without their permission, for instance. And if a property owner has the moral standing to insist that others keep off of her property, why may a state not similarly demand that outsiders not enter its territory? This alone does not show that states do in fact occupy a position of dominion analogous to that of a property owner, of course, but it does suggest the promise of doing so if we can provide an argument for why states may limit immigration. In my view, states do not *own* their land, but legitimate states have a right of jurisdiction over their territory, and this enables us to provide an argument on behalf of a state's right to control its membership.

I believe that the strongest argument for a legitimate state's right to exclude outsiders can be built on three foundational premises: (1) legitimate states are entitled to self-determination, (2) freedom of association is an integral component of self-determination, and (3) freedom of association entitles one to refuse to associate with others as one sees fit.[2] Based on this reasoning, I conclude that, just as an individual's right to self-determination explains why an individual may choose whether or not to marry any given suitor, the citizens of a legitimate state are free collectively to offer or refuse membership in their political community to any given prospective immigrant.

It is not difficult to establish the truth of the second and third premises. To see that freedom of association is integral to self-determination and that enjoying freedom of association requires that one be free to refuse to associate with others, we need only imagine a setting in which one's father, say, has sole discretion to choose his children's marital partners. Whatever one might think of this type of arrangement, it clearly does not respect rights to self-determination. Freedom of association involves more than merely the right to get married; it includes the right to reject any and all suitors one prefers not to marry, and this explains why those of us who value individual autonomy take such offense at institutions which give parents the authority to force spouses on their children.

But while few deny that individuals have a right to freedom of association in the marital realm, some may question whether corporate political entities could have such a right. To see that states are entitled to an analogous sphere of political self-determination, think of a country like Norway and its relations

---

[2] I develop and defend this argument at greatest length in my book, co-authored with Phillip Cole, *Debating the Ethics of Immigration: Is There a Right to Exclude?* (New York: Oxford University Press, 2011).

with Sweden and the European Union. Norway does not belong to the EU, but it enjoys close relations with many European countries, including Sweden, from whom it seceded in 1905. But now imagine that Sweden (inspired, perhaps, by the reunification of Germany) wanted to reunite with Norway or that the EU wanted Norway to join its ranks. Would Sweden or the EU have the right to unilaterally annex Norway, or would it be impermissible for them to do so without Norway's consent? It seems clear that neither Sweden nor the EU is morally entitled to unilaterally incorporate Norway. If either wants to merge with Norway, it may invite Norway to join forces, but Norway is free to either accept or decline such an invitation. Indeed, even if it is clear to all that the Norwegians would be better off after the merger, it remains Norway's decision to make, and no other country or external organization may permissibly force itself onto Norway without its consent. But if Norway's right to self-determination entitles it to refuse to associate with other corporate political entities like Sweden or the European Union, then why is Norway not similarly within its rights to refuse to associate with any given Swedish or European citizen? It seems to me that, just as an individual has a right to determine whom (if anyone) he or she would like to marry, a group of fellow-citizens has a right to determine whom (if anyone) it would like to invite into its political community. And just as an individual's freedom of association entitles one to remain single, a legitimate state's freedom of association entitles it to exclude all foreigners from its political community.

Here an obvious objection presents itself: Is it not misleading to compare having discretion over one's partner in marriage to the selection of potential immigrants? After all, while having the option to refuse potential associates is plainly paramount in marital relations, it seems of little consequence within the relatively impersonal context of political life.

In response to this worry, I admit that freedom of association is considerably more important in intimate relations. Acknowledging this is unproblematic, however, since it amounts to conceding only that rights to freedom of association can be more valuable in intimate contexts, not that they do not exist elsewhere. At most, then, this objection merely highlights that it may require more to defeat the presumptive right in intimate contexts. Notice, however, that there are many non-intimate associations where we rightly value freedom of association very highly. Religious associations in which people attend to matters of conscience and political groups through which members express themselves can often be large and impersonal, and yet we are extremely reluctant to restrict their associative rights.

Despite the admitted lack of intimacy, freedom of association is also clearly important for political states. To appreciate this, notice that even members of relatively insignificant associations like golf clubs are often (understandably) concerned about their control over potential members. These members typically care about their club's membership rules, *even though they will never be forced to play golf with any particular member,* for at least two sets of reasons. First and most obviously, the size of the club affects one's experience as a member. In the case of a private golf club, for instance, some may want to expand membership, so that each individual will be required to pay less in dues, whereas others might be against adding new members for fear that the increased number of golfers will result in limited access to, and more wear and tear on, the golf course. In short, whereas some might be motivated to cut costs, others will be happy to pay higher fees for a more exclusive golfing experience. Second and perhaps less obviously, members care about the rules for adding new members because all new members will subsequently have a say in how the club is organized. In other words, caring about one's experience as a club member gives one reason to care about the rules for admitting new members, because, once admitted, these new members will typically have a say in determining the future course of the club.

And if the reasons to concern oneself with the membership rules of one's golf club are straightforward, there is nothing curious about people caring so much about the rules governing who may enter their political communities (even though a citizen will typically never meet, let alone have anything approaching intimate relations with, the vast majority of her compatriots). Indeed, there are a number of obvious reasons why citizens would care deeply about how many and which type of immigrants can enter their country. Even if we put to one side all concerns about the state's culture, economy, and political functioning, for instance, people's lives are obviously affected by substantial shifts in population density, so it seems only natural that citizens who like higher population density would welcome huge numbers of immigrants, while those with contrary tastes would prefer a more exclusionary policy. And in the real world, of course, a substantial influx of foreigners will also invariably affect the host state's cultural makeup, the way its economy functions, and/or how its political system operates. And let me be clear: I am not assuming that any of these changes will necessarily be for the worse. More modestly, I am emphasizing only that citizens will often care deeply about their country's culture, economy, and political arrangements, and thus, depending upon their particular preferences, may well seek more or fewer immigrants, or perhaps more or fewer immigrants of a given linguistic, cultural, economic, and/or political profile.

In the case of Mexican immigrants into the United States, for instance, it is not the least bit surprising that some favor a more open policy, while others lobby for the government to stem what they regard as a "flood" of unwelcome newcomers. Without taking a stand on this particular controversy, I wish to stress only the obvious point that, even with large anonymous groups like contemporary bureaucratic states, the number and types of constituents can often have a pronounced affect upon what it is like to be a member of these groups. Thus, unless one questions why anyone would care about their experience as citizens, there is no reason to doubt that we should be so concerned about our country's immigration policy. What is more, as in the case of golf clubs, the crucial point is that—whether one interacts personally with them or not—one's fellow-citizens play roles in charting the course that one's country takes. And since a country's immigration policy determines who has the opportunity to join the current citizens in shaping the country's future, this policy will matter enormously to any citizen who cares what course her political community will take.

This connection between a group's membership and its future direction underscores why freedom of association is such an integral component of self-determination. No collective can be fully self-determining without enjoying freedom of association because, when the members of a group can change, an essential part of group self-determination is exercising control over what the "self" is. To appreciate this point, consider again the controversy over Mexican immigration into the United States. It is not merely that large numbers of these immigrants would almost certainly change the culture of those areas where they tend to relocate *en masse*, it is also that (if legally admitted and given the standard voting rights of citizenship) these new members will help determine future laws in the United States, including its immigration policy toward additional potential immigrants. Thus, if I am right that legitimate states are entitled to political self-determination, there appears to be every reason to conclude that this privileged position of sovereignty includes a weighty presumptive right to freedom of association, a right which entitles these countries to include or exclude foreigners as they see fit.

To recapitulate the core points of our discussion to this point: One cannot adequately capture why it is in principle wrong for an external body such as Sweden or the EU to forcibly annex a country like Norway without invoking a state's right to political self-determination. But if legitimate political regimes enjoy a sphere of self-determination which allows them to refuse relations with foreign countries and international organizations, it seems only natural to conclude that they are similarly entitled to decline to associate with individual foreigners. Thus, any regime which satisfactorily protects and respects human rights is entitled to unilaterally design and enforce its own immigration policy. In sum, just as an individual has the right to determine whom (if anyone) she would like to marry, a group of fellow-citizens has a right to determine whom (if anyone) it would like to invite into its political community. And just as an individual's freedom of association entitles one to remain single, a corporate political entity's freedom of association entitles it to exclude all foreigners.

My argument on behalf of a legitimate state's presumptive right to design and enforce its own immigration policy might be contested on any number of fronts.[3] I shall consider several potential objections in Section 5.2. For now, I conclude only that, if my argument stands up to scrutiny, then it explains why legitimate states may have a right to control immigration. If so, then just as a property owner does not necessarily violate a second party's right to free movement when she denies this person access to her land, a political collective need not violate a prospective immigrant's right to freedom of movement when it forcibly excludes this potential migrant from moving onto its territory. Unless one implausibly construes freedom of movement in perfectly general and absolute terms, introducing competing values like political self-determination illustrates why legitimate states, rather than individual outsiders, can occupy the privileged position of dominion over immigration.

Let us now consider emigration. In light of the foregoing analysis, we are well positioned to construct a straightforward case on behalf of an individual's right to exit. To begin, recall our discussion of Norway's possible merger with Sweden or the EU. As I explained above, Norway's right to self-determination explains why neither Sweden nor the European Union may forcibly annex Norway without its consent. The pivotal idea, of course, is that freedom of association entails more than merely the right to associate, it includes the right to refuse to associate with others. But notice: Just as Norway would be within its rights to decline an invitation to join the European Union, the EU is also entitled to keep Norway out. In other words, no matter how desperately Norway might like to join this collective, the EU has a presumptive right to exclude Norway, which explains why Norway may not unilaterally insert itself into the group. The fact that freedom of association is a two-way street is crucial, of course, because it suggests that, just as Norway is entitled to decide which individuals it would like to invite into its political collective, the individuals also have a right to accept or decline this invitation. And if individuals have a right to refuse to associate with the state, then this suggests that we should have a right to exit. Thus, just as freedom of association grounds a legitimate state's right to control immigration, it explains the individual's dominion over emigration. It is also worth noting that an individual's presumptive right to emigrate is buttressed by freedom of movement because, while a state's right to restrict immigration grounded in freedom of association must compete with an individual's right to freedom of movement, freedom of association and freedom of movement both weigh in favor of an

---

[3] For excellent critical discussions of my argument, see Michael Blake, "Immigration, Association, and Antidiscrimination," *Ethics* 122 (2012), 748–62; Eric Cavallero, "Association and Asylum," *Philosophical Studies* 169 (2014), 133–41; Sarah Fine, "Freedom of Association Is Not the Answer," *Ethics* 120 (2010), 538–56; and Shelley Wilcox, "Do Duties to Outsiders Entail Open Borders? A Reply to Wellman," *Philosophical Studies* 169 (2014), 123–32.

individual's right to emigrate. If anything, then, an individual's right to emigrate seems to have a stronger basis than a state's right to limit immigration, and this might explain why so few question an individual's right to exit her country.

As we will see in the next two sections, there are a variety of grounds on which one might contest the arguments I have offered here. For now, though, we may conclude that freedom of association provides the normative building blocks with which we can construct at least presumptive cases on behalf of a legitimate state's right to control immigration and the individual's discretion over emigration. Thus, even though freedom of movement would seem to recommend a symmetrical stance on the rights to enter and exit, international law's asymmetric position on these rights appears defensible.

5.2 The Right to Enter

One obvious rejoinder to the arguments sketched above is that I have profoundly underestimated the value and scope of the right to free movement. Phillip Cole, for example, is a leading proponent of a relatively unrestricted human right to freedom of movement who has argued along these lines. In addition to providing positive arguments on behalf of adopting a symmetrical position regarding the rights to enter and exit, he has raised a number of extremely sophisticated objections to my argument based on freedom of association.[4] In this section I would like to focus on Cole's contentions that (1) the human right to freedom of movement takes precedence over a state's right to self-determination; (2) permitting states to limit immigration leaves us with no principled grounds on which to object to their limiting internal migration; and (3) one cannot consistently endorse the right to emigrate without also affirming the right to immigrate. Let us consider these in turn.

First, without denying the value of political self-determination, Cole insists that countries may not limit immigration because an individual's right to freedom of movement outweighs a state's claim to freedom of association. As Cole sees it, a state cannot invoke self-determination to justify behavior which violates human rights, and because there is a human right to freedom of movement, it follows that no state may permissibly enforce immigration restrictions which limit freedom of movement.[5]

Because I understand a state to be legitimate just in case it satisfactorily protects the human rights of its constituents and respects the human rights of

---

[4] In particular, see chs. 12 and 13 of *Debating the Ethics of Immigration*.
[5] For another argument in defense of a human right to immigrate, see Kieran Oberman's contribution to this volume.

everyone else, and because I suggest that only legitimate states have a right to political self-determination, I am in no position to contest the claim that a state cannot defend any behavior that violates human rights merely by appealing to self-determination. And given that I agree that there is a human right to freedom of movement, I clearly must not take this first argument lightly. I am ultimately unpersuaded by this criticism, however, because it relies upon what I regard as an implausibly expansive understanding of the human right to freedom of movement.

To appreciate my concerns about the more expansive construal of the human right to freedom of movement, think again of the property owner's right to keep others off of her land. As was noted earlier, it seems highly implausible to suppose that my right to freedom of movement ordinarily allows me to enter your home without your permission.[6] The fact that we think a property owner's right typically prevails in these circumstances reveals the implausibility of conceiving of the right to free movement as perfectly general and absolute. More modestly, it seems sensible to understand this right as entitling each of us to a *sufficient* degree of freedom of movement.[7] Think, for instance, of Robert Nozick's example of a person whose home is completely surrounded by the private property of others, so that (unless she has a helicopter) she cannot leave her own land without trespassing upon the property of those around her.[8] Nozick rightly concludes that this arrangement would violate the Lockean proviso. The lesson to be gleaned from this example, I think, is that no system of property rights can be legitimate unless it provides those affected with sufficient room for free movement. This lesson certainly accords with both our judgment that a property owner's claim normally prevails over a typical person's claim to freedom of movement and our conviction that Nozick's imprisoned individual's right to freedom of movement would outweigh the property rights of those who own the land

---

[6] There might be extreme circumstances in which I could permissibly enter your home without your permission, but presumably these cases would involve some type of emergency and thus the justification for my intrusion would stem from something other than my right to freedom of movement.

[7] As David Miller explains, "The point here is that liberal societies in general offer their members *sufficient* freedom of movement to protect the interests that the human right to free movement is intended to protect, even though the extent of free movement is very far from absolute." David Miller, "Immigration: The Case for Limits" in Andrew I. Cohen and Christopher Heath Wellman (eds.), *Contemporary Debates in Applied Ethics* (Malden, MA: Blackwell Publishing, 2005), pp. 193–205 at p. 195. Also see Miller's contribution to this volume, in which he elaborates on that argument.

[8] As Nozick acknowledges in a footnote on page 55 of *Anarchy, State and Utopia* (New York: Basic Books, 1974), "The possibility of surrounding an individual presents a difficulty for a libertarian theory that contemplates private ownership of all roads and streets with no public ways of access. A person might trap another by purchasing the land around him, leaving him no way to leave without trespass."

around her, but it raises the obvious question of when a person's range of movement is *sufficient.*

I do not know how to incontrovertibly answer this question with any great precision, but we may be able to make some preliminary (and for our purposes adequate) progress by reflecting on what we mean by a human right.[9] On my understanding, human rights are a subset of moral rights which are distinguished by their connection to our fundamental interests or basic needs. More specifically, I would say that human rights are claims to protections against the standard threats to living a minimally decent human life in contemporary society. To assert a human right to freedom of movement, then, is to allege that one standard way in which one might be unable to live a minimally decent life would be if one were prevented from moving around to such a degree that one could, among other things, gain an education, support oneself and one's family, practice one's religion, and socialize with a reasonable variety of others. And the existence of this human right entails that we must not design institutions that would avoidably leave people without sufficient freedom of movement. Thus, just as a system of property rights would be illegitimate if it regularly prevented people from leaving their, say, one-acre pieces of land, a political system would be illegitimate if it kept citizens effectively imprisoned within similarly sized states. Importantly, though, an individual's claim to sufficient freedom of movement is consistent with a variety of types of systems of property rights that extensively limit freedom of movement, and it is consistent with a global system of territorially districted states which regularly prohibit people from moving into the country of their choice. In sum, because one clearly can have sufficient freedom (where sufficiency is cashed out in terms of human rights, which in turn are understood as protections against escaping the standard threats to living a minimally decent life) without having free rein to move all over the globe, we cannot infer the impermissibility of immigration restrictions from the presence of a human right to freedom of movement. If states were tiny, single-acre entities and people were regularly prevented from leaving the state in which they were born, then this arrangement would clearly (and egregiously) run afoul of the right to freedom of movement. But if states are sufficiently large and/or there is adequate opportunity to move from one state to another, then we cannot object to this arrangement on the grounds that it is incompatible with freedom of movement. And while we might object to the geopolitical status quo on any number of other grounds, it seems to me implausible to allege that existing states are insufficiently large and porous to migration so as to violate the human right to freedom of movement.

---

[9] On this issue, see Kieran Oberman's and David Miller's chapters in this volume. As the quote in note 7 indicates, Miller also pursues this line in "Immigration: The Case for Limits."

One way to counter my response to Cole's first argument would be to question my construal of the right to freedom of movement. Just as I alleged that Cole's understanding of the right to freedom of movement is too expansive, one might protest that conceiving of freedom of movement in light of my very narrow conception of human rights leads to an implausibly restricted right to free movement.[10] It is worth exploring this potential objection now, because it leads us directly into Cole's second argument. In particular, Cole has suggested that if one conceives of freedom of movement in terms of my (overly narrow) account of human rights, then one is left unable to condemn those countries which restrict internal migration. But surely this is unacceptable. As Joseph Carens writes, "No liberal state restricts internal mobility. Those states that do restrict internal mobility are criticized for denying basic human freedoms."[11]

To motivate this objection, consider my own situation as someone who lives in St. Louis, a city along the western bank of the Mississippi River. The Mississippi River runs through the middle of the United States, cutting the country into two roughly equal parts. Imagine that the government instituted a new law prohibiting those of us who live west of the Mississippi from moving east of the river. Virtually everyone agrees states may not permissibly place restrictions on internal migration, but it is not clear how I could object to such a policy. Given that I cash out the right to freedom of movement in the language of human rights, and given that I define human rights in terms of avoiding the standard threats to living a minimally decent life, it is hard to see how I could object that such a law leaves me with insufficient freedom of movement. After all, I remain free to move anywhere I like west of the Mississippi, so how can I plausibly claim that I cannot live a minimally decent life merely because I am legally barred from migrating east of the river?

I must confess that I am far from comfortable with this implication. As a liberal political theorist, I begin by assuming that states should treat all of their constituents as free and equal citizens. And given this presumption in favor of individual freedom (and equality), I would object to a restriction of individual liberty such as this unless it was necessary to advance some compelling state interest. At most, though, this shows that there may be a *liberal* right to freedom of movement which entitles one to move freely within one's country, but because I define state legitimacy in terms of human (rather than liberal) rights, the existence of this liberal right does not allow me to condemn a state

---

[10] Cole raises other, very thoughtful reservations about such a "minimalist" account of human rights on pages 293–7 of *Debating the Ethics of Immigration*. For further discussion regarding the scope of the human right to freedom of movement, see Oberman's contribution to this volume.

[11] Joseph Carens, "Aliens and Citizens: The Case for Open Borders," *Review of Politics* 49 (1987), 251–73 at p. 267.

which restricts internal migration as illegitimate. In the end, then, I must acknowledge that I do not believe that my human rights would in fact be violated by such a law.

I understand that this conclusion is highly revisionist of the standard thinking on internal migration, but to see why this revision does not constitute a *reductio ad absurdum*, consider what we might say about secession and its aftermath. In particular, do those Americans living in the territory to the east of the Mississippi River have a moral right to secede from their western compatriots? And if they did secede, would there be anything problematic about limiting immigration by their former compatriots? Personally, I believe that the Easterners have a right to secede and that they would subsequently have the right to limit Westerners' immigration. I recognize that this permissive stance on secession is highly controversial, but it seems much less controversial to allege that such an act of unilateral state-breaking would violate no human rights. (Think of it this way: unless one is prepared to (implausibly) say that human rights would be violated if East and West Germany mutually decided to once again go their separate political ways, then why think that anyone's rights would be violated if the political divorce was not mutual?) And if my human rights would not be violated by my inability to migrate east of the Mississippi after the East seceded from the West, then why would my human rights be violated by my inability to move east of the Mississippi within the current context?

So while I am a card-carrying liberal who would prefer a world in which all regimes treat their constituents as free and equal citizens, I do not think that states cannot be legitimate unless they are fully liberal. I distinguish between human and liberal rights (with the latter being much more extensive) and understand a state to be legitimate just as long as it protects and respects human rights. As a liberal, then, I would criticize any state that restricted free movement without sufficient justification, but I do not think it is problematic to conclude that such a state does not necessarily violate the human rights of its constituents.

Let us now consider a third objection to my argument: the contention that the right to exit entails a corresponding right to enter.[12] As was evident above, I motivate a legitimate state's right to freedom of association by invoking an analogy with marriage. That is, I contend that, just as an individual has the right to determine whom (if anyone) she would like to marry, the citizens of a legitimate state have the right to determine whom (if anyone) they would like

---

[12] Cole alleges that "one cannot consistently assert that there is a fundamental human right to emigration but no such right to immigration; the liberal asymmetry position is not merely ethically, but also conceptually, incoherent." Phillip Cole, *Philosophies of Exclusion* (Edinburgh: Edinburgh University Press, 2000), p. 46.

to invite into their political community. And just as an individual's freedom of association entitles one to remain single, a corporate political entity's freedom of association entitles it to exclude all foreigners. One might worry that this analogy between marriage and immigration is inapt because the rights to exit and enter a political state are connected in a way that the rights to enter and exit a marriage are not. It is worth quoting Cole at length here:

> However, when one exits a marriage, one does not need to have another marriage to enter, and this is the same with many associations—the right of exit does not require that one has another association to enter into. There is, if you like, a "space" one can enter without difficulty, and where one can remain indefinitely. One never needs to enter into marriage, or a golf club, or any of the other kinds of association that are often appealed to in the immigration debate. This is why it is plausible to suppose that here the right to exit does not entail a right of entry, because the right of exit *does not depend on entry elsewhere.*
>
> This is dramatically and importantly not the case when it comes to nation-states. Exit from this kind of association *does* depend on being able to enter another one, both territorially and civicly. There is a "space" of statelessness, but it is not one anybody would wish to enter—it is deeply problematic and dangerous, and nobody can develop their life prospects in that space to any degree. While it is plausible to suppose that the right of exit does not entail a right of entry into the other kinds of associations, like marriages and golf clubs, because there is no need to enter another association in order to enact the right to leave, in the case of the nation-state there is a need to enter another association in order to enact the right to leave, and so in this case it is plausible to suppose that the right of exit does imply the right of entry.[13]

This is a particularly forceful argument, because it denies neither the importance of freedom of association nor its relevance to political states. More minimally, it questions only whether those of us who take for granted the right to emigrate can consistently appeal to these values to ground a state's right to limit immigration. And because I affirm an individual's right to exit a state, I must take this objection seriously.

In response to this objection, I am inclined to switch from thinking exclusively of marriage to talking about families more generally. Whether one finds this change helpful may well depend upon one's thoughts about orphanages. Let me explain.

I agree that each of us needs a state to protect us. Ideally, on my view, everyone would live in a stable liberal democracy. At the very least, however, each of us needs a state to protect us from the standard threats to living a minimally decent human life. In other words, we all want a state that can satisfactorily secure our basic human rights. Interestingly, we can make

---

[13] Wellman and Cole, *Debating the Ethics of Immigration*, pp. 203–4. By permission of Oxford University Press.

analogous claims about families. Ideally, all young children would be raised in loving, enlightened, and financially secure families, but at the very least, each of us needs competent and conscientious adults who are assigned to see that our basic needs are met. Assuming that this is correct, it is worth musing a bit about our responsibilities to young orphans. Imagine, for instance, that the parents next door to Donna and me die, leaving their two-year-old twins behind. Clearly, Donna and I must care for these young girls, but it is not obvious that we must adopt them. If we merely took them in until we could find another suitable family to raise them, for example, presumably we would have violated no moral duties to these children. Imagine, however, that things are more complicated. Suppose that there are numerous orphans, and there are not enough families willing to take them in. Would it be morally permissible in these circumstances for those adults who would prefer not to adopt children to pool their funds to build and staff an orphanage for these children? Assuming that this orphanage took sufficiently good care of these young children, I think this option would be morally permissible, even if these children would have been better off had they been raised in nuclear families in adoptive homes.

If this is right, we might characterize the situation as follows. Every young child needs protective and nurturing care, and these needs obligate the rest of us to do our fair share to see that all children are receiving the requisite attention. As long as one is doing one's fair share, one is not morally required to do any more, even if there remain orphans who have been neither adopted nor admitted into sufficiently good orphanages. What is more, given that one can do one's share by donating sufficient funds to orphanages, no matter how many needy orphans there are, morality never requires one to adopt a child if one would prefer not to. In other words, even though the needs of young children indisputably generate moral duties to do our fair share to ensure that all orphans receive satisfactory care, these duties are distinct and can be kept separate from a family's right to freedom of association.

Assuming that this is correct, the implications for the morality of immigration control may vindicate my claims about a legitimate state's right to exclude outsiders. To appreciate these implications, it is important to first divide those who want to immigrate into two groups, depending upon whether or not their current state satisfactorily protects their human rights. My views regarding those who belong to states which adequately protect them against the standard threats to living minimally decent human lives is relatively straightforward: I concede that their right to exit their own states may be of little to no value if few or no other states are willing to let them enter, but this strikes me as no more conceptually incoherent or morally problematic than a person whose right to get married is of little to no value because she can find few or no people interested in marrying her.

As Cole's extended quote above reminds us, though, we should not be so sanguine about a person whose current state does not protect her human rights. While I think it is conceptually coherent to say that someone in this situation who has few, if any, options to immigrate elsewhere can have a right to exit which is of little to no value, this situation is undeniably much more morally worrisome. And the reason for this seems clear: just as every small child needs to be cared for, each of us needs to be sufficiently institutionally protected, and thus it is deeply problematic if someone has no effective option to leave a state which does not satisfactorily protect her from the standard threats to living a minimally decent human life. And just as a young child's need for personal care can obligate others to help provide this assistance, a foreigner's need for political protection can obligate others to ensure that this imperiled foreigner gets the requisite political protection. The most obvious way to help such a person, of course, is to allow her to enter one's country. But as the case of adoption illustrates, this is not the only way to help. Just as Donna and I would have fully discharged all of our duties to our orphan neighbors if we had either found them a satisfactory adoptive home or taken them to an orphanage where they would receive adequate care, a country that would prefer not to allow an imperiled foreigner to immigrate may permissibly exclude her as long as it finds another satisfactory political community willing to take her in. And if we can discharge our duties to orphans by contributing our fair share of money to orphanages, it is not clear why a country that would prefer to jealously protect its borders cannot fully discharge its responsibilities to needy foreigners by contributing its fair share to help reform rogue and failed states which are currently unwilling and/or unable to protect the basic rights of their constituents.[14]

If this is right, we should understand the morality of attending to the political needs of vulnerable foreigners as analogous to the ethics of helping young children. Every inhabitant of a failed or rogue state needs institutional protection, and these needs obligate the rest of us to do our fair share to see that everyone is sufficiently institutionally protected. As long as one is doing one's fair share, one is not morally required to do any more, even if there remain foreigners who have no effective means of exiting their failed or rogue state. What is more, given that one can do one's share by donating sufficient funds to the construction of adequate political institutions elsewhere, no

---

[14] For the sake of argument, let us assume that I am wrong. That is, let us grant *arguendo* that the citizens in wealthy liberal democracies cannot satisfactorily discharge their duties to foreigners in failed or rogue states in any manner other than allowing these imperiled outsiders to immigrate. Even so, this would not vindicate a right to enter grounded in freedom of movement, because the right to immigrate would be justified instead by the perilous circumstances. This position parallels our earlier observation (in note 6) that one might in extreme circumstances have a right to enter someone's home without her permission, but the permissibility of entering in these types of cases must be attributed to something other than a general right to free movement.

matter how many needy foreigners there are, morality never requires a legitimate state to allow a needy foreigner to immigrate if it would prefer not to. In other words, even though the needs of imperiled foreigners indisputably generate moral duties to do our fair share to ensure that everyone is satisfactorily institutionally protected, these duties are distinct and can be kept separate from a country's right to freedom of association.

In sum, as much as some of us may lament being either unmarried or in a bad marriage, Cole is certainly correct to point out that these circumstances simply do not compare to being in a failed or rogue state in which "nobody can develop their life prospects in that space to any degree." One's marital situation might well be psychologically painful, but it is typically not as perilous as being subject to a state that is either unable to protect or unwilling to respect your basic human rights. And given this, we should be cautious about transposing our conclusions about freedom of association in the marital realm to the dramatically different sphere of immigration. But if the preceding analysis is correct, our considered convictions about the importance of freedom of association in domestic affairs may reliably guide our understanding of the morality of immigration after all. In other words, our judgment that families can be well within their rights to exclude needy orphans supports the judgment that legitimate states may in some circumstances (i.e., if they have already done a sufficient amount to address the problems of those vulnerable to failed and rogue states) permissibly exclude even the most desperate foreigners. As a consequence, I am not ultimately persuaded by the criticism of my analogy, and I reject the claim that one cannot consistently affirm an individual's right to exit without also committing to the right to enter.

In the end, then, I remain unmoved by the three objections that (1) the human right to freedom of movement necessarily overrides a state's claim to limit the rights of outsiders to enter, (2) giving states the discretion to restrict immigration leaves one unable to criticize countries that limit internal migration, and (3) consistency requires those who endorse the right to emigrate to similarly affirm an individual's right to immigrate. Once one recognizes both that the right to freedom of movement is properly understood as a claim to a sufficient degree of free movement and that one can enjoy an adequate level of this freedom without being allowed to roam freely all over the globe, it becomes clear that acknowledging this right need not conflict with legitimate states' enjoying broad discretion over their immigration policies.

5.3 The Right to Exit

Whereas advocates for a robust right to free movement contest a state's right to restrict immigration, others have questioned whether international law is right to give individuals such free rein to emigrate. Thus, just as one might lobby for a symmetrical position wherein individuals may choose both to emigrate and immigrate, there is room to defend the contrary symmetrical stance, in which the state may limit emigration just as strictly as it controls immigration. Lea Ypi explores this possibility when she defends what she calls "the general principle in migration," which says that "if restrictions on freedom of movement could ever be justified, such restrictions ought to take equal account of justice in immigration and justice in emigration."[15] In other words, "if R provides a valid reason for restricting incoming freedom of movement, R also provides a valid reason for restricting outgoing freedom of movement."[16]

This challenge is a welcome contribution to the burgeoning literature on the ethics of migration because it pushes those of us pretheoretically inclined to accept international law's asymmetrical position to actually defend what we have traditionally taken for granted: everyone has an unqualified right to emigrate. What is more, providing this defense may not be easy, because as Ypi points out, any of the consequences a state might cite to limit immigration can also be cited to prohibit emigration. If a prospective host state is entitled to restrict immigration on the grounds that this influx will negatively affect its economy, culture, or political functioning, for instance, then why do these same effects not equally entitle a state to limit emigration? In the absence of arguments to the contrary, symmetry would seem to entail that political states are equally entitled to limit emigration and immigration.

Given my arguments in Section 5.1, it is tempting here to invoke freedom of association to explain why states have asymmetric dominion over the rights to enter and exit. This is especially tempting because I understand freedom of association to be a much more robust right than Ypi seems to. I say this because I found her discussion of this right curious. Consider, for instance, her analysis of the following example:

> A soccer team is a kind of voluntary association formed in order to play football. It requires, among other things, denying access to people who don't know how to kick a ball and also placing numerical limits on participation—i.e. restricting the team to a number of eleven players. We would not think it morally problematic if members of that association were to exclude any willing candidates either on grounds that they cannot play football or because the team already has eleven members.[17]

I would analyze the situation very differently. I think people who want to play soccer together can associate more or less on any terms they choose. If they

[15] Lea Ypi, "Justice in Migration: A Closed Border Utopia?," *Journal of Political Philosophy* 16 (2008), 391–418 at p. 391.
[16] Ypi, "Justice in Migration: A Closed Border Utopia?," p. 391.
[17] Ypi, "Justice in Migration: A Closed Border Utopia?," pp. 403–4.

want to include others who do not know how to kick and exclude those who do, that is their prerogative. And if they want to play with more or fewer than eleven players per side, they are entitled to do this as well. Imagine, for instance, that I am watching with envy as two groups of eleven players compete against each other. And suppose that one of them injures herself and exits the game, leaving her ten former teammates to compete against eleven. And finally, imagine that I happen to be no better or worse at soccer than those twenty-one players. If I asked to join the game as a substitute for the injured player, would they be obligated to include me? I do not see why. It may not be terribly friendly of them to say that they would prefer to play exclusively amongst themselves, but it strikes me that they would be well within their rights to do so. Thus, while I might implore them to reconsider on the grounds that my participation would likely improve their game, I cannot rightfully object that they have no legitimate grounds on which to exclude me. (Just as I alleged earlier that Norway has the right to decline the European Union's invitation even if Norwegians would be discernibly better off within the union, I insist that these soccer players retain their rights to exclude me even if their game would improve as a result of my inclusion.)

And if the shoe were on the other foot, if these others wanted me to join their game, freedom of association would similarly entitle me to decline. Imagine that after the one person gets hurt, the other twenty-one players turn to me and ask me to take the injured player's place. Even if I were a comparably skilled soccer player who generally enjoyed playing, I would be well within my rights to decline their invitation. Etiquette may suggest that I should offer some reason as to why I am currently unavailable, but morality does not require that I must have some pressing engagement in order to decline. I would be well within my rights to refuse to play for any reason whatsoever. And if freedom of association allows the group to refuse to associate with me and me to refuse to associate with the group, then why does it not equally permit me to stop associating once I have started? In other words, why may I not simply quit the game for whatever reason I want? And if I am at liberty to quit playing soccer with others, why am I not equally entitled to discontinue politically associating with my compatriots? Thus, freedom of association would seem to guarantee my right to renounce my citizenship and emigrate.

This line of thinking is tempting, but Ypi's argument suggests that it may be incorrect. It may be incorrect because, while freedom of association does give one broad discretion to refuse to associate with others, it may not necessarily give one the right to *dis*associate from those with whom one is currently associating. To emphasize: freedom of association may well entitle one to choose whether and/or with whom to initiate an association among willing others, but it does not automatically entitle one to *stop* associating with one's current associates. Consider my marriage with Donna, for instance. Given that Donna was willing to marry me, freedom of association explains why I could choose whether or not to marry her, but it does not necessarily entail the right to now divorce her. Whether or not (and/or under what conditions) I may withdraw from this marriage depends upon the nature and content of the obligation which binds me to the association. And given that I solemnly promised her that I would stay with her for the rest of my life, it seems pretty clear that I am obligated not to leave her. Thus, while freedom of association may well explain why I was once morally entitled to choose whether or not to associate with Donna, it does not necessarily give me the right to leave her now.

Transposing this observation to the state, we have reason to think that my arguments in the first section in defense of the asymmetry between the rights to enter and exit may have been far too quick. Even if freedom of association explains why states have broad discretion over outsiders' rights to enter, because emigration involves *dis*associating, freedom of association may not conclusively establish an insider's right to emigrate. If citizens have duties to their states and/or compatriots which entail that they have no right to leave, then perhaps states enjoy broad discretion to restrict emigration.[18]

But notice: while the right to freedom of association may not automatically entail that citizens have the right to exit, neither does it imply that they do not. The obvious question, then, seems to be "what political obligations do citizens have not to leave?" In the case of my marriage to Donna, I explicitly waived my right to exit when I publicly promised not to leave the marriage, no matter how badly things soured. Most of us have made no such promise to our compatriots, though, so if there is a general duty not to emigrate, it must have some other source. Ypi suggests that this duty might be explained in terms of fairness; after all, citizens typically benefit enormously from societies, so it seems unfair not to remain and do one's share to contribute to the future provision of these benefits. As Ypi explains,

> It is precisely the provision of goods such as personal security, guarantees on property, the enforceability of contracts, education and healthcare (to mention but some) that justifies the request that capable citizens make a productive contribution to society. Enjoying benefits made available by the state through the cooperative work of one's fellow-citizens yet being unwilling to share one's efforts with them in return, amounts to an unfair exploitation of the work of others for one's unilateral advantage.[19]

---

[18] For detailed discussion of this issue, see Anna Stilz's contribution to this volume.
[19] Ypi, "Justice in Migration: A Closed Border Utopia?," p. 408.

She thus concludes that "Justice in emigration requires limiting the outflow of more productive groups since it is precisely their exit which will most likely affect negatively sending societies."[20]

To couch Ypi's point within the context of my earlier response, we might explain her argument as follows: Just as I acknowledged the value of freedom of movement but argued that this right might be outweighed by freedom of association, Ypi can concede the presumptive rights to free movement and freedom of association but insist that both of these values must give way to the demands of justice. After all, presumably our disinclination to suppose that one's right to freedom of movement entitles one to enter another's home without her permission stems from our recognition that no one has a right to *unjustly* move freely. So, unless I want to insist that freedom of association (or perhaps freedom of association combined with freedom of movement) necessarily trumps justice, it appears as though Ypi can happily concede my more robust conception of freedom of association and still deny that individuals necessarily have the right to emigrate.

I agree that one has no right to act unjustly, so I will not pursue the idea that freedom of association somehow prevails over the demands of justice. Two other potential responses to Ypi's argument appear more promising, though. The first is to deny that the fairness principle in fact generates any duties of distributive justice among compatriots. The second is to insist that one's duties of distributive justice can be discharged in a way that is compatible with exercising one's rights to freedom of association. Let us consider each of these in turn.

As we saw above, Ypi's pivotal claim is that "Enjoying benefits made available by the state through the cooperative work of one's fellow-citizens yet being unwilling to share one's efforts with them in return, amounts to an unfair exploitation of the work of others for one's unilateral advantage."[21] Given the powerful arguments authors like John Simmons have mounted against the fair play theory of political obligation, however, should we not be skeptical of the allegation that those who emigrate may be unfairly exploiting their compatriots?[22] Put simply, the worry about invoking fairness as a source for our duty to obey the law is that one cannot become morally bound by the mere receipt of benefits; one must freely accept them. This requirement of free acceptance is thought to rule out obligation in the political sphere, however, because free acceptance typically requires having the option to reject

---

[20] Ypi, "Justice in Migration: A Closed Border Utopia?," p. 409.

[21] Ypi, "Justice in Migration: A Closed Border Utopia?," p. 408.

[22] John Simmons, *Moral Principles and Political Obligations* (Princeton, NJ: Princeton University Press, 1979).

the benefits in question, and political benefits are foisted upon all constituents within the territorial boundaries irrespective of their consent.

For the sake of argument, let us assume that the principle of fairness cannot explain the duty to obey the law. Even if this is so, it does not follow that Ypi cannot invoke fairness to establish her very different conclusion that at least some of us may have special duties to our compatriots. To see why this is so, notice that critics like John Simmons do not deny that fairness is a genuine moral principle; more minimally, the problem is thought to be that fairness cannot explain why *all of us* have a duty to obey the law. And because we are looking for an account which can explain why everyone is politically bound, fairness cannot be the answer. But notice: one need not allege that *everyone* has a duty which prohibits them from emigrating; in order to deny that all are free to emigrate one need only show that *some of us* have incurred special obligations to our compatriots. And because I do not know how to go about establishing that *none* of us has special obligations to her compatriots, I think we should not press the first potential objection, which involves denying that fairness creates any duties of distributive justice among fellow-citizens.

Thus, let us presume it is correct that fairness explains why at least some citizens may have special duties to their compatriots. Even if we grant all of this, however, it would not necessarily follow that highly educated and talented citizens, for example, may not permissibly emigrate. To see why, consider again my marriage. Clearly I have a special obligation to Donna—after all, I promised her that I would stay with her for better or for worse. Even so, many deny that I have a duty not to leave her. Rather, most think that I have only a duty to continue to care for her if I do divorce her. (Perhaps I must pay her alimony after our separation, for example.) Similarly, even if a publicly educated doctor in Ghana has special obligations to her state and/or compatriots, for instance, perhaps this implies not that she may not emigrate, but only that she must repay these debts if she chooses to emigrate. For instance, perhaps she must compensate the state for the costs of her education or even pay a competent doctor to immigrate and practice medicine within Ghana.

To confirm this conclusion, imagine that the doctor had no interest in leaving Ghana but wanted to change professions.[23] What if the doctor wanted to quit medicine in order to pursue a career in philosophy, for instance? Would she be morally obligated to continue to practice medicine, or would it be permissible for her to change professions, perhaps on the condition that she repay the costs of education or even pay a comparably trained foreign doctor to come work in her place? I presume that this doctor could permissibly

---

[23] Gillian Brock discusses the issue of medical practitioners emigrating from countries where such specialists are already in desperately short supply in *Global Justice* (Oxford: Oxford University Press, 2009).

change professions. But if she would do no wrong in leaving medicine to study philosophy in Ghana, why may she not leave Ghana to practice medicine (or study philosophy) elsewhere?

In sum, Ypi's argument forces us to recognize that freedom of association does not necessarily justify an unqualified right to emigrate, because there may be political obligations or duties of distributive justice which explain why citizens should not leave their current political association. But even if these duties exist, it is likely that they would merely place conditions on a citizen's departure, not that they would prohibit it altogether.[24]

5.4 Conclusion

If one invokes freedom of association, it is not difficult to provide an initial defense of international law's asymmetric position on the rights to enter and exit. As the arguments considered above illustrate, however, a proper appreciation for freedom of movement and the necessity of treating our compatriots fairly make defending a legitimate state's moral dominion over immigration and an individual right to emigrate much more difficult than one might initially suspect. In the end, though, I believe that recognizing that our duties of distributive justice can be fully discharged in a variety of ways that are consistent with exercising our rights to free association enables one to defend international law's support for both a state's right to limit immigration and an individual's right to emigrate.[25]

References

Blake, Michael, "Immigration, Association, and Antidiscrimination," *Ethics* 122 (2012), 748–62.

Brock, Gillian, *Global Justice* (Oxford: Oxford University Press, 2009).

[24] It is worth noting that, although I endorse an asymmetrical stance regarding the rights to enter and exit, I have utilized symmetrical responses to symmetry-based challenges to my views. That is, whether in reaction to Cole's claim about our duties to imperiled outsiders or Ypi's claim about our duties to fellow insiders, I have not denied the duty in question. Rather, my response in both cases has been to emphasize that our rights to freedom of association are distinct, and can be kept separate from, our duties of distributive justice. Thus, even if Cole is correct that we must help imperiled foreigners, I have suggested that we can do our fair share without necessarily allowing any outsiders into our political communities; and even if Ypi is correct to suppose that fairness generates debts to our fellow-citizens, I have urged that there are ways to repay our compatriots without necessarily remaining in the political community.

[25] I am extremely grateful to Sarah Fine and Lea Ypi for inviting me to participate in their wonderful conference and to contribute an essay to this volume. I would also like to thank them for their helpful comments on an earlier version of this essay.

Carens, Joseph H., "Aliens and Citizens: The Case for Open Borders," *Review of Politics* 49 (1987), 251–73.

Cavallero, Eric, "Association and Asylum," *Philosophical Studies* 169 (2014), 133–41.

Cole, Phillip, *Philosophies of Exclusion* (Edinburgh: Edinburgh University Press, 2000).

Fine, Sarah, "Freedom of Association Is Not the Answer," *Ethics* 120 (2010), 538–56.

Miller, David, "Immigration: The Case for Limits" in Andrew I. Cohen and Christopher Heath Wellman (eds.), *Contemporary Debates in Applied Ethics* (Malden, MA: Blackwell Publishing, 2005), pp. 193–205.

Nozick, Robert, *Anarchy, State and Utopia* (New York: Basic Books, 1974).

Simmons, A. John, *Moral Principles and Political Obligations* (Princeton, NJ: Princeton University Press, 1979).

Wellman, Christopher Heath and Phillip Cole, *Debating the Ethics of Immigration: Is There a Right to Exclude?* (New York: Oxford University Press, 2011).

Wilcox, Shelley, "Do Duties to Outsiders Entail Open Borders? A Reply to Wellman," *Philosophical Studies* 169 (2014), 123–32.

Ypi, Lea, "Justice in Migration: A Closed Border Utopia?," *Journal of Political Philosophy* 16 (2008), 391–418.

Part II
Migration, Equality, and Justice

6

The Special-Obligations Challenge to More Open Borders

Arash Abizadeh

One of the most powerful normative arguments for more open state borders appeals to a conception of justice as requiring equality of treatment. On this conception, justice requires treating each human being as an equal—not the same or equally, since different persons have different needs, interests, or capacities, but with equal concern and respect.[1] Many cosmopolitan writers have thought that justice so-understood imposes significant positive distributive duties at the global level.[2] My concern here, however, is specifically with the state's exercise of political power, on which this conception of justice places at least two negative normative constraints: that the state exercise its coercive power neither in a way that prevents some human beings from pursuing opportunities adequate to meet their basic material needs, nor in a way that functions to protect and entrench the structural sources of significant material inequality amongst human beings. To treat persons as equals while coercively exercising political power requires not using that power against individuals structurally to entrench absolute levels of *poverty* or relative material *inequality*. The *justice argument* for more open borders derives from precisely these two constraints, in light of two facts: the fact of severe poverty and inequality at the global level, and the fact that migrating to wealthier polities and partaking in their societies often represents one of the

---

[1] For the distinction between equal treatment and treatment as an equal, see Ronald Dworkin, *Taking Rights Seriously: New Impression with a Reply to Critics*, 2nd edn (London: Duckworth, 1978), pp. 227, 273. For the notion of equal concern and respect, see Ronald Dworkin, "The Original Position," *The University of Chicago Law Review* 40:3 (1973), 500–33.

[2] E.g. Charles R. Beitz, *Political Theory and International Relations*, 2nd edn (Princeton, NJ: Princeton University Press, 1999); Pablo Gilabert, *From Global Poverty to Global Equality: A Philosophical Exploration* (Oxford: Oxford University Press, 2012).

best opportunities for individuals from globally poor regions to alleviate their poverty and improve their relative material standing. On this conception of justice, there is a pro tanto constraint requiring the state not coercively to prevent migrants from globally poor societies from entering the territories of wealthier societies, partaking in them, and benefitting from the associated opportunities for advancement.[3]

An important challenge to the justice argument seeks to motivate border restrictions against foreigners, even while remaining committed to treating persons as equals, by appeal to the putative special obligations amongst compatriots. A number of authors have argued that in virtue of their special relationships, citizens of wealthier polities—and, by implication, their representative state institutions—have special obligations of justice to show special concern for their own most disadvantaged compatriots, even to the detriment of the global poor who are (often significantly) worse off.[4] Proponents of the *special-obligations challenge* to the justice argument for more open borders apply this conclusion directly to the borders of wealthier states. Thus Stephen Macedo argues that where more open borders would harm the domestic poor, citizens of wealthy polities have a special obligation to them to restrict immigration; citing the work of the economist George Borjas, he suggests that in the U.S. immigration has indeed harmed the country's poorest citizens.[5]

---

[3] I am concerned primarily with territorial (rather than civic) borders here. The justice or equality argument stands alongside the *liberty argument* as one of the two most prominent arguments in the literature for more open borders. For an overview of the literature, see Arash Abizadeh, "Closed Borders, Human Rights, and Democratic Legitimation" in David Hollenbach (ed.), *Driven From Home: Human Rights and the New Realities of Forced Migration* (Washington, DC: Georgetown University Press, 2010); Veit Bader, "The Ethics of Immigration," *Constellations* 12:3 (2005), 331–61. For a defense and specification of the claim that boundary controls subject foreigners to coercive political power, see Arash Abizadeh, "Democratic Legitimacy and State Coercion: A Reply to David Miller," *Political Theory* 38:1 (2010), 121–30. It is true that, as I have construed the justice argument here, it refers to the coercive restriction of liberties, but it remains distinct from the liberty argument insofar as it is fundamentally concerned with what is required to treat persons as equals (with implications for how persons may be coerced), rather than merely with the range of opportunities available to persons.

[4] See, e.g., Richard W. Miller, "Cosmopolitan Respect and Patriotic Concern," *Philosophy & Public Affairs* 27:3 (1998), 202–24. See also David Miller, *On Nationality* (Oxford: Clarendon Press, 1995), who grounds special obligations in the fact of shared nationality, rather than citizenship per se. In more recent work Richard Miller has argued that there are special relationships that hold globally and that ground significant duties at the global level. See Richard W. Miller, *Globalizing Justice: The Ethics of Poverty and Power* (Oxford: Oxford University Press, 2010).

[5] Stephen Macedo, "The Moral Dilemma of U.S. Immigration Policy: Open Borders Versus Social Justice?" in Carol M. Swain (ed.), *Debating Immigration* (New York: Cambridge University Press, 2007), pp. 63–82. Macedo does not assert that these special obligations provide an all-things-considered reason to restrict immigration; they may be outweighed by other considerations. See also James Woodward, "Commentary: Liberalism and Migration" in Brian Barry and Robert E. Goodin (eds.), *Free Movement: Ethical Issues in the Transnational Migration of People and of Money* (University Park, PA: Pennsylvania State University Press, 1992); John Isbister, "A Liberal Argument for Border Controls: Reply to Carens," *International Migration Review* 34:2 (2000), 629–35; Carol M. Swain, "Response to Joseph Carens's 'Case for Amnesty',￼" *Boston Review* 34:3 (May/June) (2009).

The special-obligations challenge therefore relies on three normative and one empirical premises: that special obligations are compatible with treating all persons as equals; that compatriots owe each other special obligations; that compatriotic special obligations justify restricting immigration if immigration would harm the domestic poor; and, finally, that as a matter of empirical fact immigration (especially by low-skilled workers) does harm the domestic poor. I concede the first two normative premises: that justice, understood to require treating others as equals, is compatible with special obligations; and that there may indeed exist compatriotic special obligations. For the sake of argument, in this chapter I also take for granted the fourth, empirical premise.[6] My purpose in this chapter is to refute the special-obligations challenge by focusing on its third normative premise. I challenge the third premise by interrogating what precisely constitutes the relationship and/or set of interactions that are supposed to ground compatriotic special obligations that, in turn, are supposed to justify restricting immigration. There are two distinct questions here: one concerns the nature and scope of the relationships/interactions that putatively ground compatriotic special obligations; another concerns the ability of such special obligations to motivate more closed borders. The literature on special obligations provides essentially three types of answer to the first question: the first focuses on the *social* aspects of compatriots' relationships and interactions, the second on specifically *civic* features constitutive of citizenship itself, and the third on the *political* relation of joint responsibility for the exercise of power over persons. I take up each in turn, and argue either that the feature in question does not ground special obligations, or that the special obligations do not justify restricting immigration.

6.1 Special Obligations: Additive and Prioritizing

The paradigm case of a relationship grounding special obligations is between parent and child. A father, for example, has a special obligation to his daughter to show special concern for her well-being, in a way that he does not to other people's children. This special obligation arises from the nature of their relationship, and the fact that human beings have reason to value some relationships non-instrumentally. There is nothing unjust about this: the special (unequal) concern for one's own daughter does not presume that her life is more valuable than the lives of others; it simply presumes that one

---

[6] But see Arash Abizadeh, Manish Pandey, and Sohrab Abizadeh, "Wage Competition and the Special-Obligations Challenge to More Open Borders," *Politics, Philosophy & Economics* 14:3 (2015), 255–69, where we argue that the empirical evidence suggests that immigration has no significant negative impact on the wages of low-skilled workers in wealthy polities, except for in the case of previous cohorts of immigrants.

(legitimately) values the relationship non-instrumentally. Thus, as Richard Miller has emphasized, treating others as equals requires equal respect but not always equal concern: to show special concern for some is compatible with treating others as equals, since valuing some relationships non-instrumentally is potentially constitutive of every person's well-being, and part of what it is to value one's special relations non-instrumentally just is to attend to their interests more generously than one is required to attend to those of others.[7]

A number of political philosophers have argued that compatriots are involved in a set of relationships and/or interactions that, like familial or friendship relations, ground a set of special obligations. In evaluating this claim, however, we must be careful to distinguish between two different types of special obligation. An *additive* special obligation simply adds to (or strengthens) the general duties that one already has to others. It requires one to sacrifice, on behalf of the special other, one's *own* interests to a greater degree (or across a greater range of circumstances) than one would otherwise have had to do. A *prioritizing* special obligation, by contrast, obligates one to prioritize the interests of some over those of others, without requiring a greater (or more robust) level of overall self-sacrifice. The paradigmatic way in which a prioritizing special obligation arises is via the perfection of an imperfect general duty. Assume, for example, that one has a general imperfect duty to help at least some persons in need, but one is not duty-bound to help everyone in need. A prioritizing special obligation that perfects such a duty towards one's friend would obligate one to help her, when she is in need, *rather than* other persons in need. Note that the prioritizing special obligation here does not merely arise for the purely instrumental consideration that, if everyone were to prioritize their friends in this way, individuals' general duties would be most efficiently discharged overall; rather, it arises because respecting the non-instrumental value of the relation obligates one to prioritize one's friend (independently of instrumental considerations of overall efficiency).[8] Additive and prioritizing special obligations can of course be combined, as they arguably are in the parent–child relationship. But they are not the same.

---

[7] Miller, "Cosmopolitan Respect and Patriotic Concern." On the non-instrumental value of special relationships grounding special obligations, see Samuel Scheffler, *Boundaries and Allegiances: Problems of Justice and Responsibility in Liberal Thought* (Oxford: Oxford University Press, 2001); Arash Abizadeh and Pablo Gilabert, "Is There a Genuine Tension between Cosmopolitan Egalitarianism and Special Responsibilities?," *Philosophical Studies* 138:3 (2008), 348–65. Miller and Abizadeh & Gilabert argue, against Scheffler, that special obligations are compatible with a cosmopolitan account of justice and equality, thus rejecting the view that taking special obligations seriously requires abandoning an impartialist account of morality.

[8] In other words, the model of prioritizing I have in mind here is not an instance of the "assigned responsibility model" defended by Robert E. Goodin, "What Is So Special about Our Fellow Countrymen?," *Ethics* 98:4 (1988), 663–86, and criticized by Scheffler, *Boundaries and Allegiances*, amongst others, for providing a merely instrumentalist derivation of special obligations.

It is important to see that the special-obligations challenge requires prioritizing, not merely additive, special obligations amongst compatriots: to motivate more closed borders, compatriotic special obligations must justify prioritizing compatriots in a way that overcomes the two pro tanto general duties of justice owed to the foreign poor. In particular, they must overcome the pro tanto constraint with which we began: the duties not to use coercive state power against persons in a way that serves structurally to entrench their absolute levels of poverty or relative material inequality. The question is precisely what feature of compatriots' relations and/or interactions could ground such *prioritizing* special obligations amongst themselves (and against foreigners).

6.2 Residence: Social Relationships and Interactions

Rather than focusing directly on *civic* features that constitute the institution and practice of citizenship itself, a number of writers argue for compatriotic special obligations on the basis of *social* features of citizens' mutual relationships and interactions. There are at least four reasons why, on the basis of such features, it might be thought that citizens, and the political society of which they are a member, have special obligations towards their compatriots: because fellow citizens jointly (1) participate in a territorially bounded, *mutually beneficial scheme* of cooperation; (2) have profound or *fundamental interests* especially vulnerable to the state's exercise of power; (3) are *subject to coercion* by the state and its laws; and (4) have pervasive and roughly *equal stakes* in the territorially bounded political society and the dense network of laws by which its citizens are governed.

A territorially based, law-governed political society may, for normative purposes, be modeled as a mutually beneficial scheme of social cooperation insofar as the state's laws enable its participants to act individually on the basis of regularized patterns of behavior and expectations, to act collectively in the pursuit of joint projects, and to benefit thereby. This is a familiar thought in Rawlsian political philosophy. Richard Dagger has argued that a requirement of *reciprocity*, grounded in a principle of fair play, implies that participants in such a politically ordered scheme of social cooperation owe special obligations to each other to prioritize each others' needs over the needs of others.[9] There

---

[9] Richard Dagger, "Rights, Boundaries, and the Bonds of Community: A Qualified Defense of Moral Parochialism," *American Political Science Review* 79:2 (1985), 436–47. See also the reciprocity argument advanced by Brian Barry, "Humanity and Justice in Global Perspective" in J. Roland Pennock and John W. Chapman (eds.), *Ethics, Economics, and the Law*, Nomos 24 (New York: New York University Press, 1982), pp. 219–52.

are several problems with this argument and with appealing to it to motivate the special-obligations challenge.

First, to the extent that the reciprocity argument succeeds in grounding special obligations, it excludes unproductive and infirm persons incapable of adequately participating in the scheme of social cooperation. Yet if society owes special obligations to its most disadvantaged, surely such obligations are especially owed to those so extremely disadvantaged that they cannot contribute to the provision of mutual benefits.[10] Second, that one cooperate with others to produce mutually beneficial outcomes is often a moral duty or obligation—rather than a precondition for such duties or obligations to arise. Hence special obligations would arise only if pre-existing general duties have been adequately fulfilled.[11] This is related to the first point: of course it is perfectly understandable why fair play would require that participants in a scheme of social cooperation treat each other with equal concern and respect; what is unclear from Dagger's argument is why it would excuse cooperators from treating *others* with equal concern as well.

The third problem is also related: the conclusion about prioritizing co-participants conflates additive and prioritizing special obligations. The argument for why participation in a scheme of social cooperation grounds special obligations to co-participants justifies additive, but not prioritizing, special obligations: it justifies *additional* responsibilities of concern for co-participants, but not a moral liberty to discharge one's special obligations to co-participants at the expense of general duties one might otherwise have to non-participants.[12] This point undermines the attempt to marshal the reciprocity argument on behalf of immigration restrictions, because that attempt would amount to claiming that the state is justified in coercively excluding some from a mutually beneficial scheme in which they desire to partake, on the basis of the fact that current participants have been benefitting each other. This is comprehensible as an appeal to self-interest, but not to justice or special obligations. Additive special obligations to poorer members need not, in any case, be discharged at the expense of shirking pre-existing general duties to disadvantaged non-members.[13]

---

[10] For this objection, see Goodin, "What Is So Special about Our Fellow Countrymen?," p. 683. See also Miller, *Globalizing Justice*, p. 36, explicitly addressing Dagger's argument. For Rawls' concern over this lacuna in his theory of justice, see John Rawls, *Justice as Fairness: A Restatement*, ed. Erin Kelly (Cambridge, MA: Harvard University Press, 2001), p. 176, note 59.

[11] Arash Abizadeh, "Cooperation, Pervasive Impact, and Coercion: On the Scope (not Site) of Distributive Justice," *Philosophy & Public Affairs* 35:4 (2007), 318–58 at pp. 336–7.

[12] Compare this with what Scheffler calls the "distributive objection" to special responsibilities. Scheffler, *Boundaries and Allegiances*.

[13] If, all other things equal, immigration harms poorer residents, then better off residents can discharge their additive special obligations to them by compensating them or contributing to the alleviation of the domestic structural causes of their social disadvantages (i.e., by making all other things not equal). See also Andrea Sangiovanni, "Global Justice, Reciprocity, and the State,"

Dagger's argument also helps to bring out a more general feature of attempts to ground compatriotic special obligations in the social, rather than constitutively civic, features of citizens' relationships and interactions. Although Dagger speaks of special obligations amongst fellow *citizens*, in fact his argument, if successful, would further extend to all those who *reside* within a state's territory, regardless of citizenship status. That is because mere residence, even without citizenship status, often enables human beings to participate in and contribute to a wide range of social and economic activities governed by the modern state. Dagger's exposition conflates two dimensions of the state: the modern state is constituted by both *territorial* boundaries, encompassing the geographical area over which it claims territorial jurisdiction, and *civic* boundaries, encompassing the persons who are its recognized members and over which it claims personal jurisdiction. In virtue of the first dimension, the modern state claims jurisdiction over all those who *reside* within its territory; in virtue of the second dimension, it claims jurisdiction over all those who are its *citizens*. It is true that if—as John Rawls assumed in his *Theory of Justice*—territorial boundaries were hermetically sealed, then, assuming birthright citizenship, territorial and civic boundaries would in practice coincide.[14] Indeed, the normative literature on distributive justice, even when specifically attending to the question of global justice, has tended to proceed as if the categories of resident and citizen can be treated as equivalent.[15] But the fact of interstate migration, combined with the massive amount of coercive state power expended on regulating it, renders this equivocation perilous for any adequate treatment of global justice—especially one focused on the justice of regimes of border control themselves. The point is not specific to Dagger: insofar as the modern state organizes and structures social relations and activities *territorially* (and not just in terms of membership), any attempt to ground special obligations on social features—rather than on the civic features that directly constitute the institution and practice of citizenship itself—will tend to suggest special obligations amongst territorial *residents* rather than just citizens. Therefore, those who ground special obligations in social features at least implicitly end up defending a modified version of the special-obligations challenge: strictly speaking, that special obligations amongst *residents* (rather than or in addition to citizens) justify immigration restrictions.[16]

Philosophy & Public Affairs 35:1 (2007), 3–39 at p. 38. Sangiovanni also advances a reciprocity account, but argues that such an account implies that "immigrants have a prima facie claim to open borders."

[14] John Rawls, *A Theory of Justice* (Cambridge, MA: Harvard University Press, 1971).

[15] See, e.g., Michael Blake, "Distributive Justice, State Coercion, and Autonomy," *Philosophy and Public Affairs* 30:3 (2002), 257–96.

[16] On the importance of the residence versus citizenship distinction, see also Sarah Song's contribution to this volume.

A second potential argument grounds special obligations in the putative fact that the fundamental interests of residents, especially long-term residents, are especially vulnerable to the state's exercise of political power. Joseph Carens, for example, has argued that long-term residents, even if unauthorized, become "members" of society in the sense that their "fundamental human interests" come to depend on their territorial presence and participation in the society: they "form their deepest human connections where they live" since they are formed by the society and develop ties of friendship and family there. The state owes it to (long-term) residents to consider, especially in its territorial and civic boundary laws, these fundamental interests precisely because they are so profoundly vulnerable to the state's exercise of power. Carens himself does not use this argument to motivate the special-obligations challenge, and he is right not to do so. As the migrant experience makes painfully obvious, territorially located social ties are not the only fundamental human interests. Migrants frequently leave behind all existing local social ties, in the hope of realizing other fundamental interests: life, limb, liberty, material well-being, opportunities to cultivate new social ties, and so on. And to the extent that these fundamental interests of non-resident, would-be immigrants are also vulnerable to the state's regime of border control, nothing in Carens' argument justifies lesser concern for *these* interests than those of residents.[17]

A third argument is that a state has special obligations of distributive justice to those individuals whom it subjects to ongoing coercion. Michael Blake has argued, for example, that comparative principles of distributive justice (i.e., principles yielding the obligation to alleviate relative material inequality as opposed to absolute deprivations) arise "only between people who share the coercive mechanisms of a state."[18] This is because, Blake argues, ongoing state coercion requires a justification consistent with respect for the autonomy of those subjected to it, and it is only the need for this kind of justification that requires concern with relative material deprivations. The state therefore has a special obligation of concern for material inequality only towards its own residents.[19] Yet even if this kind of argument were ultimately successful, it could not motivate the special-obligations challenge to more open borders: one can hardly justify subjecting foreigners to an ongoing and coercive regime

---

[17] Joseph H. Carens, "The Case for Amnesty: Time Erodes the State's Right to Deport," *Boston Review* 34:3 (May/June) (2009); available from <http://bostonreview.net/forum/case-amnesty-joseph-carens>; Arash Abizadeh, "Response to Joseph Carens's 'Case for Amnesty'," *Boston Review* 34:3 (May/June) (2009); available from <http://bostonreview.net/forum/case-amnesty/if-moral-duties-apply-domestic-noncitizens-they-apply-all-noncitizens-arash-abizadeh>. See also Sarah Song's contribution to this volume.

[18] Blake, "Distributive Justice, State Coercion, and Autonomy," p. 276.

[19] Blake himself does not use the language of special obligations. He also spells out his argument in terms of citizens, but he explicitly assumes that all and only citizens are residents.

of border control on the grounds that, since they are *not* subject to ongoing coercion, the state must prioritize the interests of those whom it does so subject. The very fact of border coercion undermines the argument's application here.[20]

A variation on this argument appeals not to the brute fact of coercion per se, but to the dense network of coercive laws that govern residents and citizens who, by virtue of their residence or citizenship, have pervasive and roughly equal stakes in the ongoing good of the territorially bounded society governed by those laws. On the equal-stakeholder view, a polity owes special consideration in determining its boundary laws to those who have a pervasive and roughly equal stake in—and are therefore presumptively committed to—the polity's ongoing well-being. Presumably (long-term) residents and citizens meet this condition, while non-resident foreigners do not.[21] The problem with this argument as a challenge to more open borders, however, is that it begs the question at hand. If equal stakes are themselves a function of shared residence (or citizenship), one cannot cite the fact of equal stakes to justify a view about who *should* be permitted to share residence (or citizenship) and have equal stakes and who not. That would be like saying—as historically it was said, of course—that only those whom the laws already count as property holders should be permitted to participate in determining the laws regulating property holdings. To justify a particular regime of border control, we need a *justification* for who should be permitted to have equal stakes in the society by virtue of residence in it, not a *description* of who already has equal stakes in the society by virtue of residence in it.[22] If whether or not someone has equal stakes in a society depends on how coercive state power is exercised over boundaries, then the fact of equal stakes cannot be cited as a justification for how the state exercises its power over boundaries.

---

[20] For a more extensive critique of Blake's argument, see Abizadeh, "Cooperation, Pervasive Impact, and Coercion," which argues that the interstate regime of border controls undermines Blake's general conclusion that comparative principles of distributive justice are owed only to citizens/residents. For an analysis of the nature of border coercion, see Abizadeh, "Democratic Legitimacy and State Coercion."

[21] For versions of an equal-stakeholder principle, see Thomas Christiano, *The Constitution of Equality: Democratic Authority and its Limits* (Oxford: Oxford University Press, 2008), pp. 80–1; Rainer Bauböck, "The Rights and Duties of External Citizenship," *Citizenship Studies* 13:5 (2009), 475–99. Note, however, that Christiano's and Bauböck's concerns are different than mine: rather than citing equal stakes as a ground for special obligations, they cite it as a ground for a right of democratic say (Christiano) or claim to citizenship (Bauböck).

[22] The interstate regime of sovereign state recognition does not provide the required justification: the combination of vastly different power relations amongst states and vastly different life prospects that states offer to their residents means that the outcomes of interstate recognition straightforwardly fail to meet the standard of equal respect for persons.

6.3 Citizenship: Civic Relationships and Interactions

Partisans of the special-obligations challenge such as Macedo usually appeal, at least officially, to the very category of citizenship itself—comprising a decidedly *civic* set of relationships and interactions—as the ground of compatriotic special obligations. The modern category of citizenship has been associated with at least four dimensions: first, and at the very least, the legal *status* of membership in a polity; second, the set of *rights* legally attached to that status; third, the fact of civic and political *participation* along with its attendant set of civic responsibilities and virtues; and fourth, a sense of *identification* with the polity or its members.[23]

The first two dimensions of citizenship do not by themselves furnish promising grounds for special obligations amongst citizens—especially not special obligations that justify immigration restrictions. This is because, when asking for a justification for a particular regime of border control, we are looking for a justification, not a *description*, of the differential legal statuses and rights (of entry and work, for example) attributed to different persons—a justification consistent with treating persons as equals. To say that the state is justified in coercively imposing laws that deny some individuals entry simply because it imposes such laws fails to express equal respect for each: it amounts to a status quo bias that begs the question against criticisms of current legal arrangements. This is perhaps why partisans of the special-obligations challenge focus on the other two dimensions of citizenship, that is, participation and/or identification. What is required, in each case, is a justification for special obligations that avoids the status quo bias. I take up each of these dimensions in turn, in reverse order.

There are at least two problems with appealing to mutual *identification* amongst compatriots to motivate the special-obligations challenge to more open borders.[24] First, even if subjective identification *were* itself the proper grounds for prioritizing special obligations, as a matter of fact such identification often fails to hold across class lines (and the special-obligations challenge requires special obligations to poorer compatriots, across class lines).[25] Second, identification is neither necessary nor sufficient for grounding prioritizing special obligations: a father who fails to identify with his children is not thereby excused of fulfilling his special obligations towards them; and a father who identifies more strongly with another person's children is not thereby

[23] See Linda Bosniak, *The Citizen and the Alien: Dilemmas of Contemporary Membership* (Princeton, NJ: Princeton University Press, 2006).

[24] The appeal to mutual identification as a ground for special obligations is made, for example, by nationalists such as Miller, *On Nationality*, p. 65.

[25] See, e.g., Moses Shayo, "A Model of Social Identity with an Application to Political Economy: Nation, Class, and Redistribution," *American Political Science Review* 103:2 (2009), 147–74.

permitted (much less obligated) to prioritize those children over his own. The lack of identification here is a pathological hindrance to fulfilling the prioritizing special obligations he has, independently of his subjective identifications. Thus identification *either* only serves as the motivational basis for fulfilling the obligations that one already has, *or*, if it does ground special obligations, then it grounds additive, not prioritizing special obligations.

The question about *participation* is this: Why would the joint (and presumptive) participation of citizens in the state's common civic and political life constitute the sort of relationship and set of interactions that ground (prioritizing) special obligations? Thomas Nagel has argued that special obligations (of comparative distributive justice) arise amongst, and only amongst, persons who are both *subject* to and the putative *authors* of the state's coercive exercise of political power, that is, persons (1) who are subject to ongoing coercion by the same set of political institutions *and* (2) in whose name those institutions act, through the "active engagement" of their will, such that they are the "putative joint authors of the coercively imposed system." I focus here on the second condition, which invokes what Rousseau called the individual's role as "citizen" as opposed to "subject." For it is the second condition that distinguishes Nagel's account from the criterion, which we previously considered, of merely being subject to ongoing coercion (and which fails to distinguish citizens from residents, and these from non-resident foreigners subject to the state's coercive regime of border control).[26]

There are at least two ways to interpret this second condition. On the *active* interpretation, individuals are the "putative joint authors" of a coercive system of governance insofar as the state allows for, and thereby presumes, their actual participation in the political process. This is close to Macedo's view of what grounds special obligations amongst compatriots (which, in turn, justify immigration restrictions): the fact that fellow-citizens are active co-participants in shared political processes of collective self-governance, by which they create a comprehensive set of shared, binding institutions over themselves. Yet the active interpretation of Nagel's second condition perversely implies that the state could exclude some individuals over whom it exercises coercive political power from the scope of special obligations simply by also excluding them from the political process. This is perverse because it adds insult to injury: it rationalizes, for example, the denial of

---

[26] Thomas Nagel, "The Problem of Global Justice," *Philosophy & Public Affairs* 33:2 (2005), 113–47 at pp. 128–30. The people of a republic, Rousseau wrote in the *Contrat social*, "s'appellent en particulier *Citoyens* comme participans à l'autorité souveraine, et *Sujets* comme soumis aux loix de l'Etat." Jean-Jacques Rousseau, *Du contrat social*, in Bernard Gagnebin and Marcel Raymond (eds.), *Oeuvres complètes*, 5 vols., vol. 3 (Paris: Bibliothèque de la Pléiade, 1959–95), p. 362.

social rights to colonial subjects on the grounds that they are also denied political rights.[27]

Nagel himself responds to the example of colonial subjugation by adopting a less demanding, *passive* interpretation of his second condition, according to which joint authorship merely requires that the state explicitly or implicitly *claims* authorization from those whom it subjects to ongoing coercion, relying on their participation only in the weak sense of counting on their compliance with the laws. Thus Nagel claims that "there is a sense" in which colonial rule over the colonized "is being imposed in their name," since colonial rule requires the "normative engagement" of colonial subjects insofar as they are "expected to uphold as participants" the enforced system of colonial laws.[28] This passive interpretation is also how Nagel handles immigration laws (which, supposedly in contrast to colonial laws, are not "authored" by the foreigners subject to them): "Immigration policies are simply enforced against the nationals of other states; the laws are not imposed in their name, nor are they asked to accept and uphold those laws. Since no acceptance is demanded of them, no justification is required."[29] Yet this interpretation is no less perverse than the active one: it implies that a state can avoid the special responsibilities it might otherwise have to those over whom it exercises coercive political power just by exercising *sheer coercion*, with no expectation that subjects willingly comply. If the perversity of the active principle is historically illustrated by colonialism, the perversity of the passive principle is illustrated by slavery: on the passive interpretation, a purely tyrannical regime that treated human beings as slaves—stripped of legal personhood and so without legal rights or obligations, to whom the law relates as it does to animals, threatening but not normatively prescribing—would, in virtue of its very tyranny, be excused of special responsibilities to those over whom it exercises power.[30]

What renders both interpretations perverse is a fundamental mistake in how Nagel conceives of the relationship between the exercise of political power and special obligations, a mistake that re-stages the status quo bias plaguing appeals to the first two aspects of citizenship (legally recognized status and rights). The coercive exercise of political power over persons who

[27] Insofar as political participation depends on legally recognized rights of participation, the problem here is of course an echo of the problem with taking the legally recognized rights of citizens to be the basis for special obligations that, in turn, are supposed to justify the particular rights of citizens.

[28] Nagel, "The Problem of Global Justice," p. 129, n.14. Nagel's further claim that colonial rule is rightly deemed to be in the name of colonial subjects also because it "is intended to serve their interests" is hard to take seriously. It is relevant to the present argument only as an illustration of how Nagel's position adds insult to injury.

[29] Nagel, "The Problem of Global Justice," pp. 129–30.

[30] Cf. Abizadeh, "Cooperation, Pervasive Impact, and Coercion," pp. 351–2.

deserve treatment as equals does indeed give rise to special obligations. However, these obligations are owed not to the (putative) *authors* of political power, but rather those *subject* to it; the (putative) authors of political power are the *bearers*, not beneficiaries, of special responsibilities, owed to those over whom they coercively exercise power. Putative authorship is not a *precondition* that a subject of political power must (descriptively) meet before she is the beneficiary of, or is owed, special obligations; instead, that subjects be putative authors is a (normative) *demand* that the exercise of political power must meet.[31]

6.4 Exercising Power: Political Relationships and Interactions

A more promising characterization of the role of participation in grounding special obligations amongst compatriots comes from Richard Miller. Miller's account has the considerable merit of avoiding the status quo bias and problem of perversity: he recognizes that those who bear special responsibilities do so in virtue of *exercising* political power (or *authoring* or willingly *benefitting* from it), not in virtue of being subject to it. This is because for Miller the special obligations of citizenship are fundamentally grounded in a more general duty to avoid exploiting or taking advantage of persons with whom one shares a relationship or interacts—that is, a duty to use power responsibly.[32] There are consequently several reasons, according to Miller, why the most disadvantaged are owed (prioritizing) special obligations by compatriots with whom, in some sense, they jointly participate in governing a territorial state.

First, treating persons as equals—that is, treating them with equal respect—when subjecting them to political power requires exercising it in a way that provides them with sufficient reason *willingly* to uphold and comply with the state's legal norms: the coercive threat of sanctions should not be their only reason for complying. In other words, power should be exercised such that those subject to it could also be its putative "authors."[33] This implies that each

---

[31] When as a matter of empirical fact all those subject to political power are also the authors of the terms of its exercise, then of course the same persons are both the bearers and the beneficiaries (and/or the objects) of these special obligations; but it is precisely because the categories can fail to coincide that Nagel's criterion (whether in its active or passive interpretation) leads to perverse results.

[32] Miller, *Globalizing Justice*, pp. 1–2.

[33] This is, of course, a passive (or liberal) interpretation of the requirement of authorship. On the active (or democratic) interpretation, treating those subject to political power as equals requires granting them rights of participation in the political processes determining the terms of its exercise. We do not need, for the purposes of the argument here, to decide between these two interpretations; the important point here recognized by Miller is that authorship is what subjects are owed, rather than a condition they must meet before being owed.

has reason to value the willing participation of her compatriots in upholding their shared political project and, in turn, that each has reason to furnish the conditions of voluntary support and compliance.[34] Valuing one's compatriots' voluntary support, and furnishing the conditions conducive to it, requires showing special concern for the needs of disadvantaged compatriots; this is what Miller calls a special obligation of *civic friendship* or loyalty to compatriots.[35]

Second, the exercise of political power coercively structures the opportunities for self-advancement. This social structure of opportunities will inevitably be less favorable to some individuals subject to it than others; indeed, it will invariably create social *dis*advantages for some. As such, Miller argues that the authors of this social structure have a special obligation to mitigate and *compensate for the created social disadvantages* that some will inevitably face.[36]

The grounds for the first two kinds of special obligation clearly imply that the *authors* of political power are their bearers, while those *subjected* to power are their beneficiaries. Miller also suggests, however, a third kind of special obligation, the bearers of which are the willing beneficiaries of the public provision of goods. He notes that citizens participate in advancing "prosperity in their sovereign territory through public and publicly funded facilities," and that although this public provision benefits everyone, it necessarily benefits some more than others. As such, Miller argues, those who richly prosper from the joint public provision of opportunities owe an obligation of special concern to compatriots who, through no fault of their own, do not. This is a special obligation of *fair public provision*.[37]

The question is whether any of these three putative special obligations of citizenship could justify immigration restrictions.[38] The first point to notice is

---

[34] Stress should be placed on the last clause of this sentence. Miller himself tends to characterize the special obligations as owed to those who *actually* willingly support, or have a *duty* to support, the political order. But both the imperative to avoid the problem of perversity and the logic of Miller's argument support the different formulation given above, as an obligation owed to those who *should be given reason* to support it willingly. This is the correct upshot of Miller's suggestion that civic friendship is rightly extended to the congenitally handicapped who (physically) *cannot* do much to support the political order, however much they might wish to do so. (Miller himself here turns from relying on actual, willing participation to emphasizing the duty to participate when feasible.) See Miller, *Globalizing Justice*, pp. 54–6.

[35] Miller, *Globalizing Justice*, pp. 43–6. According to Miller, "Cosmopolitan Respect and Patriotic Concern," pp. 210–13, furnishing the conditions for willing support and compliance requires special concern because the levels of social trust necessary to motivate voluntary support and compliance would otherwise be eroded.

[36] Miller, *Globalizing Justice*, pp. 48–54. I have switched the order of Miller's second and third grounds for special obligations.

[37] Miller, *Globalizing Justice*, pp. 46–8.

[38] Miller also proposes a fourth ground for special obligations amongst compatriots, which he calls *territorial trusteeship*, in order to motivate special concern for those, such as indigenous peoples, who reside in a territory but who do not, in the relevant sense, participate in the political order. Miller, *Globalizing Justice*, pp. 56–7. However, once one formulates the special obligation of civic friendship as I have (not as concerning those who *do* willingly uphold, or

that as a direct consequence of recognizing that such special obligations are borne by the authors of power and the beneficiaries of public provision, and are owed to those subject to power or who contribute to public provision, Miller is in fact forced to define the relation of shared citizenship not in terms of the state's civic boundaries but its territorial boundaries, that is, he is forced to include not just legally recognized citizens but also long-term *residents* within the class of "compatriots" to whom these special obligations are owed. This is not simply because long-term residents are subject to ongoing political coercion: Miller suggests that being (jointly) subject to political coercion by itself, as in the case of being subject to minimal police functions that protect basic human rights, does not add anything to the general duties one already has or is owed by others. Rather, special obligations arise because long-term residents (1) should be provided with reason willingly to comply with the coercive network of laws to which they are subject and that go beyond minimal, basic human rights protections,[39] (2) potentially suffer from socially created disadvantages, and (3) may fail to benefit equally from the public provision of goods to which they contribute.

The problem is that none of these three grounds can motivate the special-obligations challenge to more open borders. Consider, first, the special obligation of civic friendship. The special obligation fundamentally derives from the duty to wield coercive political power in a way that gives those subject to it sufficient reason *willingly* to uphold and comply with the legal norms to which they are subject. Yet foreigners subject to the coercive regime of border control of a wealthy polity would have sufficient reason willingly to uphold and comply with that regime only if their absolute poverty and relative material inequality had *already* been alleviated. Citizens would be able to author border coercion against foreigners, while treating them with equal respect, only to the extent that they show equal concern for their absolute and relative levels of poverty.

Consider, second, the special obligation to compensate socially imposed disadvantages. As Miller himself acknowledges, border coercion does create social disadvantages for non-resident foreigners, by systematically thwarting

---

have a *duty* to uphold, the political order, but concerning those whom, in virtue of exercising political power over them, the political society *ought to give sufficient reason* to uphold that order), then Miller's fourth ground becomes redundant.

[39] The reference to the basic human rights protected by minimal police functions is not explicit in Miller's account, but it is necessary for the argument to run through. To stand to reason, the claim must be that a coercive scheme that solely provides goods whose public provision is itself a demand of justice does not add to pre-existing general obligations; it merely realizes them. What might add new, special obligations is a scheme that provides goods not already demanded by justice (or other source of general duties). Otherwise the public provision argument would run afoul of the status quo bias that plagues, for example, the account of reciprocity in Barry, "Humanity and Justice in Global Perspective." See Abizadeh, "Cooperation, Pervasive Impact, and Coercion," pp. 336–7.

their efforts to partake of social opportunities available only within the state's territory. Yet Miller claims that any resulting duty of justice to open borders would be outweighed by the (prioritizing) special concern owed to disadvantaged compatriots (i.e., long-term residents). This is because as "compared with the strong determination of structures of advantage and disadvantage within a country by the laws of that country, immigration restrictions play a relatively minor role, eliminating [only] some means of getting ahead." Miller's argument, however, fails to appreciate the specific character of border laws: they are gatekeepers for the *vast majority* of the opportunities that domestic laws structure for those inside the territory. Miller's argument is, as a result, self-defeating: the more that *domestic* laws determine the structure of advantages and disadvantages for residents domestically, the more *border* laws consequently determine the structure of advantages and disadvantages for non-residents globally, since they determine access to the majority of opportunities structured domestically. This is a direct result of the territorial dimension of the jurisdictional claims of the modern state.[40]

Consider, third, the special obligation of fair public provision (which echoes Dagger's reciprocity argument above). First, as we have already seen in relation to Dagger's reciprocity argument, a cooperative scheme of public provision can generate special obligations amongst co-participants, but these are additive special obligations, not prioritizing ones. Additive obligations may warrant special concern for the needs of co-participants, but not at the expense of fulfilling one's general duties to others: prioritizing can come into play only if one's general duties to others are fulfilled. Additive special obligations therefore do not justify favoring the needs of poorer compatriots over the needs of foreigners who are even worse off and who suffer from *absolute* levels of poverty. Second, and more importantly, fair public provision cannot motivate the special-obligations challenge to more open borders even in the case of foreigners who are relatively worse off than the domestic poor but who do not suffer from absolute poverty. This is because fair public provision requires ensuring that, *amongst those participating in the cooperative scheme of public provision*, those who benefit disproportionately compensate those who do not. The requirement says nothing, however, about who should be permitted to participate. Yet that is precisely what the special-obligations challenge to more open borders requires saying: it requires a justification for coercively

---

[40] Miller, *Globalizing Justice*, p. 53. Miller also argues that while "the citizenry of a developed country bears exclusive political responsibility for disadvantages imposed among compatriots," its responsibility for excluding the global poor from a developed economy is a fraction proportional to the number of developed countries as a whole. This argument raises complicated issues of collective responsibility; in any case, it is available only to a polity that is at least doing its fair share, amongst developed countries, of opening its borders—and perhaps only to a polity that is committed to developing a collective scheme of more open borders jointly with other developed countries.

excluding some individuals from the opportunity to contribute to and benefit from a cooperative scheme of public provision. The requirement of fair public provision provides no such justification.[41]

6.5 Conclusion

I have argued that the most promising putative grounds for compatriotic special obligations fail to challenge the justice argument for more open borders. Either they do not in fact ground such obligations or, if they do, they ground additive but not prioritizing special obligations. Either way, the challenge to the justice argument for more open borders fails.

It might be thought, however, that under conditions of resource scarcity or limited capacities, the distinction on which part of my argument relies, between additive and prioritizing special obligations, will at some point break down. What if one acquires additive special obligations to some but, due to limited resources or capacities, is able to discharge the obligations only by shirking one's general duties to others? That is, what if one can no longer "add" without prioritizing? I have proceeded as if, in cases of conflict between additive special obligations and general duties, the normative force of the former is conditional on the fulfillment of (or is at least outweighed by) the latter. It might be objected, however, that in principle there may be cases in which one's additive special obligations have priority, and in such cases, when one's resources or capacities have reached their limit, one might be justified in discharging additive special obligations by prioritizing one's near and dear.

I concede that such circumstances may arise: given limited resources or capacities, one may face a genuine choice between fulfilling one's additive special obligations and general duties, and it is conceivable that in some cases the latter do not have moral priority over the former.[42] But two further questions must be addressed before this concession could be harnessed for the special-obligations challenge to more open borders.

First, we must specify the circumstances under which additive special obligations really do have priority over (or outweigh) general duties. The problem for the special-obligations challenge is that the most plausible candidates for

---

[41] It might be argued, of course, that *late* participants in a cooperative scheme of public provision would not be able to contribute their fair share—for example, older immigrants would benefit from, without being able proportionately to contribute to, a publicly funded healthcare system. See, e.g., Joseph Heath, "Immigration, Multiculturalism, and the Social Contract," *Canadian Journal of Law and Jurisprudence* 10:2 (1997), 343–61. Such an objection wrongly assumes, however, that fairness requires that one benefit from public provision only in proportion to one's contributions. (Consider again the case of the infirm.)

[42] See Abizadeh and Gilabert, "Is There a Genuine Tension?," pp. 361–3.

such priority involve trade-offs between special obligations grounded in particularly deep or robust special relations, on the one hand, and positive general duties, on the other. The case of borders, however, stumbles on both conditions. The ties of family and friendship, for example, are particularly deep relationships, both because they are intimate and because they are almost universally and non-instrumentally valued by all human beings, regardless of their particular conception of the good. But relations of citizenship are neither intimate nor universally valued, and when they are valued, they are often valued in purely instrumental ways. Moreover, the general duties in question, whose pro tanto force the special-obligations challenge must overcome, are not positive duties of assistance but, rather, negative duties. Indeed, they are especially robust negative duties: we are dealing with negative constraints on the ways in which state power, including state violence and coercion, may be deployed against persons treated as equals.

Second, even if citizenship were a robust special relation, and the additive special obligations it grounded could in principle take priority over deeply grounded, robust negative general duties, prioritizing would only be required and permitted when the bearers of the special obligations and general duties have reached their limit in terms of the resources and capacity to fulfill both. Hence to vindicate the special-obligations challenge to more open borders, one would need to show that wealthy polities have indeed reached such a limit: that the only possible way for them to discharge their additive special obligations to their domestic poor would be to impose immigration restrictions. But if it remains possible for such polities to discharge these special obligations by other morally permissible means—if, for example, whatever effects immigration might have on the domestic poor could be offset by greater contributions from the well-off, to finance greater domestic redistribution or to mitigate the domestic structural causes of class inequality—then the limit has not been reached. I take it to be obvious that contemporary wealthy polities are far from having reached any such limit. There is consequently no justification for discharging additive special obligations owed to the domestic poor by violating, in relation to foreigners, the two negative constraints of justice with which I began.[43]

[43] I am grateful to Sarah Fine, Pablo Gilabert, Richard Miller, Vijay Phulwani, Alex Sager, Lea Ypi, and participants at the conference on Migration in Legal and Political Theory, CRASSH, University of Cambridge, October 28–29, 2011, the Immigration Speaker Series, Cornell University, March 8, 2013, and the American Philosophical Association, Pacific Division, San Francisco, March 27–31, 2013, for comments, and to SSHRC for funding.

References

Abizadeh, Arash, "Cooperation, Pervasive Impact, and Coercion: On the Scope (not Site) of Distributive Justice," *Philosophy & Public Affairs* 35:4 (2007), 318–58.

Abizadeh, Arash, "Response to Joseph Carens's 'Case for Amnesty'," *Boston Review* 34:3 (May/June) (2009). Available from <http://bostonreview.net/forum/case-amnesty/if-moral-duties-apply-domestic-noncitizens-they-apply-all-noncitizens-arash-abizadeh>.

Abizadeh, Arash, "Closed Borders, Human Rights, and Democratic Legitimation" in David Hollenbach (ed.), *Driven From Home: Human Rights and the New Realities of Forced Migration* (Washington, DC: Georgetown University Press, 2010), pp. 147–66.

Abizadeh, Arash, "Democratic Legitimacy and State Coercion: A Reply to David Miller," *Political Theory* 38:1 (2010), 121–30.

Abizadeh, Arash and Pablo Gilabert, "Is There a Genuine Tension between Cosmopolitan Egalitarianism and Special Responsibilities?," *Philosophical Studies* 138: 3 (2008), 348–65.

Abizadeh, Arash, Manish Pandey, and Sohrab Abizadeh, "Wage Competition and the Special-Obligations Challenge to More Open Borders," *Politics, Philosophy & Economics* 14:3 (2015), 255–69.

Bader, Veit, "The Ethics of Immigration," *Constellations* 12:3 (2005), 331–61.

Barry, Brian, "Humanity and Justice in Global Perspective" in J. Roland Pennock and John W. Chapman (eds.), *Ethics, Economics, and the Law*, Nomos 24 (New York: New York University Press, 1982), pp. 219–52.

Bauböck, Rainer, "The Rights and Duties of External Citizenship," *Citizenship Studies* 13:5 (2009), 475–99.

Beitz, Charles R., *Political Theory and International Relations*. 2nd edn. (Princeton, NJ: Princeton University Press, 1999).

Blake, Michael, "Distributive Justice, State Coercion, and Autonomy," *Philosophy and Public Affairs* 30:3 (2002), 257–96.

Bosniak, Linda, *The Citizen and the Alien: Dilemmas of Contemporary Membership* (Princeton, NJ: Princeton University Press, 2006).

Carens, Joseph H., "The Case for Amnesty: Time Erodes the State's Right to Deport," *Boston Review* 34:3 (May/June) (2009). Available from <http://bostonreview.net/forum/case-amnesty-joseph-carens>.

Christiano, Thomas, *The Constitution of Equality: Democratic Authority and its Limits* (Oxford: Oxford University Press, 2008).

Dagger, Richard, "Rights, Boundaries, and the Bonds of Community: A Qualified Defense of Moral Parochialism," *American Political Science Review* 79:2 (1985), 436–47.

Dworkin, Ronald, "The Original Position," *The University of Chicago Law Review* 40:3 (1973), 500–33.

Dworkin, Ronald, *Taking Rights Seriously: New Impression with a Reply to Critics*. 2nd edn. (London: Duckworth, 1978).

Gilabert, Pablo, *From Global Poverty to Global Equality: A Philosophical Exploration* (Oxford: Oxford University Press, 2012).

Goodin, Robert E., "What Is So Special about Our Fellow Countrymen?," *Ethics* 98:4 (1988), 663–86.

Heath, Joseph, "Immigration, Multiculturalism, and the Social Contract," *Canadian Journal of Law and Jurisprudence* 10:2 (1997): 343–61.

Isbister, John, "A Liberal Argument for Border Controls: Reply to Carens," *International Migration Review* 34:2 (2000), 629–35.

Macedo, Stephen, "The Moral Dilemma of U.S. Immigration Policy: Open Borders Versus Social Justice?" in Carol M. Swain (ed.), *Debating Immigration* (New York: Cambridge University Press, 2007), pp. 63–82.

Miller, David, *On Nationality* (Oxford: Clarendon Press, 1995).

Miller, Richard W., "Cosmopolitan Respect and Patriotic Concern," *Philosophy & Public Affairs* 27:3 (1998), 202–24.

Miller, Richard W., *Globalizing Justice: The Ethics of Poverty and Power* (Oxford: Oxford University Press, 2010).

Nagel, Thomas, "The Problem of Global Justice," *Philosophy & Public Affairs* 33:2 (2005), 113–47.

Rawls, John, *A Theory of Justice* (Cambridge, MA: Harvard University Press, 1971).

Rawls, John, *Justice as Fairness: A Restatement*, ed. Erin Kelly (Cambridge, MA: Harvard University Press, 2001).

Rousseau, Jean-Jacques, *Du contrat social* in Bernard Gagnebin and Marcel Raymond (eds.), *Oeuvres completes*, 5 vols. Vol. 3 (Paris: Bibliothèque de la Pléiade, 1959–95).

Sangiovanni, Andrea, "Global Justice, Reciprocity, and the State," *Philosophy & Public Affairs* 35:1 (2007), 3–39.

Scheffler, Samuel, *Boundaries and Allegiances: Problems of Justice and Responsibility in Liberal Thought* (Oxford: Oxford University Press, 2001).

Shayo, Moses, "A Model of Social Identity with an Application to Political Economy: Nation, Class, and Redistribution," *American Political Science Review* 103:2 (2009), 147–74.

Swain, Carol M., "Response to Joseph Carens's 'Case for Amnesty'," *Boston Review* 34:3 (May/June) (2009).

Woodward, James, "Commentary: Liberalism and Migration" in Brian Barry and Robert E. Goodin (eds.), *Free Movement: Ethical Issues in the Transnational Migration of People and of Money* (University Park, PA: Pennsylvania State University Press, 1992), pp. 59–84.

7

Immigration and Discrimination

Sarah Fine

> *The modern world has seen and been shaped by the most ghastly and inhumane forms of racial domination imaginable, and despite the apparent consensus today that racism is wrong, some still suffer because of racial injustice and its historical consequences. So, in light of our discussion of racism and racial discrimination, we might say that the appropriate response to racial injustice is to abolish or reform any institution that operates on the basis of, or is otherwise distorted by, racism.*[1]

7.1 Introduction

One of my more memorable moments as an undergraduate arose during a discussion with a fellow student on the subject of our respective dissertation topics. I explained that I was writing a normative political theory piece critically examining the ethics of immigration restrictions, and I introduced my argument in favor of more open borders. The student listened carefully, paused thoughtfully, looked at me quizzically, and then asked, "Are you mad? Have you ever been to Leicester? There isn't a white face in the place."

The conversation was a stark reminder, if ever one were needed, of the often vast chasm between philosophical and "popular" discussions of immigration controls. Race and ethnicity, ever present in popular debate on the subject of migration, are, as Phillip Cole notes, "more or less absent" from the philosophical literature.[2] Compared with popular political discussions, the

[1] Tommie Shelby, "Race" in David Estlund (ed.), *The Oxford Handbook of Political Philosophy* (New York: Oxford University Press, 2012), pp. 336–53 at p. 346.

[2] Christopher Heath Wellman and Phillip Cole, *Debating the Ethics of Immigration: Is there a Right to Exclude?* (New York: Oxford University Press, 2011), p. 217. For an excellent exception, see Joseph H. Carens, "Nationalism and the Exclusion of Immigrants: Lessons from Australian

contemporary philosophical debate is conducted in a relatively sanitized discourse and within fairly narrow, predominantly liberal, parameters. No one engaged in the philosophical debate endorses immigration policies exactly as they stand; rather, all participants are in agreement that many existing immigration restrictions and practices are unjust. In addition, although it is frequently, if misleadingly, cast as a debate between advocates of closed borders and proponents of open borders, practically everyone in the philosophical literature agrees that there are *some* contexts in which it is permissible to exclude *some* prospective entrants, and that there are *some* practices of exclusion which are always, or almost always, impermissible.[3] This is where race and ethnicity tend to make a brief appearance: there is near consensus that states are not permitted to discriminate between candidates for admission on grounds of race and ethnicity.[4] Different theorists offer different reasons for objecting to this form of discrimination, but tend to concur that, in Michael Dummett's words, "whatever the principles governing immigration policy should be, a first requirement for it to be just is that it should not be racially discriminatory."[5] Yet that, for many theorists, is the beginning and the end of the discussion of race and ethnicity in the context of migration ethics.

I want to explore what is revealed about the ethics of immigration controls when we move race and ethnicity from the margins to the forefront of our analysis. I start with a few words on terminology, before outlining the absolutely central role of race and ethnicity in the history and politics of immigration restrictions. Next, I turn my attention to normative arguments that seek to defend some form of immigration restrictions while also denying the permissibility of discriminating between prospective immigrants on grounds of race or ethnicity. I consider what is necessary in order for these arguments to marry those objectives, and I proceed to highlight the serious challenges

---

Immigration Policy" in Mark Gibney (ed.), *Open Borders? Closed Societies? The Ethical and Political Issues* (Westport, CT: Greenwood Press, 1988), pp. 41–60. Samuel Scheffler also touches on some of these issues in Samuel Scheffler, "Immigration and the Significance of Culture," *Philosophy & Public Affairs* 35:2 (2007), 93–125. Race and ethnicity get fairly short shrift in contemporary normative political theory more generally. Exceptions include K. Anthony Appiah and Amy Gutmann, *Color Conscious: The Political Morality of Race* (Princeton, NJ: Princeton University Press, 1996), and Carole Pateman and Charles W. Mills, *Contract and Domination* (Cambridge: Polity Press, 2007). See also this interesting discussion: Desmond King, "Symposium: Contract and Domination by Carole Pateman and Charles W. Mills," *Journal of Political Ideologies* 13:3 (2008), 227–62.

[3] For example, see, on the one hand, Joseph H. Carens, "Aliens and Citizens: The Case for Open Borders," *The Review of Politics* 49:2 (1987), 251–73, e.g. pp. 259–60; and on the other hand Christopher Heath Wellman, "Immigration and Freedom of Association," *Ethics* 119:1 (2008), 109–41, esp. p. 140.

[4] Near consensus, but not complete consensus, as we shall see.

[5] Michael Dummett, *On Immigration and Refugees* (London and New York: Routledge, 2001), p. 61.

that arise. Making race and ethnicity the focus of our analysis not only serves to shed light on one particularly troubling feature of immigration controls as we know them; it also offers an additional angle from which to evaluate the wider coherence and appeal of arguments in support of the state's right to exclude would-be immigrants. Furthermore, this exercise illustrates the ways in which arguments in political philosophy might be informed and affected by addressing the history of the institutions under discussion.

7.2 Immigration, Race, and Ethnicity

First, let us pause briefly to examine some of the concepts that feature in this discussion. Race, racism, and ethnicity are all much debated, contentious terms, and so it will be helpful to have some working definitions for the purposes of the chapter. Race is a particularly difficult and controversial concept. For various reasons—not least its historical (and, many think, inextricable) connection to the comprehensively discredited idea that there is a natural hierarchy of biologically distinct races and that there are racial, "biobehavioral essences"—a number of theorists maintain that the term "race" should not be used at all.[6] After all, if we reject the idea that natural, biologically distinct human "races" exist, and if "race" is commonly understood in this biological, naturalistic sense, then it may seem that we ought to stop using the term "race" altogether. A significant number of other theorists, however, including the influential philosopher of race, Charles W. Mills, argue that while we must reject as false the discredited biological, naturalistic concept of race, we can and even ought to continue to talk of race. But here race is understood as a social construct, the existence of which is no less "real" for being social rather than natural. The racial category to which we are assigned (and with which we come to be identified) can and often does profoundly affect and frame our social and political lives. It configures our experiences in ways that serve to disadvantage some and advantage others. As Mills puts it, "race is a *contingently* deep reality that structures our particular social universe, having a social objectivity and causal significance that arise out of *our* particular history."[7] That is the sense in which I am using the

---

[6] Or at least that, in time, we should hope to move away from the use of the term. See, for example, Lawrence Blum, *I'm not a Racist, But ... The Moral Quandary of Race* (Ithaca, NY: Cornell University Press, 2002), in which Blum suggests the use of "racialized group." See also Appiah's contribution in Appiah and Gutmann, *Color Conscious*. For further discussion see Robert Miles, *Racism* (London: Routledge, 1989). On racialism and biobehavioral essences, see Ron Mallon, "'Race': Normative, Not Metaphysical or Semantic," *Ethics* 116:3 (2006), 525–51, esp. pp. 528–9.

[7] Charles W. Mills, *Blackness Visible: Essays on Philosophy and Race* (Ithaca, NY: Cornell University Press, 1998), p. 48, author's emphasis.

concept of "race," as a social construct with profound social and political effects, one of which is that it forms the basis for particular modes of discrimination. Note, then, that when we use the concept of race in this way, we are implicitly acknowledging that "race" and racial categorizations are products of a particular system of social and political relations, which assign people to these groupings; the groupings themselves vary across time and place, in different systems of social and political relations.[8]

I employ the term ethnicity to refer to perceived distinctions between people primarily based on beliefs about shared history and culture. I will understand racism, in a fairly broad sense, to refer to hostile treatment specifically connected to perceived racial difference, accompanied by a perception of hierarchy.[9] I use racial and ethnic discrimination to refer to differential treatment on grounds of perceived racial or ethnic difference, which can occur in the absence of explicit and/or intentional hostility and sense of hierarchy.[10] I am going to focus on the kind of discrimination which serves to *disadvantage* members of the perceived racial or ethnic group, rather than to advantage or favor or compensate them.[11]

Now, this chapter goes against the grain of much current, political discussion of immigration, which often seeks to detach discussions of the rights and wrongs of immigration policies and practices from the highly charged subject of racism, and racial and ethnic discrimination. In Britain, we are all familiar with the common refrain that ordinary, decent people are wary of voicing their legitimate immigration concerns for fear of being labeled "racist." The usual line is that we need a sensible, "honest" debate about immigration, and that accusations of racism shut down reasonable debate by silencing dissent. The Conservative Party played on just that sentiment during the 2005 general election, with their campaign poster, "Are you thinking what we're thinking? It's not racist to impose limits on immigration."[12]

---

[8] For instance, as Mills emphasizes, the same person may be categorized as "black" in the United States, and as "brown" or "white" in the Caribbean and Latin America. See Mills, *Blackness Visible*, pp. 46–7. See also Scheffler's "Immigration and the Significance of Culture," especially pp. 95–6, where he discusses his grandfather Yidel's arrival in the United States in 1914, at which time Yidel is determined to be of "Hebrew" race.

[9] See David Mason, *Race and Ethnicity in Modern Britain* (Oxford: Oxford University Press, 2000), esp. ch. 2; Blum, *I'm not a Racist, But...*, esp. ch. 1.

[10] For more detailed debates about this terminology, see Appiah and Gutmann, *Color Conscious*; Leonard Harris (ed.), *Racism* (New York: Humanity Books, 1999); Blum, *I'm not a Racist, But...*

[11] For further discussion of different kinds of discrimination, see Shelby, "Race," where he highlights the distinction between "treating a person differently (e.g., denying her an important opportunity) on the grounds that she is a member of an inferior race" and "treating her differently (e.g., compensating her for an injustice she has suffered) on the grounds that she has been wronged because *others* believe she is a member of an inferior race," p. 344, author's emphasis. See also the illuminating discussion in Kasper Lippert-Rasmussen, "The Badness of Discrimination," *Ethical Theory and Moral Practice* 9:2 (2006), 167–85, in which Rasmussen offers a taxonomy of discrimination.

[12] See Martin Kettle, "Are you thinking what I'm thinking about the election?," *The Guardian*, March 8, 2005.

It is important to remember, though, that the act of "talking about limiting immigration" has not acquired a bad name out of nowhere. The undeniable truth is that racism and racial and ethnic discrimination cast a long shadow over the history and politics of immigration controls. Dummett goes so far as to argue that "the principal actual motivation for exclusionist immigration policies is, of course, racial prejudice, or sometimes more general prejudice against foreigners, which, when present, is always felt more intensely against those who are of or are thought to be of, a different race."[13] Whether or not he is right that this remains the *principal* motivation, it is indisputable that, at various times and in various places, prejudice of this sort at least has been a significant part of the motivation for exclusionist immigration policies. Indeed, over the centuries, issues relating to race and ethnicity have been at the very heart of immigration policies across the world.

It is no exaggeration to claim that the modern system of immigration controls, so much a part of the present political landscape in liberal democracies, was born of racism—of hostility to those perceived as inferior races. While political communities of all shapes and sizes always have taken measures (often ineffectual) to exclude unwanted outsiders, and to expel unwanted insiders, the kinds of state centralized, bureaucratized forms of immigration restriction that we know today were inventions of the late nineteenth and early twentieth centuries. As many historians of immigration have noted, the nineteenth century was "the great age of global mobility" and a time of "remarkable freedom of movement."[14] For example, the Convention of Peking in 1860 was an agreement between the British and Chinese to allow free movement and protection across the two Empires, and the Burlingame Treaty agreed between China and the United States in 1868 "went even further in recognizing freedom of movement and migration as universal rights."[15] However, as Desmond King highlights in relation to the United States, "from broadly accepting all comers in the nineteenth century, in the twentieth century American immigration policy became restrictive and selective."[16] Marilyn Lake and Henry Reynolds detail the ways in which immigration controls "became a version of racial segregation on an international scale" at the end of the nineteenth century and beginning of the twentieth.[17] From increasingly animated opposition to the presence of Chinese workers in Australia and the United States, and the introduction of ever tougher

---

[13] Dummett, *On Immigration and Refugees*, p. 58.

[14] Marilyn Lake and Henry Reynolds, *Drawing the Global Color Line: White Men's Countries and the International Challenge of Racial Equality* (Cambridge: Cambridge University Press, 2008), p. 23.

[15] Lake and Reynolds, *Drawing the Global Color Line*, pp. 25–6.

[16] Desmond King, *In the Name of Liberalism: Illiberal Social Policy in the United States and Britain* (Oxford: Oxford University Press, 1999), p. 97.

[17] Lake and Reynolds, *Drawing the Global Color Line*, p. 5.

immigration restrictions directed against them, to discussions of deporting black Americans to Africa, and excluding them from the franchise (following the example of South Africa), it is clear that immigration and naturalization restrictions came to serve as a means for supporting and maintaining "white" rule and limiting racial and ethnic heterogeneity within self-identifying "Anglo-Saxon" states. The popular and intellectual debates regarding migration and naturalization were framed in racial terms. For instance, Chinese laborers were maligned as "docile," "servile," and "unfit" for self-government.[18] Furthermore, as Lake and Reynolds contend, "opponents of Chinese migration forged a sense of transnational community, identifying white men as under siege."[19]

In the British case, to note just two striking examples, the Aliens Act of 1905 (which is usually described as the country's first significant, centralized move to establish immigration controls during peacetime) was designed ostensibly to control the entry of certain groups of "undesirable" and "destitute" foreigners. Effectively, it was aimed at targeting the large number of impoverished Jews fleeing pogroms in Eastern Europe.[20] Similarly, the Commonwealth Immigrants Act of 1962 was a response to popular calls to limit the number of citizens from the so-called "New" (i.e., non-white) Commonwealth settling in mainland Britain.[21] In fact, sociologist David Mason maintains that, since 1962, the common theme in British immigration legislation has been the attempt "to close the door to dark-skinned potential migrants, while keeping it open to 'whites' from the countries of the Old Commonwealth and South Africa."[22]

Mention of the Commonwealth (the member states of which are primarily former territories of the British Empire) reminds us that the role played by race and ethnicity in the history and politics of immigration restrictions goes beyond, and deeper than, the underlying racism, discrimination, and prejudice of various admissions policies. Indeed, as Cole emphasizes, we must keep in mind the enduring effects of the long era of European colonialism and empire, during which time Europeans "controlled a migration regime in which they had the power to travel the world and exploit resources and people, and to determine the flow of resources and people to particular places

---

[18] Lake and Reynolds, *Drawing the Global Color Line*, p. 27.

[19] Lake and Reynolds, *Drawing the Global Color Line*, p. 28.

[20] Dummett, *On Immigration and Refugees*, pp. 3–4; Mason, *Race and Ethnicity in Modern Britain*, p. 24.

[21] Mason, *Race and Ethnicity in Modern Britain*, p. 26.

[22] Mason, *Race and Ethnicity in Modern Britain*, p. 29. On racism in British immigration legislation, see Paul Gilroy, *"There Ain't No Black in the Union Jack": The Cultural Politics of Race and Nation* (Chicago: University of Chicago Press, 1987); Floya Anthias and Nira Yuval Davis with Harriet Cain, *Racialized Boundaries: Race, Nation, Gender, Colour, and Class and the Anti-Racist Struggle* (London: Routledge, 1992), esp. ch. 2.

to further their own interests."[23] The postcolonial international state system and forms of global governance, as Cole and many others stress, still bear the scars of that history. Its legacy is felt, for instance, in the political instability of various former colonies, and in the gross economic, social, and political inequalities between the Global South and North—factors which impel large numbers of people to try to leave their countries of origin.[24] The injustices of empire and colonialism are perpetuated now as countries of the Global North attempt to close their borders to poor immigrants from the South.

In fact, colonialism, empire, migration, and race are even more intricately intertwined. The nineteenth century witnessed the emergence of Social Darwinism, which posited the existence of a natural hierarchy of human groups—biologically distinct "races"—and this supposed science was widely employed to justify white domination, conquest, empire, and non-white slavery.[25] For instance, self-styled "Anglo-Saxon" white men, as Lake and Reynolds highlight, "claimed a special right to lands in the 'temperate zone', claims made against their Indigenous inhabitants and all those people they would designate as 'non-white'...They shared an English-speaking culture and newly ascendant democratic politics, priding themselves, as Anglo-Saxons, on a distinctive capacity, indeed a genius, for self-government."[26] Moreover, on the reverse side, Lake and Reynolds argue that "international campaigns for racial equality and human rights often began as a response to the barriers to mobility and other racial discriminations enacted by New World democracies in the nineteenth century."[27]

In short, race, racism, and racial and ethnic discrimination are embedded in the history of migration, in public responses to immigrants, in the apparatus of immigration controls, and in migration flows. And this is not just a regrettable historical fact; it remains true, even pervasive. Although so-called liberal democratic states today would deny that their immigration policies directly discriminate on racial and ethnic grounds, and discrimination of that sort is widely condemned as unacceptable, it is not at all difficult to find clear

[23] Wellman and Cole, *Debating the Ethics of Immigration*, p. 221.

[24] For further discussion of the legacies of European and American Empire, see, for example, James Tully, "Lineages of Contemporary Imperialism" in Duncan Kelly (ed.), *Lineages of Empire: The Historical Roots of British Imperial Thought* (Oxford: Oxford University Press, 2009), pp. 3–29.

[25] Mason, *Race and Ethnicity in Modern Britain*, p. 7; Appiah and Gutmann, *Color Conscious*. On the concept of human "races" as inescapably linked to the history of white domination, see also Charles W. Mills, "Realizing (through Racializing) Pogge" in Alison M. Jaggar (ed.), *Thomas Pogge and his Critics* (Cambridge: Polity Press, 2010), pp. 151–74 at p. 157.

[26] Lake and Reynolds, *Drawing the Global Color Line*, p. 6. For more on the pervasive ideology of Anglo-Saxonism, see Duncan Bell, *The Idea of Greater Britain: Empire and the Future of World Order, 1860–1900* (Princeton, NJ: Princeton University Press, 2007); Duncan Bell, "Beyond the Sovereign State: Isopolitan Citizenship, Race, and Anglo-American Union," *Political Studies* 62:2 (2014), 418–34.

[27] Lake and Reynolds, *Drawing the Global Color Line*, p. 10.

examples of such discrimination. For instance, in 2009, France deported 10,000 Roma to Romania and Bulgaria, a move which drew criticism from the United Nations Committee on the Elimination of Racial Discrimination, and which was described by the European Union's Justice Commissioner as a "disgrace"; the Commission reportedly requested "proof to support France's claim that it was not deliberately targeting Roma."[28] Accusations of racism and discrimination are frequently leveled at Australia's policies regarding asylum seekers, and, again, the UN's Committee on the Elimination of Racial Discrimination has raised serious concerns about the country's treatment of asylum seekers and refugees.[29]

Often, the clear targeting of particular groups is thinly veiled behind what states see as more legitimate, "acceptable" policy objectives, such as securing their borders from foreign terror threats, or from large numbers of undocumented migrants, or for the protection of the migrants themselves. The French government naturally denied that it was specifically targeting Roma—instead, it claimed to be clamping down on illegal activities, such as the proliferation of illegal Roma sites. In a further example, we might point to the increasingly restrictive U.S. response to Mexican immigration.[30] Or another pertinent case was the British government's proposal in 2013 to impose a £3000 "migrant bond"—forfeited if visitors were to overstay their visas—on short-term visitors to the country. According to reports, in the proposed pilot scheme the bonds would be targeted at those considered to be at "high risk" of overstaying. The pilot was expected to apply to visitors from India, Bangladesh, Ghana, Pakistan, Nigeria, and Sri Lanka (all members of the Commonwealth).[31]

Moreover, immigrants regularly report racist experiences at the hands of immigration officials and enforcement officers. Official examinations into the handling of detainees at immigration detention centers in Britain have "recorded a catalogue of racist behavior in the system."[32] The Equality and Human Rights Commission challenged the Home Office with regard to raids conducted in 2013 to detect undocumented migrants, in response to reports

---

[28] See BBC News, "France Roma Expulsions," October 19, 2010, <http://www.bbc.co.uk/news/world-europe-11027288>.

[29] Human Rights Law Centre, "Race Discrimination: UN Committee Releases Report and Recommendations on Australia," <http://hrlc.org.au/race-discrimination-un-committee-releases-report-and-recommendations-on-australia-28-august-2010/>.

[30] For an interesting analysis of the US case, see Rogers M. Smith, "Living in a Promiseland? Mexican Immigration and American Obligations," *Perspectives on Politics* 9:3 (2011), 545–57.

[31] The proposal attracted serious criticism at home and abroad, and even from some prominent figures within the coalition government. It was later shelved. See Elizabeth Rigby, "Business Secretary Vince Cable Attacks £3000 Migrant Bond Plans," *Financial Times*, July 29, 2013.

[32] Tania Branigan, "Racism at immigration centres revealed in report," *The Guardian*, January 4, 2008.

that officials only targeted "non-white" people.[33] In addition, even policies which are seemingly "neutral" with regard to race and ethnicity frequently have entirely foreseeable discriminatory effects, as in the well-documented British attempts to close legal migration channels to non-skilled non-EU citizens.

That is just a brief introduction to a small selection of the myriad, prominent, direct, and indirect ways in which racism and racial and ethnic discrimination feature in the history and politics of immigration and immigration restrictions. So what does and should all this mean for debates about the ethics of migration in political philosophy? How should philosophers respond to and engage with these facts on the ground? Given the persistence of racism, and (direct and indirect) racial and ethnic discrimination in immigration practices and debates, these questions have particular urgency, as well as potential political potency.

7.3 Immigration Controls and Racism

The shameful history of immigration controls has led some philosophers, commentators, and activists to conclude that such controls are inherently, inexorably racist. They had racist beginnings and continue, directly and indirectly, to promote or permit racist ends.[34] As I have indicated thus far, there appears to be much truth in this statement as a description of immigration controls as we know and have known them. Cole contends that "the history of racism in immigration ... shows that the tendency of states to use their right to exclude on racist, and other morally repugnant, grounds, has been a common feature" and he worries that we have "no way of ruling out that kind of application" in practice.[35] Cole seems absolutely right to be worried about immigration controls in practice. We do not have experience of untarnished restrictive immigration policies. To repeat part of the opening quotation from Tommie Shelby, "in light of our discussion of racism and racial discrimination, we might say that the appropriate response to racial injustice is to abolish or reform any institution that operates on the basis of, or is otherwise distorted by, racism."[36] In the case of immigration controls, might we seek reform, or is something more drastic required?

[33] Oliver Wright and Oscar Quine, "Home Office may have broken the law in 'racist' spot checks on suspected illegal immigrants—and may have questioned domestic violence victims," *The Independent*, August 3, 2013.

[34] See, for example, Teresa Hayter, *Open Borders: The Case Against Immigration Controls* (London: Pluto Press, 2000), p. 21: "Immigration controls embody, legitimate, and institutionalise racism." And p. 165: "Immigration controls are inherently racist."

[35] Wellman and Cole, *Debating the Ethics of Immigration*, p. 219.

[36] Shelby, "Race," p. 346.

It appears as though the most obvious means of distancing migration policy from that racist legacy is to remove all barriers to entry, as Teresa Hayter argues; indeed Hayter believes that this is the only way to make the clear break.[37] This would not be the final word on the issue of racism and immigration, since the removal of barriers to entry would prompt a new set of related questions, for example about balancing the interests of existing residents (especially victims of racial injustice) against the interests of newcomers, but at least it would act to "abolish ... [an] institution that operates on the basis of, or is otherwise distorted by, racism."[38]

For many commentators and philosophers, though, presumably the "abolition" move would amount to throwing the baby out with the bathwater; they would argue that we should not reject immigration controls entirely, *simply* in virtue of their murky past and present. After all, a large number of social and political institutions have an extremely, comparably murky past (and present, some would add)—just think of marriage, or the Catholic Church, or the nation, to name but three examples—and yet a lot of people would not wish to reject these entirely, simply in virtue of that past.[39] Perhaps these institutions have virtues that can be separated from that past, and salvaged for good and/or necessary use in the present and future.

The challenge, therefore, is greatest for those political philosophers who wish to take the reformist route, and seek to defend the state's moral right to exclude would-be immigrants from their territories, while at the same time condemning racism and denying the permissibility of excluding perspective immigrants on grounds of race or ethnicity. How might a political philosopher defend the state's right to impose immigration controls in such a way that succeeds in breaking away from the familiar racist, discriminatory pattern of past and present practice?

To assist us in our analysis, we might begin by stipulating some minimal, essential, interrelated requirements for a defense of the state's right to impose immigration restrictions which effectively establishes that kind of break. (1) The defense should *acknowledge* what we might label the "racial discrimination in immigration restrictions" problem—not just explicit, direct racism and discrimination, but also implicit and indirect forms, as well as the ways in which policies may have discriminatory effects. It seems absolutely imperative that any argument in favor of the state's right to exclude would-be immigrants that seeks to break from the past should be able to

[37] Hayter, *Open Borders*.
[38] Shelby, "Race," p. 346. I thank Andrea Tivig for raising this point. For a discussion of whether policies of affirmative action should be extended to ethnic minority immigrants, see her unpublished paper "Just add, do not stir? Immigrants and Affirmative Action."
[39] For an abolitionist approach to these institutions, see Jacqueline Stevens, *States Without Nations: Citizenship for Mortals* (New York: Columbia University Press, 2010).

recognize racial discrimination *as* a problem that always has beset immigration restrictions in the world as we know it. Yet that is not sufficient, on its own. (2) The defense also should be able to *diagnose* racial discrimination in immigration restrictions as a problem. It is not enough just to call it a problem; it also should be able to explain what exactly makes it a problem, and in a way that is consistent with the defense of the state's right to exclude. (3) The defense should be able offer a *prescription* for avoiding the problem of racial discrimination in immigration restrictions. It should seek to show how and why restrictions of the sort permitted according to the argument do not or would not perpetuate the familiar problem. These requirements are interrelated, because—as we shall see—the failure of a defense to satisfy any one of them may call into question its ability to satisfy the others. With those basic requirements in mind, let us turn to the debate regarding the ethics of migration in contemporary political philosophy.

7.4 The Ethics of Immigration Restrictions

Some contemporary normative political theorists certainly think that it is possible to develop a defensible argument in support of the state's right to restrict immigration. In recent decades, a number of mainstream political theorists, including Michael Blake, David Miller, Ryan Pevnick, John Rawls, Michael Walzer, and Christopher Heath Wellman, among others, have offered a variety of arguments in support of some (more or less extensive) form of right to exclude would-be immigrants, and from a broadly "liberal" standpoint.[40] I mean "liberal" here in a very loose sense, and aim primarily to emphasize that these accounts would all see in the history of immigration policy much injustice.

Without elaborating on the precise details of, and differences between, the various accounts here,[41] to generalize, they all share the basic conviction that self-determining communities are entitled to a certain degree of control over immigration—the emphasis may be on the right to exclude as essential to self-determination, or to the ability to protect the national culture(s), for example.

---

[40] Michael Blake, "Immigration" in R. G. Frey and Christopher Heath Wellman (eds.), *A Companion to Applied Ethics* (Oxford: Blackwell, 2005), pp. 224–37; David Miller, "Immigration: The Case for Limits" in Andrew I. Cohen and Christopher Heath Wellman (eds.), *Contemporary Debates in Applied Ethics* (Oxford: Blackwell, 2005), pp. 193–206; Ryan Pevnick, *Immigration and the Constraints of Justice: Between Open Borders and Absolute Sovereignty* (New York: Cambridge University Press, 2011); John Rawls, *The Law of Peoples* (Cambridge, MA: Harvard University Press, 1999), esp. p. 39; Michael Walzer, *Spheres of Justice: A Defense of Pluralism and Equality* (New York: Basic Books, 1983), esp. ch. 2; Wellman, "Immigration and Freedom of Association."

[41] See Sarah Fine, *Immigration and the Right to Exclude* (Oxford: Oxford University Press, forthcoming) for in-depth analysis.

None of these accounts supports the state's right to complete discretion over immigration decisions; all these theorists believe that there are limits to legitimate forms of exclusion. Furthermore, on closer inspection, for some theorists these limits actually substantially restrict the state's discretion vis-à-vis admissions policy. To what extent do these accounts meet the requirements for defending the state's right to impose immigration controls while breaking away from the problem of racial discrimination in immigration restrictions so prominent in past and present practice? To recap, I proposed that (1) the defense should acknowledge that problem; (2) it should be able to diagnose it as a problem; and (3) it should be able offer a prescription for avoiding the problem.

I should note right away that Walzer's argument is possibly the "odd one out" of this group, since he does not declare that discriminating between immigrants on racial and ethnic grounds is impermissible. Indeed, he highlights cases and circumstances in which he suggests it might be permissible. In his discussion of the infamous "White Australia" immigration policy—Australia's attempt, from the beginning of the twentieth century, to exclude "non-whites" from the country in the quest to create a "white" nation—Walzer's only clear objection to the policy seems to be that Australians were holding onto an abundance of territory while refusing admission to people in need.[42] In a well-known passage, he writes:

> Space on that scale is a luxury ... Assuming, then, that there actually is superfluous land, the claim of necessity [from those clamoring for entry] would force a political community like that of White Australia to confront a radical choice. Its members could yield land for the sake of homogeneity, or they could give up homogeneity (agree to the creation of a multiracial society) for the sake of the land. And those would be their only choices. White Australia could survive only as Little Australia.[43]

The implication is that it may be permissible for states without land in abundance to select immigrants on grounds of race and ethnicity, and even to reject the claims of those in need. Furthermore, it may be permissible for states with land in abundance to select between non-"necessitous" cases on grounds of race and ethnicity. Walzer does deny that a discriminatory policy of that kind would be acceptable in all cases. For example, the "claim of American advocates of restricted immigration (in 1920, say) that they were defending a homogenous white and Protestant country" is one that Walzer calls "unjust" and "inaccurate." Here the issue, according to Walzer, is that the United States was already a "pluralist society," and "the moral realities of that

---

[42] For further discussion of "White Australia," see Lake and Reynolds, *Drawing the Global Colour Line*, ch. 6, and Carens, "Nationalism and the Exclusion of Immigrants."

[43] Walzer, *Spheres of Justice*, p. 47.

society ought to have guided the legislators of the 1920s."[44] The suggestion is that the judgment would have been different, though, were the United States actually already homogenous in the relevant sense.[45]

What is more, Walzer argues that there is a "family" or "kinship" aspect to states: "citizens often believe themselves morally bound to open the doors of their country—not to anyone who wants to come, perhaps, but to a particular group of outsiders, recognized as national or ethnic 'relatives'." He adds that "sometimes, under the auspices of the state, we take in fellow citizens to whom we are not related ..., but our more spontaneous beneficence is directed at our own kith and kin."[46] The bottom line for Walzer is that political communities are entitled to decide their own admission policies for themselves, in accordance with their own objectives, subject to some constraints (such as certain claims of necessity, up to a point), but there certainly seems to be no outright prohibition on ethnically and racially discriminatory admissions criteria. So Walzer's argument does not meet the requirements outlined above, and nor does he aim for it to meet them.

7.5 Discrimination Always Impermissible?

By contrast, two other prominent figures in the debate, Miller (who defends the state's right to exclude would-be immigrants, particularly in connection with the protection of national culture) and Wellman (who argues that the state has a right to freedom of association, which includes a right to refuse admission to would-be members), appear intent on meeting all three of the minimal requirements I outlined for supporting the state's right to exclude prospective immigrants, in such a way that succeeds in breaking away from the problematic past. With regard to the first requirement, they both clearly acknowledge the history of racial discrimination in immigration restrictions as a problem. Wellman mentions "long histories of egregious prejudice."[47] Miller describes the "fascists and racists who believe that it is wrong in principle for their political community to admit immigrants who do not conform to the approved cultural or racial stereotype," and who make it difficult for others to debate the ethics of immigration restrictions in reasonable terms.[48]

---

[44] Walzer, *Spheres of Justice*, p. 40.
[45] Walzer only makes passing reference to Australia's Aboriginal population, in *Spheres of Justice*, p. 46. Didn't the presence of Australia's "non-white" citizens render the claims of White Australia advocates "unjust" and "inaccurate," too?
[46] Walzer, *Spheres of Justice*, p. 41.
[47] Wellman and Cole, *Debating the Ethics of Immigration*, p. 143.
[48] Miller, "Immigration: The Case for Limits," p. 193.

In relation to the third requirement, they both are explicit that, while states are entitled to restrict immigration, they should not be permitted to exclude would-be immigrants on grounds of race or ethnicity. Miller, for example, explains that "even if states are not obliged to pursue an open door policy with respect to potential immigrants who are not refugees, they are bound to adopt an immigration policy that is fair, in the sense that it gives good reasons for allowing some but not others to enter."[49] He argues that, while there may be "reasonable grounds for an immigration policy designed to favor speakers of the national language" in those "exceptional cases" where "the national culture is already weak," he rejects the use of cultural selection criteria other than language. Ultimately, he concludes that "although national values and national priorities can reasonably be invoked when deciding *how many* immigrants to take in over any given period of time, when it comes to selecting among the applicants, only 'neutral' criteria such as the particular skills a person has can legitimately be used."[50] Wellman appears to allow the state more discretion. He puts forward the controversial argument that "legitimate states are entitled to reject all potential immigrants, even those desperately seeking asylum from corrupt governments."[51] Nonetheless, at the same time he maintains that "no state may exclude potential immigrants" on religious, ethnic, or racial grounds (and in a later piece he adds gender and nationality to that list).[52]

In both of these well-known accounts, then, there is an attempt (1) to acknowledge the problem, and (2) to offer a prescription for avoiding it in the future, namely by stipulating that states should not be permitted to discriminate between would-be immigrants on grounds of race and ethnicity. That much is the bare minimum we might expect from any defense of the state's right to exclude which wishes to maintain that immigration restrictions need not perpetuate the familiar problem of racial discrimination. Do these attempts succeed in meeting the requirements?

With regard to the third requirement, it is clear that prohibiting racial and ethnic discrimination in admissions decisions is not on its own *sufficient* to signal a break away from the morally problematic history of immigration controls in the world as we know it. Just as feminists long have argued that sexism and sex inequality cannot be eliminated from political theories simply with an "add women and stir" approach, so the racism endemic in immigration controls cannot be eliminated simply with a "remove racial and ethnic

---

[49] David Miller, "Immigrants, Nations, and Citizenship," *The Journal of Political Philosophy* 16:4 (2008), 371–90 at p. 388.

[50] Miller, "Immigrants, Nations, and Citizenship," p. 389, emphasis added.

[51] Wellman, "Immigration and Freedom of Association," p. 141.

[52] Wellman, "Immigration and Freedom of Association," p. 140; Wellman and Cole, *Debating the Ethics of Immigration*, p. 150.

discrimination and stir" approach.[53] Given the facts that the current state system is undeniably, and to a large extent, the product of European and American colonialism and empire (as well as war and conquest), and that immigration policies have been built upon and around racist objectives, a break away from that history requires, among other things, addressing the question of responsibility for past injustices, the legacy of these injustices, and the extent to which even policies that are apparently "neutral" with regard to race and ethnicity work to perpetuate those injustices and have entirely foreseen, if not intended, discriminatory consequences in a system that remains structurally unjust. In other words, if these arguments are designed to support some form of immigration restrictions in our world, then in order to represent a thorough departure from past and present wrongs, those wrongs must be addressed explicitly in the context of migration ethics. Evidently, for instance, there is an urgent need to consider the requirements of rectificatory justice in conjunction with the ethics of immigration controls.[54]

At this juncture, though, one might object that issues of rectification, urgent as they may be, need not concern all political philosophers defending the state's moral right to exclude would-be immigrants. Pevnick, for example, alludes to this when he briefly raises the question of rectification in relation to the ownership claims of states: "I just want to insist that although there are surely particular claims made by states that ought to be rejected as a result of identifiable historical injustices, concerns regarding such injustices do not cast doubt on [my] position as a whole."[55] As political philosophers, the objection might go, we know that racism and discrimination figure prominently in the history and politics of immigration controls (as they do in the history and politics of many other state institutions, such as police services and the military), but in this line of work we are not telling—or need not tell—a story about the past or seeking to defend current practices. We are, and must be, acutely aware of the injustices perpetuated all around us, but we are engaged in a philosophical and normative endeavor, in an attempt to focus on how things *ought* to be, on what we *should* do. In our theorizing, we are not bound by existing practices and institutions. In this context, we are entitled to take institutions, deconstruct and reconstruct them, and to consider whether they might be justifiable, useful, necessary, permissible, required under the

---

[53] See, for example, Susan Moller Okin, *Women in Western Political Thought* (Princeton, NJ: Princeton University Press, 1979); Carole Pateman, *The Sexual Contract* (Stanford, CA: Stanford University Press, 1988). See also Mills, "Realizing (through Racializing) Pogge."

[54] Mills argues that the prevalence of "flagrant racial and gender injustice" demands that contemporary political philosophy should focus on rectificatory justice. Mills, "Realizing (through Racializing) Pogge," p. 171. On obligations of rectificatory justice more generally, see Daniel Butt, *Rectifying International Injustice: Principles of Compensation and Restitution Between Nations* (Oxford: Oxford University Press, 2008).

[55] Pevnick, *Immigration and the Constraints of Justice*, p. 43.

right conditions. We are not really (or not exactly, entirely) talking about *this* messy, unjust world.

To reflect upon this in more detail, Michael Blake offers us a useful point of departure, when considering the relationship between certain kinds of political philosophy, political institutions, and facts about the messy real world. Blake distinguishes between two types—ideal types—of theorizing, which he calls "noninstitutional theory" and "institutional theory."[56] Noninstitutional theory involves "abstracting away from the institutions we currently have, and asking what sorts of institutions we would endorse if we were starting from scratch," whereas institutional theory asks "what the institutions we currently have would have to do to be justified." As he explains, institutional theory "would ask not whether we ought to have developed such a world, but what the various states we have now must do for their powers to be justifiable."[57] This distinction does not map onto that between ideal and non-ideal theory,[58] for as Blake emphasizes, "both noninstitutional and institutional forms of ideal theory exist," and further, he argues that ideal theory of the institutional kind "is the most likely to give us guidance in the real world; it does this not by accepting nonideal conditions, but by showing us how our institutions might be justified under ideal circumstances."[59]

Contemporary normative arguments which seek to defend the state's right to exclude in some capacity appear to be engaging in a form of institutional theory, according to Blake's formulation—taking an institution or set of institutions we currently have (in this case, territorial states with borders over which they claim rights to control the movement of people) and not asking "whether we ought to have developed such a world," but rather what these would have to do to be justified. There are elements of ideal theory in some of these accounts, offering justifications for immigration restrictions under "ideal circumstances," and there are also examples of non-ideal theorizing. An obvious case of the latter is the debate relating to refugees, since the very existence of refugees presupposes the perpetration of injustice and non-compliance with obligations.[60]

Thus, if these theoretical defenses of the state's right to exclude are examining familiar institutions, but are considering how those institutions might be justified under ideal circumstances—circumstances quite different from the

---

[56] Michael Blake, "Distributive Justice, State Coercion, and Autonomy," *Philosophy and Public Affairs* 30:3 (2001), 257–96.

[57] Blake, "Distributive Justice, State Coercion, and Autonomy," pp. 261–2.

[58] For the classic discussion of the ideal/non-ideal distinction, see Rawls, *The Law of Peoples*, esp. p. 5.

[59] Blake, "Distributive Justice, State Coercion, and Autonomy," pp. 263–4, n.7.

[60] On the treatment of refugees, see Miller, "Immigration: The Case for Limits," pp. 202–3; Pevnick, *Immigration and the Constraints of Justice*, pp. 90–6; and Wellman, "Immigration and Freedom of Association," pp. 129–30.

ones with which we are familiar—then perhaps this way of theorizing about immigration restrictions itself is far enough removed from the world as we know it for the history of immigration control not to pose a serious concern. Perhaps all that is required in this context is the prohibition against direct discrimination on grounds of race or ethnicity in admissions policies. They might suggest that some form of right to exclude is defensible in principle, under the correct conditions, but these arguments in support of a right to exclude are not applicable in the here and now, in the world as we know it, in circumstances far from ideal.

There is another significant complication, though. We might note that the prohibition against direct discrimination on grounds of race itself presupposes a background, a history, of racism, and racial injustice. As Mills emphasizes in his critique of Rawls' treatment of race, "a social ontology in which races are existent is a social ontology in which the basic structure is *already* racialized" and "in an ideal society, it would not merely be the case that no race or gender would be discriminated against, but that, more radically, races would not even exist."[61] That the theorists in question seek to prohibit racial discrimination signals an acknowledgment of the fact that we live in a world in which racial categories have been used to disadvantage, stigmatize, oppress, dominate, enslave, and to justify various kinds of social, political, and economic inequalities. The idea that racial discrimination is unacceptable already rests on the existence of a socially constructed category, race, which signifies particular forms of unjust practices. The prohibition against racial discrimination itself has not emerged from nowhere. It has a well-known history—one that is inextricably linked to the uses and effects of discriminatory policies in the past.

In any event, it is not obvious that these accounts can or would *like* to make the case that they are not designed to apply to the world as we know it. Consider this extract from Miller's work on the subject, for example:

> I shall outline two good reasons that states may have for restricting immigration. One has to do with preserving culture, the other with controlling population. I don't claim that these reasons will apply to every state, but they do apply to many liberal democracies that are currently having to decide how to respond to potentially very large flows of immigrants from less economically developed societies.[62]

In other words, it seems clear that his argument is designed to apply in some sense to (and draw on the experiences of) a selection of actually existing states. In fact, if we look again at Blake's formulation, there appears to be a significant ambiguity in his description of institutional theory, and this ambiguity also

---

[61] Mills, "Realizing (through Racializing) Pogge," p. 157.
[62] Miller, "Immigration: The Case for Limits," p. 199.

affects theoretical defenses of the state's right to exclude. According to Blake, institutional theory "would ask not whether we ought to have developed such a world, but *what the various states we have now* must do for their powers to be justifiable."[63] The "various states we have now" could refer to existing states—France, Japan, New Zealand, and so on—with their current borders and populations, and that is sometimes what Blake seems to mean. Or the "various states we have now" could refer just to the familiar concept—for example, something like institutions that claim a monopoly of the legitimate use of violence—and that is at other times what Blake seems to mean. If the question is what existing states must do for their powers to be justifiable, then there is no way to ignore the relevance of past injustice and the often troubling history of the institutions under discussion. At the very least, it calls for an account of how such injustices may have been superseded, for example.

To signal that they represent a clear departure from the morally problematic history of immigration restrictions, therefore, and meet the third requirement, it is not enough for defenses of the right to exclude just to rule out direct discrimination on racial or ethnic grounds. More must be said about the context in question—here and now?—and particularly about how to address past injustice. In fact, without adequately addressing the issue of how to avoid perpetuating the discriminatory effects of past practice, these accounts are also in danger of failing to meet the first, basic requirement—that of acknowledging the problem of racism, insofar as it remains a problem to this day, even in those states which overtly deny the permissibility of racial and ethnic discrimination in immigration policy. It might be the case that those who wish to defend the state's right to exclude are able to answer these two challenges, but it would appear that the subject demands far more attention than it has received to date.

7.6 Why is Discrimination a Problem?

The deepest and most substantial challenges for these accounts, however, emerge in the course of trying to meet the second requirement: that the defense also should be able to diagnose racial discrimination in immigration restrictions as a problem, and in a way that is consistent with the underlying defense of the state's right to exclude. In relation to this second requirement, Wellman is completely frank about the difficulties he faces in search for an argument, a diagnosis of the problem, that he finds compelling. He draws attention to the crucial question which poses a challenge for his own defense

---

[63] Blake, "Distributive Justice, State Coercion, and Autonomy," p. 262, emphasis added.

of the state's right to exclude would-be immigrants: "Assuming that states have the right to control who, if anyone, may enter their territories, does it follow that a country may adopt a policy that explicitly excludes people based upon their race, religion or ethnicity?"[64]

In the course of his search for a satisfactory position, he reviews Walzer's response to "White Australia," with its focus on weighing the interests of "White Australians" in maintaining vast tracts of underpopulated land for themselves, versus the interests of needy strangers.[65] Walzer, Wellman concludes, "appears to believe that, while Australia was not at liberty to simply turn its back upon needy nonwhites, there is nothing inherently unjust about an immigration policy that discriminates based upon race."[66]

Tellingly, Wellman finds himself torn. On the one hand, he is drawn to Walzer's position, because it seems to cohere with his argument in defense of the state's right to exclude would-be immigrants. On the other hand, Walzer's position obviously does not cohere with his intuition that "there must be something wrong with a country's denying admission on the basis of race."[67] He explains:

> As much as I abhor racism, I believe that racist individuals cannot permissibly be forced to marry someone (or adopt a child) outside of their race. And if the importance of freedom of association entitles racist individuals to marry exclusively within their race, why does it not similarly entitle racist citizens to exclude immigrants based upon race? At the very least, one must explain why the immigration case is dissimilar to the marital one. In the end, though, I reject Walzer's position because I think that such an explanation can be furnished.[68]

And so Wellman leans towards the argument that discriminating between would-be immigrants on racial or ethnic grounds is always impermissible. He also considers one of Miller's arguments, that discrimination between candidates for admission on racial or ethnic grounds is problematic because it is insulting to those at whom the discrimination is directed.[69] As Miller puts it:

> What cannot be defended under any circumstances is discrimination on grounds of race, sex, or, in most instances, religion—religion could be a relevant criterion only where it continues to form an essential part of the public culture, as in the case of the state of Israel...If nation-states are allowed to decide how many immigrants to admit in the first place, why can't they pick and choose among

---

[64] Wellman, "Immigration and Freedom of Association," p. 137.

[65] Walzer, *Spheres of Justice*, pp. 46–8; Wellman, "Immigration and Freedom of Association," p. 138.

[66] Wellman, "Immigration and Freedom of Association," p. 138.

[67] Wellman and Cole, *Debating the Ethics of Immigration*, pp. 143–4.

[68] Wellman, "Immigration and Freedom of Association," p. 138.

[69] Wellman, "Immigration and Freedom of Association," pp. 138–9.

potential immigrants on whatever grounds they like—admitting only red-haired women if that is what their current membership prefers? I have tried to hold a balance between the interest that the migrants have in entering the country they want to live in, and the interest that political communities have in determining their own character. Although the first of these interests is not strong enough to justify a right of migration, it is still substantial, and so the immigrants who are refused entry are owed an explanation. To be told that they are the wrong race, or sex (or have the wrong hair color) is insulting, given that these features do not connect to anything of real significance to the society they want to join. Even tennis clubs are not entitled to discriminate among applications on grounds such as these.[70]

Ultimately, Wellman rejects Miller's arguments, though, because he believes that people do not have a right not to be insulted in that way.[71]

Is Wellman right to reject Miller's argument that the problem with racial and ethnic discrimination in immigration restrictions is that it is insulting to the applicants? Is the "insulting" charge a diagnosis of the problem that coheres with these defenses of the state's right to exclude? In response, the insulting charge seems to include both too much and too little. It seems to include too much, particularly on the terms of Miller's own argument, if what counts as "insulting" depends on a subjective judgment or feeling. Unskilled workers, for instance, might be insulted by a state's decision to block their entry on grounds of their lack of desirable skills—perhaps they might find it judges their worth to the society on the basis of a factor beyond their control, or deems them less valuable contributors to the community, thereby undermining their self-esteem, and so forth. But Miller argues that the state may be justified in pursuing the kind of policy which discriminates between applicants on the basis of their skills.[72]

On the reverse side, it also seems not to go far enough. "To be told that they are the wrong race, or sex (or have the wrong hair color)," Miller claims, "is insulting, *given that these features do not connect to anything of real significance to the society they want to join.*"[73] This appears to suggest that if race, for example, *did* connect to something "of real significance" to the receiving country, then the would-be immigrant's complaint would lose its force. As Joseph Carens points out, however, this is precisely the sort of argument that was used by defenders of the White Australia policy. Their goal was to create a racially "homogenous" nation, and they offered various justifications in pursuit of

[70] Miller, "Immigration: The Case for Limits," p. 204.

[71] Wellman, "Immigration and Freedom of Association," p. 139.

[72] Miller, "Immigration: The Case for Limits," p. 204: "Next in order of priority come those with the skills and talents that are needed by the receiving community."

[73] Miller, "Immigration: The Case for Limits," p. 204, emphasis added.

that goal.[74] In the late nineteenth and early twentieth centuries, all manner of influential intellectuals (perhaps most notably historian and liberal politician James Bryce) popularized the view that functioning democracies must be racially homogeneous.[75] To them, the quest to maintain a racially homogenous country was perfectly acceptable.

Furthermore, that it is "insulting" does not seem to get at the heart of what is wrong with racially discriminatory immigration policies. If we turn back to the White Australia case, we might note that the Japanese government railed against the immigration restrictions which sought to exclude "non-white" migrants. They certainly found such restrictions insulting. However, as Lake and Reynolds point out, the insult to them was rooted not in being excluded because they were not "white." Rather, their objection was to being grouped together with the subjects of other countries, including China, whom the Japanese considered inferior in terms of "morality" and advancement of "civilization." Lake and Reynolds highlight that "Japan, too, had a deep investment in racial hierarchy, their diplomats regularly demanding recognition of their superiority to other Asian peoples."[76] In short, that racially discriminatory immigration policies are insulting does not offer a satisfactory diagnosis of the problem.[77]

Instead, Wellman moves in the direction of a position similar to that of Michael Blake, which focuses on the way in which discriminatory immigration policies affect existing citizens, rather than the excluded would-be immigrants. Since "we have a special duty to respect our fellow citizens as equal partners in the political cooperative," Wellman argues, a state is not permitted to "institute an immigration policy which excludes entry to members of a given race because such a policy would wrongly disrespect those citizens in the dispreferred category."[78]

This diagnosis of the problem seems to be consistent with Wellman's overarching argument in support of a right to exclude—the constraint on the state's freedom to discriminate between applicants is related to the rights of the citizens themselves. However, as in Walzer's argument, it makes the permissibility of discriminatory entry criteria entirely dependent on the facts of the matter. Discrimination is wrong only in particular contexts. Recall that Walzer also maintained that it would be unjust to apply racially discriminatory criteria when the state in question is already "pluralist." In Wellman's case, racist criteria are only problematic to the extent that people in what

---

[74] Carens, "Nationalism and the Exclusion of Immigrants," p. 45.

[75] See Lake and Reynolds, *Drawing the Global Color Line*, ch. 2.

[76] Lake and Reynolds, *Drawing the Global Color Line*, p. 145.

[77] For an interesting philosophical exploration of insults, see Jerome Neu, *Sticks and Stones: The Philosophy of Insults* (New York: Oxford University Press, 2008).

[78] Wellman, "Immigration and Freedom of Association," p. 139; Blake, "Immigration," p. 233.

Wellman calls the "dispreferred category" are already citizens of the state. He attempts to fashion this as a general objection to discriminating between candidates for reasons of race and ethnicity, by arguing that *"no state* is completely without minorities who would be disrespected by an immigration policy which invoked racial/ethnic/religious categories" and so *"no state* may exclude potential immigrants on these types of criteria."[79] Such an assumption about existing states is questionable, certainly with respect to more remote countries. Either way, it leaves open, at least in theory, the possibility that a state would do no wrong in discriminating between prospective immigrants on grounds of race or ethnicity if members of the relevant group were not already citizens—and this was precisely Wellman's objection to Walzer's position. Suppose a state successfully cleansed its territory of all ethnic, racial, and religious minorities, clearly perpetrating a great injustice against those minority groups. And suppose later that same state instituted an immigration policy which discriminated between prospective entrants on ethnic, racial, and religious grounds. Who exactly is wronged by that immigration policy, now that the state has no ethnic minority citizens?

Elsewhere Miller also focuses on the way in which discrimination wrongs current citizens:

> Were states today to try to select immigrants on grounds of ethnicity, as many states have done in the past, they would be seen to violate the equal citizenship status of their existing ethnic minorities. By giving preference to those of a particular ethnocultural background, the state unavoidably declares that the culture in question is superior, thereby undermining its attempts to treat all cultures even-handedly in its domestic policy.[80]

Miller widens the category of those who would be wronged: he seems to be suggesting that any kind of ethnic discrimination in admissions policy wrongs any and all members of ethnic minorities.

Again, though, the argument that racial and ethnic discrimination in admissions policies is impermissible because of the way it treats existing citizens does not seem sufficient to meet the requirement of diagnosing the problem, and in a way that coheres with the overall defense of the state's right to exclude. Certainly, existing citizens who are members of the targeted group are insulted, treated as second-class citizens, wronged by this kind of discrimination. That is beyond doubt. Indeed, this actually calls into question Miller's claim about discriminating on grounds of religion ("religion could be a relevant criterion only where it continues to form an essential part of the public

---

[79] Wellman, "Immigration and Freedom of Association," p. 140, emphasis added.
[80] Miller, "Immigrants, Nations, and Citizenship," p. 19.

culture, as in the case of the state of Israel").[81] Wouldn't use of religion as an admissions criterion risk violating "the equal citizenship status" of members of other religious groups? Even more concerning, though, is the fact that we know how ill-defined and indistinct the concepts of "race," "ethnicity," "religion," and even "nationality" are and have been in practice. Jews, for instance, have been described and have self-identified as a race, an ethnic group, a religious group, and a nation. Which groupings count as "races" now? Which count as "ethnic minorities"? Are religious groups to be defined exclusively by faith? Which kinds of discriminatory practices are ruled in and which are ruled out when religion is deemed a relevant criterion in admissions policies? These questions are significant. They remind us once again that simply ruling out "racial" and "ethnic" discrimination in immigration policies is not sufficient to acknowledge, address, and avoid perpetuating the problem in question, at least as long as these categories are vague and shifting, and open to interpretation and abuse. We need to hear more about how we are to understand and use the concepts under discussion. Moreover, this emphasizes the importance of exploring the extent to which a blanket ban on racial and ethnic discrimination in immigration policies coheres with the rest of an argument in defense of a state's right to exclude. In Miller's case, why might religion be an acceptable criterion in admissions decisions "if it continues to form an essential part of the public culture," whereas presumably race is always unacceptable, no matter what part it plays in the public culture?

Revealingly, more recently Wellman himself has decided that his earlier position—discriminatory immigration policies are wrong insofar as they fail to respect fellow-citizens as equals—is inadequate. He writes, "while I still think there must be something wrong with any immigration policy that distinguishes among applicants on the basis of criteria such as race, gender, religion, or nationality..., I must confess that I do not yet have a full satisfactory justification for this conclusion."[82] He accepts that he fails to meet what I have labeled the second requirement for defending the state's right to impose immigration controls in a way that succeeds in breaking away from this particular problem of past and present practice, that the argument should be able to diagnose racial discrimination in immigration restrictions as a problem, in a way that is consistent with the defense of the state's right to exclude. It is no surprise, of course, that he starts from the strong intuition that there must be something wrong with an immigration policy which discriminates between prospective entrants on grounds such as race, but perhaps it also should not come as a surprise that he has difficulty marrying

---

[81] Miller, "Immigrants, Nations, and Citizenship," p. 19.
[82] Wellman and Cole, *Debating the Ethics of Immigration*, p. 150; also pp. 143–4.

that intuition with an uncompromising argument in favor of the state's right to exclude.

In order to acknowledge the problem, and to avoid perpetuating it in future, while also trying to reform the blemished institution in question, what we desperately need is an argument that properly diagnoses the problem in the first place. However, if a defense of the state's right to exclude cannot diagnose ethnic and racial discrimination in immigration policy as a problem in a way that is consistent with that defense, then presumably one part of the argument has got to give. Which is it to be?

7.7 Conclusion

Race, racism, and racial and ethnic discrimination are intertwined with the history of immigration restrictions in such a way that demands urgent attention from normative political philosophers debating the ethics of migration, and particularly those seeking to defend some form of right to exclude would-be immigrants. When we move race and ethnicity from the margins to the foreground of our discussion, and we consider the history of immigration restrictions, it becomes clear how much work is still to be done. I have sought to indicate the significant challenges involved in distancing immigration restrictions from that history, and I have argued that the usual move of ruling out racial and ethnic discrimination in immigration policy simply is not sufficient.[83]

References

Anthias, Floya and Nira Yuval Davis with Harriet Cain, *Racialized Boundaries: Race, Nation, Gender, Colour, and Class and the Anti-Racist Struggle* (London: Routledge, 1992).

Appiah, K. Anthony and Amy Gutmann, *Color Conscious: The Political Morality of Race* (Princeton, NJ: Princeton University Press, 1996).

BBC News, "France Roma Expulsions," October 19, 2010, <http://www.bbc.co.uk/news/world-europe-11027288>.

Bell, Duncan, *The Idea of Greater Britain: Empire and the Future of World Order, 1860–1900* (Princeton, NJ: Princeton University Press, 2007).

---

[83] Earlier versions of this chapter were presented at the "Migration in Legal and Political Theory: Remaining Challenges" conference, CRASSH, University of Cambridge, in October 2011, at the UCL Political Theory Seminar in November 2012, and at the UK Analytic Legal and Political Conference in Cambridge, September 2013. The questions and comments on each of those occasions were extremely helpful. Particular thanks to Duncan Bell, Amandine Catala, Richard Child, Lior Erez, Rob Jubb, Kieran Oberman, Andrea Tivig, Patrick Tomlin, Laura Valentini, and Lea Ypi. This was written while I was a research fellow at Corpus Christi College, Cambridge, and I would like to thank the Master and Fellows for that wonderful opportunity.

Bell, Duncan, "Beyond the Sovereign State: Isopolitan Citizenship, Race, and Anglo-American Union," *Political Studies* 62:2 (2014), 418–34.

Blake, Michael, "Distributive Justice, State Coercion, and Autonomy," *Philosophy and Public Affairs* 30:3 (2001), 257–96.

Blake, Michael, "Immigration" in R. G. Frey and Christopher Heath Wellman (eds.), *A Companion to Applied Ethics* (Oxford: Blackwell, 2005), pp. 224–37.

Blum, Lawrence, *I'm not a Racist, But... The Moral Quandary of Race* (Ithaca, NY: Cornell University Press, 2002).

Branigan, Tania, "Racism at immigration centres revealed in report," *The Guardian*, January 4, 2008.

Butt, Daniel, *Rectifying International Injustice: Principles of Compensation and Restitution Between Nations* (Oxford: Oxford University Press, 2008).

Carens, Joseph H., "Aliens and Citizens: The Case for Open Borders," *The Review of Politics* 49:2 (1987), 251–73.

Carens, Joseph H., "Nationalism and the Exclusion of Immigrants: Lessons from Australian Immigration Policy" in Mark Gibney (ed.), *Open Borders? Closed Societies? The Ethical and Political Issues* (Westport, CT: Greenwood Press, 1988), pp. 41–60.

Dummett, Michael, *On Immigration and Refugees* (London and New York: Routledge, 2001).

Fine, Sarah, *Immigration and the Right to Exclude* (Oxford: Oxford University Press, forthcoming).

Gilroy, Paul, *"There Ain't No Black in the Union Jack": The Cultural Politics of Race and Nation* (Chicago: University of Chicago Press, 1987).

Harris, Leonard (ed.), *Racism* (New York: Humanity Books, 1999).

Hayter, Teresa, *Open Borders: The Case Against Immigration Controls* (London: Pluto Press, 2000).

Human Rights Law Centre, "Race Discrimination: UN Committee Releases Report and Recommendations on Australia," <http://hrlc.org.au/race-discrimination-un-committee-releases-report-and-recommendations-on-australia-28-august-2010/>.

Kettle, Martin, "Are you thinking what I'm thinking about the election?," *The Guardian*, March 8, 2005.

King, Desmond, *In the Name of Liberalism: Illiberal Social Policy in the United States and Britain* (Oxford: Oxford University Press, 1999).

King, Desmond, "Symposium: Contract and Domination by Carole Pateman and Charles W. Mills," *Journal of Political Ideologies* 13:3 (2008), 227–62.

Lake, Marilyn and Henry Reynolds, *Drawing the Global Color Line: White Men's Countries and the International Challenge of Racial Equality* (Cambridge: Cambridge University Press, 2008).

Lippert-Rasmussen, Kasper, "The Badness of Discrimination," *Ethical Theory and Moral Practice* 9:2 (2006), 167–85.

Mallon, Ron, "'Race': Normative, Not Metaphysical or Semantic," *Ethics* 116:3 (2006), 525–51.

Mason, David, *Race and Ethnicity in Modern Britain* (Oxford: Oxford University Press, 2000).

Miles, Robert, *Racism* (London: Routledge, 1989).

Miller, David, "Immigration: The Case for Limits" in Andrew I. Cohen and Christopher Heath Wellman (eds.), *Contemporary Debates in Applied Ethics* (Oxford: Blackwell, 2005), pp. 193–206.

Miller, David, "Immigrants, Nations, and Citizenship," *The Journal of Political Philosophy* 16:4 (2008), 371–90.

Mills, Charles W., *Blackness Visible: Essays on Philosophy and Race* (Ithaca, NY: Cornell University Press, 1998).

Mills, Charles W., "Realizing (through Racializing) Pogge" in Alison M. Jaggar (ed.), *Thomas Pogge and his Critics* (Cambridge: Polity Press, 2010), pp. 151–74.

Moller Okin, Susan, *Women in Western Political Thought* (Princeton, NJ: Princeton University Press, 1979).

Neu, Jerome, *Sticks and Stones: The Philosophy of Insults* (New York: Oxford University Press, 2008).

Pateman, Carole, *The Sexual Contract* (Stanford, CA: Stanford University Press, 1988).

Pateman, Carole and Charles W. Mills, *Contract and Domination* (Cambridge: Polity Press, 2007).

Pevnick, Ryan, *Immigration and the Constraints of Justice: Between Open Borders and Absolute Sovereignty* (New York: Cambridge University Press, 2011).

Rawls, John, *The Law of Peoples* (Cambridge, MA: Harvard University Press, 1999).

Rigby, Elizabeth, "Business Secretary Vince Cable Attacks £3000 Migrant Bond Plans," *Financial Times,* July 29, 2013.

Scheffler, Samuel, "Immigration and the Significance of Culture," *Philosophy & Public Affairs* 35:2 (2007), 93–125.

Shelby, Tommie, "Race" in David Estlund (ed.), *The Oxford Handbook of Political Philosophy* (New York: Oxford University Press, 2012), pp. 336–53.

Smith, Rogers M., "Living in a Promiseland? Mexican Immigration and American Obligations," *Perspectives on Politics* 9:3 (2011), 545–57.

Stevens, Jacqueline, *States Without Nations: Citizenship for Mortals* (New York: Columbia University Press, 2010).

Tivig, Andrea, "Just Add, Do Not Stir? Immigrants and Affirmative Action" (manuscript).

Tully, James, "Lineages of Contemporary Imperialism" in Duncan Kelly (ed.), *Lineages of Empire: The Historical Roots of British Imperial Thought* (Oxford: Oxford University Press, 2009), pp. 3–29.

Walzer, Michael, *Spheres of Justice: A Defense of Pluralism and Equality* (New York: Basic Books, 1983).

Wellman, Christopher Heath, "Immigration and Freedom of Association," *Ethics* 119:1 (2008), 109–41.

Wellman, Christopher Heath and Phillip Cole, *Debating the Ethics of Immigration: Is there a Right to Exclude?* (New York: Oxford University Press, 2011).

Wright, Oliver and Oscar Quine, "Home Office may have broken the law in 'racist' spot checks on suspected illegal immigrants—and may have questioned domestic violence victims," *The Independent,* August 3, 2013.

8

Taking Workers as a Class

The Moral Dilemmas of Guestworker Programs

Lea Ypi

8.1 Introduction: Workers and Guests

A worker is someone who exchanges his labor for money. A *guest*worker is someone who exchanges his labor for money, as a guest. A guestworker therefore belongs, at the same time, to two distinguishable but related sets: the set of workers, who typically exchange their labor for money, and the set of migrant workers, who exchange their labor for money for a specified amount of time and in a foreign labor market.

It is often said that guestworkers are exploited, that is, that unfair advantage is taken of the position of foreign workers in domestic labor markets.[1] But are

---

[1] In what follows I shall deploy a broad definition of exploitation as taking unfair advantage (on which most existing accounts seem to rely) and then proceed to illustrate its specificities. For some relevant discussions in the context of guestworker programs, see Daniel Attas, "The Case of Guest Workers: Exploitation, Citizenship and Economic Rights," *Res Publica* 6:1 (2000), 73–92; Joseph Carens, "Live-in Domestics, Seasonal Workers, and Others Hard to Locate on the Map of Democracy," *Journal of Political Philosophy* 16:4 (2008), 419–45; Patti Tamara Lenard and Christine Straehle, "Temporary labour migration, global redistribution and democratic justice," *Politics, Philosophy & Economics* 11:2 (2012), 206–30; Robert Mayer, "Guestworkers and exploitation," *Review of Politics* 67:2 (2005), 311–34; Valeria Ottonelli and Tiziana Torresi, "Inclusivist Egalitarian Liberalism and Temporary Migration: A Dilemma," *Journal of Political Philosophy* 20:2 (2010), 202–24; Anna Stilz, "Guestworkers and second-class citizenship," *Policy and Society* 29:4 (2010), 295–307; Michael Walzer, *Spheres of Justice: a Defence of Pluralism and Equality* (Oxford: Robertson, 1983). For defenses of guestworker programs as second-best policies, see Daniel Bell, "Equal rights for foreign resident workers?," *Dissent* 48:4 (2001) 26–34 and Howard F. Chang, "Liberal Ideals and Political Feasibility: Guest-Worker Programs as Second-Best Policies," *North Carolina Journal of International Law and Commercial Regulation* 27:3 (2002), 465–81. For a general discussion on the different ways of understanding the unfairness of exploitation, see Alan Wertheimer and Matt Zwolinski, "Exploitation" in Edward N. Zalta (ed.), *The Stanford Encyclopedia of Philosophy* (Spring 2013 Edition), <http://plato.stanford.edu/archives/spr2013/entries/exploitation/>.

guestworkers exploited in virtue of being workers or of being guests or both or neither?

The answer to these questions depends in part on the moral baseline upon which we choose to focus in trying to capture the wrong of exploitation. If we link that wrong to the occurrence of domination we might think that guest-workers are exploited because they are guests rather than citizens (or permanent residents). Deprived of a significant (even if not full) range of political and social rights that normally protect citizens and permanent residents from the failures of the market and the whims of employers, they have no access to the political remedies necessary to counter economic disadvantage. Let us call this "the domination theory of exploitation."

Alternatively, if we think that an agent is exploited whenever an unequal distribution of benefits systematically follows relatively equal amounts of effort for relatively similar tasks performed, we might say that a guestworker is exploited both because he is a worker and because he is a guest. As a worker, his labor receives less than its fair share. As a guest, his labor receives less than its fair share compared to that of workers operating in similar market conditions. Call this the "egalitarian theory of exploitation."

Finally, guestworkers might be considered exploited because they operate in a market that fails to reward their labor with sufficient access to the resources they need to lead a decent life. If prospective guestworkers struggle to subsist and accept employment offers just because they couldn't afford to reject them, desperation bidding renders them vulnerable to being taken unfair advantage of. We might call this "the sufficientarian account of exploitation."

This chapter argues that neither the domination account nor the egalitarian account nor the sufficientarian account fully captures the respects in which guestworkers are exploited. To illustrate the wrong of exploitation, we should focus on workers taken collectively as a class rather than distributively as workers who are not citizens of the country in which they work. The exploitation of guestworkers is, I shall argue, a result of the collective unfreedom of workers taken together, not of guestworkers considered as a special category deserving particular normative attention. The appropriate question to ask when reflecting on the moral dilemmas of guestworkers is not whether guest-workers are exploited but whether guestworker programs are exploitative. This chapter argues that they are. The exploitative nature of guestworker programs is manifest in the way labor markets operate in a global sphere, in the way states and private employers interact with each other, and in the way the global distribution of labor negatively affects guestworkers and domestic workers alike.

It is important to emphasize from the start that I am not arguing here that guestworkers are never exploited. My point is that *even if* we concede that guestworkers are not *always* exploited, or that not *all* guestworkers are exploited, or that they are not *all* exploited in *all* circumstances, the problem of exploitation raised by certain migration practices remains a key problem. But the reasons are different from those that migration scholars typically invoke. Guestworker programs make for a curious object of enquiry. Rather than an issue to be explored in the context of a theory of just migration, they present a relevant case in which an old and seemingly outdated issue, the exploitation of the working class taken collectively, re-surfaces with all its normative force. The remedial principles to which such a perspective gives rise are principles seeking to abolish the exploitation of workers in general and not just the exploitation of guestworkers as a special category of them. The problems of guestworker programs can therefore be more effectively addressed through a theory that integrates the distribution of the benefits and burdens of freedom of movement in the broader question concerning the basic institutional structure regulating how markets operate.

8.2 The Dilemmas of Guestworker Programs

Since the invention of the passport and the institutionalization of border controls, guestworker programs have become an integral part of states' efforts to cope with transitions in industrial relations and shortages of labor supply. The first attempts to regulate the entrance of guestworkers date back to the late nineteenth century, following a process that accompanied the consolidation of the national territorial state and the related increasing hostility towards prospective immigrants.[2] Despite a short period of skepticism towards such programs in the mid-eighties, guestworker schemes are now in place in many countries of the world: Mexican agricultural workers in the U.S., Mozambiquan diamond miners in South Africa, Asian construction workers in the Middle East (especially in Saudi Arabia, Kuwait, Qatar, United Arab Emirates, and Oman), Indonesian nannies in Malaysia, and Filipino carers in Canada are only some of the relevant cases in point.[3] And there are no signs that the flux is about to stop: since 1997, the number of temporary migrants traveling to OECD countries has been growing annually by 9 percent. Migration to East and West Asia, including

---

[2] Prussia's introduction of guestworker programs occurred in the two decades following German unification, whereas migrant workers employed in the diamond and gold mines of southern Africa followed British attempts to unify British colonies, Boer Republics, and African kingdoms under British rule. See on this issue Cindy Hahamovitch, "Creating Perfect Immigrants: Guestworkers of the World in Historical Perspective 1," *Labor History* 44:1 (2003), 69–94.

[3] See Stephen Castles, "Guestworkers in Europe: A resurrection?," *International Migration Review* 40:4 (2006), 741–66 and Hahamovitch, "Creating Perfect Immigrants."

Saudi Arabia and the United Arab Emirates, has also increased by 2.5 percent per year since 1985.[4]

Notwithstanding a number of governmental and intergovernmental attempts to modify the procedures surrounding the employment of guest-workers (especially in the EU area), the conditions of their arrival and the contracts regulating their stay have only superficially changed. Guestworkers are neither long-term migrants nor short-term visitors.[5] The conditions of their temporary settlement are regulated through negotiations between sending and receiving societies, and they are only allowed to remain in the host state for specified amounts of time. They are also typically denied access to the same political and social benefits granted to citizens (and often also permanent residents). On the one hand, it is claimed, guestworker programs continue to serve well the interests of states experiencing industrial change, shortages in specific sectors of the labor market, and demographic shifts, especially popu-lation ageing and increasing decline in fertility rates. On the other hand, the conditions under which they are able to achieve these aims remain concern-ing. Most guestworkers cannot participate in elections, cannot claim access to public subsidies (e.g., unemployment benefits), cannot join collective bargain-ing processes, and are in general deprived of the right to have a say on the terms according to which the host political community requires them to conduct their lives. They are entitled to fewer benefits of membership even compared to other immigrant workers, for example, compared to students who have decided to settle and work in the receiving state, compared to refugees or compared to immigrants who have gained entrance as a result of practices of family reunification (to mention but some of the most prominent categories). Unlike these other noncitizens, guestworkers are either typically tied to one particular work sector or the terms of their visas prevent them from changing employers. They often cannot apply for permanent residence and eventually citizenship, they are denied the right to apply for family reunification, and they are subject to being deported from the country if they lose their jobs.[6]

Applauded by employers, politicians, and policymakers and often mis-trusted by ordinary citizens, guestworker programs are likely to provoke bitter

---

[4] Dovelyn Agunias and Kathleen Newland, "Circular Migration and Development: Trends, Policy, Routes, and Ways Forward," <http://www.migrationpolicy.org/research/circular-migration-and-development-trends-policy-routes-and-ways-forward>, accessed July 16, 2015.

[5] See Castles, "Guestworkers in Europe: A resurrection?."

[6] See on this issue Martin Ruhs and Philip Martin, "Numbers vs. Rights: Trade-Offs and Guest Worker Programs," *International Migration Review* 42:1 (2008), 249–65 at p. 251. See also Stephen Castles and Godula Kosack, *Immigrant Workers and Class Structure in Western Europe* (Oxford: Oxford University Press, 1985); James Hollifield, *Immigrants, Markets, and States: The Political Economy of Postwar Europe* (Cambridge, MA: Harvard University Press, 1992); and Rachel Salazar Parrenas, *Servants of Globalization: Women, Migration and Domestic Work* (Stanford, CA: Stanford University Press, 2001).

controversy both when they are rejected and when they are endorsed.[7] Some see them as providing de facto coverage to a regime of second-class citizenship that exploits the contribution of workers but offers them no membership benefits to negotiate the terms of that contribution or to counter the bargaining disadvantage they face in potentially hostile labor environments. Others see them as a perhaps non-ideal but nevertheless acceptable form of economic support for workers who can migrate for a specific amount of time to save money, send remittances home, and contribute to the development of their countries upon return. Assessing these arguments requires examining the terms according to which guestworkers are employed in host states, reflecting on their occupational position compared to members of receiving societies, and observing the potential benefits they receive compared to fellow-citizens who are left behind. In other words, addressing the moral dilemmas of guestworker programs has often been attempted in the context of theories of just migration-seeking to distribute fairly the benefits and burdens of freedom of movement. That may not necessarily be the most appropriate way to go. To understand why, we need to examine in some detail one of the most vexed questions that is typically raised in the context of the employment of guestworkers: the issue of their potential exploitation. As we shall see in what follows, it is when we address this question that both the moral dilemmas of guestworker programs and the shortcomings of their solutions come prominently to the fore.

8.3 Guestworkers and Domination

The fact that guestworkers are denied many of the standard membership rights typically granted to citizens (and often also permanent residents) has attracted criticism of these programs as exploitative, linking their exploitative nature to the political disenfranchisement from which guestworkers typically suffer.[8] Being deprived of political membership implies that guestworkers are unable to appeal to the protection of state institutions to defend themselves from abuses of power, both political and economic. Although they are required to comply with the rules of receiving states, they have no equal say in the making of these rules and no chance of shaping them to improve their bargaining position. They are subjected to the laws but banned from authoring them. Political inequality leaves guestworkers in a vulnerable condition

---

[7] For an informative discussion of the attitudes of the American public towards temporary work programs, see Ilias Shayerah, Katherine Fennelly, and Christopher M. Federico, "American Attitudes toward Guest Worker Policies," *International Migration Review* 42:4 (2008), 741–66.

[8] Walzer, *Spheres of Justice*, p. 59.

and exposes them to the possibility of others taking advantage of that condition to derive profit from it. Indeed, so the argument goes, the very point of their disenfranchised status is to prevent guestworkers from overcoming their vulnerability. For if guestworkers ceased to be treated as politically unequal, they would be just like domestic workers, and the programs in which they take part would no longer serve only the interests of employers in the host state. On this view, the exploitation of guestworkers depends on the status of second-class citizens to which they are confined.

Of course being politically disenfranchised is not a sufficient condition for declaring guestworkers an exploited category. Political domination does not causally explain the occurrence of exploitation. Moreover, guestworkers are visitors, and like all other visitors (tourists and students, for example), it is reasonable, all things considered, to ask them to comply with the rules of the country in which they are admitted. We do not find problematic the fact that tourists are required to obey traffic laws in the countries that they visit, nor do we ever try to campaign to give them a say in the making of such laws. However, some might argue here that, unlike tourists and students, guestworkers are deprived of the benefits of political membership whilst being asked to contribute to the system that creates and upholds such benefits.[9] It is the contribution that guestworkers make to the production of public goods in receiving societies without being able to claim back equal political benefits that renders them vulnerable to being exploited in the receiving state.

But why should we always expect the context in which a productive contribution is made and that where equal benefits are claimed to overlap so neatly with each other? The argument from cooperation in the production of certain goods would have more force if guestworkers were deprived of the benefits of citizenship altogether, not necessarily if they were deprived of such benefits in a particular host country but continued to retain access to them in their home states. There might be good reasons for thinking that overlap is desirable but surely more needs to be said on whether the mere absence of it clearly indicates the presence of exploitation.

To see this point, consider the following example. David, a prominent academic from Oxford, has been invited to give a series of keynote lectures at the University of Toronto. The series lasts for one month and, although David is guaranteed accommodation on campus during that period, he has no right to borrowing facilities from the library, no access to a University of Toronto email address, and no entitlement to attend meetings of the academic board. He is of course working hard to prepare his lectures and contributing to upholding the standards of teaching and research at the University of

---

[9] See on this issue Carens, "Live-in Domestics, Seasonal Workers, and Others Hard to Locate on the Map of Democracy" and Stilz, "Guestworkers and second-class citizenship."

Toronto. Yet the benefits he can claim during his visiting period in the department are significantly lower compared to those granted to his colleague Joe, who is a member of the department. Still, it would be difficult to insist that David is being exploited. He is a member of the University of Oxford, he can borrow from his college library, he can use his Oxford email address, and he can attend departmental meetings in his home university. He has rights of membership in the Politics department at Oxford. Although he may miss important meetings and fail to have a say on particular funding decisions during his research stay in Canada, he will be able to make up for those by being an active member of the department and influence the agenda of meetings upon his return.

One might argue here that there is a difference between being concerned for wealthy academics and their access to libraries and email accounts and worrying about poor citizens from vulnerable states who rely on their temporary migration for access to vital resources needed both in their home countries and in the host states. Yet this change of focus draws our attention to how the difference in skills and status between different categories of migrants significantly affects their vulnerability to exploitation, showing how the issue of membership may or may not matter to that assessment. Indeed, if we only focused on membership rights, we would see that, if other institutions were functioning properly, guestworkers would not lose all the protection provided by their membership rights because of their status as guests. They would remain citizens of their country of origin, they would enjoy diplomatic protection from their home countries in the host state (they're not refugees, after all!), and they would retain relevant membership entitlements (such as voting) in the places from which they came. Although they would continue to make a contribution to the economy of receiving states without being able to claim the same entitlements as citizens of those states (just like David can't claim the same entitlements as Joe at the University of Toronto even though his lectures make a productive contribution there), their work contracts would have been negotiated with the input of their home states. Despite the fact that guestworkers would not have an immediate say in making the rules with which they are asked to comply, in the long term they would contribute to modifying the criteria on the basis of which different labor agencies interact with each other.

As emphasized, all this presupposes that the institutions responsible for negotiating adequate guestworker contracts have roughly equal bargaining powers to come up with mutually advantageous terms of cooperation, and that temporary workers have ample margins of democratic participation to ensure their voice really is channeled by the appropriate mechanisms for political decision-making. In practice this is hardly ever the case. But if guestworkers end up being exploited as a result of inequalities in bargaining power between sending and receiving states or due to insufficient channels of democratic participation in their home countries, this simply strengthens the point we are trying to make. Sociopolitical disenfranchisement does not by itself explain the kind of injustice suffered by guestworkers in the countries that they visit, nor does lack of equal rights of membership suffice to illustrate why such category of people is always vulnerable to exploitation. Other factors have to be taken into account before we can establish the moral baseline on grounds of which we can show that unfair advantage can be taken from them.

8.4 Guestworkers and Egalitarianism

An alternative way to think about the exploitation of guestworkers is to reflect on their condition by observing the relative inequalities of occupational position in which temporary labor programs tend to confine them. Temporary contracts subject guestworkers to terms of employment that differ significantly from those of domestic workers. They typically work the same hours, perform the same jobs, but are simply paid less. Moreover, it is often said, unlike domestic workers, guestworkers are prevented from changing employers, cannot search for jobs different from the ones that they were initially admitted to perform, are bound to remain in a particular work sector, enjoy limited opportunities for participation in workers' unions, and have very little or no say in the possible extension of their work contracts. Guestworkers are at a relative disadvantage compared to domestic workers. Some have argued, it is precisely this relatively different position in the job market that renders them more vulnerable to exploitation compared to domestic workers. But what exactly is the baseline with regard to which we consider the process to confer an unfair advantage upon those who buy labor at the expense of those who sell it?

To answer this question, we need to look at the dynamics of supply and demand governing the exchange of labor. Those who defend the egalitarian theory of exploitation typically do so from a classical liberal economic perspective. On this view, a just price of labor is the one that emerges if supply and demand balance each other in circumstances of perfect competition, undistorted by extra-market factors. The problem, critics argue, is that guestworkers' restricted access to the labor market modifies the nature of the exchange between employers and workers. Due to the contractual constraints guestworkers face, the labor market is partially closed to them.[10] Their freedom

---

[10] See Attas, "The Case of Guest Workers: Exploitation, Citizenship and Economic Rights," pp. 75–9; and Carens, "Live-in Domestics, Seasonal Workers, and Others Hard to Locate on the Map of Democracy," pp. 430–2.

of occupational choice is severely restricted. Consequently the negotiations in which they are involved tend to favor those placed in a stronger bargaining position, for example, those that have full capacity to choose who to hire. But, unlike the domination case we examined in Section 8.3, the problem is not, inherently, one of limited access to the benefits of political membership. The problem is rather that, due to their socio-economic placement in society, guestworkers are treated unfairly because they accept jobs remunerated at a price which is lower than the equilibrium price for their labor in the absence of those restrictions. Exploitation consists in employers profiting more and workers obtaining less for their labor than they would if they were to exchange their labor in perfectly competitive markets.

Those who endorse this perspective typically emphasize that one of its advantages consists in allowing us to distinguish between denying guest-workers the full package of political membership benefits and compelling us to extend them comprehensive rights of participation in the economic sphere. Whilst fellow-citizens' right to self-determination may entitle them to deny permanent rights of political participation to temporary members, guest-workers are entitled to an inclusive list of rights usually associated to the economic sphere. More specifically, it is argued that freedom of exchange, freedom of occupational choice, freedom of movement and organization, the right to participate in collective bargaining, to strike and to claim unemploy-ment benefits and compensation for loss of income ought to be extended to guestworkers in order to allow them to remove the cause of unequal exchange for the wages they receive.[11] If guestworkers' vulnerability to exploitation is due to their limited access to the economic sphere, making that sphere fully accessible to them might sound like a plausible remedial measure.

We may wonder, however, whether drawing a sharp line of division between political and economic membership, as this argument seems to require, really serves the kind of egalitarian theory that its defenders would want to support. If we want to focus consistently on the supply and demand process generated by interactions between economic agents based in different states we also have to take seriously the conditions that trigger that process in the first place: the need to fill labor market shortages in the host society the availability of excess labor force in the sending state, and the labor market sector in which different migrants tend to be employed. And we also have to consider the voluntary, spontaneous, and impersonal nature of labor exchange in a *global*, rather than simply domestic circumstances.

This brings our attention to an issue which is crucial to assessing whether guestworkers are exploited within the egalitarian theory we have

[11] See Attas, "The Case of Guest Workers: Exploitation, Citizenship and Economic Rights," p. 77.

just outlined: the link between the conditions on the basis of which guest-workers are admitted and the demand for labor and features of the labor market in the host state. Empirical analysis suggests that not all guestworker contracts are the same; not only do they vary from country to country, but they also depend significantly on the kinds of jobs that guestworkers are performing. This argument fits well with an important body of research in labor economics illustrating the effects of the structural segmentation of labor markets on the conditions of people operating in different labor environments. As many economic historians and theorists have documented, the division between "primary" and "secondary" labor markets that emerged following the transition from competitive to monopolistic capital was accompanied by a sharp differentiation in the conditions of labor for workers performing different tasks, depending on the relative stability of the labor environment. Typically, jobs involving the corporate sector where long-term planning and a stable market environment were required ended up better paid, with greater opportunities for skill refinement within the corporate structure and higher levels of promotion compared to jobs that were cyclical, seasonal, or otherwise unstable.[12] The distinction between high- and low-skilled migration with which we tend to capture the different working conditions of different categories of temporary workers fits well with this pattern. Highly skilled migrants tend to be employed in primary market sectors where the demand for labor is higher and the occupational conditions under which they are admitted are far superior to those of migrants employed in secondary markets. Here, as many authors suggest, the international market for skilled and highly skilled workers is characterized by "excess" demand for labor.[13] An increasing number of developed countries compete with each other for a relatively small pool of qualified workers, for example, specialists in management, information and communication technology, and people working in the health sector.[14] In this case economic exclusion does not always follow recruitment of temporary labor, and freedom of occupational choice may or may not be curtailed. Moreover their position compared to other domestic workers is not necessarily one of disadvantage. Whether temporary workers can be considered exploited or not depends on the kind of labor force a

[12] See on this issue Michael Reich, David M. Gordon, and Richard C. Edwards, "Dual Labor Markets: A Theory of Labor Market Segmentation," *The American Economic Review* 63:2 (May 1973), 359–65 and for a pioneering discussion of the distinction between primary and secondary markets, Peter B. Doeringer and Michael J. Piore, *Internal Labor Markets and Manpower Analysis* (Armonk, NY: M.E. Sharpe, 1985).

[13] For a discussion of the specific issues raised by the migration of highly skilled workers, see Ayelet Shachar, "Selecting by Merit: The Brave New World of Stratified Mobility," in this volume. See also Allan M. Findlay, "Skilled Transients: The Invisible Fenomenon?" in Robin Cohen (ed.), *The Cambridge Survey of World Migration* (New York: Cambridge University Press, 1995), pp. 515–22.

[14] Castles, "Guestworkers in Europe: A resurrection?," p. 749.

country is looking for and the sector in which that labor force will be placed. Temporary workers employed in the primary sector can often decide whether or not to accept the contracts offered to them. Qualified migrants can choose among a number of potential host states, and their choice of destination depends both on prospective earnings and on the future terms of employment in the receiving states.

Some examples might be useful to illustrate this point. Canada and Australia, two countries that have traditionally focused their admissions policy on the recruitment of skilled workers, provide them with rights similar to those of permanent residents. Likewise, the UK's Highly Skilled Migrant Programme offers qualified migrants the right to apply for permanent residence after only five years of residence in the UK. Ireland has also recently been involved with the introduction of a long-term residence status to attract migrants with skills in short supply. In contrast, Germany's "Green Card" program designed to attract IT workers offered a five-year work permit rather than permanent residency status, and did not succeed in obtaining similar numbers of applications compared to countries with more flexible policies.[15] States and employers seeking to hire skilled migrant workers are likely to offer them not only high wages but also comprehensive entitlements, often resulting in high-skilled migrants having more rather than less freedom of occupational choice both compared to domestic workers and to other migrants employed in more unstable sectors of the labor market.

These examples illustrate that there are no clear-cut conclusions to be drawn from an all-purpose comparison of guestworkers to domestic workers regardless of their position in the domestic and global economy. The relationship between exclusion and inclusion in the economic sphere is itself dependent upon the prior evolution of the process of supply and demand that governs the admission of guestworkers and the labor segment to which that process applies. But if this argument is correct, it is not clear how we can ground an account of temporary workers' exploitation on the issue of economic exclusion without considering the conditions of their labor, themselves dependent on the sector in which labor is employed. If a country seeks to recruit workers in a primary sector where the demand is relatively high but the supply is low, chances are that guestworkers will be admitted on very inclusive terms. If a country is facing labor shortages in a secondary work sector, employers will be enabled by structural market factors to make successful offers at rates lower than domestic ones. As with all market-based processes, the nature of this transaction is spontaneous, voluntary, and hard to criticize precisely for that reason. The process of supply and demand governing the admission of

---

[15] I owe these examples to Ruhs and Martin, "Numbers vs. Rights: Trade-Offs and Guest Worker Programs," p. 254 who also provide more references to the relevant data.

guestworkers limits the numbers of those to whom full economic inclusion can be offered and makes the charge of exploitation difficult to apply to all temporary workers and without further qualification.[16] Exclusion from the socio-economic sphere is not an intrinsic feature of all guestworker programs; neither is the exploitation of all foreign workers its unavoidable outcome.

8.5 Guestworkers and Sufficiency

One final strategy for reflecting on the exploitation of guestworkers is to think of the baseline for a transaction qualifying as fair or unfair as a sufficiency criterion. This allows us to bracket the issue of temporary labor performed by high-skilled migrants and focus on secondary market sectors where guestworkers are employed to perform jobs that are difficult, dirty, and dangerous. They lack the security and welfare guarantees that would allow them to cope with such hazardous occupational circumstances, and they are vulnerable to being taken unfair advantage of because they have nothing else remotely acceptable to opt for. According to the sufficientarian account, exploitation takes place when the following two conditions occur. Firstly, an agent is made an offer that he could not refuse, on pain of being left with not enough resources to lead a minimally decent life.[17] Secondly, the transaction is less beneficial or more costly than it would be if the agent started to bargain from a position of sufficiency (i.e., he had enough to begin with).[18]

As defenders of sufficientarian accounts often admit, establishing how much is "enough" in this case is far from trivial. There seem to be two candidate options: one which focuses on the sending state, and one which focuses on the receiving state. Since guestworkers are only employed for a specific amount of time and typically enter host states with the intention of returning home at the end of their contract, it might seem that the appropriate baseline to start with is the position of a worker in the sending state.[19] If agents have enough in their own country, they can choose whether to accept an offer of work abroad or to remain in that country. If their decision to move is constrained by not having enough to survive in the home country then it

---

[16] See for an empirical discussion of this point also Rupa Chanda, "Movement of natural persons and the GATS," *World Economy* 24:5 (2001), 631–54.

[17] "Resources" is here a generic term employed to refer to whatever unit of distribution we might prefer, i.e., primary goods, opportunities, capabilities, etc.

[18] See on this issue Mayer, "Guestworkers and exploitation," p. 321.

[19] For an influential empirical analysis that emphasizes how the decision to migrate is influenced more by the relative position of prospective migrants in their home community than by the desire to improve absolute deprivation, see Oded Stark and J. Edward Taylor, "Relative Deprivation and International Migration," *Demography* 26:1 (February 1989), 1–14, and also Oded Stark and J. Edward Taylor, "Migration Incentives, Migration Types: The Role of Relative Deprivation," *The Economic Journal* 101:408 (September 1991), 1163–78.

does not seem to constitute a genuine choice. And if one accepts an offer because he has no other choice, then we might say that someone is vulnerable to being taken advantage of in the host state. The prospective guestworker accepts an offer he could not refuse, on pain of being left with an insufficient amount of resources for himself or his family to survive.

If on the other hand, someone already has sufficient resources at their disposal in the home state, they are free to decline the offer if they do not find it acceptable. Their agreement to the terms of the contract in this case might be considered mutually beneficial. For defenders of sufficientarian accounts, the relevant counterfactual to consider is what a worker earning above the threshold of sufficiency in the labor-exporting nation would choose to do. As one author puts it, "we judge their exploitability by whether they will have enough if they do not migrate, and we judge exploitable workers to be exploited if they gain less than one with enough at home would be likely to accept."[20]

Interestingly, however, when we raise the issue of guestworkers' exploitation with a sufficientarian criterion in mind, empirical evidence leaves us with only a few relevant cases. Prospective guestworkers, studies show, do not represent the bottom social strata in sending societies and tend to negotiate from a position in which sufficiency demands are met. The lowest-earning citizens often lack the knowledge, skills, and means necessary to even take the risk of emigrating. Those that fall below the threshold of sufficiency typically rule themselves out of the prospective pool of candidates, a pool which involves citizens normally placed in the middle of the social stratification hierarchy. Unable to afford the transportation costs and risks involved in leaving everything behind, the poorest citizens of poor states are much more likely to starve at home. This also explains why, for example, in a continent like Africa, with rampant poverty and the highest concentration of absolutely poor citizens in the world, emigration rates recently have in fact declined.[21]

All this implies that those real life workers who decide to accept temporary foreign contracts negotiate from a position in which sufficientarian criteria are met. Even though they are prepared to waive some rights for a period of time in exchange for better pay, they do not act so on pain of continuing to lead a life in which their own survival is at risk. As some of the evidence from the West German guestworker program of the sixties and seventies indicates, Turkish guestworkers who moved to Germany had on average better skills, comparatively higher levels of education, and sufficient financial means

---

[20] See Mayer, "Guestworkers and exploitation," p. 322.

[21] In 1970 Africa supplied 12 percent of the world's migrant population but by 2000 that share had declined to 9 percent of the global migrant stock, see International Organization For Migration, "International Migration Trends," *World Migration 2005: Costs and Benefits of International Migration* (2005), 379–404 at p. 391.

available to be able to survive in their home states. The standard guestworker earned four times more than domestic workers before departure and six times as much as them during his stay.[22]

A similar trend appears also in some of the more recent cases of guestworker programs. Empirical studies in the female migrant population of two of the major labor-exporting nations, Mexico and the Philippines, revealed that a majority of their guestworkers were educated and, prior to leaving these countries, occupied clerical, retail, or professional positions with income rates that did not put them in a position of desperate bidding when it came to seeking jobs and accepting offers from abroad.[23] This is also why in both these countries, despite much hope that guestworker programs would provide a win–win solution helping relieve domestic unemployment in sending societies and fill labor shortages in host states, this did not turn out to be the case. Prospective guestworkers already had jobs guaranteeing that their sufficiency demands were met in their home states, and their skills were not easy to replace. Unemployment rates remained the same.[24] Those most vulnerable citizens who would have most desperately needed temporary contracts to ensure the survival of themselves and their families tended to stay where they were.

This is perhaps the most troubling feature of the relation between migration and poverty: the more extreme the conditions of deprivation, the less people tend to move. Emigration rates are lowest in the least developed countries, and the phenomenon of survival migration of the poorest is local and regional at most, rarely involving changing states.[25] Historical examples also confirm this point: in the case of the Irish potato famine taking place between 1845 and 1850 and which triggered one of the greatest migratory flows experienced in Irish history, the most deprived families tended to starve in place.[26] Typically, only those who are not absolutely deprived where they are and have sufficient means at their disposal—skills, savings, foreign contacts, or all of these in combination—can afford the risks involved in transport and the costs of settlement in a completely different environment. And whilst the conditions

---

[22] See on this issue Suzanne Paine, *Exporting Workers: the Turkish case* (London: Cambridge University Press, 1974) and also the discussion in Mayer, "Guestworkers and exploitation."

[23] See on this issue Janet Henshall Momsen, *Gender, Migration, and Domestic Service* (New York: Routledge, 1999); see also the normative discussion in Stilz, "Guestworkers and second-class citizenship."

[24] Bhimal Ghosh, "Economic effects of international migration: A synoptic overview," *World Migration 2005: Costs and Benefits of International Migration* (Darya Ganj, New Delhi: Academic, 2005), pp. 163–83.

[25] Ronald Skeldon, "Migration and poverty: Some issues in the context of Asia," *World Migration 2005: Costs and Benefits of International Migration* (Darya Ganj, New Delhi: Academic, 2005), pp. 253–68.

[26] Kerby Miller, *Emigrants and Exiles: Ireland and the Irish exodus to North America* (New York: Oxford University Press, 1985).

of such guestworkers are not optimal, their starting position does not appear as one of desperation. Their choice is not constrained by unavoidable necessity. To be sure, guestworkers are still required to make significant sacrifices, be they living away from their families, having to integrate in a new country, or getting to know a foreign labor market. But their decisions are made in the context of a number of options available, and they are not threatened with not having enough to survive.

A similar predicament has led some to conclude that unless guestworkers fail to access sufficient resources to lead a minimally decent life in their home countries, the offers they receive are not of an exploitative kind.[27] But we need to distinguish two questions here. The first is whether guestworkers are exploited. The second is whether guestworker programs are exploitative. If we keep these two questions separate, the answer to them might well end up being different. Even if not all guestworkers are exploited, some workers will be. And even if not all workers are exploited distributively, as individuals, they may still be exploited collectively, as members of the working class.

8.6 Taking Workers as a Class

To explore the possibility of class exploitation as a result of guestworker programs, we need to reflect on their impact on workers' wages in labor-importing nations. A number of empirical studies suggest that guestworkers agree to exchange their labor for wages and employment conditions that are normally higher than those prevailing in their countries of origin but, as we saw earlier, small by the standards of host countries. Employers themselves often acknowledge that the kinds of wages and employment conditions offered to guestworkers are often too low to be considered acceptable by most local workers.[28] Hence, even if we abstract from the fact that guestworkers agree to exchange their labor for wages that improve their relative position in the country of origin, the effect of these contracts on offers received by domestic workers represents a concerning trend. Even if we concede that guestworkers make their decisions in a context of choice sufficient to undermine the view that offers made to them are of an exploitative kind, the same cannot be said for domestic workers. The context of choice for them ends up being significantly restricted as a result. Unless we take sufficiency thresholds to overlap perfectly, what is enough in one context may not be

[27] For this conclusion, see Mayer, "Guestworkers and exploitation" and Stilz, "Guestworkers and second-class citizenship."
[28] Martin Ruhs and Bridget Anderson, *Who Needs Migrant Workers?: Labour shortages, immigration, and public policy* (Oxford: Oxford University Press, 2010).

enough in another. After the admission of guestworkers, domestic workers have to choose between wage offers significantly lower compared to what they might have previously considered enough.[29] Even more worrying is that their acceptance of such offers could mark the beginning of a nasty trend towards leveling down. The relative inequality in the position from which guestworkers negotiate their contracts means that they are unable to hold out for higher wages.

It is of course unjust that guestworkers have to face such constraints even though, as I argued above, the kind of injustice they suffer is not one of direct exploitation. But something additional is concerning us here. Foreign workers take up temporary work only temporarily. That is to say, the reference group with which they tend to compare themselves remains that of their source communities, since the intention is to leave after a period of time.[30] It is therefore understandable that guestworkers apply the standards of their host community to the state they visit, accepting conditions of life and work (whether in housing, healthcare, or labor standards) that to domestic workers would seem unacceptable. But if guestworkers are prepared to work for much lower rates of pay, corresponding to standards that they derive from home societies, their wages will drive down the equilibrium wages of everyone employed in secondary labor markets. This means that the standards of sufficiency in host states will end up being lower, putting at a bargaining disadvantage all workers who will continue to live in such host states (whether native born or resident migrants) provided they continue to seek employment in similar segments of the labor market.

Does this mean that domestic workers are exploited? I suggest that it does. To see this point we need to apply the same analysis of exploitation through which we assessed the case of guestworkers to workers in receiving societies. We emphasized earlier that a person is vulnerable to being exploited if he is made an offer which he could not reject, on pain of being left with not enough. In the case of guestworkers, the relevant counterfactual with reference to which to assess the threshold of sufficiency was their position in home states. If they reject the offer of employment in a new state and are still left with a sufficient amount in their home country, then they have some margin of choice and therefore cannot be considered exploited. But what should be the counterfactual situation with reference to which to assess thresholds of sufficiency in the case of domestic workers?

---

[29] For an empirical analysis of the competition between foreign workers and domestic workers employed in secondary labor markets, see George J. Borjas, *Heaven's Door: Immigration Policy and the American Economy* (Princeton, NJ: Princeton University Press, 2001).

[30] See on this issue Stark and Taylor, "Relative Deprivation and International Migration."

There seem to be two options here, one which includes guestworkers in that assessment and one which ignores them. The first one implies that the threshold should be the same for both temporary and domestic workers. If a guestworker accepts the offer given the sufficiency constraints mentioned above, then a domestic worker should accept it too. But as we saw, the main consideration in the case of guestworkers is based on their position prior to entering the host state and the threshold of what is considered enough applies to how they fare before they make a decision to migrate. Yet it would be unfair to hold domestic workers to the same standard. Sufficiency thresholds vary from country to country, and what is enough in one context may not be enough in another.[31]

To see the point, consider the following example. Compare the position of two students who attend German language courses at the same school but at two different levels: a basic level and an intermediate level. At the end of the year there is an exam and the pass mark for progressing to the next level is the same for both students, say 55. Even though the mark is the same, the level of competency in German required by students attending these different classes is completely different. One has to show that he can construct simple sentences, be able to ask for directions in the street, orient himself with a restaurant menu, and so on. The other has to be able to understand a more complex television program, show that she is able to grasp the main ideas being discussed, and articulate an opinion in however simple terms. Clearly what is considered "enough" knowledge of German in these two groups is likely to display a great deal of difference. And it would be absurd, as well as unfair, to expect the student from the basic level class to obtain a pass at the end of an exam which has been designed to test the knowledge of members in the intermediate course.

A similar argument could be made with respect to the situation of domestic and guestworkers. Life in different countries means that expectations of what might be considered sufficient in each of them are likely to differ significantly. A wage that might contribute to significant savings in one state could barely sustain a family in a different market environment. It would therefore be as absurd to conclude that wages that are acceptable to a Philippine worker because they are more than sufficient to conduct a minimally decent life in say, Manila, are also sufficient to survive living permanently in London. The counterfactual circumstances should be constructed in a different way.

A more plausible alternative might therefore be to assess the sufficiency threshold of domestic workers whilst abstracting from the impact of guestworkers in host societies. In this case, the relevant counterfactual evidence

---

[31] For a longer discussion of the relation between absolute and relative deprivation, see Lea Ypi, *Global Justice and Avant-Garde Political Agency* (Oxford: Oxford University Press, 2012), ch. 5.

might require comparison with the typical wages of similarly placed domestic employees prior to the admission of guestworkers. All other things being equal, we could then define an offer as exploitative if a domestic worker accepts a job which is paid less than it would have been before guestworkers entered the job market. A domestic worker is subjected to unfair treatment if he has to negotiate his wage from a position with fewer resources than a worker with equal skills and ability, and performing the same job, would have received prior to the admission of guestworkers. An offer could then be considered exploitative if the agent who makes the offer benefits from it, and if the agent to whom the offer is made loses more or benefits less than he might have done in those counterfactual circumstances. As in the case of guestworkers, we judge an offer to be exploitative by whether the agent will be left with enough if he does not take the job. But in contrast to how we proceeded in the guestworkers case, in the case of the domestic worker we establish the sufficiency threshold by looking at what the domestic worker would have earned prior to the admission of guestworkers (all other things being equal). If we see that domestic workers earn less, we can say that they are exploited.

We can conclude from this discussion that guestworker programs may be exploitative even if they don't actually exploit all guestworkers, as such. What makes guestworker programs exploitative is that they contribute to a global competition for labor driven by the desperation bidding of those who have only their labor to sell. They help employers and firms increase profits at the expense of adverse effects on local wages and by leveling down. Guestworker programs pit workers off against each other, ensuring that what expands options for some workers at the same time increases constraints for others. In the end, even if workers are not exploited distributively, as citizens of different states, they may be exploited collectively, as members of the working class.

8.7 On Workers and Guests: Some Objections

One objection to the argument we have just tried to advance might be that it relies on the existence of a competitive dynamic between foreign and domestic workers, which in reality might be absent. If we bracket skilled migration, guestworkers, one often hears, are admitted to fill labor shortages for jobs that local workers typically don't want, such as catering, agricultural labor, the building sectors, cleaning services, or caring for the sick and the elderly. Since there are not enough domestic workers interested in taking up employment in either of these occupational spheres, so the argument goes, the issue of their exploitation does not arise at all. If there simply aren't enough local workers earning similar wages to compare with guestworkers, the idea that guestworker programs might contribute to leveling down could safely be put to one side.

The standard answer to this objection is that since labor demand is socially caused, the poor wages, degrading work conditions, and lower social status typically associated with jobs performed by guestworkers are precisely what makes locals distance themselves from such jobs. If the conditions and status associated with them were substantially improved, local workers would be more willing to take offers of employment in similar sectors.[32] This would in turn also contribute to sending marginal employers out of business, to increase investment in labor-saving technologies, and to benefit producers (especially agricultural producers) in developing countries who would no longer compete with large companies deploying cheap labor.[33]

Although this answer is plausible, it does not really confront the objection we are examining. That objection insists that where competition between domestic and foreign workers is absent, we have no reason to be concerned with what happens to local standards of sufficiency. In this sense, reflecting on what might occur in the future, if and when wages rise, is irrelevant to address a challenge that only applies to present circumstances. A better strategy for answering this objection might be therefore to confront head-on the evidence upon which it is grounded: the claim that domestic workers and foreigners do not compete with each other for the same dirty, dangerous, and difficult jobs. To criticize that assumption, we might appeal to examples from two paradigmatic guestworker cases with which the empirical literature is often concerned: the Bracero program in the United States and the employment of guestworkers in Germany. Both provide important insights into the relationship between domestic and temporary laborers in low-skilled work sectors. And both are helpful to reveal the upsetting effect of differential contracts on unionized workers and the sufficiency standards on the basis of which they negotiate.

In the case of the Bracero program, the costs to domestic labor of hiring cheap Mexican labor to work in the Californian agricultural sector became increasingly clear after 1964, when the program officially came to an end. Although unions had always voiced concerns about the effects of importing foreign labor on local earnings, the extent to which the Bracero program had depressed wages was evident from the unprecedented rise in agricultural workers' wages that was experienced between 1964 and 1980 (when illegal

---

[32] See on this Carens, "Live-in Domestics, Seasonal Workers, and Others Hard to Locate on the Map of Democracy" and Castles, "Guestworkers in Europe: A resurrection?."

[33] See on this issue Castles, "Guestworkers in Europe: A resurrection?," p. 761.

immigration became a new threat).[34] To mention but one prominent example, in the San Joaquin Valley of California, near Delano, Cesar Chavez and his United Farm Workers Union conducted an extremely effective campaign against local table grape growers culminating in a 40 percent increase, bringing wages from $1.25 to $1.75 an hour. In the days when Bracero workers were available to break the grape-pickers' strike, this would not have been possible.[35]

The difficult relationship between temporary foreign workers and local labor unions is also illustrated in a number of studies involving laborers employed in Germany in the years following the country's reunification. A study of the Berlin building industry showed that even though 25 percent of unemployed people in Berlin had been construction workers by 1996, employers preferred to hire foreign contract workers to maximize profit. This competition had adverse effects especially on unionized building workers, many of whom were long-term foreign residents.[36] In contrast to the model of long-term employment, where the workplace and the trade union were sites of inter-ethnic communication and integration, domestic and guestworkers were now competing against each other.[37] Similar outcomes could be observed also in other contexts. As recent studies of the American job market have indicated, the wages of workers without high school education have declined as a result of low-skilled immigrant pressure, and those most affected are resident immigrants in low-wage jobs and less-educated American workers, including the unemployed.[38]

It is therefore hard to maintain that because guestworkers and domestic workers are not interested in the same jobs, the latter are not vulnerable to exploitation. However, one could still object at this point that our argument focuses too much on the short-term negative impact of guestworker programs without considering their long-term positive effects. These typically include contributing to economic growth in host states, helping sending societies through remittances and other forms of support, and providing guestworkers with chances to increase their earnings and gain skills and experiences through work in a different state. Notice, however, that all these allegedly positive features rely on the long-term promise of economic growth. Yet growth and exploitation are perfectly compatible with each other. Even if one takes the long-term view some economists might prefer us to take, there

---

[34] Philip Martin, "Mexican Workers and U.S. Agriculture: The Revolving Door," *International Migration Review* 36:4 (2002), 1124–42.

[35] Philip Martin and Michael Teitelbaum, "The Mirage of Mexican Guest Workers," *Foreign Affairs* 80:6 (2001), 117–31 at p. 124.

[36] Castles, "Guestworkers in Europe: A resurrection?," p. 751.

[37] Castles, "Guestworkers in Europe: A resurrection?," p. 751.

[38] Ghosh, "Economic effects of international migration: A synoptic overview," p. 169.

are no guarantees that a fair distribution of the extra wealth generated by migration will follow economic growth. Absent that distributional perspective, what is the guarantee that those at the very bottom of the social hierarchy will not continue to be exposed to exploitation? If improved opportunities for some come at the price of others being deprived of the same, indeed can develop precisely on that assumption (recall that short-term sacrifices are required for long-term gains) even if some individual workers might benefit, the structural conditions of collective exploitation will likely remain the same.

8.8 Conclusion

Guestworker programs pose many dilemmas. Conspicuous among those is the issue of whether guestworkers are exploited. A cursory look at the daily newspapers indicates that they are treated dismally: guestworkers work long hours, carry out difficult jobs, and receive very little recognition (both financial and social) for the services they perform.[39] Yet, when we turn to the issue from a normative perspective we seem to have trouble capturing what is the moral standard with regard to which we consider guestworkers to be taken unfair advantage of. If we rely on a domination theory of exploitation, lack of access to the benefits of citizenship does not seem sufficient to distinguish between collective political entitlements one should always have access to and others that it is acceptable to waive, at least for a time. If we rely on an egalitarian theory, we neglect how global processes of supply and demand might respond differently to different skills under offer, changing the equilibrium price for labor, and making exploitative practices often very hard to identify. If we rely on a sufficientarian theory we hit against considerable empirical evidence suggesting that guestworkers negotiate their employment offers from positions above the threshold of sufficiency, and that it is either those who stay at home or those who are affected in host societies who are normally left with not enough.

All this is not to say that guestworkers are never exploited. The point is that even if we have trouble capturing precisely in what way they are exploited, even if not all guestworkers, not everywhere, and not all the time are exploited, guestworker programs can still be considered structurally exploitative. They may not always exploit individual guestworkers as such but they take unfair

[39] For a very recent report of the conditions in which guestworkers are employed all over the European Union, see an article just appeared in the Belgium daily newspaper *Le Soir*, entitled: "Les nouveaux esclaves sont parmi nous" (The new Slaves are among us), <http://archives.lesoir.be/les-nouveaux-esclaves-sont-parmi-nous-20-euros_t-20111018-01MG25.html?query=traite+des+%EAtres&firstHit=0&by=10&sort=datedesc&when=-1&queryor=traite+des+%EAtres&pos=1&all=37299&nav=1>.

advantage of the position of workers in both sending and receiving societies. Even if each individual guestworker has enough employment choice to rule out that they can be taken unfair advantage of, this is only possible on condition that others don't exercise the same choice.

The case of guestworkers therefore provides a good empirical lens through which to examine a problem that has long been discussed in political theory: the issue of proletarian unfreedom.[40] As many authors have shown, what makes the proletariat unfree as a collective is the fact that the freedom of each individual worker is contingent upon others not exercising their similarly contingent freedom. The structural conditions under which workers are forced to sell their labor are such that the offers one agent is individually free to pursue necessarily restrict the space for others taking advantage of similar options. Therefore, even if each worker is individually free to exit their collective exploitative condition, he suffers with others in circumstances that have often also been defined as circumstances of "collective unfreedom."[41]

The implications of this point are important for the kind of normative framework in which we choose to place the issue of guestworkers. So far, the question has been raised in the context of theories reflecting on the issue of justice in migration, that is, the distribution of benefits and burdens between migrants (in this case guestworkers), citizens of sending societies, and citizens of receiving societies. But if the problem with guestworker programs is not so much the condition of individual guestworkers but the way in which such programs narrow the options of workers in general, the fact that workers happen to be separated by boundaries and that they belong to different states is a matter of secondary importance. Taking seriously the distinction between domestic and foreign workers and asking members of one group to make sacrifices for the sake of members in the other is unlikely to be a very productive route for ending the exploitation of workers as a collective. The questions we should be asking instead are those that focus on the status of workers in general, the circumstances in which they are forced to accept certain wages, the sort of incentives that reward employers and firms seeking to hire cheap labor, and the institutional arrangements that govern the trade of labor and the accumulation of capital in the global market. Even if guestworker programs don't exploit each individual guestworker, they operate in a global institutional structure that exploits workers as members of a collective: the collective composed by all those who sell their labor for a living or, to put it in

---

[40] G.A. Cohen, "The Structure of Proletarian Unfreedom," *Philosophy & Public Affairs* 12:1 (1983), 3–33.
[41] Cohen, "The Structure of Proletarian Unfreedom," p. 11.

more familiar terms, the collective we refer to with the term "working class." To reflect on the remedial principles required to end their exploitation is to engage with a radically different way of thinking about the production and distribution of labor and with a different ideal of how global markets ought to operate.[42]

References

Agunias, Dovelyn and Kathleen Newland, "Circular Migration and Development: Trends, Policy, Routes, and Ways Forward," <http://www.migrationpolicy.org/re search/circular-migration-and-development-trends-policy-routes-and-ways-forward>, accessed July 16, 2015.

Attas, Daniel, "The Case of Guest Workers: Exploitation, Citizenship and Economic Rights," *Res Publica* 6:1 (2000), 73–92.

Bell, Daniel, "Equal Rights For Foreign Resident Workers?," *Dissent* 48:4 (2001), 26–34.

Borjas, George J., *Heaven's Door: Immigration Policy and the American Economy* (Princeton, NJ: Princeton University Press, 2001).

Carens, Joseph H., "Live-in Domestics, Seasonal Workers, and Others Hard to Locate on the Map of Democracy," *Journal of Political Philosophy* 16:4 (2008), 419–45.

Castles, Stephen, "Guestworkers in Europe: A Resurrection?," *International Migration Review* 40:4 (2006), 741–66.

Castles, Stephen and Godula Kosack, *Immigrant Workers and Class Structure in Western Europe* (Oxford: Oxford University Press, 1985).

Chanda, Rupa, "Movement of Natural Persons and the GATS," *World Economy* 24:5 (2001), 631–54.

Chang, Howard F., "Liberal Ideals and Political Feasibility: Guest-Worker Programs as Second-Best Policies," *North Carolina Journal of International Law and Commercial Regulation* 27:3 (2002), 465–81.

Cohen, G. A., "The Structure of Proletarian Unfreedom," *Philosophy & Public Affairs* 12:1 (1983), 3–33.

Doeringer, Peter B. and Michael J. Piore, *Internal Labor Markets and Manpower Analysis* (Armonk, NY: M.E. Sharpe, 1985).

Findlay, Allan M., "Skilled Transients: The Invisible Fenomenon?" in Robin Cohen (ed.), *The Cambridge Survey of World Migration* (New York: Cambridge University Press, 1995), pp. 515–22.

Ghosh, Bhimal, "Economic Effects of International Migration: A Synoptic Overview," *World Migration 2005: Costs and Benefits of International Migration* (Darya Ganj, New Delhi: Academic, 2005), pp. 163–83.

Hahamovitch, Cindy, "Creating Perfect Immigrants: Guestworkers of the World in Historical Perspective 1," *Labor History* 44:1 (2003), 69–94.

[42] I am grateful to Sarah Fine, Bob Goodin, Patti Lenard, and the anonymous reviewers of Oxford University Press for very helpful written comments on a previous version of this chapter.

Hollifield, James, *Immigrants, Markets, and States: The Political Economy of Postwar Europe* (Cambridge, MA: Harvard University Press, 1992).

International Organization for Migration, "International Migration Trends," *World Migration 2005: Costs and Benefits of International Migration* (2005), 379–404.

Lenard, Patti Tamara and Christine Straehle, "Temporary Labour Migration, Global Redistribution and Democratic Justice," *Politics, Philosophy & Economics* 11:2 (2012), 206–30.

Mayer, Robert, "Guestworkers and exploitation," *Review of Politics* 67:2 (2005), 311–34.

Miller, Kerby, *Emigrants and Exiles: Ireland and the Irish Exodus to North America* (New York: Oxford University Press, 1985).

Momsen, Janet Henshall, *Gender, Migration, and Domestic Service* (New York: Routledge, 1999).

Ottonelli, Valeria and Tiziana Torresi, "Inclusivist Egalitarian Liberalism and Temporary Migration: A Dilemma," *Journal of Political Philosophy* 20:2 (2010), 202–24.

Paine, Suzanne, *Exporting Workers: The Turkish Case* (London: Cambridge University Press, 1974).

Reich, Michael, David M. Gordon, and Richard C. Edwards, "Dual Labor Markets: A Theory of Labor Market Segmentation," *The American Economic Review* 63:2 (1973), 359–65.

Ruhs, Martin and Bridget Anderson, *Who Needs Migrant Workers? Labour Shortages, Immigration, And Public Policy* (Oxford: Oxford University Press, 2010).

Ruhs, Martin and Philip Martin, "Numbers vs. Rights: Trade-Offs and Guest Worker Programs," *International Migration Review* 42:1 (2008), 249–65.

Salazar Parrenas, Rachel, *Servants of Globalization: Women, Migration and Domestic Work* (Stanford, CA: Stanford University Press, 2001).

Shayerah, Ilias, Katherine Fennelly, and Christopher M. Federico, "American Attitudes toward Guest Worker Policies," *International Migration Review* 42:4 (2008), 741–66.

Skeldon, Ronald, "Migration and Poverty: Some Issues in the Context of Asia," *World Migration 2005: Costs and Benefits of International Migration* (Darya Ganj, New Delhi: Academic, 2005), pp. 253–68.

Stark, Oded and J. Edward Taylor, "Relative Deprivation and International Migration," *Demography* 26:1 (February 1989), 1–14.

Stark, Oded and J. Edward Taylor, "Migration Incentives, Migration Types: The Role of Relative Deprivation," *The Economic Journal* 101:408 (September 1991), 1163–78.

Stilz, Anna, "Guestworkers and Second Class Citizenship," *Policy and Society* 29:4 (2010), 295–307.

Walzer, Michael, *Spheres of Justice: a Defence of Pluralism and Equality* (Oxford: Robertson, 1983).

Wertheimer, Alan and Matt Zwolinski, "Exploitation" in Edward N. Zalta (ed.), *The Stanford Encyclopedia of Philosophy* (Spring 2013 Edition), <http://plato.stanford.edu/archives/spr2013/entries/exploitation/>.

Ypi, Lea, *Global Justice and Avant-Garde Political Agency* (Oxford: Oxford University Press, 2012).

9

Selecting By Merit

The Brave New World of Stratified Mobility

Ayelet Shachar

Immigration is often referred to as the "last bastion of sovereignty" in the rising tides of globalization. Accordingly, much of the scholarship on immigration is still country-specific and gives significant weight to domestic-centered factors in shaping a country's immigration law and policy. This chapter takes a different approach. While acknowledging these classic considerations of identity and belonging, it conducts an inquiry into the skill-based selection criteria adopted by immigrant-receiving countries, and in doing so reveals a surprising picture: states are *interacting* with one another in increasingly complex ways, not only to reinvent migration control policies, but also to reconfigure their membership boundaries.[1] Such interaction may take a restrictivist and enforcement-oriented direction, as in the creation of Frontex as a supranational agency operating on behalf of European Union member states to control and police the external perimeter of Europe. Or, instead of anything resembling the cartelization of international immigrant flows, it may generate an increasingly vigorous competition among states, each seeking to recruit and attract to its respective jurisdiction the world's best and brightest.[2] In recent years, this global race for talent has gained tremendous

[1] Looking at migration as a process shaped by states, within a broad cross-national perspective, fits in the tradition bequeathed by international migration scholars such as the late Aristide Zolberg. See Aristide Zolberg, "Matters of State: Theorizing Immigration Policy" in Charles Hirschman, Philip Kasinitz, and Josh DeWind (eds.), *The Handbook of International Migration* (New York: Russell Sage, 2000), pp. 71–93.

[2] My focus throughout this discussion is on international labor-market migration, rather than family-based migration or the humanitarian obligations of states to refugees, asylum seekers, trafficked persons, undocumented migrants, or other vulnerable persons. Within the broad range of international labor-market migration streams, highly skilled migration programs fall squarely

momentum, but the significance of the new reality it represents—the opportunities it creates and the risks it poses—remains largely unnoticed and under-theorized in the literature. This chapter begins to fill the gap.

Across the globe, countries are vying to outbid one another to attract highly skilled migrants with extraordinary talent. In this dynamic and competitive environment, immigration policymakers (operating primarily but not exclusively at the national level) constantly learn from, or simply "borrow" and refine, the innovations of their counterparts. This represents an *uncoordinated* response by nations to the perception that, in the knowledge-based global economy, "the resource that is in greatest scarcity is human capital." Indeed, countries are willing to go as far as to invest membership in exceptionally talented individuals—in the arts, sciences, sports, technology, innovation, and the like—in order to gain or sustain a comparative advantage. Pressure is mounting in this competitive scramble, as no country wants to be left behind.[3] Each wants to reap the expected benefits—economic, cultural, and reputational—associated with the infusion of immigrants with abundant human capital to their respective jurisdictions. Call this the new paradigm of *selecting by merit*, in contrast with the traditional pattern that Christian Joppke has provactivally termed *selecting by origin*.[4]

This transformation—"from origin to merit" (to paraphrase Henry Maine's catchphrase "from status to contract")—is vitally significant, as it touches upon some of the most foundational and sensitive issues that any society must address: how to define who belongs, or ought to belong, within its circle of members. The global race for talent, which reflects the zenith of the logic of selecting by merit, opens up the otherwise heavily bolted gates of admission to those who have acquired the specialized skills and human capital now valued by states operating in a more competitive and global knowledge-based economy. Many of those who benefit from the shift to selecting-by-merit hail from the global south, and, as such, would likely have been categorically barred from access to membership under the old regime of selecting-by-origin, which officially subscribed to racially discriminatory immigration laws until as late as the mid-1960s.[5] At the same time, the rise of managed migration regimes as

---

into the category of "discretionary immigration." See Michael Blake, "Discretionary Immigration," *Philosophical Topics* 30:2 (2002), 273–89.

[3] Ben Wildavsky, *The Great Brain Race: How Global Universities Are Reshaping the World* (Princeton, NJ: Princeton University Press, 2010).

[4] Triadafilos Triadafilopoulos and Craig D. Smith, "Introduction," in Triadafilos Triadafilopoulos (ed.), *Wanted and Welcome: Policies for Highly Skilled Immigrants in Comparative Perspective* (New York: Springer, 2013), pp. 1–12. See also Christian Joppke, *Selecting by Origin: Ethnic Migration in the Liberal State* (Cambridge, MA: Harvard University Press, 2005).

[5] The long history of anti-Asian immigration and naturalization laws in the United States—the birthplace of today's global race for talent—is well documented. For a concise overview, see Gabriel J. Chin, "The Civil Rights Revolution Comes to Immigration Law: A New Look at the Immigration and Nationality Act of 1965," *North Carolina Law Review* 75 (1996), 273–345.

part of today's global race for talent also entrenches new inequalities and stratifications. These tensions and contradictions inform and motivate my analysis here.

This chapter focuses on the highly skilled, exploring the centrality of state action in facilitating the competitive scramble to lure "those with brains, skills, and talent," before turning to address the core legal and ethical conundrums associated with these dramatic yet under-theorized developments.[6] The details vary, but even countries that have experienced a backlash against multiculturalism tend to grant privileged access to those who possess remarkable prowess and a proven track record of success in their fields of expertise.[7] The effects of this process of "picking winners" become particularly evident when we focus on those at the top echelons of the talent pyramid—virtuoso artists, brilliant scientists, elite athletes—who possess precisely the kind of "added value" that competitive states covet most.[8] The willingness of governments—our public trustees of citizenship—to grant membership goods as part of the transaction to lure the "top crop" among the best

---

[6] Darrel M. West, *Brain Gain: Rethinking U.S. Immigration Policy* (Washington, DC: Brookings Institute, 2010), p. 131.

[7] Interestingly, related reconfigurations are simultaneously occurring in emigrant-sending countries themselves. Whereas in the past, skilled emigrants were regarded as lost causes who had "exited" their home national community, the new era of competitive immigration regimes has changed countries' attitudes towards their own emigrants. These individuals are now treated as long-lost sons and daughters who have made a sacrifice by working and living abroad. Emigration countries are adopting more flexible approaches to dual citizenship and designing various rules that allow successful emigrants to maintain their membership ties with their home nation, thus engaging in the same game of trying to reap the benefits of highly skilled migration. Their position represents a mirror image of the talent-for-citizenship exchange in the receiving state: the sending country is offering the emigrant (who, despite leaving the home community, may still feel attached to it) what we might call a "preservation of membership" entitlement. The emigration state now enthusiastically uses its control over the definition of political membership in the home country as a tool to maintain and strengthen ties with those who have settled abroad. See Kim Barry, "Home and Away: The Construction of Citizenship in an Emigration Context," *New York Law Review* 81 (2006), 11–59. How this is achieved varies among countries, but it may involve reforms to dual-citizenship rules, investment laws, and even the granting of voting rights to emigrants who permanently reside abroad. This raises complex and still unresolved puzzles about the relationship between powerful and successful citizens abroad and their countrymen and women who reside in the country of origin. Some perceive these recent developments as overdue and redemptive, giving due credit and respect to the efforts undertaken by those who have left, while at the same time encouraging them to continue to contribute handsomely to the home country. For others, they represent a vexing illustration of how asymmetry is formalized between those residing outside the country, who get to enjoy rights to political participation across borders, and those who stay, who must contend with the brunt of the corresponding political duties—potentially eroding the ideal of democratic equality and control. I thank Sarah Fine and Lea Ypi for their insights on this point.

[8] For further discussion, see Ayelet Shachar, "Picking Winners: Olympic Citizenship and the Global Race for Talent," *Yale Law Journal* 120:8 (2011), 2088–139; Ayelet Shachar and Ran Hirschl, "Recruiting 'Super Talent': The New World of Selective Migration Regimes," *Indiana Journal of Global Legal Studies* 20:1 (2013), 71–107.

and brightest here becomes a metric for signaling the perceived value of the recruited knowledge migrant to the recruiting country.[9]

The discussion is divided into two main parts. The first is devoted to identifying the core legal mechanisms and major turning points that have shaped the global race for talent from the perspective of immigrant-recruiting nations. I will also briefly examine related developments in emigrant-sending countries. In shedding light on the surge in skills-centered selective migration regimes, I explore why policymakers are eagerly intervening in the "global market" for the highly skilled, and discuss how interjurisdictional competition raises the stakes for the countries involved. This permits theorizing about the core elements of the nascent paradigm of selecting-by-merit while taking into account the crucial role of human-capital valuation in shaping and molding selective migration priorities and the discursive casting of the highly skilled as the new breed of "desired" migrants. This is a shift that is associated with deeper transformations in the conception of citizenship that place on a pedestal those who actively contribute and successfully integrate into the membership community.

In the second part of the discussion, I explore the main conceptual and ethical puzzles associated with the global race for talent, and reflect on the potential implications of these fast-paced developments on the very future of citizenship in the twenty-first century. More specifically, I will explore two kinds of arguments: an argument grounded in fairness (which analytically can be subcategorized as: (1) fairness to other streams of migrants, (2) fairness to those who stay in the country of origin, and (3) fairness to those who already reside in the receiving society); and an argument based on a concern with the erosion of the ideal of citizenship as a political relation grounded in equality rather than competition.

9.1 The Paradigm Shift: Selecting by Merit, not Origin

Immigration today is among the most controversial and high-profile topics in the public domain. It touches on foundational questions about how we live together as members of a shared political community and where we draw the lines of inclusion and exclusion. These issues are fraught with disagreement and open to legal and ethical contestation. Recent years have witnessed a renaissance of sorts in the field of citizenship and migration studies. Contemporary scholars approach the topic from a variety of disciplinary perspectives,

---

[9] This can be seen as a new twist on the classic Lockean labor theory, where manual or agricultural labor is replaced with sophisticated knowledge economy equivalents, and applied to the acquisition of membership status in the state rather than of property in cultivated land.

from political philosophers to neoclassical economists, to critical geographers studying the spatial dimensions and inequalities manifested in patterns of mobility across borders. These perspectives reveal a largely bifurcated international migration order: movement and membership are becoming more readily available for some while increasingly sliding out of reach for the majority of "standard" would-be immigrants, who face more and more hurdles to lawfully entering the once-promised lands of migration.[10]

This tension between restrictive closure (for the many) and selective openness (for the few) provides the context for my inquiry into the rise of the global race for talent and the interjurisdictional zeal involved in finding the most sophisticated methods for identifying, selecting, and luring the so-called best and brightest (a term of art regularly used by policymakers worldwide). This is a new phase in the checkered history of migration. As Aristide Zolberg famously documented, even countries like the United States that purport to be open to anyone who wishes to come have in fact long treated immigration as part of a social-engineered narrative of nation-building.[11] In today's global knowledge economy, what is desired are those who can shore up the human capital reserve of the nation. This makes the study of competitive immigration regimes for the highly skilled ever more vital and fascinating. We can investigate the question of why this paradigm shift toward managed and selective migration—with the global race for talent at its apex—has occurred, and why it has occurred now, from several perspectives.

The political economist would begin the inquiry by highlighting that, unlike other factors going into innovation and production, talent is distinctive: it is encapsulated in individuals. As such, it cannot be codified, duplicated, sold, or easily transferred from one person to another. In other words, it is the *human* in "human capital" that makes it a unique and irreplaceable factor of production and a quality-of-life multiplier in the new knowledge economy. Faced with more opportunities, and with a longer list of destination countries wooing and enticing them, it is only rational for skilled migrants with abundant human capital—people with aspirations and proven adaptability to new

---

[10] Catherine Dauvergne, *Making People Illegal: What Globalization Means for Migration and Law* (Cambridge: Cambridge University Press, 2008); Christian Joppke, "Comparative Citizenship? A Restrictive Turn in Europe," *Law and Ethics of Human Rights* 2:1 (2008), 1–41; Valsamis Mitsilega, "Immigration Control in an Era of Globalization: Deflecting Foreigners, Weakening Citizens, Strengthening the State," *Indiana Journal of Global Legal Studies* 19:1 (2012), 3–60; Ayelet Shachar, "Citizenship" in Michel Rosenfeld and András Sajó (eds.), *Oxford Handbook of Comparative Constitutional Law* (Oxford: Oxford University Press, 2012), pp. 1002–19.

[11] Aristide R. Zolberg, *A Nation by Design: Immigration Policy in the Fashioning of America* (Cambridge, MA: Harvard University Press, 2006). Zolberg's analysis focuses on domestic factors, where certain social and economic interest groups manifest preferences for, and seek to influence the design of admission policies that favor, certain kinds of migrants over others, whereas I focus on the interjurisdictional dimension and how the global competition among states affects the design of their respective selecting-by-merit admission and settlement programs.

challenges—to redirect their patterns of international movement in response to competitive governmental offers.

The social historian would add that people with extraordinary talent have always enjoyed greater mobility across borders, while emphasizing that the specific set of desired skills and occupations has changed "according to the time period, location, and nature of the technologies in use."[12] In nineteenth-century America, artisans and craft workers were seen as highly skilled, whereas today the highly skilled are the sharpest minds, the keenest entrepreneurs, the prodigious innovators. But, not only has the *definition* of talent and valued skills changed, so has the *scale* and *intensity* of the competition, which now involves more countries and regions as well as ever-increasing stakes. As the International Migration Outlook summarily stated, the "competition for talent [now] goes well beyond the OECD area."[13]

The empiricist would observe that, contrary to the predictions of postnationalists, countries have not "lost control" over their membership boundaries, but instead have significantly changed how control is manifested.[14] States and their governments, operating alone or in concert, have been hard at work to (re)assert their authority over determining whom to admit, whom to turn back, and whom to keep at bay. Legal strategies to recruit the highly skilled play a vital role in this larger process of redesigning membership categories and regaining control over borders, turning such ideational shifts into actionable plans. By continually "retooling and recalibrating" selective skills-based admission avenues to attract the best and brightest, governments engaged in the global race for talent have demonstrated their willingness and their ability to intervene in the market for the highly skilled.[15] Adding to this is that leading countries are increasingly learning from and emulating one another in the international competition for highly skilled immigrants. In this selective and stratified mobility market, membership goods—including fast-tracked access to permanent residence and the granting of citizenship as the ultimate prize—are turned into "incentive packages" tailored by governments to attract the new brand of desired migrants. We typically think of citizenship and immigration as an identity-laden and domestically centered policy arena, steeped in questions of membership and belonging. Alas, no state is an island, and the legal measures adopted by *other* countries can lead to interdependent

---

[12] Joseph P. Ferrie, "A Historical Perspective on Highly-Skilled Immigrants to the United States, 1820–1920" in Barry R. Chiswick (ed.), *High-Skilled Immigration in a Global Labor Market* (Washington, DC: The AEI Press, 2010), pp. 15–49.

[13] SOPEMI, International Migration Outlook 2011, 1.

[14] Scholars of migration studies and international relations sharply disagree on whether the nation-state is in decline, or whether it has enough resources to reinvent itself in the current era of globalization.

[15] A concrete example of this broader pattern is found in the increased recruitment of international students by competitors in the global race for talent.

causality whereby, in developing their own strategies, countries factor in the already-tested policies or projected responses of their major competitors in the global race for talent. Policymakers who specialize in targeted migration regimes for the highly skilled routinely engage in transnational "borrowing"—or simply "importing"—of the innovations of their counterparts.[16]

This pattern can be best demonstrated with the example of the point-system rubric, a prevalent mechanism for selecting-by-merit, which originated in Canada and has since spread to the four corners of the world. Under the point system, applicants are assigned a cumulative numeric value determined by assessing a set of predefined factors, such as the applicant's highest educational degree, professional experience, linguistic proficiency, and adaptability. The origins of the point system are rooted in the late 1960s policy overhaul that repealed the old system of selecting-by-origin by introducing new skills-based criteria designed to select immigrants on the basis of their professional and educational achievements as well as potential ability to contribute to the country's economy and labor markets. In sharp contrast with the previous system that distinguished among potential entrants on the basis of national origins, under the point system "applicants' ethnic and racial backgrounds were no longer to be considered in determining their eligibility for admission to Canada."[17] In a classic example of interjurisdictional emulation, the point system was later adopted in Australia as part of that country's formal abolishment of its infamous "White Australia" policy.[18] It has since been "copied and pasted" (with relevant local variations) in various other countries, including, most recently, Denmark, Singapore, Hong Kong, and the United Kingdom.[19] A variant of the point system was proposed (but never adopted) in the United States as part of the major legislative overhaul of America's notoriously cumbersome and byzantine immigrant-selection system. The introduction of a merit-based point system would have represented not only an instance of interjurisdictional borrowing along the model of competitive immigration regimes,

---

[16] On the rich literature on policy emulation and diffusion, see e.g., Beth A. Simmons, Frank Dobbin, and Geoffrey Garrett (eds.), *The Global Diffusion of Markets and Democracy* (Cambridge: Cambridge University Press, 2008). On competitive immigration regimes, Ayelet Shachar, "The Race for Talent: Highly Skilled Migrants and Competitive Immigration Regimes," *New York University Law Review* 81:1 (2006), 148–206.

[17] See Triadafilos Triadafilopoulos, "Dismantling White Canada: Race, Rights, and the Origins of the Points System" in Triadafilos Triadafilopoulos (ed.), *Wanted and Welcome: Policies for Highly Skilled Immigrants in Comparative Perspective* (New York: Springer, 2013), pp. 15–37 at p. 16.

[18] On this change and its impact on Australia's contemporary "gatekeeping" function, which has shifted to an emphasis on language and social class, as well as occupational skills, see Gwenda Tavan, *The Long, Slow Death of White Australia* (Melbourne: Scribe Publications, 2005).

[19] As could be expected, each jurisdiction slightly adjusts the point system to fit its own specific local demands and trajectories. In Germany, for example, a proposed bill that introduced the point system (which ultimately did not become part of the law) would have given points to individuals with ethno-national ties to Germany, reflecting the *volkish* aspect of German identity that still resonates even with its more liberalized interpretations of citizenship and membership.

but also a concerted effort by the United States to strike back and reclaim its once-legendary position as the world's leading "IQ magnet" for the highly skilled.

Unlike international efforts to harmonize or increase coordination across borders, the global race for talent results from *non*-cooperation among fiercely competitive jurisdictions seeking the prize of the best and brightest among the highly skilled. The core stakeholders in this multiplayer game—recruiting nations, knowledge migrants, and countries of origin—have become increasingly sophisticated, and the competitive scramble now involves a range of different tiers, establishing a "talent pyramid" of skilled migrants who are recruited at different stages of their professional careers. At the top of the talent pyramid we find high-achieving migrants with a track record of international achievements. They are in an enviable position in today's global race for talent: they are perceived to know where they are wanted. For this reason, they can vote with their feet, which increases the pressure on recruiting nations to lavish them with attractive settlement packages.[20] But this privilege applies primarily to those with the potential to "substantially benefit prospectively the national economy, cultural or educational interests, or the welfare of the [country]," as is required, for example, under American immigration law provisions of the selective EB-1 (employment-based first preference) admission category that immediately grants the successful applicant a green card—and with it the freedom to establish herself in the United States—while waiving standard requirements for gaining an employment offer or a domestic sponsor. In the United Kingdom, "exceptionally talented individuals in the fields of science, humanities, engineering and the arts" are invited to join in under the new Tier 1 exceptional talent category. And the list goes on. Even based on this brief description, the talent pyramid can be seen to reflect a "scale of attractiveness" according to which the more desired the immigrant is, the faster she will be given an opportunity to lawfully enter the country and embark on a fast-tracked path to its membership rewards. This is part of a subtle yet potentially dramatic redefinition of citizenship connected with the rise of the new selection-by-merit paradigm of "value added" human mobility and membership.[21]

The exponential growth of the global race for talent means that it is no longer necessarily tied to, or motivated by, cyclical domestic skills shortages. Rather, it is about "building [a] future through well-managed entry and

---

[20] The choice of destination for these migrants is of course neither unlimited nor necessarily determinative. It is likely that language, networking, family ties, and postcolonial channels of migration play a role in shaping the directionality of human mobility, although emergent patterns of "super diversity"—a condition that refers to small and scattered multiple-origin global migration flows—reveals a level of complexity that surpasses previous experiences and predictions. See Stephen Vertovec, "Super-Diversity and its Implications," *Ethnic and Racial Studies* 30:6 (2007), 1024–54.

[21] See Shachar and Hirschl, "Recruiting 'Super Talent'."

settlement of people."[22] Today's skills-based migration priorities reflect a technocratic, econometric, and managerial logic that aims to bring an air of objectivity (through measures such as the point-system rubric) into the otherwise deeply charged and politicized terrain of discretionary immigration.[23] By setting human capital criteria for selecting *whom* to admit, governments signal their clear preference for a particular class of immigrants—educated, cultivated, innovative, and productive individuals—so as to meet the impetus to "maximize the economic benefits that skilled immigration can provide." Of course, these functional and efficiency-based standards obscure the less convenient "gatekeeping" ramifications that come with selecting-by-merit, such as the inevitable head start it gives to those with greater access to higher education, sustained records of paid employment, multilinguistic proficiency, and so on (in short, what sociologists would term as the social class advantage), a point to which I return later in the discussion.[24] At this stage, suffice it to say that as a matter of political expediency in the face of growing public support for ever restrictive immigration policies, the focus on the highly skilled allows governments leeway to respond to international competitive pressures while domestically conveying a message of control, and to signal to those with high-demand skills and extraordinary talent that they are "wanted and welcome."[25]

Indeed, government officials are willing to go as far as to redraw the boundaries of membership and tender citizenship in an expedited fashion for those at the top echelons of the talent pyramid. To provide but one particularly visible illustration of this pattern at work, consider the intersection of sports, nationality, and grand international events that bring together athletes from around the world as individual competitors *and* members of national teams. In anticipation of the London 2012 Summer Olympics, for example, medal-contender athletes were recruited and bestowed fast-track citizenship grants by talent-hungry nations. Some of these nationality swaps, as they are known in the athletics world, were approved only ten days prior to the Games'

---

[22] Australia, Joint Standing Committee on Migration 2011, Inquiry into Multiculturalism in Australia, DIAC, Submission no. 150, May 2011.

[23] As mentioned earlier, the category of discretionary migration does *not* apply to refugees, asylum seekers, and other humanitarian claimants who have a special legal and moral standing vis-à-vis the state in which they seek a safe haven. See Blake, "Discretionary Immigration."

[24] The point system is often described by immigration officials as a "transparent and objective method of selecting skilled migrants with the skills and attributes" that are valued by the admitting society. While facially neutral and formally open to all, the point-system assessment scheme is not free from biases. For example, it privileges the breadwinner over the homemaker, the professional over the non-professional, the "productive" over the "dependent," and so on. These binary oppositions historically traced gender-based distinctions, which favored the full-time (male) wage earner over the stay-at-home (female) spouse who did not formally engage in the paid labor market.

[25] I am here borrowing from the title of a collection of essays on highly skilled immigrants edited by Triadafilos Triadafilopoulos: *Wanted and Welcome*.

opening ceremony.[26] Proactively "snatching" top talent from other countries or offering a soft landing for rising stars who seek to leave their home countries is, of course, not limited to elite sports. This strategy is also utilized to advance national interests in academia, science, technology, arts, and media. Internationally, this practice of "picking winners" has become more common than ever; it can lead to situations in which individuals serve as ambassadors for a nation to which they have nothing but the flimsiest of links. This "bartering" of membership goods raises significant fairness and global inequality concerns, addressed in the following section. It also brings into sharp focus additional dilemmas at the heart of the global talent hunt. These include the blurring of allegiance with commodification, the dilution of citizenship-as-membership by proliferating form-over-substance grants, and the conflation of the language of national pride with neoclassical economic principles that treat human capital as a factor of production able to generate significant branding and reputation gains. The advent of savvy and sophisticated skills-based migration routes thus intriguingly demonstrates both the erosion and the revitalization of a country's control over its membership boundaries (alas, along more strategic and instrumental lines), since it takes agency and governmental action to attract and retain these highly skilled migrants: the very same talent pool in high demand that other competitive nations wish to lure to their respective jurisdictions.

9.2 Theoretical and Ethical Conundrums

In the previous pages, I have provided a glimpse into the vigor and zeal of the fast-growing worldwide competition for talent. Counterintuitively, and under conditions of uncertainty, national immigration agencies (and increasingly local and regional officials, too) have reasserted themselves as significant players in the global market in the highly skilled. They have done this by developing the logic of competitive immigration regimes, maintaining tight control over their power to govern legal entry, and conferring membership goods to attract highly skilled migrants perceived as "assets." This last point is significant. Granting full and formal membership in the political community remains the only good that even the mightiest economic conglomerate cannot offer to the skilled migrant. Only governments can allocate access to, and the security of, citizenship.

The global race for talent, with its increasingly calculated and instrumental approach to selecting-by-merit, provides us with a new lens through which to

---

[26] I discuss this pattern in detail in Shachar, "Picking Winners."

observe the centrality of competitive states—the fashionable alarms about their decline notwithstanding—in controlling and allocating membership goods. Challenging the prevalent view that states have "lost control" over border and membership boundaries, the recent changes identified here illuminate a more nuanced and complicated picture. Clearly, the extensity, intensity, and velocity of today's globalization transactions generate a more competitive environment for the cross-border recruitment of the highly skilled.[27] The crucial point, however, is that *governments*, too, by fine-tuning immigration categories and procedures, have played an active role in facilitating the flow of human talent across borders. This has important ethical ramifications, strident ones, since the state is held to stricter standards of justification and democratic accountability than markets and amorphous globalization forces.

This paradigm shift, which is only beginning to gain wider scholarly recognition, presents several conceptual and normative puzzles which I formulate here as grounds for further research with the potential to bridge the empirical and ethical aspects of migration studies. There are at least three different issues at stake: (1) Does giving priority in the citizenship line to those with brains, talent, and special skills erode the basic egalitarian thrust of political membership?; (2) In a world still characterized by severe inequalities across borders and regions, are receiving countries under any obligation (moral, or potentially legal as well) to "compensate" sending countries for their potentially severe loss of institution builders, innovators, and reformers?; (3) Within admitting countries, is there a risk that reliance on the recruitment of highly skilled migrants will lead to decreased public investment in cultivating homegrown talent through educational and related measures benefitting the domestic population, or that the emphasis on high-demand skills will crowd out other streams of migrants that have not achieved the merit requirement of exceptional ability?[28] These challenges, which I briefly address in the following pages, reveal the potential use and abuse of citizenship as a recruitment tool in the worldwide hunt for talent. They also reveal the evolving matrix of interactions among sending and receiving countries, the nascent tensions between mobile and sedentary populations, and ultimately, the issues of inequality and stratification in cross-border mobility, and the influence of market-oriented concepts in reshaping traditional understandings of citizenship.

---

[27] David Held et al. list extensity, intensity, and velocity as three of the four elements of today's globalization era. See David Held, Anthony McGrew, David Goldblatt, and Jonathan Perraton (eds.), *Global Transformations: Politics, Economics and Culture* (Stanford, CA: Stanford University Press, 1999), pp. 14–28.

[28] For some discussion of these and related considerations, see Anna Stilz's chapter in this volume. On the broader question of legitimate selection criteria, see the chapter by Sarah Fine.

I will divide these challenges into two categories of normative argument: the fairness argument (which analytically can be broken into distinct subcategories: fairness to other would-be immigrants; to the population of the admitting country; and to those who stay in the country of origin); and an argument based on a concern with the erosion of the ideal of citizenship as a political relation grounded in equality rather than competition. By exploring these arguments we also come to see more clearly the political and distributive aspects of the global race for talent. I address each in turn.

Fairness. When speaking about fairness in the immigration context, the initial task we face is to discern the scope and scale of the comparative unit: should we take as our baseline the distribution of sovereignty among states under the current international system, or should we focus on subnational and supranational alternatives, or perhaps begin with a global welfare matrix? The choice of scale will determine which dimensions of equality and inequality we capture, potentially affecting our conclusion as to what is fair and just. As a simplifying heuristic let us assume, for the foreseeable future, a world of regulated human mobility in which recognized and independent states, acting alone or in concert, remain the primary units of political organization and border control. Taking the existing order as a background condition for our normative evaluation is congruent with the strategy adopted by other leading political and legal theorists.[29] It permits us to take into account existing tensions and assess the trade-offs that may arise when states exercise their prerogative to selectively recruit whom to admit. In such a world, there are at least three possible communities of reference that we ought to consider: fairness to other streams of international migrants; fairness to the population of the home country; and fairness to the population of the receiving community.

9.2.1 *Fairness to other potential migrants*

The main concern here is that while granting new opportunities to the world's mobile knowledge migrants, the emphasis on skills-based migration streams may "crowd out" other bases for admission.[30] This argument assumes,

---

[29] This is what Joseph Carens refers to as the engagement with the "conventional normative view on immigration." See Joseph H. Carens, *The Ethics of Immigration* (Oxford: Oxford University Press, 2013).

[30] Political scientists, development economists, and demographers of international migration traditionally have emphasized a different "crowding out" concern, namely that associated with network migration (also referred to in the literature as chain migration or secondary migration) of family members, friends, and relatives of the original migrants who have settled in the new country. The main theoretical insight here is that once it passes a threshold or tipping point, "migration becomes self-perpetuating because each act of migration itself creates the social structure needed to sustain it." See Douglas S. Massey, Joaquin Arango, Graeme Hugo, Ali

however, a zero-sum relationship between the different categories of international migration, something that has to be proven and not merely purported. In fact, no country relies exclusively on skills-based selection programs. Even immigrant-receiving societies that rely on the human-capital accretion model and have made it a centerpiece of their selective admission policy, such as Australia and Canada, have never treated it as the sole purpose of their immigration law and policy. Rather, they have always maintained multiple streams, or pathways, to membership, including family-reunification, employment-based, and humanitarian streams.[31] They have done so to fulfill certain ethical and legal obligations (especially in reference to refugees, asylum seekers, trafficked persons, and the like) and partly as a matter of political expediency.[32] Immigration is a contentious issue everywhere, and as Gary Freeman and others have shown, elected officials face significant pressures from competing lobby and interest groups, including business organizations, labor unions, and so-called ethnic lobbies.[33] These pressures make it nearly impossible to have an immigration policy that is limited to a singular admission route.

Still, the critic might argue that the competition to lure those with an abundance of talent and human capital underwrites the new political economy of wanted-and-welcomed migration. Preference is given to marketable skills and talent over the moral claims of those with vulnerabilities and needs. The potential to bring tangible results and increased reputational value to the recruiting nation distinguishes suitable from unsuitable candidates.[34] It is the reliance on the language of economic growth and innovation that allows talent and human capital to seem neutral and unobjectionable as criteria for selection. So the concern here may have more to do with a conceptual shift and prioritization of certain marketable skills that are valued in the knowledge economy, something that some segments of society—those who have had access to higher education or specialized professional training (whether in the countries of origin or destination)—gain more readily than others. This adds

Kouaouci, Adela Pellegrino, and J. Edward Taylor, "Theories of International Migration: A Review and Appraisal," *Population and Development Review* 19:3 (2005), 431–66.

[31] In addition, their skills-based immigration categories also include immediate admission to the applicant's immediate relatives (spouse and children) as part of the talent-for-citizenship exchange.

[32] The humanitarian stream is not part of the "discretionary migration" framework in which the global race for talent operates. As such, at least in principle, it is immune to the effects of placing greater faith in human capital admission criteria. In practice we might worry about a slippage or erosion at the edges of the legal parameters governing humanitarian migration as well.

[33] Gary P. Freeman, "Modes of Immigrant Politics in Liberal Democratic States," *International Migration Review* 29:44 (1995), 881–902.

[34] See Bill Jordan and Franck Duvell, *Migration: The Boundaries of Equality and Justice* (Cambridge: Polity Press, 2003), pp. 91–5.

considerations of skills selectively and social class to the presumably objective and universal selection matrix embedded in the point system or related merit-based assessment criteria that are adhered to with zeal by the competitors in the global race for talent. In this brave new world of stratified mobility, explicit discrimination on prohibited grounds such as race, ethnicity, and national origin is strictly prohibited. But that doesn't imply that all are equally welcome. Even among the highly skilled, as we have already seen, those at the top echelon of the talent pyramid enjoy faster and smoother routes to admission and membership.

At the level of theory building, we must acknowledge, however, that we are dealing here with *would-be* entrants, whom even Joseph Carens describes as "potential immigrants who have no specific moral claim to admittance."[35] This realization requires us to step back and take in the fuller picture. Even these privileged beneficiaries must earn—through their extraordinary talent and achievement—what is automatically assigned as a result of nothing but fortuitous station of birth to those who "naturally" belong to the admitting society. Although discredited in all other fields of law, it is birthright—not migration—that remains the primary route for citizenship acquisition. Some are born to sweet delight, others to endless night. In our world, the latter is far more common. Only a minuscule minority of the global population—estimated at 3 percent of the world's population—partakes in international migration, and those who do are neither the poorest nor the neediest locally or globally. Instead of engaging in a tactic of divide-and-conquer among the meager numbers of those who have managed to move (and thereby to defy their ascribed lot in the birthright lottery), we need to push the question back one step further and ask whether in the absence of migration, the persistent and dramatic inequalities in life chances that attach to the reliance on birthright in the distribution of membership by virtue of circumstances that none of us control—namely, where or to whom we are born—are justified in the first place. This is a task I have taken on elsewhere and will not discuss in detail here, but I mention it to clarify the kind of questions that should occupy us in reimagining mobility and justice for the twenty-first century, a reimagining that must take place on a larger canvas and not fall into the dangerous trap of finger-pointing among migration categories.[36] Further complicating matters is the harsh legal reality that in today's world, each of us has a right to *exit*

---

[35] Carens, *The Ethics of Immigration*, p. 179. Undocumented migrants are another category of de facto would-be entrants, but they fall beyond the scope of this chapter because they are not officially selected by states through standard admission routes.

[36] For a detailed analysis of the legal, normative, and distributive consequences of reliance on ascription in membership allocation by birth, see Ayelet Shachar, *The Birthright Lottery: Citizenship and Global Inequality* (Cambridge, MA: Harvard University Press, 2009). For a different take on birthright citizenship, see Joseph Carens in this volume.

our ascribed home country but no corresponding right to *enter* a political community to which we do not yet belong as members.[37] The force of the fairness argument among would-be migrants is thus significantly diminished as soon as we recognize that in a world of regulated borders (like our own), *no one* has a guaranteed shot at gaining access to membership by virtue of volition or want.

As long as human mobility remains so strictly regulated, we must also be cautious not to assume a causal link between the instrumental and strategic considerations that fuel the fires of talent migration and the stricter mobility-curbing measures imposed upon other streams of migration. The two processes may occur contemporaneously, but that does not establish that the former is the cause of the latter, or vice versa. The harsh policies adopted by many European countries in recent years that have led them to tighten family admission, intercept asylum seekers at open sea, and place culturally infused barriers on certain third-country nationals (for example, the Netherlands' pre-admission screening test) reflect the troubling return of the demons of exclusion, or what has aptly been labeled the new "restrictive turn" in immigration control.[38] These re-emerging patterns reflect a long and dark history of migration that cannot plausibly (or chronologically) be the "result" of the rise of the global race for talent. These different streams of migration appear to be rationalized and socially constructed in strikingly different terms of discourse: "l'*immigration choisie*" as opposed to the "*l'immigration subie*," as the French would put it.[39] With the rising anti-immigrant sentiment, members of the latter category are pejoratively presented in political discourse as holding immutable cultural differences that make them unassimilable, quintessential "Others," whereas selective migration is presented as a culture-free zone that is treated functionally and technocratically as a measure to advance the country's economic, reputational, and scientific advantage. If anything, the rise of merit-based admission categories and the fine-grained developments of managed migration that I have discussed in the previous sections are more likely the result of, rather than the cause of, these shifting sentiments in immigrant-receiving countries. Politicians and policymakers alike are attracted to skills-based migration programs as a panacea for what they see as the failure of previous policies.

---

[37] The only exception to this general rule is the special case of refugees and asylum seekers who cannot be deported, based on a well-founded fear of persecution, to their country of origin or their last place of abode. On this topic, see Anna Stilz's and Christopher Heath Wellman's contributions to this volume.

[38] See Joppke, "Comparative Citizenship?."

[39] Triadafilopoulos and Smith, "Introduction," p. 4.

9.2.2 *Fairness to the countries of origin*

With the advent of the global race for talent and the formal removal of race- and national origins–based restrictions to mobility, many of the highly skilled who are drawn by the promise of permanent residence and eventual citizenship in a stable, rule-of-law society hail from poorer and less developed countries, especially those in Asia and Africa. It seems unjust that countries that are already struggling to fulfill their basic obligations towards their own citizenry should invest their scarce resources (educational and otherwise) to help their best and brightest, only to see those potential institution builders, innovators, and democratic reformers lured to the greener pastures of more affluent recruiting nations. Even the most brilliant athlete, scientist, or innovator needs a community in order to succeed; the social-cooperative efforts and public investments made by the home countries in skilled emigrants are of relevance here: "[p]eople don't rise from nothing" as Malcolm Gladwell so vividly illustrates in *Outliers*.[40]

Some have suggested a protectionist response to this predicament, recommending a restriction on the mobility of highly skilled migrants in order to help home countries develop an adequate response.[41] This is a band-aid approach that does nothing to address the root causes of the problems that lead skilled emigrants to consider leaving their world behind in the first place. It also stands in tension with individual freedom and human mobility in that it "locks up" people in the polity into which they happen to have been born. It amounts uncomfortably closely to assigning "ownership" of individuals' cultivation and refinement of their human capital to some anonymous governmental authority to assign as it sees fit.[42] On this account, the collective (utilitarian) interest in having a skilled migrant stay in the country of origin ought to trump other considerations, including individual liberty. Alas, if we go down this path, where do we stop? Who decides whose freedoms and skills are to be owned by others, and distributed according to some macro-efficiency plan? And why force the doctor, the lawyer, the teacher from the poorer country to remain in it forever, while freeing equally qualified professionals born in more affluent societies from any responsibility to improve, to the best

---

[40] Malcolm Gladwell, *Outliers: The Story of Success* (New York: Little, Brown and Company, 2008), p. 19.

[41] The most commonly cited examples relate to the mobility of healthcare workers.

[42] It is not raw talent per se (which is arguably arbitrary from a moral point of view) that is tracked and valued by selective skills-based admission routes, but the result of the concentrated effort that goes into developing one's human capital, which is, as Charles Beitz convincingly argues (in his critique of John Rawls' position), bound up with identity and therefore protected by considerations of personal liberty. See Charles R. Beitz, *Political Theory and International Relations* (Princeton, NJ: Princeton University Press; revised edition 1999, originally published 1979), pp. 138–9. For further discussion, see Ayelet Shachar and Ran Hirschl, "On Citizenship, States and Markets," *Journal of Political Philosophy* 22:2 (2014), 231–57.

of their ability, the situation of the world's neediest? This protectionist argument therefore only further accentuates (rather than minimizes) the ramification of the birthright lottery. It places yet additional restrictions and obstacles to mobility on members of less well-off polities. As one commentator succinctly put it, referring to the American context, "could we [justly] say to a Ghanaian doctor that she must return to her country while an immigrant Russian doctor is allowed to settle down and start a new life?"[43] This kind of distinction, if rationalized on the basis of national origins, or worse, race, comes close to amounting to prohibited grounds.

The anti-mobility stance also seems to ignore the simple fact that it is individuals and households, and not some abstracted economic function of a social-welfare-utility unit to be maximized in the service of the home country, who move—migrants who are part of communities, who are dreamers, who may be dispossessed, who may feel pushed into a corner, or who may fit the designation of "exceptional people" (to borrow from the title of a recent bestseller on the history of immigration).[44] Whatever their story, those who engage in migration, even privileged emigrants at the top of the talent pyramid, take a tremendous risk by leaving their whole world behind, whether permanently or temporarily. Once we bring this human dimension into the analysis, we can no longer categorically assert that it is ethically imperative that we restrict or prohibit the mobility of the highly skilled based on some implied commitment (if not "indenture") to the society into which they happened to have been born. This would amount to allowing considerations of social utility to trump, categorically and by definition, competing interests of liberty and freedom.

Such an approach also misguidedly removes another crucial question from the table: namely, whether competitive states engaged in the active recruitment of the highly skilled have a responsibility to "offset" the losses suffered in those places skilled migrants leave behind. While there are significant knowledge transfers ("brain circulation") and other forms of investment that skilled emigrants contribute handsomely to their home countries, the responsibility for shaping and implementing immigration policy lies squarely with governments, especially when they proactively create supply-side admission schemes to lure knowledge migrants in the global race for talent. Accordingly, they should be key players in any attempt to systemically and more fairly address the consequences of skilled emigration as between sending and receiving countries. Instead of restricting mobility, it is possible to imagine fresher ideas, such as creating a link between seizing home countries' talent and

---

[43] Jagdish Bhagwati, "The Brain-Drain Panic Returns," *Project Syndicate*, January 27, 2012.

[44] See Ian Goldin, Geoffrey Cameron, and Meera Balarajan, *Exceptional People: How Immigration Shaped Our World and Will Define Our Future* (Princeton, NJ: Princeton University Press, 2011).

establishing structural channels for giving back, for instance, by investing in infrastructure, education, health, anti-corruption, and democratic empowerment in the communities from which emigrants hail, under the guidance of democratic deliberation informed by local insights and needs.

In the early days of the brain-drain discussion, the focus was on whether highly skilled emigrants should redirect a share of their newfound bounty (material or symbolic) back to their home country, and if so, whether this should amount to a voluntary or mandatory obligation. Today, it is evident that the transfer of knowledge and skills is less unidirectional than was initially assumed. We witness complex patterns of transnational relocation, circular migration, time-limited resettlement, and even "reverse brain drain" (from developed to less developed countries). Many successful emigrants and their progeny who have settled abroad maintain a multiplicity of connections with their home country; the bulk of these are retained without any formal obligation to do so. Remittance flows are a prime example. Economists are quick to point out that remittances now have a value more than three times that of official development assistance, and that they provide cash (or in-kind) transfers directly to resident households.[45] But diaspora communities do more than send back cash or its equivalent. They also engage in technological and knowledge transfers, cultural transmission, start-up investments, and so on. While it may well be correct to assume that some of those who have left would have contributed more to their home societies had they stayed (the counterfactual hypothetical), the normative issue is, as I have already mentioned, slightly different. It asks whether talent-recruiting nations, as beneficiaries of skilled emigration from the rest of the world, are under any obligation (moral or eventually legal, as well) to counterbalance the consequences of their actions, especially if an unintended consequence of the global race for talent is to drain sending countries of their most promising institution builders, innovators, and democratic reformers. Even if remittances are sent back home, the development effects of talent emigration run deeper than what monetary and knowledge transfers (important as they are) can offset.

Shifting the focus from skilled migrants themselves to the governments that actively recruit them (with the assistance of various third-party intermediaries, be they employers, international recruitment agencies, and so on) is a first step. We already established that the anti-mobility stance that advocates banning or significantly restricting the mobility of international talent is unnecessarily harsh and punitive, amplifying rather than minimizing brute luck. It unfairly places an added burden on those hailing from the huge swaths

---

[45] There is a debate in the economics literature about how these remittances are spent by recipients in the home countries, and whether they increase household consumption or reduce the level and severity of poverty and improve health and education expenditures.

of the world's population that already bear the brunt of unequal mobility and opportunity. The ethical resolution does not lie in giving each birthright community a veto to override the migration choices of its members (or more accurately the very few of its members who will gain a chance to lawfully enter another country on the strength of their skills and specialized knowledge). Although space limitations do not permit me to develop possible policy alternatives here, suffice it to say that a more comprehensive approach will require addressing the competing interests at stake. The global race for talent, as the name indicates, is characterized by *inter*jurisdictional flows, innovation, and emulation. It is anything but static and fixed. In this multiplayer context, it seems anachronistic to pin the responsibility for improving the dire situation in the home country solely on the skilled migrant herself, as recommended by those holding the anti-mobility stance.[46] Better to involve the multiple stakeholders in the global race for talent—including government agencies in the receiving country, the migrant's future employers, intermediaries that may have helped facilitate the transaction, local and regional non-governmental organizations, and the international community at large—in efforts to make whole the country of origin, and ideally to increase opportunities for the vast majority of people worldwide who will not move, but may be indirectly affected by the benefits and possible costs of relocation of the highly skilled. This can be achieved through inter-state, regional, or even international initiatives for bringing considerations of migration and development more closely together. It also permits us to begin constructively to address the "citizenship premium" of the birthright lottery as part of the brain-drain debate, taking into account the growing tensions that may arise between the sedentary or mobile segments of the global population.

9.2.3 *Fairness to the population of the recruiting nation*

Discussions of human mobility in the context of the global race for talent often neglect to address questions of membership and mobility as seen from the perspective of residents of the home countries that seek to recruit and retain knowledge migrants. But what is at stake for those who are already members of the political community that welcomes in the highly skilled? It is to be expected that certain segments of society would benefit more from this practice than others, but there is another concern that does not relate to

[46] My position here differs from the Bhagwati tax, which places the burden of compensation on the emigrant herself, but does not challenge the underlying motivation to find creative ways to permit skilled migration (the freedom and individual choice dimension) while allowing the country of origin to share in the spoils that the mobility of the highly skilled can generate, for instance, through remittances, knowledge and skills transfers, political engagement of the diaspora, and so on.

immediate returns, but to a deeper realignment. The basic concern is that if the world's best and brightest can be "imported" at will, with governments fast-tracking admission to those they covet on the basis of an expected return—material, reputation, or otherwise—we might see decreased attention paid to the kind of persistent, long-term investment that is required in order to build up a creative and professional workforce to meet the challenges of the knowledge economy in the twenty-first century and to cultivate home-grown talent in arts, athletics, sciences, and the like. As a matter of realpolitik, the surest recipe to build popular opposition to skilled migration is to appear to haphazardly waive residency and other naturalization requirements, which sensibly operate as a buffer to ensure that those who gain the prize of citizenship in the talent-recruiting country have indeed made it their new home.

Policymakers who ignore such charged issues do so at their own peril. Emerging economies that have experienced a particularly high ratio of international-to-local talent, such as Singapore and Hong Kong, now invest a tremendous amount of social capital in ensuring that such tensions, if they arise, are proactively addressed. Even market-oriented democracies such as the United States are paying heed. A recent legislative proposal to "staple" a green card to the STEM degrees of advanced international graduate students to facilitate their absorption into the local market is a fitting example. Such a reform, if adopted, would set numerical limits on STEM green cards while simultaneously developing a domestic "pipeline" of U.S.-born and -trained workers with advanced skills and training.[47] Such legislation would also see fees collected by the federal government from employers who wish to recruit the highly skilled reallocated to grant programs that support and enhance domestic students' STEM education and employee retraining within the United States. This is a concrete illustration of measures required to ensure that the recruitment of highly skilled international migrants does not discount the commitment to local talent in the short or long term. The more pertinent general point is that the significant spoils and benefits associated with highly skilled migration to recruiting nations must benefit the average citizen, not just jetsetters, top universities, and corporate headquarters. Another crucial fairness measure would be to require that those who have gained fast-track admission due to their extraordinary abilities and

---

[47] In part, as in food or energy security, no country should ever voluntarily place itself at the mercy of the volatility and risk of an international market that it cannot control. For this reason, building up a robust domestic "brainstock" is in the interest of the local population and various levels of government. Otherwise, they risk political fracture and the economic risk of becoming dependent upon (or "addicted" to) the inflow of international talent, which may eventually dry up or change course to other, more attractive destinations, or back to the countries of origin should their economic fate improve, as we have seen with the "reverse brain drain" to China and India in recent years.

high-demand skills must nevertheless "earn" their civic and membership goods, just like anyone else, by laying roots in the society that has given them a new home and a host of new opportunities.

On balance, many of the doomsday-style predictions about trade-offs and tensions that come with an increase in highly skilled migration are inflated and exaggerated. If anything, the profile of the highly skilled as "net contributors" to job creation and economic growth lends greater fuel to those advocating selective admission through designated pathways for knowledge and talent migrants.[48] Given the concern to ensure that the domestic workforce is not given short shrift, it would be prudent to see major private- and public-sector stakeholders, including the high-technology industries that are often the most vocal advocates for, and direct beneficiaries of the turn to, skills-based admission programs, do their share and participate in discharging the fairness obligation towards the local population, for instance, by providing retraining programs or other valuable education initiatives to stimulate renewal and more varied access points to the pipelines that eventually build up the talent reservoirs of competitive states and markets.

In sum, rather than preaching either the anti-mobility stance that advocates limiting the mobility choices of those who have drawn the shorter straw in the birthright lottery, or the anti-statist position that calls for demolishing citizenship-centered structures of membership, greater promise lies in recognizing that while skilled migration is not a zero-sum game—neither among different streams of migrants, nor between sending and receiving countries, nor between long-term investment in local populations and short-term gains from fast-tracking international talent—the fact remains that the costs and benefits of highly skilled migration are unevenly distributed, both *within* and *across* jurisdictions. To address these real and pressing challenges, we will require both political will and creative visions for our collective life as members of viable political communities in the twenty-first century.

Another measure to offset the inequalities built into selective mobility regimes would be to insist that the core benefits that make human capital the centerpiece of these new competitive migration regimes—including the knowledge, innovation, and experience gained by the infusion of local markets with international talent—should be diffused more fairly and consistently to the various communities to which the highly skilled belong. The underlying commitment is to greater freedom of mobility for individuals (rejecting calls for making the international migration system even more

---

[48] In the United States, studies have focused on the economic impact of foreign-born STEM students trained in American universities, establishing that they have made disproportionate contributions to the creation of new jobs for domestic workers, patent production, and research and development in both industry and university.

restrictive than it is today) while at the same time minimizing the unfairness or adverse effects. These kinds of responses strive to balance the values of freedom, fairness, and community intertwined in this debate, and to articulate the distributive matrix of opportunities and responsibilities affecting mobile and immobile segments of the population, countries of origin, and admitting nations, all of which are operating in a more closely interconnected world.

9.3 Eroding the Ideal of Equal Citizenship

Immigration is not just about crossing borders; it is also about entering communities. If having extraordinary talent or performing strongly on a point-system grid will come to signify the new hard-to-attain gold standard for allotting access to membership for those not born as citizens, then by process of osmosis of ideas and practices we may eventually witness its impact stretch and expand to other realms of decision-making about "who belongs," and according to what criteria. It is one thing for a country to legitimately seek to draw in the best and brightest, or to fast-track in the visa line talent migrants of the caliber of Russian-born star soprano Anna Netrebko (the recipient of expedited Austrian citizenship on the basis of her exceptional artistic merit), or to draw scientific genius so as to strengthen a country's research institutions and facilities. It is quite another to turn merit and extraordinary talent into a core criterion for admission and settlement. It is in this regard that the still nascent move from selecting-by-origin to selecting-by-merit poses significant challenges, both philosophical and applied.

The surge in selective migration also alerts us to a deeper transformation, one that cannot be easily averted even if we miraculously manage to address the multiple dimensions of the fairness argument discussed above. At issue is the potential eroding or diluting effect of bringing market-valuation of talent and exchange into assigning and allocating "membership goods"—be they an entry visa, a residence permit, and ultimately, citizenship itself. As Michael Sandel powerfully argues, this kind of objection (which he refers to as "corruption" in the moral sense) focuses on "the character of the goods themselves and the norms that should govern them."[49] The global race for talent clearly privileges those who have perfected and honed their skills. It does not reward raw talent per se, but captures instead elements of determination, hard work,

[49] The distinction between fairness and "corruption" is drawn from Michael J. Sandel, *What Money Can't Buy: The Moral Limits of Markets* (New York: Farrar, Straus and Girous, 2012), pp. 111–13. Debra Satz, too, emphasizes the importance of evaluating not only the logic that governs the distribution of certain goods, but also the social and political relationships that such goods may sustain and support. See Debra Satz, *Why Some Things Should Not be for Sale: The Moral Limits of Markets* (Oxford: Oxford University Press, 2010).

and adaptability, traits that some countries' point systems directly reward.[50] This model vision does not stand in tension with perfectionist conceptions of citizenship, but it does pose serious hazards to democratic and egalitarian notions which at least formally assign membership to individuals *irrespective* of how innovative, talented, or accomplished they may (or may not) be. The emphasis on more calculated interpretations of membership thus sets talent-for-citizenship apart from more ideational understandings of membership and belonging. Thinking about citizenship as a multilayered "bundle" of rights, identity, and legal standing, it becomes clear that how (or based on what criteria) people become members of the political community is a crucial question with far-reaching ramifications for the individuals involved and even the very future of citizenship as grounded in social and political—and not merely market—relations. **This makes the critical study of the transition from origin to merit ever more vital.**

9.4 Concluding Remarks

At present, as I hope to have shown, the vigorously competitive global race for talent offers an exception to an otherwise punitive and increasingly restrictive regime of tightly regulated mobility across borders. Even if the "huddled masses yearning to breathe free, the wretched refuse of your teeming shore"—immortalized in Emma Lazarus' *The New Colossus*—wanted to relocate and start afresh in America (or any other symbolic land of immigration), they would be disheartened to learn that promised golden gate is increasingly closed shut. In such a world, in which mobility remains difficult to achieve, the promise of acquiring access to and membership in a well-off society is a major draw, especially for those coming from a teeming shore. Contrary to the predictions of postnationalists and others suggesting the imminent erosion of borders and bounded membership, it is precisely the security and dignity of membership that makes the talent-for-citizenship exchange into an opportune tool used by the talent-hungry nations in their competitive interjurisdictional scramble to attract and retain the best and brightest.

To their credit, selective migration regimes are officially color-, race-, gender-, and national-origin blind, which is not a minor point given the exclusionary history of world migration. However, the global race for talent is not stratification-free. It reflects a vision of an ideal citizen who is creative and contributory, who has been able to maximize her talent and turn herself into a

---

[50] The distribution of raw talent and economic conditions into which one is born can also deeply affect the ability to gain education later in life, and hence skills-based migration can be seen as correlated to, although not the cause of, such larger patterns of inequality.

"net benefit" for her new society. If we think of immigration policy as a porous membrane that in part reflects and discloses the qualities a polity values in its members-to-be, then it tells us something important about the state of citizenship today and about our collective identity. It demonstrates just how far we have gone down the path toward a winner-takes-all society, even at the immeasurable risk of eroding our increasingly fragile understandings of citizenship that are still infused (at least in theory if not always in practice) with ideals of democracy and equality, not just power and prowess.[51]

While we cannot read the tea leaves of the changed landscape of citizenship, we can sketch the contours of the dystopian future to which it could potentially lead: a neo-mercantilist world in which the rush to fast-track prized recruits undercuts other important commitments. In this dystopian future, the specter rises of political relations morphing into more calculated transactions (much like processes of stratification in other spheres of social life), subtly yet persistently undercutting the commitment to on-a-par membership that has been at the heart and soul of our modern democratic, civic republican, and liberal conceptions of citizenship. Fortunately, this is not yet a fait accompli. Forestalling it further, however, will require many brave voices objecting to and pushing back against the totalizing impact of turning human capital into make-or-break criteria for cross-border human mobility. The matter is neither beyond human control nor immune to resistance. There is no reason, for instance, to assume a priori that skilled migration streams are not compatible with other justifications for migration. Each has its own central guiding principle. Family reunification, for example, takes into account the human dignity and value of exercising the right to family life.[52] Humanitarian admission is grounded in ethics and a sense of our shared humanity and vulnerability, and specifically in the baseline legal obligation of non-refoulement as codified in the Refugee Convention. Temporary migrants are increasingly recruited to do the necessary but often difficult, degrading, and dangerous (the infamous 3D categorization) work that the local population is loath to do, at least so long as it is accompanied by meager pay and tarnished cultural value. The highly skilled fill a different niche: that of accumulating the nation's human capital and the innovation,

---

[51] For staunch critiques of these internal transformations of social citizenship and the imbalances of power in the American economic and political system, see e.g., Margaret R. Sommers, *Genealogies of Citizenship: Markets, Statelessness, and the Rights to Have Rights* (Cambridge: Cambridge University Press, 2008); Jacob S. Hacker and Paul Pierson, *Winner-Take-All Politics: How Washington Made the Rich Richer—And Turned Its Back on the Middle Class* (New York: Simon and Shuster, 2012).

[52] In Europe, this value finds explicit expression in Article 8 of the European Convention on Human Rights and the jurisprudence of the European Court of Human Rights. States have at times resisted this jurisprudence or tried to find ways to limit its impact, but the obligation remains valid and enforceable.

creativity, and growth that are presumed to come with it. While they may partly overlap and intersect, these different streams serve different purposes and follow distinctive logics. There is no principled reason to presuppose that any of these, standing alone, can respond to the full spectrum of human motivations for mobility, nor to the range of pluralistic demands and values that the modern state is expected to respect. None of these migration streams ought to be given priority or exclusivity. They can (and should) operate side by side in a negotiated *modus vivendi*.

The major risk lies elsewhere. Except in Lake Wobegon, the slide toward a vision of society where "all are above average" means that some will be left behind, if not completely outside, the new market-oriented boundaries of membership and belonging.

References

Australia, Joint Standing Committee on Migration 2011, Inquiry into Multiculturalism in Australia, DIAC, Submission no. 150, May 2011.

Barry, Kim, "Home and Away: The Construction of Citizenship in an Emigration Context," *New York Law Review* 81 (2006), 11–59.

Beitz, Charles R., *Political Theory and International Relations* (Princeton, NJ: Princeton University Press; revised edition 1999, originally published 1979).

Bhagwati, Jagdish, "The Brain-Drain Panic Returns," *Project Syndicate*, January 27, 2012. Available at <http://www.project-syndicate.org/commentary/the-brain-drain-panic-returns>.

Blake, Michael, "Discretionary Immigration," *Philosophical Topics* 30:2 (2002), 273–89.

Carens, Joseph H., *The Ethics of Immigration* (Oxford: Oxford University Press, 2013).

Chin, Gabriel J., "The Civil Rights Revolution Comes to Immigration Law: A New Look at the Immigration and Nationality Act of 1965," *North Carolina Law Review* 75 (1996), 273–345.

Dauvergne, Catherine, *Making People Illegal: What Globalization Means for Migration and Law* (Cambridge: Cambridge University Press, 2008).

Ferrie, Joseph P., "A Historical Perspective on Highly-Skilled Immigrants to the United States, 1820–1920" in Barry R. Chiswick (ed.), *High-Skilled Immigration in a Global Labor Market* (Washington, DC: The AEI Press, 2010), pp. 15–49.

Freeman, Gary P., "Modes of Immigrant Politics in Liberal Democratic States," *International Migration Review* 29:44 (1995), 881–902.

Gladwell, Malcolm, *Outliers: The Story of Success* (New York: Little, Brown and Company, 2008).

Goldin, Ian, Geoffrey Cameron, and Meera Balarajan, *Exceptional People: How Immigration Shaped Our World and Will Define Our Future* (Princeton, NJ: Princeton University Press, 2011).

Hacker, Jacob S. and Paul Pierson, *Winner-Take-All Politics: How Washington Made the Rich Richer—And Turned Its Back on the Middle Class* (New York: Simon and Shuster, 2012).

Held, David, Anthony McGrew, David Goldblatt, and Jonathan Perraton (eds.), *Global Transformations: Politics, Economics and Culture* (Stanford, CA: Stanford University Press, 1999).

Joppke, Christian, *Selecting by Origin: Ethnic Migration in the Liberal State* (Cambridge, MA: Harvard University Press, 2005).

Joppke, Christian, "Comparative Citizenship? A Restrictive Turn in Europe," *Law and Ethics of Human Rights* 2:1 (2008), 1–41.

Jordan, Bill and Franck Duvell, *Migration: The Boundaries of Equality and Justice* (Cambridge: Polity Press, 2003).

Massey, Douglas S., Joaquin Arango, Graeme Hugo, Ali Kouaouci, Adela Pellegrino, and J. Edward Taylor, "Theories of International Migration: A Review and Appraisal," *Population and Development Review* 19:3 (2005), 431–66.

Mitsilega, Valsamis, "Immigration Control in an Era of Globalization: Deflecting Foreigners, Weakening Citizens, Strengthening the State," *Indiana Journal of Global Legal Studies* 19:1 (2012), 3–60.

Sandel, Michael J., *What Money Can't Buy: The Moral Limits of Markets* (New York: Farrar, Straus and Girous, 2012).

Satz, Debra, *Why Some Things Should Not be for Sale: The Moral Limits of Markets* (Oxford: Oxford University Press, 2010).

Shachar, Ayelet, "The Race for Talent: Highly Skilled Migrants and Competitive Immigration Regimes," *New York University Law Review* 81:1 (2006), 148–206.

Shachar, Ayelet, *The Birthright Lottery: Citizenship and Global Inequality* (Cambridge, MA: Harvard University Press, 2009).

Shachar, Ayelet, "Picking Winners: Olympic Citizenship and the Global Race for Talent," *Yale Law Journal* 120:8 (2011), 2088–139.

Shachar, Ayelet, "Citizenship" in Michel Rosenfeld and András Sajó (eds.), *Oxford Handbook of Comparative Constitutional Law* (Oxford: Oxford University Press, 2012), pp. 1002–19.

Shachar, Ayelet and Ran Hirschl, "Recruiting 'Super Talent': The New World of Selective Migration Regimes," *Indiana Journal of Global Legal Studies* 20:1 (2013), 71–107.

Shachar, Ayelet and Ran Hirschl, "On Citizenship, States and Markets," *Journal of Political Philosophy* 22:2 (2014), 231–57.

Simmons, Beth A., Frank Dobbin, and Geoffrey Garrett (eds.), *The Global Diffusion of Markets and Democracy* (Cambridge: Cambridge University Press, 2008).

Sommers, Margaret R., *Genealogies of Citizenship: Markets, Statelessness, and the Rights to Have Rights* (Cambridge: Cambridge University Press, 2008).

SOPEMI, International Migration Outlook 2011.

Tavan, Gwenda, *The Long, Slow Death of White Australia* (Melbourne: Scribe Publications, 2005).

Triadafilopoulos, Triadafilos, "Dismantling White Canada: Race, Rights, and the Origins of the Points System" in Triadafilos Triadafilopoulos (ed.), *Wanted and Welcome:*

Policies for Highly Skilled Immigrants in Comparative Perspective (New York: Springer, 2013), pp. 15–37.

Triadafilopoulos, Triadafilos and Craig D. Smith, "Introduction" in Triadafilos Triadafilopoulos (ed.), *Wanted and Welcome: Policies for Highly Skilled Immigrants in Comparative Perspective* (New York: Springer, 2013), pp. 1–12.

Vertovec, Stephen, "Super-Diversity and its Implications," *Ethnic and Racial Studies* 30:6 (2007), 1024–54.

West, Darrel M., *Brain Gain: Rethinking U.S. Immigration Policy* (Washington, DC: Brookings Institute, 2010).

Wildavsky, Ben, *The Great Brain Race: How Global Universities Are Reshaping the World* (Princeton, NJ: Princeton University Press, 2010).

Zolberg, Aristide, "Matters of State: Theorizing Immigration Policy" in Charles Hirschman, Philip Kasinitz, and Josh DeWind (eds.), *The Handbook of International Migration* (New York: Russell Sage, 2000), pp. 71–93.

Zolberg, Aristide R., *A Nation by Design: Immigration Policy in the Fashioning of America* (Cambridge, MA: Harvard University Press, 2006).

Part III
Migration and Membership

10

In Defense of Birthright Citizenship

Joseph H. Carens

In 1987, in constructing an argument for open borders, I wrote the following:

> Citizenship in Western liberal democracies is the modern equivalent of feudal privilege—an inherited status that greatly enhances one's life chances. Like feudal birthright privileges, restrictive citizenship is hard to justify when one thinks about it closely.[1]

Many readers, quite understandably, took this passage to mean that I thought birthright citizenship was intrinsically unjust.

In this chapter I want to rehabilitate the reputation of birthright citizenship. I want to show that birthright citizenship makes moral sense as a practice in liberal democratic states, so long as it is extended to the children of settled immigrants as well as to the children of citizens. In developing this argument, I am not repudiating the criticisms of global inequality and restrictions on migration that I made in my 1987 article and that many others have made before and since. I am simply trying to make it clearer that the fundamental problem with respect to the relationship between citizenship on the one hand and international inequality and constraints on human freedom on the other is not that individuals are given an initial citizenship at birth but rather that they are not free to change that citizenship later by moving to another state and taking up its citizenship if they wish to do so.[2] In the original article, I observed, "To assign citizenship on the basis of birth might be an acceptable procedure, but only if it did not preclude individuals from making different choices later when they reached maturity."[3] In this article

---

[1] Joseph H. Carens, "Aliens and Citizens: The Case for Open Borders," *The Review of Politics* 49:2 (1987), 251–73 at p. 252.

[2] Does this clarification undercut the analogy that I drew with feudalism in the original article? I don't think so for reasons that I will develop in the last section of the chapter.

[3] Carens, "Aliens and Citizens," pp. 261–2.

I want to explain why assigning citizenship on the basis of birth is not only an acceptable procedure but indeed one that is morally required in a liberal democratic state.[4]

Questions about birthright citizenship arise not only in the context of principled debates about open borders and global justice but also in the context of policy debates about how contemporary liberal democratic states should treat immigrants and their descendants. Some liberal democratic states grant citizenship at birth to the children of settled immigrants. Others do not. The key question in this context is whether each liberal democracy is morally free to determine for itself the criteria it will use in granting citizenship at birth or whether there are standards of justice that set moral limits to state discretion on this issue. The central claim of this chapter is that justice requires that contemporary liberal democratic states grant citizenship at birth to the descendants of settled immigrants.

Policy debates about birthright citizenship usually take place against a background in which it is taken for granted that states have the moral right to exercise discretionary control over immigration and that there is nothing morally problematic about the division of the world into independent sovereign states with vast differences of freedom and equality between them. As a defender of open borders, I disagree with these background assumptions. Nevertheless, I think it is useful to consider the question of birthright citizenship first within the constraints of these assumptions because they express a conventional view about the state's right to control immigration and the legitimacy of the current world order that is widely shared. After exploring the issue of birthright citizenship within these constraints, I will argue in the last section of the chapter that the basic moral principles that govern birthright citizenship under these constraints would also apply in a world that had open borders and much greater equality between states.

For reasons of space, I limit my discussion here to children who are born in the state to which their immigrant parents have moved and whose parents are legal permanent residents of that state.[5]

---

[4] In a 1992 article restating the open borders argument, I said, "The initial allocation of citizenship on the basis of birthplace, parentage, or some combination thereof is not objectionable from a liberal egalitarian perspective. Indeed it is morally required because children are born into a community with others with ties that should be acknowledged." See Joseph H. Carens, "Migration and Morality: A Liberal Egalitarian Perspective" in Brian Barry and Robert E. Goodin (eds.), *Free Movement: Ethical Issues in the Transnational Migration of People and of Money* (University Park, PA: Pennsylvania State University Press, 1992), pp. 25–47. This essay is an elaboration of that claim.

[5] In the larger work from which this chapter is drawn, I consider a broader range of questions about access to citizenship, at birth and afterwards, including questions about access for children whose parents are not legal residents.

My discussion in this chapter focuses on immigrants' access to citizenship as a legal status.[6] Some may feel that is too narrow. After all, citizenship also has psychological, social, and political dimensions. It involves participation and identity as well as legal rights and duties.[7] Even within the framework of a general commitment to liberal democracy, there are many different conceptions of citizenship. Some might say therefore that it is impossible to determine who should be a citizen until we have a theory of citizenship, some comprehensive understanding of what citizenship is, and what it entails.

I disagree. I do not think that we have to settle the broader questions about how we should understand citizenship before addressing the question of what justice requires with respect to access to citizenship as a legal status. The importance of citizenship as a legal status is often exaggerated, and we could imagine other ways of institutionalizing many of the functions now performed by citizenship as a legal status.[8] Nevertheless, the legal status of citizenship does matter in some important respects now. Above all, it is through the granting of legal status as a citizen that a modern state officially recognizes someone as a member of the political community. That provides the anchor for my reflections. I will argue that there are moral principles that govern access to the legal status of citizenship and that apply to every contemporary democratic state in Europe and North America. These principles set normative limits on the morally acceptable range of conceptions of citizenship, at least within the context of a commitment to democracy.

10.1 Birth and Belonging

Most people in liberal democratic states become citizens automatically at the moment of birth. Birthright citizenship is such a familiar political and legal practice that it is hard even to notice it.[9] Indeed, it seems so natural that when immigrants acquire citizenship after arriving in their new state, we call the

---

[6] Citizenship as a legal status is called "nationality" in international law and in some academic discussions. I prefer to use the term "citizenship," despite its other connotations because that is the word used most often in public discussions of the questions I am considering here, at least in the English-speaking world. The term "nationality" has its own complexities in a world in which many states contain more than one nation, sometimes ones that receive official recognition of some sort.

[7] For a discussion of the psychological and participatory dimensions of citizenship, see Joseph H. Carens, *Culture, Citizenship, and Community: A Contextual Exploration of Justice as Evenhandedness* (Oxford: Oxford University Press, 2000), ch. 7.

[8] See Stephen H. Legomsky, "Why Citizenship?," *Virginia Journal of International Law* 35 (1994), 279–300. See Peter J. Spiro, *Beyond Citizenship* (New York: Oxford University Press, 2008) for an argument about how globalization has transformed what citizenship can be and can do.

[9] Two recent works that seek to make the practice of birthright citizenship and the questions it raises much more visible are Ayelet Shachar, *The Birthright Lottery* (Cambridge, MA: Harvard University Press, 2009) and Jacqueline Stevens, *States without Nations: Citizenship for Mortals* (New York: Columbia University Press, 2010). See also the earlier critique of birthright citizenship in Peter

process "naturalization." But, of course, legal citizenship is not a natural category. People acquire citizenship as a result of the rules of a political practice, not as the natural outcome of being born.

Does birthright citizenship make sense morally? In some ways granting citizenship at birth seems like an odd practice from a democratic perspective.[10] When democratic theorists ask who should be included in the citizenry—and it is a question that is often neglected—they usually emphasize factors like ongoing subjection to the laws or long-term residence in a state and participation in its civil society, and they appeal to norms like consent to authority and participation in decisions that affect one's interests.[11] These sorts of considerations do play an important role when we think about the issue of naturalization for adult immigrants, but they cannot easily be applied to babies. Newborns have no past (outside the womb) so one cannot appeal to their experience as a justification for granting them citizenship. They cannot be political agents, deliberating among political alternatives and exercising political will through voting and running for office. So, we cannot appeal directly to their right to consent or to participate as a justification for granting them citizenship. Why do we confer citizenship on newborn infants?

H. Schuck and Rogers M. Smith, *Citizenship without Consent: Illegal Aliens in the American Polity* (New Haven, CT: Yale University Press, 1985).

[10] A number of scholars have argued that birthright citizenship is in tension with liberal democratic values, most notably Schuck and Smith, *Citizenship without Consent*; Shachar, *The Birthright Lottery*; and Stevens, *States without Nations*. These critiques focus on two issues: (1) the claim that there is a deep tension between the liberal commitment to consent as the foundation of legitimate authority and the practice of automatically assigning citizenship at birth; (2) the claim that there is an intrinsic link between birthright citizenship and international inequality. As I indicated at the outset, I am sympathetic to the critique of international inequality, but I think that it is a mistake to see this as intrinsically linked to the practice of birthright citizenship for reasons I will discuss in the last section of the paper. By contrast, I think the attempt to make the acquisition of citizenship a voluntary matter for everyone misconstrues the place of consent in democratic theory. I have developed this argument at length in Joseph Carens, "Who Belongs? Theoretical and Legal Questions About Birthright Citizenship in the United States," *University of Toronto Law Journal* 37:4 (1987), 413–43, which is a critique of Schuck and Smith. Here I leave the criticism of the consent argument aside in order to focus on the positive reasons for allocating citizenship at birth.

[11] For discussions of how these factors affect the question of who should be included in the demos, see Frederick Whelan, "Citizenship and Free Movement: An Open Admission Policy?" in Mark Gibney (ed.), *Open Borders? Closed Societies? The Ethical and Political Issues* (Westport, CT: Greenwood Press, 1988), pp. 3–39; Robert A. Dahl, *Democracy and its Critics* (New Haven, CT: Yale University Press, 1989); and Rainer Bauböck, *Transnational Citizenship: Membership and Rights in International Migration* (Aldershot: Edward Elgar, 1994). Ruth Rubio-Marin, *Immigration as a Democratic Challenge* (Cambridge: Cambridge University Press, 2000) provides an excellent overview of these issues. My own earliest discussions of this topic focused on the same considerations. See Joseph H. Carens, "Membership and Morality: Admission to Citizenship in Liberal Democratic States" in W. R. Brubaker (ed.), *Immigration and the Politics of Citizenship in Europe and North America* (Lanham, MD: German Marshall Fund and University Press of America, 1989), pp. 31–49 and Joseph H. Carens, "Why Naturalization Should Be Easy: A Response to Noah Pickus" in Noah M. Jeddiah Pickus (ed.), *Immigration and Citizenship in the 21st Century* (Lanham, MD: Rowman and Littlefield, 1998), pp. 141–6.

We could offer a formalistic answer to this question, noting the need for passports and diplomatic protection if parents take their minor children abroad, but these are legal technicalities that do not go to the heart of the matter. Most young children don't travel abroad. There is more than the facilitation and protection of international travel at stake in the acquisition of citizenship even by the very young.

A somewhat better answer is that even infants are moral persons. They cannot (yet) exercise political agency but they can be and are bearers of legal rights. So, the state has a duty to recognize them as moral persons and to protect their rights. Someone might say that the state acknowledges this duty by making the babies citizens.

This approach draws appropriate attention to the moral status of babies as persons and to the duty of the state to recognize that moral status by granting babies legal rights, but it does not yet explain why those legal rights should include the status of citizenship. After all, the state has a duty to respect the moral personhood and protect the legal rights of all those within its jurisdiction, even temporary visitors. It does not have to make them citizens to do this.

Someone might say that the state has to make babies citizens because being without citizenship, being stateless, is a precarious and vulnerable condition in the modern world. There is considerable truth to that, although it is also a claim that is often overstated. In any event, the need for a child to have citizenship in some state does not explain why a particular state ought to grant citizenship to a particular child. So, we are back at the question of why states confer citizenship at birth on *particular* infants and why they should do so.

The answer to that question has to lie in our sense of the moral relevance of the connections that are established at birth between a particular baby and a particular political community. Let's look first at the sorts of connections that make it obligatory for liberal democratic states to grant citizenship at birth to the children of citizens. This will enable us to see that the children of immigrants have similar sorts of connections and so similar moral claims to birthright citizenship.

10.2 The Children of Resident Citizens

Consider first children who are born to parents who are citizens of the state where their children are born and who live in that state as well. In other words, the baby's parents are resident citizens. Every democratic state grants citizenship automatically to such children at birth.[12] Some readers may be inclined

---

[12] I am deliberately avoiding discussion of whether the children of resident citizens acquire legal citizenship at birth through a legal rule that focuses on descent (*ius sanguinis*) or one that focuses on birthplace (*ius soli*). The children of resident citizens always qualify under both sorts of rules.

to say "Of course!" (or something less polite). It may seem intuitively obvious that this practice makes moral sense, but I want to make the underlying rationale explicit, and that rationale is not self-evident. As I noted above, birthright citizenship is not a natural phenomenon. It is a political practice, even when it concerns the children of resident citizens. What justifies this practice from a liberal democratic perspective?

Some will want to point out that granting citizenship at birth to the children of resident citizens is in the state's interest. That is a highly plausible claim, although anyone with a little imagination could come up with circumstances under which a state might find it in its interest not to grant citizenship to the children of some segment of its resident citizen population. In any event, my question is not why states follow this practice but whether they are morally obliged to do so. The fact that a policy is in the state's interest does not even prove that the policy is morally permissible, and I want to know whether it is not only morally permissible but also morally required. Would a state act wrongly, from a liberal democratic perspective, if it did not grant citizenship to the children of resident citizens? Is this something that justice requires? My answer to both of these questions is "yes." The challenge is to explain why.

Babies do not appear upon the earth unconnected to other human beings.[13] A baby emerges physically from her mother, of course, but she enters a social world. From the outset, she has various sorts of relationships and belongs to various sorts of human communities. She is connected to people, most intimately to parents and siblings, and through them to friends and more distant family members. Of course, these connections vary enormously. Her family may have one parent or two; the parent(s) may or may not be physically related to her; the extended social network may be large or small, intense or diffuse; it may or may not involve a religious or a cultural community into which she is welcomed as a new member. Unless a child is very unlucky, however, she will, from the moment of her birth, have connections to other human beings who feel an interest in and a responsibility for her well-being (even though the degree of interest and responsibility will vary enormously across individuals and communities). In various ways, these connections will affect not only the child's well-being but also her identity. Who we are depends in large part on how we see ourselves in relation to others, and how they see us.

One important relationship for a new baby is her relationship with a particular political community, namely, the state where she lives. We are embodied creatures. Most of our activities take place within some physical

---

[13] For a discussion of why it is important to think about relationships when talking about rights and justice, see Jennifer Nedelsky, *Law's Relations: A Relational Theory of Self, Autonomy and Law* (New York: Oxford University Press, 2011).

space. In the modern world, the physical spaces in which people live are organized politically primarily as territories governed by states.[14] So, even though a baby cannot exercise any agency, the state where she lives matters a lot to her life. As I noted above, the state can and should recognize her as a person and a bearer of rights. Beyond that, the state where she lives inevitably structures, secures, and promotes her relationships with other human beings, including her family, in various ways. Indeed, the state has a fallback responsibility for the baby's well-being in case of a catastrophic failure of familial relationships (e.g., parental death, violence, or abandonment). In addition, the state has a wide range of responsibilities for the welfare and security of those living within its territory (though, of course, particular states interpret and implement these responsibilities in different ways).

When a baby is born to parents who are resident citizens, it is reasonable to expect that she will grow up in that state and receive her social formation there and that her life chances and choices will be affected in central ways by that state's laws and policies. She cannot exercise political agency at birth, but she will be able to do so as an adult. If she is to play that role properly, she should see herself prospectively in it as she is growing up. She needs to know that she is entitled to a voice in the community where she lives and that her voice will matter. In addition, political communities are also an important source of identity for many, perhaps most, people in the modern world. A baby born to resident citizens is likely to develop a strong sense of identification with the political community in which she lives and in which her parents are citizens. She is likely to see herself and be seen by others as someone who belongs in that community. All of these circumstances shape her relationship with the state where she is born from the outset. They give her a fundamental interest in being recognized immediately as a member of the political community. Granting her citizenship at birth is a way of recognizing that relationship and giving it legal backing.

But why is citizenship the appropriate way of recognizing this relationship? As I said before, in the modern world, citizenship is the legal status by which we recognize a human being as an official member of the political community. This is not a necessary truth about how citizenship has to be constructed, but it is a fact about what citizenship means in contemporary democracies. Similarly, it is an important feature of the way we have constructed citizenship that it is a status that can be held by children as well as adults. Even human beings who are too young to exercise all of the rights or bear all of the duties that

---

[14] Federal arrangements complicate this picture, but for the sake of simplicity I will leave that complication aside.

adult citizens bear can be citizens.[15] The legal differences between adults and children should probably lead us to be more careful in deploying the rhetoric of equal citizenship because that rhetoric sometimes obscures children from our view. Nevertheless, the language of equal citizenship does capture an important truth about the relationship between citizen children and their political community. A young citizen will automatically acquire all of the rights and face all of the duties of an adult citizen once she reaches the age of maturity.[16] She does not have to pass any tests or meet any standards to qualify for full citizenship. She is recognized as a full member, in important respects, even before she is capable of agency or in possession of all of the rights of an adult citizen. These facts about what the legal status of citizenship entails are what make it the appropriate way to give legal recognition to the baby's relationship to the state.

Someone might object that birthright citizenship rests upon expectations that may not be fulfilled. The child's parents may take her abroad to live. If this happens after the child has spent several years in the state, it is clearly irrelevant. The child will have developed her own connections to the political community and will have been profoundly shaped by her upbringing within the state, even if she has not yet reached adulthood. But what if they leave while she is still quite young? She may never develop the anticipated deep connections with the political community.

The objection is true but unimportant in the absence of some plausible story about why this is likely to happen with great frequency and why it would create problems for the political community, even if it did. If a child of resident citizens gets birthright citizenship and then leaves at a young age with her parents and grows up abroad, this simply means that the state has extended citizenship and the right to return to the political community to someone who was not raised there as had been expected. Relationships are always vulnerable to the possibility of disruption and disconnection. That is not a good enough reason to make only tentative commitments. It would be wrong for a state to hand out citizenship capriciously or randomly, but no great harm is done to the community or to any individual if a state grants citizenship to someone whom it expects to live within its boundaries on an ongoing basis but who turns out, for whatever reason, not to do so. On the other hand, it is harmful to people not to be recognized as members of, and

---

[15] One can argue, as some people in the children's rights movement do, that some of the limitations on minors are unjust, that they should have more say about how their lives go and gain more legal rights at a younger age than is now the case, at least in some states. These are often good arguments, but they do have limits. No one claims that infants should be entitled to vote.

[16] In the text I am implicitly assuming that the citizens in question (child and adult) reside in the state where they hold citizenship. I explore some of the complications of non-residence later in the chapter.

granted the legal status of citizenship in, a political community to which they belong. In a liberal democratic state, citizenship policy should err on the side of inclusion. The fact that some children of resident citizens may leave is not a sufficient reason to deny citizenship to all of them.[17]

In sum, birthright citizenship for the children of resident citizens makes moral sense as a practice because it acknowledges the realities of the child's relationship to the community and the fundamental interest she has in maintaining that relationship. In a liberal democratic framework, the state is morally obliged to take these sorts of fundamental interests into account in its citizenship policies.[18] Granting citizenship at birth to the children of resident citizens is not just an administrative device that serves the state's interests. It is a moral imperative. It would be unjust to do otherwise.

In thinking about the moral logic underlying birthright citizenship for the children of resident citizens, we should pay almost as much attention to the things that the state does not take into account as to the ones it does. In the actual practice of contemporary liberal democratic states, all that matters is that the baby's parents are citizens of the state where the baby is born and that they live there. Nothing depends upon the baby's further ancestry. The transmission of citizenship to children of resident citizens is not contingent upon what language the child's parents speak at home, what their political, religious, and moral views are, how patriotic they feel, how they live their lives, or what they believe or value in general. These considerations and many others might be relevant if one were thinking about questions of belonging and exclusion from a sociological perspective, but they don't matter when the question is about the transmission of citizenship at birth.

Limiting what is relevant to birthright citizenship for the children of resident citizens is not some radical philosophical proposal. It is the way existing legal regimes treat this question in every liberal democratic state. And so they should. The fundamental liberal democratic principles of equal citizenship and respect for individual rights clearly exclude the idea of basing access to citizenship on

---

[17] Bauböck makes a similar point about the inevitability of some variation in degrees of connection: "citizenship status and rights cannot be tailored to fit individual interests and circumstances, but must apply in a wholesale way to categories of individuals whose relation with a political authority creates a presumptive interest in membership." See Rainer Bauböck, "The Rights and Duties of External Citizenship," *Citizenship Studies* 13:5 (2009), 475–99 at p. 484.

[18] The arguments for birthright citizenship for the children of resident citizens imply that any child who was born in another country but is adopted by resident citizens should be granted citizenship at the moment of adoption because that is the moment (rather than birth) when the child enters the family. From a moral perspective, a child who is adopted into her family automatically becomes a member of her new parents' political community. She has just as strong a moral claim to official recognition of that membership through a grant of legal citizenship as a child who is born into her family. The fact that the adopted child may have another citizenship is entirely irrelevant from a moral perspective for reasons that I explore in the larger work from which this is drawn.

ethnicity. And at birth, children have no cultural commitments or values or beliefs, so it is not possible to assign citizenship to them on the basis of such factors.[19] This means that the prerequisites for an undisputed right to the acquisition of citizenship at birth may legitimately involve only certain forms of connection to the community—important forms of connection but also ones that are limited in their content. They may involve only questions about one's birthplace and about the legal status and residence of one's parents.

10.3 The Children of Emigrant Citizens

I have focused so far on children born in a state to citizen parents who live there. That is, statistically, the normal case. But there is another group of citizens to consider—emigrant citizens, that is, people who have moved abroad but retain their citizenship in their country of origin. Let's call them emigrants for short. What sort of access should the children of emigrants have to citizenship in their parents' country of origin, at least if that country is a liberal democracy?

Let's start again with actual practice. So far as I have been able to determine, every country in Europe and North America grants some sort of birthright entitlement to citizenship to children born abroad to emigrants.[20] Often the child of emigrants simply becomes a citizen of her parents' country of origin at birth as a matter of law. Sometimes, the child has access to citizenship as an optional right. For example, the parents have to register the child with a consulate or fill out some form in order for her to gain citizenship status. In a few cases this transmission of parental citizenship is made contingent upon

[19] Even though infants have no cultural commitments, one could argue that the state counts on citizen parents to inculcate the norms, attitudes, and dispositions required for citizenship in their children. That expectation may well be an important component of the way in which a political culture is maintained and transmitted. However, the normative question here is whether it would be morally justifiable for a democratic state to use some means to assess whether citizen parents had actually succeeded in their educational responsibilities and whether it would be morally permissible for the state to exclude from citizenship those children who did not pass the state's tests. I assume that no one who claims to be committed to liberal democratic principles today would be prepared to defend that sort of exclusionary testing of the citizenship qualifications of the children of citizens, though we can find versions of this in the practices of democratic states in the past.

[20] See Patrick Weil, "Access to Citizenship: A Comparison of Twenty-Five Nationality Laws" in T. Alexander Aleinikoff and Douglas Klusmeyer (eds.), *Citizenship Today: Global Perspectives and Practices* (Washington, DC: Carnegie Endowment for International Peace, 2001), pp. 17–35. For an updated and more detailed version see Costica Dumbrova, "Nationality, Citizenship, and Ethno-Cultural Membership," European University Institute, unpublished PhD thesis, 2012. Citizens who live abroad can be described as emigrants (from their home country's perspective) but their children are not emigrants since they have never lived in their parents' country of origin, just as they are not properly described as immigrants in the country of their birth if they have never lived anywhere else.

the child spending some time living in the country of parental origin before a certain age. Whether or not the children of emigrants have to meet some conditions to retain or activate their birthright citizenship in their parents' country of origin, their own capacity to pass on that citizenship to their own children may be limited in significant ways.

Let me illustrate from my own experience. My wife Jenny and I are American citizens. We were both born and raised in the United States and began our working careers there. We moved to Canada to pursue professional opportunities, and our two sons were born in Canada. Because of our American citizenship, our children automatically became American citizens at birth, even though they also obtained Canadian citizenship at birth because Canada grants citizenship to anyone born on Canadian territory. Their American citizenship is not contingent. In other words, they will not lose their American citizenship unless they voluntarily renounce it. But their American citizenship differs from ours in one important way. Their capacity to pass on American citizenship to their own children is limited. If one of our sons has a child who is born outside the United States (and whose other parent is not an American), the child will not become an American citizen at birth—or indeed have any claim to American citizenship—unless our son has lived in the United States for a few years before his child is born. Many states adopt policies that are like this in order to limit the indefinite transmission of citizenship to people who live in another state. Few countries have an unqualified policy of granting citizenship to children on the basis of descent no matter how remote the children's connection with people who have actually lived in the country.

What should we make of this practice of granting birthright citizenship to the children of emigrants but limiting its subsequent transmission?[21] I think this sort of policy is not only morally permissible, but also morally required, at least within a certain discretionary range.

One possible justification for the practice is that it is a way for states to meet their general obligation to avoid statelessness. Unfortunately, this line of argument implicitly presupposes what it is supposed to explain, namely why a particular state has a duty to grant citizenship at birth to a particular child. Emigrant parents have left their state's territory and are subject to its jurisdiction only in limited ways. Why is their state obliged to extend citizenship to their children? That is not a rhetorical question but rather one designed to draw attention to the fact that the answer is not self-evident. There is an answer, I think, and I try to identify that answer in what follows, but it is

---

[21] The best philosophical discussion of the issues raised by emigrants (and external citizenship generally) is Bauböck, "The Rights and Duties of External Citizenship." See also Bauböck, *Transnational Citizenship*.

appropriate to ask for an explicit account. We cannot easily appeal to the international convention on statelessness to justify this practice of granting citizenship to the children of emigrants. The convention assigns the responsibility to avoid statelessness first to the state of birth, at least when that is also the state of residence. It is only if that state fails to adopt appropriate rules regarding the acquisition of nationality that the duty falls upon the state of parental citizenship. If meeting the duty to avoid statelessness were the sole motivation for a policy of granting citizenship to the children of emigrants, one would expect much more contingent, qualified policies than we see in practice. Note also that the duties assigned by the convention on statelessness both to the state of residence and to the state of parental origin implicitly presuppose the moral relevance of social connections between particular individuals and particular states.

If preventing statelessness were the only reason for the practice of granting citizenship to the children of emigrant citizens, it would seem hard to explain why these children acquire their parents' citizenship even if they also obtain citizenship at birth in the state where their family lives. That is often the case, as my children's experience illustrates. So, I think we have to look for a deeper rationale.

Leaving aside questions about the merits of specific rules, I think the general pattern of granting birthright citizenship to the children of emigrant citizens makes moral sense from a liberal democratic perspective. It reflects the same normative logic that underlies birthright citizenship for the children of resident citizens, namely that moral claims to a particular citizenship at birth derive from the baby's connections to that political community and the ways in which those connections are likely to affect her interests and her identity. In other words, having parents who are citizens matters morally to a child's claim to citizenship not because it means that the child has blood ties to the wider political community but because it means that the child has important social connections to the community.

By definition, a child born abroad to emigrants is not connected to her parents' political community through birthplace and residence. In that respect, her claims to birthright citizenship are weaker than the claims of a child born in the state where her parents are citizens. Nevertheless, her claims are still strong enough to warrant recognizing her as a member of the community. A baby born abroad will have important ties to her parents' original political community through her immediate family, not because of some imagined genetic link to citizens outside her family but because of her social situation and her existing and potential relationships. She has a reasonable prospect of growing up in the state if her parents decide to return there. In the meantime, she will almost certainly have relatives there whom the family will visit, and she is likely to acquire cultural and emotional ties to the country through her parents. Her parents' identities are likely to be shaped in powerful ways by the country they have left, and they may well want to pass that identity on to their child.

At the same time, states are, above all, territorial communities. Citizenship status should not become too disconnected from that fact. The emigrants themselves have a direct connection to the state, having lived on its territory. The potential for the children to live there, if their parents take them back, is strong enough to justify their citizenship. But if the children don't live there, it's less plausible to pass on citizenship to a generation twice removed from the one that did live there.

Let me again illustrate these general points from my own experience. As I noted, our sons acquired Canadian citizenship at birth. Nevertheless, it was very important to us that our children also have American citizenship. For one thing, our children were born relatively soon after we moved to Canada. We still saw ourselves then primarily as Americans rather than Canadians, and we wanted our children to have an American identity as well as a Canadian one. We were not certain that we would stay in Canada permanently. Our children's American citizenship guaranteed that we would have the legal right to move the entire family "back" to the United States if we wanted to do so. In fact we loved our jobs, we loved living in Toronto and in Canada, and over time we came to see ourselves as Canadian (as well as American). Things could have turned out differently, however. Moreover, when we moved to Canada, almost all of our close relatives were in the United States, including my parents and siblings and Jenny's parents and siblings. We returned frequently for visits. As a practical matter the fact that we all had American passports made family travel easier. A more fundamental issue was that the children would have had a right to move to the United States to live with relatives there if both of us had died while they were young. So, from our perspective, the fact that our children had acquired American citizenship at birth protected their (and our) vital interests, interests that were rooted in the lives we had led in the United States.[22] On the other hand, having grown up in Canada and having

---

[22] One objection to the argument that the children of emigrants have a moral claim to citizenship in their parents' country of origin because of the ways in which their interests and identity may depend upon their recognition as members of that community is that other people may have much more vital interests at stake in gaining recognition as members than the children of emigrants do. For example, people from a poor state might have a much more vital interest in gaining American citizenship than my children who, after all, are already in a privileged position as Canadian citizens. This objection implicitly rests upon a challenge to the presuppositions that I adopted at the beginning of the chapter regarding the moral legitimacy of the existing international order and the rights of states to control admissions. I do not want to consider that challenge here for reasons of space. I do think that the challenge introduces an important line of inquiry, and I explore it in the larger work from which this is drawn, though I argue there that this way of framing the issue is ultimately misguided. I will explain at the end of this chapter why my conclusions about birthright citizenship would still largely apply in a world of open borders.

Canadian citizenship, our sons see themselves primarily as Canadians. If they do not move to the United States, their own connections to the United States will be far more limited than the connections that Jenny and I had and have, and their identification with the United States much more attenuated. America was home for both of us for a long time. It has never been home for them. So, their moral claims to pass on their American citizenship to their own children are much weaker than our claims to pass on our American citizenship to them.

The relative importance of children gaining citizenship in their emigrant parents' country of origin varies from case to case, depending on a wide range of individual and social circumstances, even among children who remain permanently in the state where they were born. Some have such strong connections to their parents' original country that it really is a second home, perhaps even their primary home in their identity and affections (though this is rare for children who are treated decently in the land where they live). For others, it is just a vague point of reference in their parents' past (though this, too, is rare if the parents left voluntarily as adults). Most fall somewhere in between these extremes. In any event, there is no plausible way to construct birthright citizenship rules that respond to these individual variations.

As we have already seen in discussing birthright citizenship for the children of resident citizens, a state cannot avoid adopting rules regarding the transmission of citizenship whose underlying rationale rests in part on generalizations, probabilities, and expectations about human lives and relationships. Given this indeterminacy and the fact that the children of emigrants have weaker moral claims to birthright citizenship than the children of resident citizens, it is reasonable for different states to make somewhat different judgments about the relative importance of their connections with the children of emigrants and to adopt somewhat different policies regarding the transmission of citizenship to them. Like the United States, many states grant the children of emigrants a simple and unqualified citizenship at birth, while setting further conditions on the transmission of that citizenship to their own children. That is clearly a morally permissible policy, given the analysis I have offered, but so would be a policy that was somewhat more restrictive or somewhat more expansive. For example, it is also morally permissible in my view for states to grant only a right to citizenship and to require some form of registration for this right to be activated. This is one way of ensuring that the parents actually want their children to gain citizenship in their land of origin. By the same token, it would not be morally wrong for a state to adopt a somewhat less restrictive policy than the American one, for example by permitting the children of emigrants to pass on citizenship to their own children automatically.

While there are no precise moral boundaries to the rules regulating the transmission of citizenship to the children of emigrants, the range of morally permissible rules is not unlimited. On the one hand, the children of emigrants normally have sufficient ties to their parents' community of origin to warrant some effective access to citizenship in that country. It would be unjust to exclude them altogether, even in cases where this would not leave them stateless. As we have seen, every democratic state does in fact grant the children of emigrants some sort of birthright claim to citizenship. On the other hand, states should not be unduly expansive in granting citizenship to descendants of emigrants who have no other tie to the political community than their ancestry. Normally the grandchildren of immigrants have much weaker ties to their grandparents' country of origin than the children do and the great-grandchildren few if any ties. It would be wrong to regard citizenship in a democracy as a sort of feudal title or property right that could be passed on from one generation to the next regardless of where the heirs actually lived their lives.[23] Unlimited transmission of citizenship through generations living outside the country would reflect an ethnic conception of political community that would be difficult to reconcile with democratic principles. As the proximity to an ancestor who lived in the country decreases, so too does the plausibility of any justification for automatically granting citizenship.[24]

10.4 Children of Immigrants

If the account I have offered of the moral logic underlying birthright citizenship for the children of citizens is correct, it has important implications for the question of access to citizenship for the children of immigrants: children who are born in a liberal democratic state in which their parents have settled as legal immigrants should acquire citizenship automatically at birth because they, too, have sufficient ties to the community to merit recognition as members. Indeed because they have been born in the state and are likely to be raised there, they normally have even stronger ties to the political

---

[23] For a critique of the practice of birthright citizenship on the grounds that it treats citizenship like property, see Shachar, *The Birthright Lottery*.

[24] Like almost every principle, the one I have just enunciated about limiting the transmission of citizenship is subject to qualification under certain circumstances. For example, if the original emigrants have been forced into exile and their children have been unable to return, a newly established (or restored) democratic state might be justified in extending access to citizenship to later generations born abroad. Some states in Eastern Europe adopted policies of this sort in the wake of the collapse of the Soviet Union. Similarly, if descendants of emigrants were subject to persecution because of their ancestral origins, the state of (ancestral) origin might be justified in extending to the descendants offers of admission and access to citizenship. Again this reflects real historical circumstances, though the question of what would be justifiable in any particular case would require a detailed analysis that I cannot provide here.

community and so stronger claims to birthright citizenship than the children of emigrant citizens (who, as we have seen, enjoy some form of birthright citizenship in every liberal democratic state).

Recall the rationale that I offered for granting citizenship at birth to the children of resident citizens. It emphasized the fact that the baby was likely to grow up in the state, to receive her social formation there, and to have her life chances and choices deeply affected by the state's policies. These considerations apply also to the children of settled immigrants. If they are reasons why the children of resident citizens should get citizenship at birth, they are also reasons why the children of immigrants should get citizenship at birth. So, too, with the cultivation of political agency. A child of immigrants should be taught from the beginning that she is entitled to a voice in the community where she lives and that her voice will matter. And so, too, with political identity. Like a child of resident citizens, a child of immigrants has a deep interest in seeing herself and in being seen by others as someone who belongs in the political community in which she lives. Finally, like resident citizens, settled immigrants may leave, returning to their country of origin or going elsewhere and taking their children with them. If a child is old enough, she will have developed her own connections to the community and so this fact will be irrelevant to her claim to citizenship. But like the children of resident citizens, some children of settled immigrants may leave at a young age and never return. As with the children or resident citizens and for the same sorts of reasons, this possibility does not provide a good enough reason to treat a child's membership in the political community as a contingent matter.

In sum, the most important circumstances shaping a child's relationship with the state from the outset are the same for a child of immigrants as they are for a child of resident citizens. So, a child of immigrants has the same sort of fundamental interest in being recognized immediately as a member of the political community.

To be sure, a child of immigrants has a somewhat weaker claim to membership than a child of resident citizens, because, in the latter case, the parents' status as citizens provides another important social connection to the political community. But as we have just seen, this is not because the political community is constituted by blood ties among the citizens. Parentage is only relevant because it is an indicator of a child's social connections to the community. From that perspective a child of immigrants has a considerably stronger set of social connections and hence a stronger claim to membership than a child born to emigrant parents. The ties that come from actually living in a state are the most powerful basis for a claim to membership. Home is where one lives, and where one lives is the crucial variable for interests and for identity, both empirically and normatively. Birthright citizenship is the only proper way to recognize the relationship between the newborn child of settled immigrants and the political community in which her family lives and in which she is expected to grow up. It is unjust not to grant citizenship at birth to the children of settled immigrants.

10.5 Birthright Citizenship in a Just World

Now consider how these arguments about birthright citizenship would be affected if we depart from the conventional view about the state's right to control immigration and the legitimacy of the current world order. One way to do this would be to imagine a world of relative economic equality between states and open borders between them on the grounds that these are the conditions required by a just world.[25] Under these conditions, birthright citizenship would no longer grant access to a privileged social position, as it does today to those born in rich liberal democratic states. Nevertheless, it would be important that children born in a state and expected to grow up there be recognized as members of the political community from the outset, for all of the reasons discussed earlier in the chapter. So, even in a world of open borders and relative equality between states, it would make sense to regard birthright citizenship for the children of resident citizens and settled immigrants as a moral imperative.

The case for birthright citizenship for the children of emigrant citizens would be a bit weaker under these ideal conditions because in a world where people were free to move, the children would not need the parents' citizenship to have the right to move to the parents' home state. On the other hand, that is only one of the vital interests that are protected by parental transmission of citizenship in the current world. In particular, to the extent that a parent is motivated by her identities and attachments, she would have just as much reason to want to transmit her membership in her community of origin to her children in a world of open borders as she does in our world today.

Even if birthright citizenship would be a legitimate, indeed, a morally required practice in a just world, can't we say that it is an illegitimate practice today because of the way in which it contributes to the maintenance of global inequality? Wasn't that the point of the analogy between citizenship today and feudal privilege?

Not quite. The central point of the analogy was that in both cases (feudalism and the modern state system) we have humanly constructed social orders that create social positions with highly different life chances, that people are assigned to these social positions at birth, and that restrictions on mobility

---

[25] For a defense of the view that these are the conditions that would characterize a just world, see Joseph H. Carens, *The Ethics of Immigration* (New York: Oxford University Press, 2013), chs. 11–13.

play a crucial role in preventing those assigned to less advantageous positions from moving to more advantageous ones. All of these key elements in the analogy still hold, if one recognizes, as I do, that it is not birthright assignment per se that is objectionable but rather the fact that the social positions are so unequal and that the opportunities for moving from one position to another are so restricted.

There are many debates about the best way to move from the existing unjust social order to one that is more just. My own view, for reasons elaborated elsewhere, is that justice requires eliminating most of the restrictions on freedom of migration across borders and on access to citizenship in the place where one lives on an ongoing basis, though I do not suggest that this is a complete solution in itself.[26]

Some of those who criticize birthright citizenship are really concerned with the need for more effective redistributive mechanisms between states. I share that concern and I agree that opening borders is not the only way, or even the best way, to address this problem. But I also think that eliminating birthright citizenship does nothing in itself to advance international redistribution. Indeed Ayelet Shachar, who makes birthright citizenship a centerpiece of her critique of global inequality, ultimately acknowledges that the practice itself is not intrinsically problematic and that she would not eliminate it.[27]

Jacqueline Stevens presents an even more radical critique of birthright citizenship, but again, in my view, her real target is something other than birthright citizenship itself, namely the way in which birthright citizenship has historically been connected with other problematic practices (such as restrictions on migration) and with ways of thinking about the political community that have destructive consequences. So far as I can see, Stevens' critique does not apply to the understanding of birthright citizenship that I have claimed is its underlying moral logic from a liberal democratic perspective. Stevens herself acknowledges that where one lives matters in terms of the claims of membership.[28]

In sum, if it is properly structured, the practice of birthright citizenship makes moral sense in the world we live in today, if we abstract from concerns with global inequality and restrictions on immigration, and it would also make moral sense in a more just world of open borders and relatively equal states.[29]

---

[26] See Carens, *The Ethics of Immigration.*

[27] See Shachar, *The Birthright Lottery.*

[28] See Stevens, *States without Nations: Citizenship for Mortals.*

[29] This chapter draws upon material presented in a slightly different way in Carens, *The Ethics of Immigration.* Several paragraphs in the text are adapted from Joseph H. Carens, "The Integration of Immigrants," *Journal of Moral Philosophy* 2:1 (April 2005), 29–46.

References

Bauböck, Rainer, *Transnational Citizenship: Membership and Rights in International Migration* (Aldershot: Edward Elgar, 1994).

Bauböck, Rainer, "The Rights and Duties of External Citizenship," *Citizenship Studies* 13:5 (2009), 475–99.

Carens, Joseph H., "Aliens and Citizens: The Case for Open Borders," *Review of Politics* 49 (1987), 251–73.

Carens, Joseph H., "Who Belongs? Theoretical and Legal Questions About Birthright Citizenship in the United States," *University of Toronto Law Journal* 37:4 (Fall 1987), 413–43.

Carens, Joseph H., "Membership and Morality: Admission to Citizenship in Liberal Democratic States" in W. R. Brubaker (ed.), *Immigration and the Politics of Citizenship in Europe and North America* (Lanham, MD: German Marshall Fund and University Press of America, 1989), pp. 31–49.

Carens, Joseph H., "Migration and Morality: A liberal egalitarian perspective" in B. Barry and R. E. Goodin (eds.), *Free Movement: Ethical Issues in the Transnational Migration of People and of Money* (University Park, PA: University of Pennsylvania Press, 1992), pp. 25–47.

Carens, Joseph H., "Why Naturalization Should Be Easy: A Response to Noah Pickus" in Noah M. Jeddiah Pickus (ed.), *Immigration and Citizenship in the 21st Century* (Lanham, MD: Rowman and Littlefield, 1998), pp. 141–6.

Carens, Joseph H., *Culture, Citizenship, and Community: A Contextual Exploration of Justice as Evenhandedness* (Oxford: Oxford University Press, 2000).

Carens, Joseph H., "The Integration of Immigrants," *Journal of Moral Philosophy* 2:1 (2005), 29–46.

Carens, Joseph H., *The Ethics of Immigration* (New York: Oxford University Press, 2013).

Dahl, Robert A., *Democracy and its Critics* (New Haven, CT: Yale University Press, 1989).

Dumbrova, Costica, "Nationality, Citizenship, and Ethno-Cultural Membership." European University Institute, unpublished PhD thesis, 2012.

Legomsky, Stephen H., "Why Citizenship?," *Virginia Journal of International Law* 35 (1994), 279–300.

Nedelsky, Jennifer, *Law's Relations: A Relational Theory of Self, Autonomy and Law* (New York: Oxford University Press, 2011).

Rubio-Marin, Ruth, *Immigration as a Democratic Challenge* (Cambridge: Cambridge University Press, 2000).

Schuck, Peter H. and Rogers M. Smith, *Citizenship without Consent: Illegal Aliens in the American Polity* (New Haven, CT: Yale University Press, 1985).

Shachar, Ayelet, *The Birthright Lottery* (Cambridge, MA: Harvard University Press, 2009).

Spiro, Peter J., *Beyond Citizenship* (New York: Oxford University Press, 2008).

Stevens, Jacqueline, *States without Nations: Citizenship for Mortals* (New York: Columbia University Press, 2010).

Weil, Patrick, "Access to Citizenship: A Comparison of Twenty-Five Nationality Laws" in T. Alexander Aleinikoff and Douglas Klusmeyer (eds.), *Citizenship Today: Global*

Perspectives and Practices (Washington, DC: Carnegie Endowment for International Peace, 2001), pp. 17–35.

Whelan, Frederick, "Citizenship and Free Movement: An Open Admission Policy?" in Mark Gibney (ed.), *Open Borders? Closed Societies? The Ethical and Political Issues* (Westport, CT: Greenwood Press, 1988), pp. 3–39.

11

The Significance of Territorial Presence and the Rights of Immigrants

Sarah Song

Contemporary philosophical debates about immigration have focused on two sets of questions. The first has to do with the control of state borders and the movement of people across them. Do states have the right to control their own borders? What, if any, limits are there on this right? Some theorists defend this right by appeal to the importance of preserving distinctive cultures or the idea of freedom of association.[1] Others have pursued the question of what the content of a liberal democratic state's immigration policy should look like: who should get in and why.[2] In this chapter, I leave aside these important questions about the grounds of the state's right to control immigration and how this right ought to be exercised in order to focus on a second set of normative questions about immigration: how a liberal democratic state should treat noncitizens who are already inside its borders.

These two sets of questions are, of course, related. If one thinks that the state has the right to control its own borders, one may also think that the state has the right to treat territorial insiders in any way it wishes. In states that aspire to liberal democratic principles, however, citizens must balance a political community's right to self-determination against a commitment to treating all persons in the territory as equals. One way of articulating the moral constraints on a liberal democratic state's right to self-determination is in terms of the value of equality. One might emphasize the moral equality of all human

---

[1] See, respectively, Michael Walzer, *Spheres of Justice: A Defense of Pluralism and Equality* (New York: Basic Books, 1983) and Christopher Heath Wellman, "Immigration and Freedom of Association," *Ethics* 119 (2008), 109–41.

[2] Joseph Carens, "Who Should Get In? The Ethics of Immigration Admissions," *Ethics & International Affairs* 17:1 (2003), 95–110.

beings to argue for basic human rights, regardless of the territorial location of individuals.[3] But others might maintain that the premise of moral equality is consistent with the view that physical presence in a state's territory should make a difference to the rights one is entitled to. This chapter explores this normative position by considering what equality requires in the treatment of noncitizens who are present in the territory of liberal democratic states. A full treatment of this topic would require showing how the demands of equality should be weighed against the state's right to self-determination, including the right to control immigration. My more modest aim is to offer pro tanto reasons for extending rights to territorially present noncitizens in a way that is consistent with treating them as equals.

This normative inquiry is important because liberal democratic states are already engaged in the practice of extending a range of rights to noncitizens in virtue of their territorial presence, but without deeper consideration of why territorial presence matters. For example, in the U.S., noncitizens are entitled to many of the same rights as citizens, including the protection of antidiscrimination law, due process rights in criminal proceedings, and access to public education and some welfare benefits. In the 1886 case, *Yick Wo v. Hopkins*, the U.S. Supreme Court first acknowledged that basic rights should be extended to all persons within the territory, regardless of their citizenship status: "[Fundamental rights] are not confined to the protection of citizens . . . These provisions are universal in their application to all persons within the territorial jurisdiction, without regard to any differences of race, of color, or of nationality."[4] That territorial presence was significant was asserted again in the 1982 case, *Plyler v. Doe*, which struck down a Texas statute barring the children of unauthorized migrants from attending public schools. The Court held that equal protection of the laws "extends to anyone, citizen or stranger, who is subject to the laws of a State, and reaches into every corner of a state's territory."[5] These legal claims to personhood are not appeals to personhood *simpliciter*—that all persons *qua* persons are entitled to equal concern and respect—but what Linda Bosniak has called claims of

---

[3] Joseph Carens' "Aliens and Citizens: The Case for Open Borders," *Review of Politics* 49:2 (1987), 251–73, reflects such a view. Yasemin Soysal's *Limits of Citizenship: Migrants and Postnational Membership in Europe* (Chicago: University of Chicago Press, 1994) and David Jacobson's *Rights across Borders: Immigration and the Decline of Citizenship* (Baltimore, MD: Johns Hopkins University Press, 1996) offer a political sociological analysis of the way states have turned in incremental fashion to international human rights law (such as the UN human rights instruments and the European Convention on Human Rights) as a basis for extending rights to migrants; one might build on their analyses to argue, from the premise of moral equality, that this is what states ought to be doing.

[4] *Yick Wo v. Hopkins*, 118 U.S. 356, 369 (1886). A decade later, in *Wong Wing v. United States*, 163 U.S. 228 (1896), the Court ruled that noncitizen criminal defendants, like citizen defendants, are entitled to the protection of the Fifth and Sixth Amendments.

[5] *Plyler v. Doe*, 457 U.S. 202, 215 (1982).

"territorial personhood"—that all *persons within the territorial jurisdiction* are entitled to some of the same protections and benefits that citizens enjoy.[6]

This chapter examines three different accounts of the normative significance of territorial presence, based on the principles of (1) affiliation, (2) fair play, and (3) coercion.[7] Each of these principles offers a way of delimiting the scope of the duties that human beings have to each other. My focus is on whether these principles can account for the special obligations that territorial insiders of a state have to one another. The claim that territorial insiders have special responsibilities toward one another rests on the following premises: (1) that there are certain kinds of relationships that ground special responsibilities, and (2) that territorial insiders share the kind of relationship that grounds special responsibilities. I assume the first premise and look to different accounts of the second premise. What kind of relationship do territorial insiders have to one another, and what sorts of rights and responsibilities does the relationship generate?

My chapter proceeds as follows. First, I analyze the three principles—affiliation, fair play, and coercion—to see how well they account for special rights and obligations of territorial insiders. While each account suffers weaknesses, I argue that the three principles, taken together, do ground a case for the special rights and obligations of different groups of territorial insiders. I then turn to consider the question of what equality requires when it comes to the treatment of territorially present noncitizens: does equality require uniform treatment, or is differential treatment permissible? I conclude by exploring the implications of my analysis for the content of the special rights and responsibilities of different groups of territorial insiders.

11.1 Affiliation

We might view territorial presence as generating special rights and responsibilities in virtue of certain kinds of *affiliations* that inhabitants of a territory share with one another. Legal scholar Hiroshi Motomura has described "immigration as affiliation" as "the view that the treatment of lawful immigrants and other noncitizens should depend on the ties that they have formed in this country."[8] The affiliation principle is also at the heart of Joseph Carens'

---

[6] Linda Bosniak, *The Citizen and the Alien* (Princeton, NJ: Princeton University Press, 2006), p. 55.

[7] This chapter is inspired by Linda Bosniak's "Being Here: Ethical Territoriality and the Rights of Immigrants," *Theoretical Inquiries in Law* 8:2 (2007), 389–410, which examines the principles of affiliation, anti-caste, and "mutuality of obligation" (or the coercion principle). I explore the affiliation and coercion principles in greater depth and consider an additional account based on fair play.

[8] Hiroshi Motomura, *Americans in Waiting: The Lost Story of Immigration and Citizenship in the United States* (Oxford: Oxford University Press, 2006), p. 11.

argument for amnesty for unauthorized migrants: "there is something deeply wrong in forcing people to leave a place where they have lived for a long time. Most people form their deepest human connections where they live—it becomes home." Webs of social connection or de facto social membership (as opposed to official legal membership) is taken to ground a case for the right to reside permanently in a state's territory. As Carens puts it, "People who live and work and raise their families in a society become members, whatever their legal status. That is why we find it hard to expel them when they are discovered."[9]

Affiliations were a central rationale for the legalization programs enacted by the U.S. Congress and signed into law by President Reagan in 1986, which extended a path to citizenship to 2.9 miliion unauthorized migrants.[10] The importance of affiliations is also reflected in U.S. immigration law in the context of deportation proceedings. Consider noncitizens admitted to the U.S. as lawful permanent residents (LPRs). LPRs who commit certain crimes are subject to deportation, but if they have lived in the U.S. as LPRs for at least five years, have seven years of continuous residence, and no commission of an aggravated felony, they may appeal to an immigration judge to cancel the deportation order.[11] The underlying rationale seems to be that the longer noncitizens are here, the deeper their affiliations, and the stronger their claim to remain. Some appeal to human rights, but most rely on familial and social ties to citizens of the host society.

What kind of affiliations should count? One answer is provided by theorists of nationalism, who emphasize the importance of ties to the nation. On David Miller's prominent theory of nationality, nations are defined as communities bound together by "natural sentiments."[12] In characterizing what is distinctive about national identity, Miller says it "requires that the people who share it should have something in common, a set of characteristics that in the past was often referred to as a 'national character,' but which I prefer to describe as a common public culture."[13] You and I share a national culture, even if we never meet, if each of us has a personal history involving the national culture, has been initiated into its traditions, and identifies with the nation. Miller emphasizes the openness of his account to immigrants: "immigration need not pose problems, provided only that the immigrants come to share a

---

[9] Joseph Carens, *Immigrants and the Right to Stay* (Cambridge, MA: MIT Press, 2010), pp. 12, 18–19.

[10] Immigrant Reform and Control Act of 1986, Public Law 99–603 (Act of November 6, 1986).

[11] Illegal Immigration Reform & Immigrant Responsibility Act of 1996 (hereafter IIRIRA), P.L. 104–208 § 240A(a), 8 U.S.C. 1229b(a) (2006).

[12] David Miller, *On Nationality* (Oxford: Oxford University Press, 1995), p. 58, n.11.

[13] Miller, *On Nationality*, p. 25.

common national identity, to which they may contribute their own distinctive ingredients."[14]

For the sake of argument, let's grant that national affiliations have ethical significance, that they are a valid source of rights and obligations. We nonetheless run into some difficulties. First, the boundaries of national affiliations don't map neatly onto territorial boundaries. Not even all citizens of a state speak the national language, and many residents, including many citizens, may lack a sense of belonging together or a strong degree of identification with the national culture. On a strict interpretation of the nationality principle, such disengagement with the national culture would undermine the "disengaged" noncitizens' access to citizenship, or in the case of "disengaged" birthright citizens, jeopardize the citizenship status they already possess. Proponents of the nationality principle might say this is as it should be. My point here is that national affiliations are an imperfect proxy for territorial presence.

Second, it seems morally perverse to require affiliation with the dominant national culture as a condition of equal treatment. Consider Chinese migrants in late-nineteenth-century America. On the nationalist view, the greater the immigrant's identification and interaction with the dominant society, the greater his claim to rights. But what if racial prejudice and inequality are barriers to integrating into the national culture as they have been in the U.S. and elsewhere? In order to claim rights, Chinese and other non-white migrants would have had to identify and affiliate with the white majority who sought to exclude them.[15]

In response, one might argue that what triggers equal concern is not affiliation with members of the dominant group but with any *local* group in the host society. Affiliations with family, friends, neighbors, and co-workers in the host society are sufficient to trigger equal concern. These local affiliations are what Carens seems to have in mind in making his case for amnesty. In practice, local, not national, affiliations are the kinds of ties that U.S. immigration law has tended to prioritize. For example, in considering appeals to deportation orders, much greater weight is given to family ties than national ties. Whether the noncitizen being deported is able to speak the language of the country to which they will go sometimes comes up, but it is a relatively minor factor. More weight is given to whether deportation would result in "extreme hardship" to their spouses, parents, or children who would be left behind.[16]

[14] Miller, *On Nationality*, p. 26.
[15] On racial discrimination in the history of immigration policy, see Sarah Fine's chapter in this volume.
[16] See, e.g., *Cruz Rendon v. Holder*, 604 F.3d 1104 (9th Cir. 2009) (minor child's specialized medical and educational needs offered as grounds for cancelling the deportation order).

The local affiliations view, however, is not free of problems either. First, it seems too weak to generate equal concern. Consider a migrant in the UK who develops friends in the UK while also maintaining ties of family and friendship with people from his home country. Why does the fact that he interacts with a group of people in the UK entitle him to equal concern from the British government if he also has affiliations of a similar kind outside the territory? In response, the local affiliations view needs to explain the nature, density, and depth of affiliations that should trigger equal concern. A proponent of the local affiliations view would have to argue something like the following: when a person's *primary* affiliations are in the host country, he is entitled to equal concern. For example, one might argue that noncitizens whose most intimate affiliates—partners, children, and other family members or close friends—are in the host state have a prima facie claim to remain in the territory.

A second problem with the local affiliations view is that ties to family, friends, and neighbors is an imperfect proxy for territorial presence, especially for the most recently arrived migrants. Carens is probably right that most people form their "deepest human connections" where they live.[17] Yet, there is some irony in grounding a case for the rights of immigrants on affiliations since the disjuncture between country of residence and the location of one's familial and other affiliations is greatest in the case of migrants, including temporary workers who leave loved ones behind in order to work and send money back home. Many immigrants will develop social ties in the host country, but most will not do this right away. Using time as a proxy for affiliation, Carens suggests that one or two years is not enough to develop substantial affiliations and fifteen to twenty years are "much more than enough." He settles upon "five years of settled residence without any criminal convictions" as sufficient "to establish anyone as a responsible member of society."[18] But before a noncitizen establishes local affiliations, on what grounds could she claim rights? Consider the case of a first-time visitor to the U.S. who has no affiliations to any residents of the host country. Under current law, such a visitor would still enjoy legal protections against unreasonable search and seizure from the moment she sets foot in the territory. Noncitizens who have just entered the territory are treated, for many legal purposes, the same as those who have lived there for years.[19] The affiliations view cannot account for the rights and responsibilities of short-term and temporary visitors.

---

[17] Carens, *Immigrants and the Right to Stay*, p. 12.

[18] Carens, *Immigrants and the Right to Stay*, pp. 20–1.

[19] Kal Raustiala argues that the logic underlying this practice is "simply spatial" ("The Geography of Justice," *Fordham Law Review* 73 (2005), 2501–60). This chapter explores the normativity of spatiality with the aim of showing that the rationales for distributing rights and responsibilities based on territorial presence is not "simply spatial."

This limitation is not a reason for rejecting the affiliation principle as an account of the significance of territorial presence. While it may not apply to the most recently arrived, it does capture the situation of many migrants. The affiliation principle is scalar, not binary. It admits of degrees. The deeper one's affiliation to the country, the greater one's entitlement to rights. This view of affiliations as a matter of degree is reflected in the U.S. Supreme Court decision, *Mathews v. Diaz*, which upheld a Social Security Act provision that excluded noncitizens from Medicare unless they had resided in the country for at least five years:

> The decision to share [the social] bounty with our guests may take into account the character of the relationship between the alien and this country: Congress may decide that as the alien's tie grows stronger, so does the strength of his claim to an equal share of that munificence ... it is unquestionably reasonable for Congress to make an alien's eligibility depend on both the character and the duration of his residence.[20]

The Court affirmed the view it had articulated earlier that the noncitizen has an "ascending scale of rights as he increases his identity with our society."[21] The affiliations view does account for some rights and responsibilities of noncitizens, typically those of longer-term residents, but it does not provide the whole story about the rights and responsibilities of territorial insiders.

11.2 Fair Play

A second way of accounting for the special rights and responsibilities of territorially present persons is the principle of "fair play" or reciprocity. On this principle, all those who participate in a scheme of social cooperation are entitled to the benefits and must bear the burdens of that scheme. Arguments about fair play presuppose a view of the state as a mutually beneficial system of social cooperation. As Rawls puts it, the basic idea is, "We are not to gain from the cooperative labors of others without doing our fair share."[22] Indeed, the modern state is the most consequential social scheme we know. Without the institutions of the modern state to make, enforce, and interpret the laws, each of us would be left to our own devices to ensure our own security and survival.

The principle of fair play has typically been invoked in debates about political obligation to answer the question of why individuals should obey

---

[20] *Mathews v. Diaz*, 426 U.S. 67, 80, 82–3 (1976).

[21] *Johnson v. Eisentrager*, 339 U.S. 763, 770 (1950).

[22] John Rawls, *A Theory of Justice* (Cambridge, MA: Belknap Press, [1971] 2005), pp. 4, 112. See also Rawls' "Legal Obligation and the Principle of Fair Play" in S. Hook (ed.), *Law and Philosophy: A Symposium* (New York: New York University Press, 1964), pp. 3–18.

the law. Here I consider the reverse—to justify obligations that the state has to individuals, or in the case of democratic states, to justify obligations that citizens have to one another as well as to noncitizens in their midst. If we think of a democratic state as the representation of the collective will or interests of the citizens who make up the state, the question then is: what obligations do democratic citizens have to newcomers who are participants in the scheme of social cooperation that is the state?

To answer, we need to consider what relationship must hold between an individual and a cooperative scheme for her to be said to be a *participant* in some significant sense. Someone who accepts benefits from the social scheme unintentionally or without knowing the moral consequences of doing so is not a participant. One might think that to be a participant in a social scheme one must have expressly or tacitly *consented* to participate. Before getting to the question of whether one can participate in a scheme without consenting to it, let me briefly say something about the problems with the consent principle for grounding the special rights and responsibilities of territorial insiders.

Consider first those inhabitants who are already citizens. As many critics of the consent principle have argued, the vast majority of citizens have never consented to citizenship. In defending a consent-based theory of citizenship, Peter Schuck and Rogers Smith seek to make consent to citizenship a real possibility by offering children born to citizens and long-term lawful resident noncitizens the opportunity to renounce citizenship when they reach the age of majority.[23] But even if a state agency were to notify birthright citizens of the opportunity to self-expatriate at age eighteen or thereabouts, the enormous costs and challenges of exiting a political community make it implausible to regard failure to self-expatriate as a sign of consent.

As for noncitizens in a state's territory, only lawful permanent residents (LPRs) can live up to the liberal ideal of consent. They enact consent in a way that native-born citizens never do. The "good, consenting immigrant," in Bonnie Honig's words, "reperform[s] the official social contract by naturalizing to citizenship."[24] In contrast, the unauthorized migrant is the "bad immigrant" whose territorial presence has not been consented to and therefore is deemed not only unworthy of membership but also ineligible for many of the rights accorded to LPRs.

---

[23] Peter Schuck and Rogers M. Smith, *Citizenship without Consent: Illegal Aliens in the American Polity* (New Haven, CT: Yale University Press, 1985). Schuck and Smith's claim is not that the native-born children of unauthorized migrants should be denied citizenship but that birthright citizenship (*jus soli*) is not constitutionally required and therefore open to democratic contestation.

[24] Bonnie Honig, *Democracy and the Foreigner* (Princeton, NJ: Princeton University Press, 2001), p. 92.

While the consent principle can ground the rights and obligations of naturalized citizens, it cannot account for all those birthright citizens who have never consented to citizenship. In light of this, we need to ask whether one can be a participant in a social scheme without giving her consent to it. In discussing the fair play principle, Rawls suggests that political obligation depends on "our having accepted and our intention to continue accepting the benefits of a just scheme of cooperation."[25] A. John Simmons distinguishes between *accepting benefits* from and *giving consent* to a social scheme. He uses the example of Jones, who opposes the neighborhood plan to dig a well for clean water. After the well is dug, however, he sneaks to the well every night and takes some water home. While Jones has accepted benefits from the well, he has not consented to it. Yet he still has an obligation to do his part within the cooperative scheme in virtue of having accepted benefits.

Unlike the consent principle, the fair play principle does not insist on a consensual or deliberate undertaking. Anticipating the objection that Jones' sneaking out at night and taking water from the well might be taken as a sign of consent, Simmons revises the example to have Smith going to the well in broad daylight and shouting, "Don't think this means I'm coming into your stupid scheme! I'll never consent to share the burdens of this enterprise!"[26] On this scenario, Jones has obligations to contribute not in virtue of having consented but in virtue of having accepted benefits from the scheme.

But how many citizens of a state have accepted the public goods provided by the state? I think we can plausibly say that using public roads is a way of willingly accepting public goods. I follow George Klosko in thinking that recipients of public goods have obligations of fair play if the goods supplied are: "(i) worth the recipients' effort in providing them; (ii) indispensable for satisfactory lives; and (iii) have benefits and burdens that are fairly distributed."[27] The state provides indispensable benefits, including protections to our physical security through national defense, maintenance of law and order, public health measures, and provisions for satisfying our basic bodily needs. My obligation to the state does not stem from my giving consent, but from the fact that I accepted and benefitted from these goods.

---

[25] Rawls, "Legal Obligation and the Duty of Fair Play," p. 10. Rawls himself rejects the idea that actual consent is necessary for us to be bound to uphold and comply with a scheme of social cooperation.

[26] A. John Simmons, *Moral Principles and Political Obligations* (Princeton, NJ: Princeton University Press, 1979), p. 127.

[27] George Klosko, *Political Obligations* (Oxford: Oxford University Press, 2005), p. 6. As Jon Quong pointed out to me, it is possible that the indispensability criterion may not be necessary to generate obligations of fair play. We may have obligations of fair play even in cases where I accept benefits that are not indispensable for my well-being. If accepting any goods produced by a scheme of social cooperation generates obligations of fair play, accepting goods that are indispensable for my well-being presents an easier case.

Not only citizens but *all residents* in a state's territory participate in the cooperative scheme of the state to varying degrees. The contributions of noncitizens can take a variety of forms. Noncitizens contribute through their labor and paying taxes. Many noncitizens, especially unauthorized migrants and temporary workers, do exhausting, grueling work that most citizens do not want to do at the wages currently on offer. This includes work in meatpacking companies and industrial farms, cleaning homes and offices, and domestic care work. Some noncitizens contribute through military service.[28] The vast majority of noncitizens also contribute by simply complying with the law. All of these contributions help sustain state institutions and the public goods they provide. On the fair play principle, it is in virtue of such contributions that noncitizens are entitled to the benefits provided by the state.

Turning to consider the scope of the fair play principle, we encounter difficulties. One might object that the fair play principle is not easily contained within the territorial boundaries of states. This is a point made in debates about global justice by critics of attempts to restrict the fair play principle within the boundaries of one state.[29] In response, it is important, first, to acknowledge the undeniable fact of global interdependence and cooperation, which is reflected in the great and increasing volume of global communications, trade, investment, and the movement of capital and labor across borders. The international economic and political relationships that states participate in suggest a global scheme of social cooperation.[30] But, second, even if we accept that there is a global scheme of social cooperation, cooperation within a state's territorial boundaries is distinctive and grounds distinctive claims and responsibilities. It is not simply that the social cooperation inside a state impacts us more profoundly and pervasively; sometimes it doesn't. Rather, the state is indispensable in securing the just background conditions that make fair transactions and agreements between individuals and groups possible in the first place.[31] A just state makes possible much more

---

[28] About 65,000 foreign-born persons serve in the U.S. military, representing about 5 percent of all active-duty personnel; one-third of the foreign-born serving in the military are not U.S. citizens. See Jeanne Batalova, "Immigrants in the U.S. Armed Forces," Migration Policy Institute (May 2008), <http://www.migrationpolicy.org/article/immigrants-us-armed-forces/>, accessed August 6, 2015.

[29] See Arash Abizadeh, "Cooperation, Pervasive Impact, and Coercion: On the Scope (not Site) of Distributive Justice," *Philosophy and Public Affairs* 35:4 (2007), 318–58.

[30] Charles Beitz, *Political Theory and International Relations* (Princeton, NJ: Princeton University Press, 1979), pp. 143–54; Joshua Cohen and Charles Sabel, "Extra Rempublicam Nulla Justitia?," *Philosophy and Public Affairs* 34:2 (2006), 147–75.

[31] John Rawls, *Justice as Fairness* (Cambridge, MA: Harvard University Press, 2001), pp. 52–4; see also John Rawls, *Political Liberalism* (New York: Columbia University Press, [1993] 2005), pp. 265–9. See also Andrea Sangiovanni, "Global Justice, Reciprocity, and the State," *Philosophy and Public Affairs* 35:1 (2007), 3–39, who develops a similar argument in terms of reciprocity.

than fair economic exchange; it provides the conditions necessary for individual autonomy through ensuring equal basic liberties, as well as equal opportunities and some minimum of income and wealth. Given the necessity of participation in a state for individual autonomy, each of us has, as Rawls puts it, a "natural duty of justice" to "comply with and to do our share in just institutions when they exist and apply to us."[32] By contributing toward the maintenance of the state in whose territory we reside, each of us is entitled to the public goods provided by that state.

What do these considerations about fair play suggest for the rights and responsibilities of noncitizens in a state's territory? Like the affiliation principle, it admits of degrees. One might take a proportional view that says the benefits one can claim should be proportional to the contributions one has made, with the proviso that anyone who contributes through simple compliance with the law is entitled to some minimum of rights and protections. On such a view, all territorial insiders who support and comply with the state have a prima facie case to some minimal share of the benefits of the cooperative scheme, for example, protection of physical security and the provision of basic goods. A more extensive set of public goods should go to those who have contributed more over a greater period of time.

The fair play principle is already reflected in law. Take, for example, the U.S. Supreme Court case, *Graham v. Richardson*. Under challenge were Arizona and Pennsylvania laws that conditioned the receipt of public assistance on being a U.S. citizen or having resided in the U.S. for at least fifteen years. Both states justified their restrictions on the basis of a "special public interest" in favoring their citizens over noncitizens in the distribution of scarce resources. The Court acknowledged that states have "a valid interest in preserving the fiscal integrity of its programs," but argued that a concern for fiscal integrity did not justify the use of "invidious distinctions":

> Aliens like citizens pay taxes and may be called into the armed forces . . . [A]liens may live within a state for many years, work in the state and contribute to the economic growth of the state . . . There can be no "special public interest" in tax revenues to which aliens have contributed on an equal basis with the residents of the States.[33]

Similarly, in a case striking down a New York requirement that state employees had to be citizens, the Court stated, "A resident alien may reside lawfully in New York for a long period of time. He must pay taxes. And he is subject to service in this country's Armed Forces."[34] The logic of fair play underlies these

---

[32] Rawls, *A Theory of Justice*, p. 334.
[33] *Graham v. Richardson*, 403 U.S. 365, 374–6 (1970).
[34] *Sugarman v. Dougall*, 413 U.S. 634, 645, 646 (1973).

cases. Although the courts have focused on lawful long-term residents, the fair play principle ought to be seen as extending to *all noncitizens*, including unauthorized migrants and some temporary workers, who in virtue of their contributions have a prima facie claim to civil rights and basic public goods.[35]

It is worth elaborating briefly on the importance of *work* as a form of contribution, which is particularly strong in the American political tradition. The connection stems in part from the history of exclusion of African Americans from the right to work and earn. As Judith Shklar observed, "The issue is not labor as such, but earning and the independence it confers. The slave is degraded not because he has to work—everyone should do that—but because he is kept rather than remunerated."[36] She points to the example of Frederick Douglass, who upon receiving his first paying job after escaping slavery, remarked:

> I was now my own master—a tremendous fact . . . The thought, "I can work! I can work for a living; I am not afraid of work; I have no Master Hugh to rob me of my earnings"—placed me in a state of independence . . . All that any man has a right to expect, ask, give or receive in this world, is *fair play*.[37]

Perhaps because the fair play rationale in American political discourse has been so focused on paid work outside the home, it raises some worrying implications. One is that the kinds of work that get counted as a "contribution" will be defined narrowly with exclusionary implications for many groups of territorially present persons, including children who don't work, noncitizen elderly adults who don't work, and economically unremunerated workers.[38] I think this objection can be answered by insisting on a broad definition of what counts as a "contribution" to the scheme of social cooperation: not only paid work in the labor market but also unpaid domestic labor and public service in local neighborhoods and communities. As Andrea Sangiovanni has suggested, the kinds of "contribution" that give rise to obligations of fair play (what he calls reciprocity) ought to be defined expansively to include contributions "paid in the coin of compliance, trust, resources, and participation."[39]

---

[35] Because unauthorized migrants have violated immigration laws, one would have to address countervailing reasons articulated by those who argue for imposing additional requirements for undocumented immigrants who wish to remain, such as paying a fine.

[36] Judith N. Shklar, *American Citizenship: The Quest for Inclusion* (Cambridge, MA: Harvard University Press, 1991), p. 94.

[37] Frederick Douglass, *The Life and Writings of Frederick Douglass*, ed. Philip S. Foner, vol. 4 (International Publishers, 1955), pp. 271–2.

[38] On this point see the discussion of reciprocity in Arash Abizadeh's contribution to this volume.

[39] Sangiovanni, "Global Justice, Reciprocity, and the State," pp. 20–1.

11.3 Coercion

A third way of accounting for the normative significance of territorial presence is in terms of autonomy and coercion. The basic idea is that because state coercion infringes on people's autonomy, all those subject to state coercion are entitled to some form of justification. Personal autonomy involves, in Joseph Raz's words, a vision of persons as "part creators of their own moral world" who "have a commitment to projects, relationships, and causes which affect the kind of life that is for them worth living."[40] Because coercion always invades personal autonomy, coercion must either be stopped or justified to those who are coerced. The most obvious form of state coercion is the imposition of criminal penalties: incarceration removes "almost all autonomous pursuits" from the prisoner.[41] As Michael Blake has argued, while coercion is most starkly present in criminal law, it abounds in private law as well. In the law of contracts, property, and torts, adjudication of disputes will involve a transfer of legal rights from the loser of the legal dispute to the winner, and the civil judgment is backed by coercive measures.[42]

What sort of justification is owed to those subject to state coercion? Some interpret the coercion principle as requiring a hypothetical justification: we ask not what is actually consented to here and now, but what would be consented to, *ex ante*, under some appropriate method of modeling rational consent. What matters is the justness of the institutions and laws through which political power is exercised. For example, in Blake's view, the justification of ongoing state coercion must take the form of state concern with the *relative* material deprivation of all those coerced. In contrast, on the democratic interpretation of the coercion principle, what is owed to those subject to state coercion is actual opportunities to participate in the political processes that decide how state power is exercised.[43] The democratic strategy of justification links personal autonomy with public autonomy: coercive infringements on personal autonomy are justified only insofar as those subject to coercion have the opportunity to govern those infringements.

As with the affiliation and fair play principles, one problem with trying to account for the normative significance of territorial presence through the coercion principle is that the scope of state coercion does not line up neatly with the boundaries of citizenship or territory. Blake restricts the scope of his arguments to *citizens*, assuming for his purposes that "the set of people bound

---

[40] Joseph Raz, *The Morality of Freedom* (Oxford: Clarendon Press, 1986), p. 154.

[41] Raz, *The Morality of Freedom*, p. 419.

[42] Michael Blake, "Distributive Justice, State Coercion, and Autonomy," *Philosophy and Public Affairs* 30:3 (2001), 257–96 at pp. 276–7.

[43] Arash Abizadeh, "Democratic Theory and Border Coercion: No Right to Unilaterally Control Your Own Borders," *Political Theory* 36:1 (2008), 37–65.

under the territorial reach of a state's laws and the set of that state's citizens are equivalent."[44] Yet, there are many people "bound under the territorial reach of a state's laws" who are not citizens. All *persons* in the territory—from tourists and temporary workers to unauthorized migrants and legal permanent residents—are subject to the criminal and civil law of the state where they find themselves. Because these noncitizens are subject to a state's legal system, they too are owed some form of justification. Arash Abizadeh has argued that the coercion principle pushes not only beyond the boundaries of *citizenship* but also beyond *territorial* boundaries. A great many foreigners beyond the territorial boundaries of a powerful state are subject to its coercion, with radically inclusionary implications: justification is owed not only to territorial inhabitants but to all foreigners subject to a state's immigration and economic policies.[45]

I think the radically inclusionary implications of the coercion principle can be resisted. First, while state coercion has a profound impact on the life chances of people outside the state's territory, we should not let these instances of extraterritorial coercion blind us to the fact that those *inside* the territory of the state are subject to profound and pervasive coercion in a way that most territorial outsiders are not. There is an important *dis-analogy* between nonresident noncitizens, on the one hand, and inhabitants of the territory, on the other: the foreigner at the border is subject only to the immigration power of the state she wishes to enter, but she is not subject to the entire legal system. The coercion principle is scalar. Different degrees and forms of coercion require different justifications. Every dimension of a territorial insider's life choices is structured by the policies of the state in which she resides; the same cannot be said of territorial outsiders who are members of other states and are therefore subject to the legal system of their home states.[46] Second, consent makes a difference here. While the vast majority of citizens simply find themselves, by the accident of birth, inside the territory of a particular state, many noncitizens have entered a host state voluntarily and have their home states to return to. Different migrants have different opportunities for exit and return, but where there is a viable exit option, the force of the coercion principle is considerably weakened as a basis for extending full and equal rights of citizenship.

[44] Blake, "Distributive Justice," p. 266, n.8.

[45] Abizadeh, "Democratic Theory and Border Coercion."

[46] I do not mean to suggest that territorial outsiders should have no voice whatsoever in the making of policies to which they are subject; they might be granted some voice. For example, Mexicans subject to U.S. economic and immigration policy would not have equal voting rights in U.S. elections, but they could reasonably demand a voice through their political representatives speaking to representatives of the U.S. government through transnational deliberative bodies.

A related concern is whether the coercion principle can distinguish among different groups of territorial insiders, including tourists, temporary workers, and long-term resident noncitizens. All seem equally liable to the criminal and civil laws of the state in which they find themselves. On the democratic interpretation of the coercion principle, all these individuals should be entitled to an equal voice in the making of the laws to which they are subject. However, coercion, like affiliation and fair play, is not an all-or-nothing affair. It admits of degrees, even inside the territorial boundaries of a state. Consider tourists or foreign students visiting the U.S. That they are subject to the host state's coercive power during their stay is undeniable. This is why they are entitled to certain basic rights and protections from the moment they set foot in the territory. But there are important differences between short-term visitors and longer-term residents. The former are in the country for a short period of time; their aspirations and life projects are bound up with their lives and networks back in their home countries. While these short-term visitors are subject to the laws of the host state during their stay, the degree of control that the host state exerts over their lives is far less than the degree of control that the host state exerts on long-term residents. To see why, we must recognize that the way in which territorial presence matters will depend in part on the person's own goals and life plans. The state has more power over the life of someone who pursues her life plan centrally inside the territory of the state than someone who is primarily engaged in short-term projects. This explains why we treat tourists and foreign students differently from long-term residents. In many cases, temporary workers are more like other short-term visitors in that they are in the country for a short period of time and their own aspirations are to return home. The longer foreign workers live and work in the host state and the more their own life plans become pervasively subject to the host state, the stronger their claim to remain becomes.

11.4 Implications for the Rights of Immigrants

Rather than defending one principle over another, my central contention is that the three principles considered above—affiliation, fair play, and coercion—work together to ground a case for the special rights and obligations of territorial insiders. The affiliation principle is perhaps the most imperfect proxy for territorial presence, especially in the case of newcomers to a state's territory. As one's affiliations with members of the host society expand and deepen, so does the extent of rights and obligations. Similarly, the fair play principle extends a greater set of rights and obligations based on the nature and extent of the contribution. The coercion principle accounts for why newcomers present in the territory are entitled to certain rights and responsibilities from the moment they set foot in the territory.

If one accepts these principles as grounds for the special rights and responsibilities of territorial insiders, the question then is: what is the content of the special rights and responsibilities of territorial insiders? Before taking up this question, we first need to consider whether all territorial insiders ought to be treated identically or whether differential treatment is permissible for different groups of territorial insiders.

11.4.1 *Equality: uniform or differential treatment?*

There is a strong presumption in contemporary liberal theory in favor of treating most, if not all, territorial insiders in exactly the same way. Call this the *uniform treatment* view. Michael Walzer implies such a view when he writes: "Men and women are either subject to the state's authority, or they are not; and if they are subject, they must be given a say, and ultimately an equal say, in what that authority does." Walzer was writing with temporary workers in mind, arguing that they "must be set on the road to citizenship." Admission into the territory must eventually come with full inclusion as equal members, which is "subject only to certain constraints of time and qualification."[47] Why?

Walzer provides two reasons. The first is shared subjection to state authority. We may think of temporary workers as guests, but they ought to be regarded as "subjects" just as citizens are. Subjection to state coercion triggers the demand for justification, which may be met through the provision of certain rights and protections. But as we saw, what is owed to those subject to state coercion is subject to debate: not necessarily full membership but a set of basic rights. Second, Walzer seeks to avoid the creation of a permanent, vulnerable caste of foreigners. This concern stems from the two historical cases that inform Walzer's theory of membership: the *metics* of ancient Greece and "guest workers" in Germany. Migrants typically perform difficult, dangerous work that is socially necessary, but they are regarded as strangers with little to no civil, social, and political rights. Because their presence in the territory is tied to employment, they live under the constant threat of deportation and their marginal economic and political position renders them vulnerable to exploitation. Reflecting on these cases, it is no surprise that Walzer concludes that temporary workers "must be set on the road to citizenship."[48]

These are serious concerns, but I think there is an alternative to the either/or choice implied by Walzer's uniform treatment approach: either inclusion of

---

[47] Walzer, *Spheres of Justice*, pp. 60–1.   [48] Walzer, *Spheres of Justice*, pp. 57, 59, 60.

guest workers as full members or acceptance of their situation as a vulnerable caste with few rights. Before elaborating an alternative proposal, let's consider the limits of the uniform treatment view.

First, Walzer's theory presupposes only one type of migration across borders—permanent resettlement—but not all movement fits this model. Some intend to migrate only temporarily, and some who intend to remain permanently do not wish to become citizens.[49] If we take seriously the agency of immigrants—the "aspirations and projects of the migrants themselves"— we see that many migrant workers do not wish to settle in the host country.[50] Temporary workers' goal of returning home is reflected in their higher rate of savings and remittances, and their willingness to accept lower-paying jobs in contrast to permanent residents.[51] If temporary workers wish to work for a time and eventually return to their home states, a group-differentiated approach that accords certain rights—but not the same rights as citizens or long-term residents—may be consistent with treating them as equals.

Second, there is the practical consideration that if the uniform treatment approach were to be implemented as a matter of policy, host societies would drastically reduce or eliminate temporary worker programs. Many egalitarians may rejoice at this, but temporary worker programs are one way of addressing global inequality. To be sure, such programs are limited tools of global redistribution because it is typically not the worst off members of a society who tend to migrate and because there are more direct means of redistributing wealth and income across countries. Yet, temporary worker programs do serve as one vehicle of global redistribution through remittances. According to the World Bank, $111 billion was remitted worldwide in 2001. About 65 percent went to developing countries, with half going to countries considered to be "lower-middle income countries." Remittances constituted over 10 percent of GDP for countries such as El Salvador, Nicaragua, Eritrea, Jamaica, and Jordan.[52]

Third, the uniform treatment view is at odds with the long-standing practice of group-differentiated rights, not only with regard to the treatment of temporary versus long-term migrants but also through policies such as pregnancy leave for women, language rights for linguistic minorities, and limited

---

[49] See Douglass S. Massey et al., *Beyond Smoke and Mirrors: Mexican Immigration in an Era of Economic Integration* (New York: Russell Sage, 2002).

[50] Valeria Ottonelli and Tiziana Torresi, "Inclusivist Egalitarian Liberalism and Temporary Migration: A Dilemma," *The Journal of Political Philosophy* 20:2 (2012), 202–24 at 208.

[51] Oded Galor and Oded Stark, "Migrants' Savings, the Probability of Return Migration and Migrants' Performance," *International Economic Review* 31 (1990), 463–7; Massey et al., *Beyond Smoke and Mirrors*.

[52] Kevin O'Neil, "Remittances from the United States in Context," Migration Policy Institute (June 2003), <http://www.migrationpolicy.org/article/remittances-united-states-context>, accessed August 6, 2015.

self-government rights for indigenous groups, all of which have been defended on grounds of egalitarian justice.[53] We need to inquire into the purpose and justification of particular cases of group-differentiated policies to see whether they are consistent with egalitarian justice. A uniform treatment approach is too sweeping in its blanket opposition to differential treatment.

Rather than viewing rights as an all-or-nothing bundle attached to citizenship status, as reflected in the uniform treatment view, we ought to consider an approach that *disaggregates* certain rights from the formal status of citizenship and extends them to noncitizens in virtue of their territorial presence.[54] There are at least two advantages to a disaggregation approach. First, it leaves open the possibility that certain practices of group-differentiated rights and responsibilities are justifiable. Second, permitting differential treatment of different groups of territorial insiders is more likely to address Walzer's concern about the domination of vulnerable groups, including temporary workers and unauthorized migrants. On the uniform treatment view, unauthorized migrants must either remain in the shadows or be granted recognition as full members. A disaggregation approach could offer a middle position that extends a range of rights to them, not in virtue of membership but in virtue of territorial presence.

11.4.2 *Which rights for which territorial insiders?*

If one adopts a strategy of disaggregation, the question then is: which rights for which territorial insiders? In closing, I provide a brief proposal to illustrate one form the disaggregation approach might take. There are at least three categories of resident noncitizens that ought to be distinguished: sojourners, residents, and members. Table 11.1 below indicates which of the three principles discussed above offers normative support for each category and provides examples of different rights claims associated with each. No doubt, some will disagree with the particular content I suggest and favor alternative content,

---

[53] See Will Kymlicka, *Multicultural Citizenship: A Liberal Theory of Minority Rights* (Oxford: Oxford University Press, 1995); Sarah Song, *Justice, Gender, and the Politics of Multiculturalism* (Cambridge: Cambridge University Press, 2007).

[54] A number of scholars have provided historical, sociological, and legal analyses of the phenomenon of the disaggregation of rights from citizenship status as civil, social, and political rights are increasingly predicated on residency. In addition to Jacobson's *Rights across Borders*, Soysal's *Limits of Citizenship*, and Bosniak's *The Citizen and the Alien* cited above, see also Seyla Benhabib's *The Rights of Others: Aliens, Residents, and Citizens* (Cambridge: Cambridge University Press, 2004) and Saskia Sassen's *Territory, Authority, Rights* (Princeton, NJ: Princeton University Press, 2008). These arguments are situated within broader arguments about the decline of nation-state sovereignty, especially in the European context. My argument is intended to offer normative grounds for domestic legal regimes to extend rights to noncitizens and does not depend on international human rights law as the sole or primary basis of the move toward disaggregation.

Table 11.1. An example of a scheme of differentiated rights

	(i) Sojourners	(ii) Residents	(iii) Members
Who	tourists, visiting students, temporary workers	long-term resident noncitizens	citizens (native-born and naturalized)
Rights	civil rights & liberties	civil rights & liberties	civil rights & liberties
	(freedom of religion, speech, & assembly; equal protection of the laws; due process rights in criminal proceedings; protection of property law and contract law)		
	basic public goods (access to public roads, emergency healthcare)	extended public goods (non-emergency healthcare, welfare benefits, basic education)	extended public goods
		right to remain in the territory	right to remain in the territory
		political rights	political rights
		(right to vote, freedom to contribute to political campaigns)	
			right to run for & hold political office
Normative Grounds	coercion	coercion, affiliation, fair play	coercion, affiliation, fair play

but my hope is that they will nonetheless see the appeal of the disaggregation approach.[55]

(I) CLAIMS OF SOJOURNERS

Sojourners include temporary workers, tourists, visiting students, and other temporary migrants who enter a state's territory after agreeing to a short-term stay. Sojourners ought to be entitled to civil rights and liberties and basic public goods. In practice, the U.S. and Western European countries already extend civil rights and basic public goods to noncitizens. In the European context, the extension of these rights is predicated on international human rights instruments, as well as the European Convention on Human Rights.[56] My point is that the coercion principle offers distinctive grounds for extending rights to sojourners.

Sojourners may seek to adjust their status from sojourner to resident on grounds of affiliation or fair play, but as I suggested above, whether such

---

[55] Ryan Pevnick has also defended a disaggregation approach in a different context (as part of a critique of the social trust argument for a state's right to exclude foreigners); he distinguishes only between claims of residence and of membership, and assigns extended public goods and political rights and duties to members only. See Ryan Pevnick, "Social Trust and the Ethics of Immigration Policy," *Journal of Political Philosophy* 17:2 (2009): 146–67. A more complete analysis than I can provide here would discuss not only the particular rights but also the obligations of different groups of territorial insiders.

[56] See Jacobson, *Rights across Borders*; Soysal, *Limits of Citizenship*.

adjustment is ultimately granted will depend on how these pro tanto reasons are weighed against the state's right to self-determination, a part of the analysis that I have not been able to provide here.[57] On the democratic interpretation of the coercion principle of the kind defended by Abizadeh, sojourners would have a prima facie case for equal rights of political participation. In my view, the constitutive and instrumental conditions of democracy, including considerations about political equality and solidarity, weigh against enfranchising sojourners.[58]

(II) CLAIMS OF RESIDENTS

Like sojourners, long-term residents are entitled to civil liberties and basic public goods. In contrast to sojourners, they are entitled to a more extensive set of rights, including the right to remain permanently in the territory, extended public goods, and rights of political participation. The affiliation and fair play principles provide pro tanto reasons for extending such rights to long-term residents, including unauthorized migrants. These principles would apply to someone who has resided, worked, and/or formed affiliations in the host country for a significant period of time, as opposed to someone who has just arrived in the territory. As in the case of sojourners, a full consideration of the rights of unauthorized migrants needs to address how their pro tanto claims based on affiliation, fair play, and coercion should be weighed against the state's right to self-determination.

On the democratic interpretation of the coercion principle, noncitizen residents would be entitled to equal rights of political participation. The concerns about knowledge, solidarity, and stability that apply to sojourners are less of a concern in the case of long-term residents. On the fair play principle, contributions to the scheme of social cooperation through working and paying taxes ground a pro tanto case for social and economic rights.

My proposal for the claims of residents diverges significantly from current law in the U.S. For example, only citizens have the right to reside permanently in the territory, which, among other things, means freedom from deportation. Federal laws prohibit noncitizens from receiving public assistance and from working in particular jobs.[59] When it comes to political rights, only citizens

---

[57] For discussion of the modern state's right to self-determination, including the right to control immigration, see my "Why Does the State Have the Right to Control Immigration," *NOMOS: Migration, Immigration, and Emigration* (forthcoming).

[58] Sarah Song, "The Boundary Problem in Democratic Theory: Why the Demos Should Be Bounded by the State," *International Theory* 4:1 (2012), 39–68.

[59] For limits on lawful permanent residents' access to public assistance, see 8 U.S.C. 1611–13, 1621–2, 1631–2 (2006), and for restrictions on employment opportunities for lawful permanent residents, see *Cabell v. Chavez-Salido*, 454 U.S. 432 (1982). One notable exception is the California legislature's passage of AB 1024, which Governor Brown signed into law in October 2013 and which authorizes the California Supreme Court to admit to the practice of law an applicant who

have the right to vote in most local and all state and federal elections.[60] In contrast, the disaggregation of citizenship status and political rights is more widespread in Europe. The 1993 Maastricht Treaty granted the right to vote to any citizen of the fifteen signatory states of the EU who resides in another EU state. Since 1993, Ireland, the Netherlands, and all the Scandinavian countries have introduced universal local franchise for all residents, independent of their nationality. New Zealand has the most inclusive policy of all countries: local and national voting rights after one year of legal residence.[61]

(III) CLAIMS OF CITIZENS

Under the disaggregation approach, many of the civil, social, and political rights which have traditionally been tied to political membership would be unbundled from citizenship status and extended in virtue of residency. Rights of political participation or access to welfare benefits would no longer be restricted to citizens as is the current practice. One right that ought to be reserved for citizens is the right to run for and hold public office. This claim requires more defense than I can provide here, but a key premise is that effective political leadership requires not only certain expertise but also a deeper level of commitment to the political community. A noncitizen resident's decision to become a citizen might be taken as a proxy, however imperfect, of the extent of her loyalty to the political community.

One important objection to my proposal for disaggregating rights from citizenship status is that it would diminish the worth of citizenship, what Peter Schuck has called the "devaluation of citizenship."[62] U.S. Senator Diane Feinstein echoed similar concerns when she expressed opposition to noncitizen voting rights in local school board elections in San Francisco, a measure that lost by a slim margin: "Allowing noncitizens to vote . . . clearly dilutes the promise of citizenship."[63] In response, it is important to acknowledge that the disaggregation approach would diminish the material worth of citizenship, but citizenship would retain symbolic importance: the shared pride and collective sentiment associated with the common history and common experiences of the political community. That it is symbolic does not mean it is insignificant. For noncitizens, the decision to become a citizen would signal a desire to belong to the political community. This would shift the

---

fulfilled all the requirements for admission to practice law but is not lawfully present in the U.S. (see <http://leginfo.legislature.ca.gov/faces/billNavClient.xhtml?bill_id=201320140AB1024>).

[60] See Alexander Keyssar, *The Right to Vote* (New York: Basic Books, 2000).

[61] Rainer Bauböck, "Expansive Citizenship—Voting beyond Territory and Membership," *PS: Political Science and Politics* 38:4 (2005), 683–7.

[62] See, e.g., Peter H. Schuck, "The Devaluation of Citizenship" in *Citizens, Strangers, and In-Betweens: Essays on Immigration and Citizenship* (Boulder, CO: Westview Press, 1998), pp. 163–75.

[63] Ron Hayduk, *Democracy for All: Restoring Immigrant Voting Rights in the United States* (New York: Routledge, 2006), p. 126.

motivational basis for noncitizens' decisions to become citizens: one would join not for the sake of the benefits attached to the status of citizenship but out of affective attachment and identification with the political community.

11.5 Conclusion

This chapter considered the question of whether and why territorial presence makes a normative difference. Taken together, the three principles examined above—affiliation, fair play, and coercion—account for the special rights and obligations of different groups of territorial insiders. Turning to the question of the particular content of the special rights and obligations, I defended an approach that *disaggregates* rights and obligations from citizenship status. As I have tried to show, liberal democratic states owe a range of rights and protections to noncitizens inside their territorial boundaries in virtue of coercion, affiliation, and fair play, and such a system of disaggregated rights is consistent with equality.[64]

References

Abizadeh, Arash, "Cooperation, Pervasive Impact, and Coercion: On the Scope (not Site) of Distributive Justice," *Philosophy and Public Affairs* 35:4 (2007), 318–58.

Abizadeh, Arash, "Democratic Theory and Border Coercion: No Right to Unilaterally Control Your Own Borders," *Political Theory* 36:1 (2008), 37–65.

Bauböck, Rainer, "Expansive Citizenship—Voting beyond Territory and Membership," *PS: Political Science and Politics* 38:4 (2005), 683–87.

Beitz, Charles, *Political Theory and International Relations* (Princeton, NJ: Princeton University Press, 1979).

Benhabib, Seyla, *The Rights of Others: Aliens, Residents, and Citizens* (Cambridge: Cambridge University Press, 2004).

Blake, Michael, "Distributive Justice, State Coercion, and Autonomy," *Philosophy and Public Affairs* 30:3 (2001), 257–96.

Bosniak, Linda, *The Citizen and the Alien* (Princeton, NJ: Princeton University Press, 2006).

Bosniak, Linda, "Being Here: Ethical Territoriality and the Rights of Immigrants," *Theoretical Inquiries in Law* 8:2 (2007), 389–410.

Carens, Joseph H., "Aliens and Citizens: The Case for Open Borders," *Review of Politics* 49:2 (1987), 251–73.

[64] For comments and discussion, I am grateful to the editors of this volume, as well as Seyla Benhabib, Linda Bosniak, Corey Brettschneider, Stephen Galoob, Bryan Garsten, Matthew Lister, Karuna Mantena, Hamsa Murthy, Paulina Ochoa Espejo, Jon Quong, Daniel Viehoff, Leti Volpp, and participants at the 2011 Law and Society Association meeting, the 2011 Princeton Program in Ethics and Public Affairs Seminar, and the 2012 Yale Political Theory Workshop.

Carens, Joseph H., "Who Should Get In? The Ethics of Immigration Admissions," *Ethics & International Affairs* 17:1 (2003), 95–110.

Carens, Joseph H., *Immigrants and the Right to Stay* (Cambridge, MA: MIT Press, 2010).

Cohen, Joshua and Charles Sabel, "Extra Rempublicam Nulla Justitia?," *Philosophy and Public Affairs* 34:2 (2006), 147–75.

Douglass, Frederick, *The Life and Writings of Frederick Douglass*, ed. Philip S. Foner, vol. 4 (New York: International Publishers, 1975).

Galor, Oded and Oded Stark, "Migrants' Savings, the Probability of Return Migration and Migrants' Performance," *International Economic Review* 31 (1990), 463–7.

Hayduk, Ron, *Democracy for All: Restoring Immigrant Voting Rights in the United States* (New York: Routledge, 2006).

Honig, Bonnie, *Democracy and the Foreigner* (Princeton, NJ: Princeton University Press, 2001).

Jacobson, David, *Rights across Borders: Immigration and the Decline of Citizenship* (Baltimore, MD: Johns Hopkins University Press, 1996).

Keyssar, Alexander, *The Right to Vote* (New York: Basic Books, 2000).

Klosko, George, *Political Obligations* (Oxford: Oxford University Press, 2005).

Kymlicka, Will, *Multicultural Citizenship: A Liberal Theory of Minority Rights* (Oxford: Oxford University Press, 1995).

Massey, Douglass S., Jorge Durand, and Nolan J. Malone, *Beyond Smoke and Mirrors: Mexican Immigration in an Era of Economic Integration* (New York: Russell Sage, 2002).

Miller, David, *On Nationality* (Oxford: Oxford University Press, 1995).

Motomura, Hiroshi, *Americans in Waiting: The Lost Story of Immigration and Citizenship in the United States* (Oxford: Oxford University Press, 2006).

O'Neil, Kevin, "Remittances from the United States in Context," *Migration Policy Institute* (June 2003), <http://www.migrationpolicy.org/article/remittances-united-states-context>.

Ottonelli, Valeria and Tiziana Torresi, "Inclusivist Egalitarian Liberalism and Temporary Migration: A Dilemma," *The Journal of Political Philosophy* 20:2 (2012), 202–24.

Pevnick, Ryan, "Social Trust and the Ethics of Immigration Policy," *Journal of Political Philosophy* 17:2 (2009), 146–67.

Raustiala, Kal, "The Geography of Justice," *Fordham Law Review* 73 (2005), 2501–60.

Rawls, John, "Legal Obligation and the Principle of Fair Play" in S. Hook (ed.), *Law and Philosophy: A Symposium* (New York: New York University Press, 1964), pp. 3–18.

Rawls, John, *Justice as Fairness* (Cambridge, MA: Harvard University Press, 2001).

Rawls, John, *A Theory of Justice* (Cambridge, MA: Belknap Press, [1971] 2005).

Rawls, John, *Political Liberalism* (New York: Columbia University Press, [1993] 2005).

Raz, Joseph, *The Morality of Freedom* (Oxford: Clarendon Press, 1986).

Sangiovanni, Andrea, "Global Justice, Reciprocity, and the State," *Philosophy and Public Affairs* 35:1 (2007), 3–39.

Sassen, Saskia, *Territory, Authority, Rights* (Princeton, NJ: Princeton University Press, 2008).

Schuck, Peter H., "The Devaluation of Citizenship" in *Citizens, Strangers, and In-Betweens: Essays on Immigration and Citizenship* (Boulder, CO: Westview Press, 1998), pp. 163–75.

Schuck, Peter H. and Rogers M. Smith, *Citizenship without Consent: Illegal Aliens in the American Polity* (New Haven, CT: Yale University Press, 1985).

Shklar, Judith N., *American Citizenship: The Quest for Inclusion* (Cambridge, MA: Harvard University Press, 1991).

Simmons, A. John, *Moral Principles and Political Obligations* (Princeton, NJ: Princeton University Press, 1979).

Song, Sarah, *Justice, Gender, and the Politics of Multiculturalism* (Cambridge: Cambridge University Press, 2007).

Song, Sarah, "The Boundary Problem in Democratic Theory: Why the Demos Should Be Bounded by the State," *International Theory* 4:1 (2012), 39–68.

Song, Sarah, "Why Does the State Have the Right to Control Immigration," *NOMOS: Migration, Immigration, and Emigration* (forthcoming).

Soysal, Yasemin, *The Limits of Citizenship: Migrants and Postnational Membership in Europe* (Chicago: University of Chicago Press, 1994).

Walzer, Michael, *Spheres of Justice: A Defense of Pluralism and Equality* (New York: Basic Books, 1983).

Wellman, Christopher Heath, "Immigration and Freedom of Association," *Ethics* 119 (2008), 109–41.

12

Are Refugees Special?

Chandran Kukathas

The stranger has no friend, unless it be a stranger[1]

12.1 Prologue: The Morality of Hospitality

His vessel crushed by Poseidon's storm after leaving Kalypso's island, Odysseus finds himself washed up on the shores of Phaiakia and, eventually, the guest of the hospitable King, Alkinoos, to whom he tells the long story of the journey that led him from Troy to Ogygia. After reaching, and quickly leaving, the land of the lotus-eaters, Odysseus relates, he and his crew came to the "country of the lawless outrageous Cyclopes." Of the inhabitants he had this to say:

> These people have no institutions, no meetings for counsels;
> rather they make their habitations in caverns hollowed
> among the peaks of the high mountains, and each one is the law
> for his own wives and children, and cares nothing about the others.[2]

Yet when he found himself trapped in the cave of Polyphemus, he had no choice but to address his suspicious host, who demanded to know what these strangers were after, "recklessly roving as pirates do," and wondered if they too proposed to "venture their lives as they wander, bringing evil to alien people?"[3] Odysseus at once tried to reassure the son of Poseidon that he and

---

[1] Sa'di, *The Gulistan or Flower Garden, of Shaikh Sadī of Shiraz*, translated by James Ross (London: J.M. Richardson, 1823 [1258]), p. 297.

[2] Homer, *The Odyssey of Homer*, translated and with an introduction by Richmond Lattimore (New York: Harper Collins, 1991), Book IX, verses 113–15: p. 140.

[3] Homer, *The Odyssey of Homer*, Book IX, 254–5: pp. 143–4.

his men intended no one any harm, and to remind him that, as strangers, they might well be considered guests:

> ...but now in turn we come to you and are suppliants
> at your knees, if you might give us a guest present or otherwise
> some gift of grace, for such is the right of strangers. Therefore
> respect the gods, O best of men. We are your suppliants,
> and Zeus the guest god, who stands behind all strangers with honours
> due them, avenges any wrong toward strangers and suppliants.[4]

The Cyclopes, of course, had no intention of showing the wanderers any hospitality, proposing only to eat them.

That Polyphemus should come to the nasty end that he did at the hands of the stranger, "Nobody," is entirely in keeping with the understanding of civilized life that lies at the core of Homer's *Odyssey*. A vital part of being civilized is knowing the duties of hospitality—and the duties owed to strangers in particular. The Cyclopes, the Lastrygonians, and Circe, among others, do not understand these duties—and come to grief. The Phaiakians, however, are model hosts, and their land is a civilized place where all is in order.

Indeed, when society is well ordered and in balance, norms of hospitality are also in balance: respected by hosts and not abused by guests. Ithaca, the Kingdom of Odysseus, however, is in a mess, the disorder of the state symbolized by the overrunning of the household by Penelope's suitors, who abuse the hospitality of their reluctant hostess while demanding a decision which will make one of them king. The task performed by the central figure of Homer's epic is to keep the household and the kingdom intact, preserving the most important values of civilized life, until Odysseus can return to settle the issue of succession.

The moral world of ancient Greece described in Homer's poetry is undoubtedly a long way away from our own. Yet there is something important, nonetheless, about the idea that hospitality and the treatment of strangers is fundamental to civilized life, and the key to the possibility of a well-ordered society. It does not seem out of place in Sa'di's thirteenth century Persia; or, for that matter, in our own time. It seems right to say that we owe a duty of hospitality to strangers, particularly when they come to us in distress: and we owe the most when they can offer us the least. "For I was an hungred, and ye gave me meat: I was thirsty and ye gave me drink: I was a stranger, and ye took me in."[5]

Intuitively compelling though this might be, however, the skeptical question must be posed: can such a norm serve us in modern society? We live, after all, in a world of many more people and many more strangers. Can a Homeric

---

[4] Homer, *The Odyssey of Homer*, Book IX, 266–71: p. 144.
[5] *St. Matthew*, Chapter 25 Verse 35.

ethics really serve us when the size of the earth's population, combined with the number of dislocating conflicts and the volume of population displacement, threaten to strain the resources and the tolerance of host peoples? As Rousseau observed, "Wherever strangers are rare, they are welcome. Nothing makes one more hospitable than seldom needing to be. It is the abundance of guests which destroys hospitality. In the time of Homer people hardly traveled, and travelers were well received everywhere."[6]

It must be conceded that the skeptic may have a point: perhaps Homeric ethics cannot be ours. Yet the ethical and political point of Homer's tale ought not to be lost either. The norms of civilized society are importantly bound up with the treatment of strangers. Our conduct before, and treatment of, those we do not immediately count among our own has an important relation to, and bearing upon, the quality of our civilization. And this reflection ought not to be lost sight of when we turn to consider what kind of an ethics we do need to deal with the strangers of the modern world, particularly when they appear before us in large numbers, fleeing persecution or tragedy and seeking refuge in places they hope will prove hospitable. What kind of an ethics do we need to deal with those so displaced—the strangers who come as refugees?

The answer we have settled upon is a political ethics according to which the movement of peoples is a matter for states to manage, with a view to protecting the interests of the state and its members, while granting special dispensation on humanitarian grounds to those whose reasons for moving are deemed special. The question addressed in this chapter is whether or not this political ethics is defensible—whether the idea of a system in which movement is controlled (and more importantly, *restricted*) but exceptions are made is either feasible or morally justifiable. Its main purpose is to cast doubt on this idea by showing that it depends upon distinctions that cannot be sustained and upon the establishment of institutions that cannot do what they proclaim. It does so by focusing on the case of refugees, who are widely regarded by states, political actors generally, immigration advocates, and theorists alike as deserving of special treatment.

12.2 Refugees as Exceptions

Modern reflection on the ethics of our relations with strangers begins with the existence of a world of states, and of individuals as members of states (with the notable exception of a small but significant minority who remain stateless). The world today is demarcated by political boundaries and so borders

---

[6] Jean-Jacques Rousseau, *Emile, or On Education*, Introduction, translation and Notes by Allan Bloom (New York: Basic Books, 1979), ch. V: p. 413.

that are increasingly closely policed. While there is movement across borders all the time, that movement is almost always complicated. To move one has generally to acquire a passport and secure a status, whether as a tourist, or a student, or a worker, or any one of dozens of possible types of person who is eligible to be granted entry into a state. Though some borders are easier to cross than others—or at least, easier for *some* people to cross—the presumption in the modern world is that "thou shall not cross" without proper authorization. Only a few borders come close to being absolutely shut, but none are fully open. The purpose of borders is to keep people out: to deny them membership of the state, or to limit their rights when they do enter, or to bar them from physical entry altogether. The ethical issue at stake is the matter of how closed or open those borders should be: who should be allowed in and who kept out? Whatever the preponderance of opinion among philosophers, the view of the state is generally that people should be kept out unless it is to the advantage (or at least, not to the disadvantage) of the state that they be admitted. No one has a right to be admitted, and the principle of free movement, if it holds at all, applies only within states, and not between states.

Nevertheless, all but the most insistent of defenders of closed borders or restricted immigration make an exception for refugees. However strong they consider the reasons for limiting the numbers, or controlling the types, of immigrants—strangers—entering a country, they concede that refugees are a special case. Michael Walzer, for example, maintains that a people's right to control membership of the state to which they belong must nonetheless be sensitive to the plight of refugees.[7] David Miller similarly argues, after making the case for immigration limits, that refugees "have a very strong, but not absolute, right to be admitted to a place of safety, a right now widely recognized in both law and political practice."[8] This is not to say that either of these theorists thinks that the claims of refugees are so great as to trump the interests of states or citizens. In the end, their views are not far from that advanced by Andrew Altman and Christopher Wellman, who argue that while states have a general "samaritan duty" to help people who land on their doorstep seeking asylum, this does not extend so far as to constitute an obligation to grant them admission or membership.[9] Nonetheless, these authors also concede that the duty to "help rescue from peril," when it can only be discharged by admission to membership of the state, would issue in a duty to admit asylum seekers,

---

[7] Michael Walzer, *Spheres of Justice: A Defense of Pluralism and Equality* (Oxford: Blackwell, 1983), pp. 43–51.

[8] David Miller, *National Responsibility and Global Justice* (Oxford: Oxford University Press, 2007), p. 227. See also David Miller, "Immigration: The Case for Limits" in Andrew I. Cohen and Christopher Heath Wellman (eds.), *Contemporary Debates in Applied Ethics* (Oxford: Blackwell, 2005), pp. 193–206 at pp. 202–3.

[9] Andrew Altman and Christopher Heath Wellman, *A Liberal Theory of International Justice* (Oxford: Oxford University Press, 2011), p. 181.

even though they think this duty holds "only if nothing was done to remedy the situation in the home state and no other state was willing to grant permanent residence."[10]

The thought that lies behind these views is that there is a very strong presumption in favor of a state having the right to, and being justified in, limiting entry into its territory. States may wish to restrict immigration for any of a number of reasons: to protect their citizens from criminals or subversives, to give some of their citizens an advantage in labor-market or business competition—or more generally to ensure it does not share too much of its wealth with outsiders, and to protect its cultural integrity. States are justified in doing so even if the costs to foreigners—would-be immigrants and non-immigrants alike (and indeed citizens who would stand to gain from immigration)—are substantial. (Thus no state thought it was under any obligation to open its borders even a little to the Haitians whose country was devastated by the 2010 earthquake that killed at least 46,000, injured more than 200,000, and left 1.5 million homeless.[11] Many stepped up with generous offers of aid, in cash and in kind, but also strengthened their border surveillance to keep fleeing Haitians out.) Yet, the thought continues, states ought to be more open to some kinds of people: those fleeing persecution, fearing for their lives. Confronted by such cases, the argument goes, states ought to relax the presumption in favor of keeping people out when the benefits of admitting them are outweighed by the costs—or at least engage in some form of recalculation that weighs the interests of the potential immigrants a little more heavily. People seeking asylum are special—not so special, perhaps, as to be regarded simply as ends in themselves, but special enough to be viewed as more substantial concerns in the calculus of value than immigrants of any other stripe. Theorists such as Walzer, Miller, Altman, and Wellman think that exceptions have to be made for special categories (and possibly for special circumstances), but the presumption in favor of states controlling movement remains.

Of course, there are many other things that could be done besides admitting asylum seekers into the state. The samaritan's duty might embrace any of a variety of possibilities, as Altman and Wellman maintain. The general duty is to rescue people from peril, and this duty can be discharged in any number of ways. It could be discharged by "sending the asylum-seekers to another state that has agreed to let them in; by establishing through military intervention a safe-haven in the asylum-seekers' home state and returning them there; by

---

[10] Altman and Wellman, *A Liberal Theory of International Justice*, p. 181. The buck lingers here.

[11] These are the more conservative figures from the U.S. Agency for International Development, rather than the official numbers published by the Haitian government. According to the Human Development Index, Haiti is the poorest country in the Americas, with an annual per capita income of a little over US$600 a year.

letting them in and granting them asylum until such time as they can be safely settled in another state or their home state." Only when all else fails does the duty to admit asylum seekers kick in. But these people are special—for in the case of refugees such a duty can eventually arise in a way that it cannot with respect to other aspiring immigrants.

Yet all this said, there is something troubling about the thought that refugees are special, and that there are certain distinctive features of their situation that impose upon us duties we do not owe others. It is troubling, first, because it suggests that we draw a line distinguishing our obligations in a way that may not make much sense, morally speaking. Second, the institutional implications of this way of approaching the plight of asylum seekers are unfortunate for it proposes that we treat them as supplicants who must prove their worthiness, thereby opening up the way for matters of humanitarian necessity to be transformed into questions of political expediency. More generally, the very idea that duties towards refugees might be special duties owed by the state is troubling because, if we understand the state properly, it is hard to see how refugees will ever be given proper moral consideration. After all, the category of refugee was created by states not so much to enable us to fulfill our duties to the distressed and unfortunate as to make it easier for us to evade them.

If this is true, then those who argue that the existing arrangements under which states are widely seen to be justified in limiting the free movement of people, while having obligations only to make exceptions for special categories of person, should just give up the fiction that the plight of refugees is a serious ethical concern. It would be more accurate and honest to concede that it is simply a matter of indifference, for, ultimately, strangers just don't count—no matter what their predicament.

To see this we should begin by looking more closely at the way the distinction between refugees and other potential migrants is drawn, to try to understand how the case for differential duties might be made—and why it cannot be sustained. We should turn then to consider why institutionalizing this distinction is unlikely to achieve the ethical ends that are supposed to be the point of this development. The historical record provides ample evidence to bear this out. From here we can turn to consider more directly the reasons why making the state the bearer of ethical duties is not likely to serve the interests of the refugees or asylum seekers to any significant degree, and is more likely to harm those interests. Out of this analysis comes just one conclusion that seems plausible: the interests of refugees and asylum seekers can only be served by an opening of state borders. To the extent that this prospect is utopian, so too is the prospect of humane treatment of those almost everyone says is special.[12]

---

[12] For some reflections on how the attempt to reform the institutions of refugee protection may itself be utopian, see William Maley, "A New Tower of Babel? Reappraising the Architecture of

12.3 Refugees versus Immigrants

To see the problem with making a moral distinction between refugees and immigrants, it would be useful to start with the definition of refugee deployed by the 1951 *United Nations Convention Relating to the Status of Refugees*, which came into force in 1954 and now has more than 120 state signatories. The Convention states that a refugee is any person who,

> owing to a well-founded fear of being persecuted for reasons of race, religion, nationality, membership of a particular social group or political opinion, is outside the country of his nationality and is unable, or owing to such fear, is unwilling to avail himself of the protection of that country; or who, not having a nationality and being outside the country of his former habitual residence as a result of such events, is unable or, owing to such fear, is unwilling to return to it. (Article 1A2)

What is most glaring about this definition is who it excludes: those fleeing their circumstances for reasons other than persecution; those who have fled but not crossed an international boundary; and those whose flight from persecution has taken them across borders but who have been persecuted for reasons other than race, religion, nationality, or social or political membership. Most Cambodians trying to escape from the Khmer Rouge did not count as refugees.

The matter of definition has been a contentious issue from the start and there have been many proposals to revise the Convention's understanding to try to include more people who seem also to be candidates for refugee status: people fleeing war, or famine, or environmental disaster, to name some obvious cases. Thus the Organization of African Unity adopted a very different definition, according to which a refugee was a person who "owing to external aggression, occupation, foreign domination or events seriously disturbing public order in either part or the whole of his country of origin or nationality, is compelled to leave his place of habitual residence in order to seek refuge in another place outside his country of nationality" (OAU Convention Governing the Specific Aspects of Refugee Problems in Africa, adopted September 10, 1969 (UNTS no.14691), Article 1(2)).[13] Bosnians fleeing civil war are thus captured by this definition in a way that they are not by the 1951 UN Convention. Yet even this definition has its limitations, since it excludes internally displaced people, and a better account may be the one offered by Matthew Gibney, who suggests that refugees are "those people who require a

Refugee Protection" in Edward Newman and Joanne van Selm (eds.), *Refugees and Forced Displacement: International Security, Human Vulnerability, and the State* (Tokyo: United Nations Press, 2003), pp. 306–29.

[13] See the discussion in Andrew Shacknove, "Who is a Refugee?," *Ethics* 95:2 (1985), 274–84 at pp. 275–6.

new state of residence, either temporarily or permanently, because if forced to return or stay at home they would, as a result of either the inadequacy or brutality of their state, be persecuted or seriously jeopardize their physical security or vital subsistence needs."[14] One particular merit of this definition is that it also includes as refugees those forced to flee in anticipation of rightly foreseeable repression. It also includes refugees *sur place*: persons who were not refugees when they left their countries, but are unable to return home because events in their country since their original temporary departure have left them with a well-founded fear of persecution should they do so.

The problem, however, is not the quality of the definition but the pursuit of the distinction that gives the definition its point. The purpose of distinguishing between refugees and immigrants is to limit and control the movement of people in a world in which free movement is not tolerated. If only some are allowed to move, the question is: who? States allow people to move in and out for a variety of reasons, most of them economic or political. Economic considerations may include the need to meet the domestic demand for labor (both skilled and unskilled), the desire to attract foreign investment capital, and the concern to change the demographic structure of the population. The importance of such economic concerns makes states less likely to welcome the poor, the illiterate, the disabled, the unskilled, the unhealthy, and the elderly.[15] Political considerations lie behind the weight given to different economic concerns. Business interests generally favor more immigration since capital benefits when there is a larger pool of labor; while labor fears that immigrants will either outcompete domestic workers or depress the general level of wages by entering the labor market. Immigration policy will always attempt to placate these two contending economic interests. But other political considerations will also obtrude. Different groups will want preferential treatment for particular classes of migrant: universities will want favorable treatment for students, families with relatives overseas will want to privilege family reunion, ethnic communities will want their own national or cultural groups given special treatment if immigrant places are limited, and lovers will want exceptions made for potential marriage partners. In a world of controlled borders, refugees must either compete with other immigrants for a limited number of places or show that the case for their admission should not be considered as a

---

[14] Matthew Gibney, "Liberal Democratic States and Responsibilities for Refugees," *American Political Science Review* 93:1 (1999), 169–81 at pp. 170–1. See also Matthew Gibney, *The Ethics and Politics of Asylum: Liberal Democracy and the Response to Refugees* (Cambridge: Cambridge University Press, 2004).

[15] A quick glance at the "points tests" administered by the Australian and Canadian governments to would-be immigrants makes the nature of the calculus very plain: there are more points to be gained for having greater language proficiency, more years of study, a sum of money to transfer, and a longer life expectancy as a potential future tax-payer. Ill health and any criminal record cancel out the points gained by having some of the other desirable assets.

part of the general case for immigrant admission: that they really are special. But how is this to be done?

It may look as though the best strategy here is simply to insist that the refugee question is a humanitarian issue, and that refugees should not be viewed as economic migrants but people whose human rights have been violated and need to be restored. Thus Yael Tamir suggests that "a clear distinction should be drawn between the rights of refugees and the rights of immigrants. Although certain restrictions on immigrants could be justified, they could never rescind the *absolute* obligation to grant refuge to individuals for as long as their lives are at risk."[16] This is an argument many refugee advocates have decided to make, in part for fear that if refugees were viewed as migrants they would be easy prey for governments looking to reduce immigration numbers.[17] But this strategy is sustainable only if such a distinction can really be drawn.[18] Unfortunately, this looks very unlikely.

One way of drawing the distinction might be to follow Tamir and say that there is an absolute obligation to grant refuge to individuals whose lives are at risk. Yet there are many difficulties with this approach. To begin with, even if we put to one side the question of whether this, or any other, obligation can be "absolute," the problem is that human circumstances are never absolute but relative. Lives may be at risk, but all lives are never equally at risk, and the degree of risk that is a cause for alarm is a matter of moral judgment. It may have been riskier to be a Jew in pre-war Berlin than to be a Hazara in Afghanistan today, but it is probably riskier to be a Hazara in Kabul than to be a *Reformasi* activist in Malaysia. The risks borne by those whose lives are at risk also vary, since some face the prospect of being killed, others face possible imprisonment, and some the loss of economic, civil, and political rights. Lives can be at risk in many ways and to varying degrees. It would not be plausible to argue that *any* level of risk triggers a right to be granted refuge; but there is no naturalistic way of determining what level of risk might.

Assuming, however, that the principle of granting refuge to those whose lives are at risk can be given some substantive content, it would have to be shown why this should favor those seeking asylum rather than those moving for reasons other than flight from persecution. Many economic migrants, after all, move because their lives, or the lives of their loved ones, are at risk. Adverse economic conditions, environmental catastrophe, or simply the poverty of their surrounding circumstances may mean that they face destitution unless they move, for their plight cannot be addressed by domestic institutions or

---

[16] Yael Tamir, *Liberal Nationalism* (Princeton, NJ: Princeton University Press, 1993), p. 159.

[17] See the discussion in Liza Schuster, *The Use and Abuse of Political Asylum in Britain and Germany* (London: Frank Cass, 2004), pp. 33–4.

[18] Though I don't want to get carried away here: in politics, truth can all too often be readily overcome by interest or power.

the help of fellow citizens. There are many refugees whose plight is more serious than that of most economic migrants; yet there are also many would-be economic migrants who face greater threats to their well-being than do some refugees. Not all economic migrants are in the same boat; nor are all refugees.

At this point the problem of definition becomes particularly acute. We could try to bolster the claim that the plight of the refugee is more serious than that of the economic migrant by narrowing the definition of refugee—perhaps appealing to a conservative reading of the 1951 Convention so that only those outside their home countries fearing persecution for very particular reasons might qualify. The trouble here is that refugee protection is bought at a high price: excluding, for example, those fleeing war zones or famine or even genocidal violence from being considered refugees. The more narrowly the term is defined the easier it might be to make refugees special, but only because there would be many fewer of them. However, if we consider this unpalatable, and think the definition should be expanded to include a greater number of types of displaced people, the difference between refugees and economic migrants will be even harder to draw.

Any attempt to show empirically that refugees, or displaced people more generally, suffer in ways that economic migrants do not, will founder on the rocks of this particular dilemma. The root of the problem is that the source of injustice, or of human suffering, is not always easy to locate. The aspiration to find the explanation that distinguishes the refugee from the human being who moves merely (*merely!*) to improve his lot is in many cases motivated by a noble concern to address the needs of those who are most vulnerable or suffer most. But, for better or for worse, suffering is dispersed too erratically for our political concepts to handle.

12.4 Institutional Solutions

One possible response to this analysis is to say that it will not do to get too caught up in conceptual niceties, for it is well known that in political life philosophical purity is not really attainable. The tragic reality of the plight of refugees, asylum seekers, or displaced people more generally, cannot be denied: the evidence is overwhelming. Even if we cannot quite account for it conceptually, the swarms of people moving in response to the predations of genocidal rulers, or rushing across borders to avoid bombs and marauding armies, supply evidence enough of a distinct phenomenon. What is needed is an institutional response that recognizes that there is a problem that must be addressed.

The institutional response we have made is that embodied in the regime defined by the 1951 Convention. However imperfectly, the argument goes, it rightly draws the distinction between refugees and immigrants. Our best bet might be simply to try to work within its terms in an effort to secure what we can for the victims of repressive states and war.[19] A regime of human rights that recognizes the rights of refugees might lack the full theoretical justification philosophers seek, but it could just work—by giving refugees the legal and moral resources they need to protect or secure their vital interests.

Unfortunately, this simply won't do. International regimes, to be sure, are political constructions rather than philosophical ones; but this is not to the advantage of the refugee or asylum seeker. On the contrary, what is all too evident is that the purpose of the institutional identification of refugees in international law was never solely to attend to the plight of the distressed and dispossessed but largely to serve the interests of states.

The 1951 UN Convention on Refugees has its origins in the Second World War, which saw hundreds of thousands of people displaced by the conflict, many of them victims and survivors of the Holocaust. Britain became home to many of these people, primarily from Eastern Europe, who were unable to return to their countries of origin. The government labeled them "displaced persons" rather than refugees, since they thought the term refugee might imply that the persons in question would not return to their home countries.[20] In 1947 the International Refugee Organization was formed and its definition of displaced persons as victims of Nazi, fascist, or quisling regimes or "persons who were considered refugees before the outbreak of the Second World War, for reasons of race, religion, nationality or political opinion" later formed the basis of the 1951 Convention understanding of refugees as persons fleeing persecution. But already the British and American governments were hesitant about using the term "refugee" for fear that it might amount to a concession that the persons in question could not return. Many people were thus allowed to stay in Britain, for example, as "European Volunteer Workers," who were supposedly admitted to help alleviate labor shortages.[21] At the very outset, even with the memory of the Holocaust fresh in the mind, the thoughts of government officials turned to the problem of how to keep people out.

On the whole, the history of the state's treatment of refugees is not an inspiring one. In the years between the wars the nations of Europe were more troubled by the inconvenience of refugee movements and invented new mechanisms to restrict their mobility. The outflow of Jewish refugees from Nazi Germany in the 1930s was met with grim resistance by states that

---

[19] For further discussion of statelessness and refugees, see the chapters by Joseph Carens and David Owen in this volume.

[20] Tony Kushner and Katharine Knox, *Refugees in an Age of Genocide: Global, Local, and National Perspectives during the Twentieth Century* (London: Frank Cass, 1999), p. 217.

[21] Kushner and Knox, *Refugees in an Age of Genocide*, p. 218.

expressed support for the principle of granting asylum but refused to grant refugees rights to any such thing. Twentieth-century states, it turned out, "were governed by Machiavellian self-interest, and liberalism served only to disguise this brutal reality."[22]

The workings of the refugee regime since the establishment of the 1951 Convention can scarcely be said to have served the interests of refugees well. Some of this is best explained by the particular interests of states, which have continued to see refugees as a problem whose impact has to be minimized rather than a moral responsibility to be discharged. Thus while the number of conventional instruments devised for the purpose of refugee protection has increased, the commitment of states to that end has, if anything, declined. The upsurge in the numbers of refugees worldwide as a result of the many political conflicts in the postwar era led to states increasingly adopting measures to restrict opportunities to seek asylum. Agnès Hurwitz identifies five kinds of policies used to achieve this end. First, there are measures to restrict access to the territory of the state by imposing fines on companies transporting undocumented aliens, by requiring visas from nationals of refugee producing countries, by posting immigration officers abroad, and by interdicting vessels at sea to prevent them from allowing refugee passengers to make landfall. Second, there are measures to limit access to asylum procedures, for example by imposing strict time limits for the lodging of asylum claims, invoking the concept of "safe country of origin" to require that claims for refugee status be processed elsewhere, and creating international zones in airports. Third, states have adopted a narrower interpretation of Article 1 of the Refugee Convention, and invented weaker forms of protection, such as temporary or subsidiary protection. Fourth, states have tried to create "safe havens" in the regions or countries of the refugee's origin in order to discourage or prevent attempts to seek asylum. Fifth, states have restricted access to welfare benefits and placed refugees in detention in order to deter arrivals.[23]

In pursuing these strategies states have effectively blurred the distinction between refugees and economic migrants by treating all asylum seekers with suspicion. Even as they have maintained the centrality of the distinction between refugees and migrants to their policies, they have weakened it by treating asylum seekers as undocumented would-be immigrants unless they can show otherwise—while making it ever more difficult for refugee claims to be established. When immigration officers have gone to refugee camps they have often gone with the aim of picking and choosing the most economically

---

[22] Schuster, *Use and Abuse of Political Asylum*, p. 89.
[23] Agnès Hurwitz, *The Collective Responsibility of States to Protect Refugees* (Oxford: Oxford University Press, 2009), pp. 18–19.

attractive potential migrants—doctors and engineers rather than women and children traumatized by war or violence.

What has emerged over the years, in what is supposed to be a refugee protection regime, is a security-driven discourse that has led to the adoption of greater and greater measures designed to "contain" the refugee problem by restricting the opportunities of asylum seekers to gain refugee status and, ultimately, admission to the state.

Of the practices used to delay, if not prevent altogether, the possibility of asylum seekers or refugees gaining admission, two are worth dwelling upon a little more carefully. The first is the confining or detaining of asylum seekers waiting to learn if they will be brought to a more permanent place of safety or waiting to learn if their application for refugee status has been successful. The enforcement of immigration controls generally has led to the development of an extensive system of prisons to deal with undocumented workers, visa over-stayers, and illegal aliens of all kinds.[24] For many victims of forced displace-ment, the search for asylum begins in refugee camps where they exist on the edge of the social world in conditions which are often little better than prison. What is too seldom recognized or acknowledged is that refugee camps have become, in effect, one of the four solutions to the refugee problem adopted by the United Nations High Commission for Refugees. The first three, official, solutions are: repatriation, integration in the country of asylum, and resettle-ment in a third country. In 2007 UNHCR reported that there were some 6.5 million people residing in refugee camps around the world (not including camps of Palestinian refugees, or those for internally displaced people in places like Sudan). Under the refugee regime, vast numbers of people live in makeshift accommodation, often in remote and inhospitable parts of the world, with plastic sheeting for extra coverings, and food that is rationed by agencies which have themselves to go begging to raise the funds to feed people who have fled for their lives. The camps are not a happy advertisement for the success of the institutionalization of refugee protection.

Yet this barely begins to get at the nature of the problem with the institu-tional response to the plight of the refugee or asylum seeker. Regardless of the conditions in the camps,[25] the people looking for help find themselves not at

---

[24] For graphic accounts of what this means in practice, see David C. Brotherton and Philip Kretsedemas (eds.), *Keeping Out the Other: A Critical Introduction to Immigration Enforcement Today* (New York: Columbia University Press, 2008).

[25] A part of the tragedy of many of the camps is the fact of abuse of the people herded into them for protection by the very people designated as their humanitarian protectors. Discussing the sexual abuses perpetrated in camps in Guinea, Liberia, and Sierra Leone, Michel Agier and Françoise Bouchet-Saulnier observed: "Designed to bring help and protection to people in danger, in some cases humanitarian action has contributed to enclosing people in spaces of exception, spaces of irresponsibility. Far from protecting the international public order, the continued existence of these spaces has reintroduced inhumanity at the heart of all societies." See their chapter, "Humanitarian Spaces, Spaces of Exception" in Fabrice Weissman (ed.), *In the*

the doorstep of agencies straining to help them but of a vast and impersonal bureaucratic structure that demands that they show—prove—that they have a case. Asylum seekers confront this problem no matter what their circumstances, and regardless of the physical or emotional state they are in. To some extent this is inescapable: bureaucratic procedures, once in place, cannot simply be waived away because some people claim that they are inappropriate or unreasonable or do not apply to them. But the human cost is worth dwelling upon. Consider the case of France, one of the countries most active in the negotiations surrounding the establishment of the 1951 Convention (but also the toughest of the early signatories since it always viewed asylum seekers as potential competitors in the French labor market). When France began to place stronger restrictions on immigration in 1974, its policy on asylum seekers became stricter and stricter as the imperative to stop the flow became increasingly urgent. Over the period of the seventies, eighties, and nineties the percentage of refugee applications granted fell from a peak of 95 percent in 1976 to 28 percent in 1989, until by 2003 only three applicants in twenty were successful.[26] Crucially, however, those who were eventually granted leave to remain in the country as bona fide refugees had first to undergo searching examinations of their histories by border agents who were also under pressure to reduce the credibility of the applicants' testimonies.

Over the years the legal and bureaucratic obstacles to presenting a case for asylum have increased and applicants have been turned into objects of suspicion, dehumanized not only by their subjection to a bewildering array of scrutinizing procedures but by the reduction of their life histories to a series of objective statements on certificates that will be used to determine whether or not the candidate merits selection. The subjective experience of the refugee is played down, discarded, or never inquired into as the emphasis is placed on whether clinical evidence is available to corroborate claims of torture or abuse that led to flight and escape. The following extract from a letter from the file of legal correspondence collated by the nongovernmental organization COMEDE supplies a striking illustration.

> Dear Sir,
>
> I write in respect of the Commission of Appeal hearing on [date]. In order for you to obtain refugee status, you *must* send me a medical certificate testifying to the

---

Shadow of "Just Wars": Violence, Politics and Humanitarian Action, quoted in Didier Fassin, "Heart of Humaneness: The Moral Economy of Humanitarian Intervention" in Didier Fassin and Mariella Pandolfi (eds.), *Contemporary States of Emergency: The Politics of Military and Humanitarian Interventions* (New York: Zone Books, 2010), pp. 269–93 at p. 292, n.52.

[26] Didier Fassin and Richard Rechtman, *The Empire of Trauma: An Inquiry into the Condition of Victimhood* (Princeton, NJ: Princeton University Press, 2009), p. 256.

traces left on your body as a result of the torture and abuse inflicted on you, particularly with respect to your eye. Please do not hesitate to contact me if you have any difficulty.

Yours sincerely . . . [27]

The dehumanizing character of the institutional apparatus that has grown up around the world to address the refugee "problem" is further evident in the conditions under which those seeking asylum are detained in those countries that incarcerate applicants until their cases are settled. In Australia the inmates of the detention centers have been driven to suicide, self-mutilation, and even to the extreme of sewing up their lips to express their sense of powerlessness.[28]

Institutionalizing the distinction between immigrant and refugee has been considered by some to be the best, or only, way of promoting the interests of asylum seekers and ensuring that their special claims were appropriately considered. The reality, however, is that the institutional distinction has accomplished no such thing. Governments have consistently seen refugees as competitor economic migrants and have therefore constantly implied that those seeking admission to a country on humanitarian grounds were nothing more than queue-jumpers trying to get around the immigration laws. As time has gone on, the institutional structures they have devised have simply made it more and more difficult for asylum seekers to bring their claims forward, and to gain the protection they seek. Institutionally, refugees have turned out not to be very special at all.

12.5 In Search of a Solution

Refugees have been identified as special for a very special reason. Nation-states and their defenders wish to maintain that immigration can rightly be restricted to the extent that the state is an ethical community that requires protection, and freedom of movement threatens to undermine it.[29] Yet the arbitrariness of such an arrangement is difficult to ignore since the opportunities people enjoy to live reasonably prosperous lives in safety differ so dramatically from one part of the world to the next—particularly when some

---

[27] Quoted in Didier Fassin, *Humanitarian Reason: A Moral History of the Present* (Berkeley: University of California Press, 2011), p. 114.

[28] See Kathy Marks, "Refugee Camp Children Sew Their Lips in Protest," *The Independent*, January 22, 2002, <http://www.independent.co.uk/news/world/australasia/refugee-camp-children-sew-their-lips-in-protest-664504.html>.

[29] For a passionate analysis of the transformative effects of immigration, and its costs and dangers, see Paul Scheffer, *Immigrant Nations*, translated by Liz Waters (Cambridge: Polity Press, 2011). For an even more passionate critique of immigration from an American perspective (albeit by an English immigrant to the United States), see Peter Brimelow, *Alien Nation: Common Sense about America's Immigration Disaster* (New York: Harper, 1996).

people are effectively denied the freedom to improve their conditions by moving to places where they might improve their lot. The birthright lottery might be a fact of life, but it is difficult to justify.[30] For this reason, liberal political theorists in particular have argued for a solution that combines limiting immigration but compensating for the restriction on free movement by greater transfers of wealth to the poor in other nations. There is a "tragic conflict" between the goal of nation-building on the one hand and the liberal commitment to equality on the other. But perhaps the tragedy can be avoided by careful, constructive planning, to transfer wealth from the rich to the poor abroad through appropriately devised global institutions.[31] As Robert Goodin puts it, "if rich countries do not want to let foreigners in, then the very least they must do is send much more money to compensate them for their being kept out."[32] Theorists such as Will Kymlicka, Thomas Pogge, and Martha Nussbaum, in different ways, advocate a transformation of global institutions, and the development of mechanisms of global redistribution, to combine nation-building with a concern for global equality.[33] The problem with refugees is that transfers of wealth cannot help those whose suffering is rooted in the breakdown of the institutions in their homelands, or the unwillingness of the powers that dominate those institutions to accept them as members of good standing. In such circumstances, it looks like an exception has to be made for this class of people, who can best be helped not by a transfer of funds but by emigration. The answer, it seems, is to allow some people to move more easily as asylum seekers or refugees rather than migrants, and to develop institutions that facilitate this.

As we have seen, however, there are two problems with this solution. First, the distinction between immigrants and asylum seekers or refugees cannot easily be drawn; and second, the history of the development of an institutional framework to deal with the plight of refugees does not suggest that it is even remotely possible to do justice to the people in question. Making

---

[30] See Ayelet Shachar, *The Birthright Lottery: Citizenship and Global Inequality* (Cambridge, MA: Harvard University Press, 2009).

[31] For a discussion of the idea of such a dilemma, see Kok-Chor Tan, *Justice Without Borders: Cosmopolitanism, Nationalism and Patriotism* (Cambridge: Cambridge University Press, 2004), pp. 123–32.

[32] Robert E. Goodin, "If People Were Money..." in Brian Barry and Robert Goodin (eds.), *Free Movement: Ethical Issues in the Transnational Migration of People and Money* (University Park, PA: Pennsylvania State University Press, 1992), pp. 6–22 at p. 9. Goodin is, however, an advocate of open borders. See Goodin, "What's so Special about our Fellow Countrymen?," *Ethics* 99:4 (1989), 663–86.

[33] See Will Kymlicka, *Politics in the Vernacular: Nationalism, Multiculturalism and Citizenship* (Oxford: Oxford University Press, 2001); Thomas Pogge (ed.), *Global Justice* (Oxford: Blackwell, 2004); Thomas Pogge, *World Poverty and Human Rights* (Oxford: Polity, 2002); Martha Nussbaum, *Creating Capabilities: The Human Development Approach* (Cambridge, MA: Harvard University Press, 2011).

refugees special neither makes sense conceptually, nor looks possible practically on the evidence we have to date.

If this is right, and there is indeed a trade-off between the ideals of nation-building and the humane treatment of the displaced people of the world, then we must either give up some of our concern with nation-building or simply admit that we are prepared to leave a great number of vulnerable people to their fate. If the fate of the wretched of the world is something we cannot ignore, however, then this means, more concretely, that we should open borders to immigrants of all kinds, thus removing the barriers to the free movement of asylum seekers and other kinds of immigrants alike. Trying to make fine-grained judgments about which kinds of distress merit concern is conceptually problematic; and trying to put these distinctions to work institutionally is more or less pointless. At best, this approach serves to do little more than assuage some consciences that something is being done. But it would be more honest simply to plead indifference.

This is not to suggest that we should simply throw our hands up in the air, and wait for the advent of a borderless world to solve the problem. Border controls are a reality, as is the existence of a refugee regime shaped by the 1951 Convention. Undoubtedly some good can be done by revising the Convention, pressing for more generous interpretations of its rules, persuading state authorities to make it easier for asylum seekers to gain the right to work, improving the conditions in detention centers (if authorities are unwilling to close them down altogether). We must, after all, be realistic, as we are repeatedly told we must. Yet we can do all this without buying into the fiction that we can readily draw the distinction between refugees and all other migrants, or that once such a distinction is made we can devise and run institutions that will serve the interests of the desperate and the destitute.

12.6 Epilogue: The Morality of Hospitality

Modern democratic societies host many people whose status in society is uncertain, asylum seekers, refugees, and undocumented migrants among them. In her study of the treatment of aliens in the democratic state, Seyla Benhabib observes that such people are effectively treated as criminals by existing polities. "The right to universal hospitality is sacrificed on the altar of state interest."[34] She goes on to suggest that we

---

[34] Seyla Benhabib, *The Rights of Others: Aliens, Residents and Citizens* (Cambridge: Cambridge University Press, 2004), p. 177.

...need to decriminalize the worldwide movement of peoples, and treat each person, whatever his or her political citizenship status, in accordance with the dignity of moral personhood. This implies acknowledging that crossing borders and seeking entry into different polities is not a criminal act but an expression of human freedom and the search for human betterment in a world which we have to share with our fellow human beings.[35]

Benhabib develops the argument that leads to this view through an analysis of Kant's understanding of the universal right of hospitality enjoyed by all peoples of the world. For all its humanity, however, Benhabib finds Kant's perspective wanting. While it recognizes an imperfect duty to help and offer shelter to those in danger of life and limb, and is generally sympathetic to the rights of all people to travel and sojourn in different lands, the structure that has emerged that enshrines Kant's thinking to some degree nonetheless views matters from the perspective of the state, rather than of world society. While it may not be possible to have a world of open borders, a case can be made for more porous ones. We can build on Kant's appreciation of the importance of hospitality, but not become trapped by sharp distinctions between citizens and aliens, members and foreigners. The aim should be to develop improved understandings of membership and citizenship which take seriously the need to incorporate those who move into the democratic polity—even if they cannot be granted the full range of citizen rights on first entry.

While I am very sympathetic to Benhabib's stance, and recognize her awareness of the tension between the demands of democratic representation on the one hand and the requirements of open admission on the other, I am not sure that a solution can be found that does not require a serious diminution in the importance of the state, and of membership of states. The problem is that states, while not merely reflections of the relations of power and the strength of particular interests in society, are nonetheless substantially precisely that. To the extent that individuals engage with any society for the first time through a confrontation with the state, they are unlikely to be met with hospitality rather than hostility. The very point of the state is to protect interests; the problem is how to widen its purview so that it serves the interest of all its members rather than the interests of those who can capture it. To turn the state into an institution that takes seriously the interests of those who are not even members might be more difficult still.

If refugees and asylum seekers are to be welcomed into any society, and shown a measure of hospitality, this will not be because the polity is welcoming but because society is so. Hospitality is, as Homer shows us in the *Odyssey*, a human relation rather than an institutional one. To the extent that we try to

---

[35] Benhabib, *The Rights of Others*, p. 177.

design institutions that perform a function that only people can, it seems unlikely that our efforts will meet with much success.[36]

References

Agier, Michel and Françoise Bouchet-Saulnier, "Humanitarian Spaces, Spaces of Exception" in Fabrice Weissman (ed.), *In the Shadow of "Just Wars": Violence, Politics and Humanitarian Action* (London: Hurst, 2004).

Altman, Andrew and Christopher Heath Wellman, *A Liberal Theory of International Justice* (Oxford: Oxford University Press, 2011).

Benhabib, Seyla, *The Rights of Others: Aliens, Residents and Citizens* (Cambridge: Cambridge University Press, 2004).

Brimelow, Peter, *Alien Nation: Common Sense about America's Immigration Disaster* (New York: Harper, 1996).

Brotherton, David C. and Philip Kretsedemas (eds.), *Keeping Out the Other: A Critical Introduction to Immigration Enforcement Today* (New York: Columbia University Press, 2008).

Fassin, Didier, "Heart of Humaneness: The Moral Economy of Humanitarian Intervention" in Didier Fassin and Mariella Pandolfi (eds.), *Contemporary States of Emergency: The Politics of Military and Humanitarian Interventions* (New York: Zone Books, 2010), pp. 269–93.

Fassin, Didier, *Humanitarian Reason: A Moral History of the Present* (Berkeley, CA: University of California Press, 2011).

Fassin, Didier and Richard Rechtman, *The Empire of Trauma: An Inquiry into the Condition of Victimhood* (Princeton, NJ: Princeton University Press, 2009).

Gibney, Matthew, "Liberal Democratic States and Responsibilities for Refugees," *American Political Science Review* 93:1 (1999), 169–81.

Gibney, Matthew, *The Ethics and Politics of Asylum: Liberal Democracy and the Response to Refugees* (Cambridge: Cambridge University Press, 2004).

Goodin, Robert E., "What's so Special about our Fellow Countrymen?," *Ethics* 99:4 (1989), 663–86.

Goodin, Robert E., "If People Were Money ..." in Brian Barry and Robert E. Goodin (eds.), *Free Movement: Ethical Issues in the Transnational Migration of People and Money* (University Park, PA: Pennsylvania State University Press, 1992), pp. 6–22.

Homer, *The Odyssey of Homer*, translated and with an introduction by Richmond Lattimore (New York: Harper Collins, 1991).

Hurwitz, Agnès, *The Collective Responsibility of States to Protect Refugees* (Oxford: Oxford University Press, 2009).

Kushner, Tony and Katharine Knox, *Refugees in an Age of Genocide: Global, Local, and National Perspectives during the Twentieth Century* (London: Frank Cass, 1999).

[36] I wish to thank Sarah Fine, Lea Ypi, Mollie Gerver, and Liza Schuster for helpful comments on an earlier draft of this chapter.

Kymlicka, Will, *Politics in the Vernacular: Nationalism, Multiculturalism and Citizenship* (Oxford: Oxford University Press, 2001).

Maley, William, "A New Tower of Babel? Reappraising the Architecture of Refugee Protection" in Edward Newman and Joanne van Selm (eds.), *Refugees and Forced Displacement: International Security, Human Vulnerability, and the State* (Tokyo: United Nations Press, 2003).

Marks, Kathy, "Refugee Camp Children Sew Their Lips in Protest," *The Independent*, January 22, 2002, accessed at <http://www.independent.co.uk/news/world/aus tralasia/refugee-camp-children-sew-their-lips-in-protest-664504.html>.

Miller, David, "Immigration: The Case for Limits" in Andrew I. Cohen and Christopher Heath Wellman (eds.), *Contemporary Debates in Applied Ethics* (Oxford: Blackwell, 2005), pp. 193–206.

Miller, David, *National Responsibility and Global Justice* (Oxford: Oxford University Press, 2007).

Nussbaum, Martha, *Creating Capabilities: The Human Development Approach* (Cambridge, MA: Harvard University Press, 2011).

Pogge, Thomas, *World Poverty and Human Rights* (Oxford: Polity, 2002).

Pogge, Thomas (ed.), *Global Justice* (Oxford: Blackwell, 2004).

Rousseau, Jean-Jacques, *Emile, or On Education*, Introduction, translation and Notes by Allan Bloom (New York: Basic Books, 1979).

Sa'di, *The Gulistan or Flower Garden, of Shaikh Sadī of Shiraz*, translated by James Ross (London: J.M. Richardson, 1823 [1258]).

Scheffer, Paul, *Immigrant Nations*, translated by Liz Waters (Cambridge: Polity Press, 2011).

Schuster, Liza, *The Use and Abuse of Political Asylum in Britain and Germany* (London: Frank Cass, 2004).

Shachar, Ayelet, *The Birthright Lottery: Citizenship and Global Inequality* (Cambridge, MA: Harvard University Press, 2009).

Shacknove, Andrew, "Who is a Refugee?," *Ethics* 95:2 (1985), 274–84.

Tamir, Yael, *Liberal Nationalism* (Princeton, NJ: Princeton University Press, 1993).

Tan, Kok-Chor, *Justice Without Borders: Cosmopolitanism, Nationalism and Patriotism* (Cambridge: Cambridge University Press, 2004).

Walzer, Michael, *Spheres of Justice: A Defense of Pluralism and Equality* (Oxford: Blackwell, 1983).

13

In Loco Civitatis

On the Normative Basis of the Institution of Refugeehood and Responsibilities for Refugees

David Owen

Hannah Arendt was perhaps the first to outline the thought of the refugee as an exemplary figure for a political order organized as a plurality of territorially bounded sovereign states. Exemplary in the sense not only that the refugee is best conceived as a distinctively modern political artifact of the international order of states, but also that the *exceptional* status of refugee is one of the political media through which the ongoing reproduction of the normative structure of this order of governance is accomplished. This normative order being characterized, most basically, by the governmental norms of (1) allocating authority over, and primary responsibility for, national citizenries to states as sovereign political agents who determine their own membership rules, and (2) non-intervention by states with respect to each other's territorial jurisdiction.[1] Arendt's thought has been both supported and elaborated by recent historical studies of the institution of refugeehood, but its

---

[1] As Nevzat Soguk has shown in *States and Strangers: Refugees and the Displacements of Statecraft* (Minneapolis: University of Minneapolis Press, 1999)—his historical analysis of the emergence and development of the figure of the refugee—the constitution of refugee regimes, like the constitution of nationality regimes, can be productively conceived as governmental practices of statecraft through which the belonging of citizens within the territorial or national order of the state is constituted and the powers of the state with respect to its citizens are legitimated in terms of its role as the agent responsible for securing their liberty and welfare. In similar vein, Emma Haddad's *The Refugee in International Society: Between Sovereigns* (Cambridge: Cambridge University Press, 2008), a study of the history of the refugee, stresses the centrality of the refugee to our global political order as an inevitable but unanticipated feature of international society which both problematizes that order and, through the international refugee regime, reproduces it.

implications for normative reflection on this modern institution have not, I think, been widely taken up.[2]

My strategy is, then, to try to defend a view of the international refugee regime which is not constructed in terms of humanitarian obligations owed to strangers but, rather, in terms of political obligations that arise as conditions of the political legitimacy of the international order of states considered as a global regime of governance, and to draw out the normative implications of this view for the institution of refugeehood and the distribution of responsibility for refugees. In other words, I want to make a case for the claim that we can rationally reconstruct the normative grounds and character of the international refugee regime in terms that require reference only to basic or minimum conditions of the legitimacy of states and of the international order of states.

The current definition of the refugee is provided by international refugee law which, strictly speaking, consists of "international and regional conventions, General Assembly resolutions and resolutions of various ad hoc groups with regional competence (e.g. the EEC Ad Hoc Group on Immigration), customary law and domestic legislation."[3] However, the primary instruments of contemporary international refugee law are the 1951 Geneva Convention Relating to the Status of Refugees (hereafter "the 1951 Convention") and the 1967 New York Protocol to the Convention Relating to the Status of Refugees (hereafter "the 1967 Protocol") and, taken together, these instruments provide the basic definition of the refugee as one who

> owing to a well-founded fear of being persecuted for reasons of race, religion, nationality [as belonging to a 'people'], membership of a social group or political opinion is outside the country of his nationality [as membership of a state] and is unable or, owing to such fear, is unwilling to avail himself of the protection of that country; or who, not having a nationality and being outside the country of his habitual residence . . . is unable, or, owing to such fear, is unwilling to return to it.[4]

Refugeehood, as I have already noted, is an *exceptional* status. A person claiming this status is entitled to a fair determination of whether they satisfy the relevant criteria specified by the 1951 Convention and, if so, the state to which they have made application has a duty to ensure that they are not exposed to the relevant threat (typically, but not necessarily, through a grant

---

[2] One important exception is Seyla Benhabib's *The Rights of Others: Aliens, Residents and Citizens* (Cambridge: Cambridge University Press, 2004), which addresses refugees in Arendtian terms.

[3] Patricia Tuitt, *False Images: Law's Construction of the Refugee* (London: Pluto Press, 1996), p. 9. Cf. Guy Goodwin-Gill and Jane Adam, *The Refugee in International Law* (Oxford: Oxford University Press, 2007).

[4] 1951 Convention Article 1 A (2) & 1967 Protocol Article 1 (2), although see the potential qualification of the geographic scope provided by Article 1 (B) 1 of the Convention and Article 1 (3) of the Protocol. The insertions are mine.

of asylum in that state).[5] What makes this status *exceptional* is that refugees are entitled to *the protection of a state which is not their own*,[6] in the context of a predominant norm of global governance that states are fundamentally responsible to, and for, their own citizens. As Matthew Gibney has noted:

> Above all else...the state is fundamentally an answer to the question of who is responsible to whom in the modern world: states are responsible to their own citizens. The survival of the state as an entity over time rests, moreover, on its ability to portray itself convincingly as an answer to such a question. As a consequence, the claims of outsiders are assessed by states, including liberal democratic ones, through a logic that deprecates the interests and needs of outsiders—a logic that is exceedingly sensitive to the potential damage to its own authority involved in forcing its citizens to incur costs for the sake of strangers. Modern states are highly resistant to the moral claims of outsiders.[7]

Since the state is a territorial organization, one form that this exceptional status can take—and the form that it currently does take—is an exemption from the norm that states have sovereign discretion over admissions into, and removals from, their territorial jurisdiction. This exemption is expressed as the duty of non-refoulement, which

> encompasses any measure attributable to the State which could have the effect of returning an asylum seeker or refugee to the frontiers of territories where his or her

---

[5] In addition to asylum seekers, there are also resettlement refugees who are already determined to satisfy the refugee requirement and are situated under the protection of the UN (for example, in "safe havens") and who await resettlement by way of quota schemes run by states such as Australia and the U.S. I will not address resettlement refugees in this chapter since they are a very small fraction of the global refugee population and they do not raise fundamental normative issues that are not also addressed by considering the more prevalent issue of asylum seeking.

[6] That is neither their state of nationality nor their state of habitual residence as specified under the 1951 Convention.

[7] Matthew Gibney, *The Ethics and Politics of Asylum: Liberal Democracy and the Response to Refugees* (Cambridge: Cambridge University Press, 2004), p. 211. Gibney supports this view by tracking the historical development of theoretical reflections on the political legitimacy of the state, from an initial focus on the security of its subjects to a position where modern states "now also claim to be agents for the protection of the ways of life of the human community over which they rule (national agents) and actors in pursuit of their citizens' economic welfare (economic agents)," these changes being related to a broader transformation in the relation between state and citizen: "the modern state's role as democratic agent" such that "increasingly the authority of the modern state has come to rest upon the claim that its actions and goals reflect not only the needs of its citizenry but also their wishes as expressed through a representative democratic process" (p. 211). From a somewhat different theoretical perspective, Hindess makes a closely related point in terms of national citizenship: citizenship is an important component of a dispersed system of governing a large, culturally diverse and interdependent world population that it operates by dividing that population into a series of discrete sub-populations and setting them against each other. Within that larger population, citizenship serves to facilitate or promote certain kinds of movement and interaction among its members and to inhibit or penalize others (Barry Hindess, "Divide and Rule: the International Character of Modern Citizenship," *European Journal of Social Theory* 1:1 (1998), 57–70 at p. 63).

life or freedom would be threatened, or where he or she is at risk of persecution, including interception, rejection at the frontier, or indirect *refoulement*.[8]

For those theorists who propose a principle of humanitarianism as a realistic ideal for refugee policy, such that we have obligations to refugees when the costs of discharging those obligations are low, the importance of this characteristic feature of the modern state as privileging the interests of its citizens is that it acts as a constraint on what can plausibly be expected of states, even liberal democratic ones, in terms of refugee protection. But this argument can also be approached in a different way if we reflect on the point that these characteristic norms are themselves constituted through the transnational relations of governance within which states are situated and which they follow, breach, adapt, and transform through their practices.

There are two points here. The first is that the practical identity of the modern state as a political actor should be conceived contextually as dependent on its location within wider relations of governance (from the 1648 Peace of Westphalia to the 1945 UN Charter). More fully, the practical identity of modern states cannot be separated from the commitments, entitlements, and obligations that comprise the normative status of statehood, where that status is constituted in and through the wider relations of governance (including relations of recognition) in which states are situated. Hence, the political legitimacy of modern states cannot be separated from the political legitimacy of these wider relations of governance. The second is that since states in their relations to each other are the primary agents through which these wider relations of governance are constituted, they are collectively outcome responsible for the character of these relations of governance and share responsibility with respect to the political legitimacy of these wider relations of governance. They share responsibility because (a) they are co-participants in a practice of governance who recognize each other as co-participants and through their activities, constitute and reconstitute the norms of the practice,[9] and (b) no participant has the unilateral power to determine these norms and every participant has the ability to modify them (however slightly) *en passant* through their conduct.[10] This does not, of course,

---

[8] Erika Feller, Volker Türk, and Frances Nicholson (eds.), *Refugee Protection in International Law: UNHCR's Global Consultations on International Protection* (Cambridge: Cambridge University Press, 2008), pp. 178–9.

[9] In David Miller, *National Responsibility and Global Justice* (Oxford: Oxford University Press, 2008), pp. 111–34, Miller distinguishes two models of collective responsibility—the like-minded model and the cooperative practice model—and we can see states as exhibiting elements of both of these ideal-typical models with respect to the practice of global governance. On sharing responsibility, see also Larry May, *Sharing Responsibility* (Chicago: Chicago University Press, 1992), especially chs. 2 and 6.

[10] For an account of the relationship between actors and norms in practices that highlights this point, see James Tully, *Public Philosophy in a New Key*, Volume 1 (Cambridge: Cambridge University Press, 2008), pp. 135–44.

entail that different states bear equal responsibility for these wider relations of governance since particular states may be (and are) more or less powerful participants in this practice of global governance (nor though does it entail that a state's portion of responsibility is proportional to its power considered as an individual agent).[11]

Drawing out these two points can help us with a puzzle that otherwise arises with respect to the modern state, namely, the question of what normative grounds *internal* to a political order characterized by a plurality of sovereign territorial states would support instituting, and giving legal expression to, the political status of refugee, that is, to a general obligation on states to offer protective refuge to any person whose own state fails to protect them in the relevant ways. To see how this puzzle arises, imagine that we do not recognize that the practical identity of the state is bound up with the wider relations of governance in which it is situated or that states share responsibility for the norms that order global governance. From such a standpoint, sovereign territorial states appear as autochthonous agents whose legitimacy is predicated on protecting the rights of their own citizenry and respecting the sovereignty of other states. Conceived thus, there is no legitimacy-based reason internal to this political order for states to institute the political status of refugee and place themselves under the obligations this entails (though there may be prudential reasons for them to adopt such a practice). Once we introduce the two points I have highlighted, however, such reasons naturally arise.

Consider that the norm that the state is responsible to, and for, its own citizens as a basic norm of this regime of global governance presupposes that, in general, states can reasonably be expected to possess the relevant dispositions and capabilities to conduct themselves in accordance with this norm, where acting in accordance with the norm can be glossed as satisfying basic legitimacy requirements. This, I suppose, includes on any plausible account acting effectively to ensure the basic security, liberty, and welfare of their citizens.[12] To the extent that some states lack such a disposition and/or capability, this constructs a legitimacy problem not only for that state but

---

[11] This latter point applies since although power is a positional good, it is also a combinable good such that the power of a given state is a function of the alliances in which it stands and can stand with respect to other such power blocs, rather than its own power considered in isolation from such relationships.

[12] I do not want to spell out a full account of legitimacy conditions but I do want to say that we can draw a distinction between basic or minimum legitimacy conditions and full or maximal legitimacy conditions and that for my purposes in this chapter it is basic legitimacy conditions that matter. It is a happy advantage of this point that basic legitimacy conditions are rather more likely to generate an overlapping consensus among different theoretical accounts. Examples of such basic legitimacy conditions are provided by Henry Shue, *Basic Rights: Subsistence, Affluence and US Foreign Policy* (2nd edition) (Princeton, NJ: Princeton University Press, 1996); John Rawls, *The Law of Peoples* (Cambridge, MA: Harvard University Press, 2001); and Miller, *National Responsibility and Global Justice*.

also for the international order of states as a global regime of governance—or, more precisely, it does so if we grant the practical possibility of a global regime of governance in which these basic rights can, in general, be universally protected. It does so since it implies that this current regime itself lacks either the disposition or capability to act effectively (in ways compatible with its normative ordering) to ensure that states are capable of, and disposed to, act in accordance with the basic norm of state legitimacy.

It might be objected here that in the case of states, we can set up a contrast between rogue states and failing states, on the one hand, and well-functioning states, on the other hand, because we know that some states can satisfy the basic legitimacy requirements in respect of their own citizens, but in the case of global orders, we lack the relevant contrast. How do we know that it is possible that there can be a global order disposed to secure the basic rights of all human beings that is capable of doing so—or vice versa? Is there a *plausible world* in which the order of global governance is such as to protect basic human rights effectively? I cannot offer here a full account of the relationships of governance, norms, actors, incentives, and opportunities in our contemporary political order in the way that would be needed to secure this counterfactual claim, but two points can support it.[13] The first, offering indirect support, is that the judgment that we can plausibly achieve a global order generally characterized by universal human rights protection is a widely shared judgment (indeed, it is presupposed by almost all contemporary theories of global justice). The second, offering more direct support, is that the trajectory of the transformations of global governance since 1945, in which the diffusion and effectivity of human rights norms has increased dramatically, gives us rational grounds to affirm the existence of such a plausible world.[14]

Supposing then that we can reasonably take human rights abuses to pose legitimacy problems for both the state in which abuse occurs and the international order of states, we can reflect that, considered generally, such legitimacy problems require that this global regime of governance develop its disposition and capabilities for acting effectively to ensure states conform to the norm,[15] where doing so may require adapting its character as a normative order. How the regime meets this requirement will depend on how it ranks the

---

[13] By "plausible world" I refer to that set of possible worlds that are relatively close to our own in the sense that there is a causal path from where we are to such a possible world that agents in our world can feasibly take.

[14] For an already classic study of the power of human rights, see Thomas Risse, Stephen C. Ropp, and Kathryn Sikkink, *The Power of Human Rights: International Norms and Domestic Change* (Cambridge: Cambridge University Press, 1999).

[15] These may include what we, narrowly, refer to as compliance mechanisms such as sanction regimes, but also mechanisms such as funding capacity-building, supporting democratization, etc., which we have good reason to believe facilitate conformity to the norm.

governmental norms that comprise it. Thus, for example, if states collectively take sovereignty/non-intervention to be the *grundnorm* of this regime of governance, this will be consequential for the types of institutions and practices characteristic of the regime.

However, even a well-developed regime of governance is likely to confront non-compliance problems, and committing to such disposition and capacity-building projects is not sufficient to deal with legitimacy problems in their concrete immediacy. What is additionally needed are what one might call "legitimacy repair" mechanisms, that is, institutional practices that act effectively to ensure that the basic security, liberty, and welfare of those subject to a non-conforming state are protected to the greatest degree possible without breaching the constitutive norms of the regime. Appropriately designed, such legitimacy-repair mechanisms can perform not only a reparative role, but also a role as governmental mechanisms for acting on the conduct of non-conforming states. The institution of refugeehood can be profitably seen as one such mechanism.

On the one hand, this institution provides a route by which a specific class of those who are subject to non-conforming states can be provided with protection in a way that is compatible with the *grundnorm* of state sovereignty/non-intervention. Currently this takes the form of, first, the duty of non-refoulement by the state of application and, second, the entitlement of the refugee to seek asylum. In this respect, at least insofar as it functions effectively, the institution of refugeehood plays a legitimacy-repair role. On the other hand, the institution of refugeehood also acts as a specific governmental mechanism. It is a communicative act through which the international order of states acknowledges its responsibility to, and for, the human population subject to its rule (and does so in a way that entrenches the norm of state responsibility precisely by asserting the exceptionality of the refugee). But it is also the medium of specific communicative acts in that, as Matthew Price has argued:

> A decision to grant asylum rests on a judgment that another state has persecuted; such a judgment is by definition critical; granting asylum, thereby, entails the expression of condemnation; and that condemnation aims at reforming the abusive state.[16]

In the remainder of this chapter, I want to develop this understanding of the normative grounds and character of the international refugee regime by bringing this rational reconstruction of its basic normative character to bear on a series of questions addressing who should be entitled to refugee status

---

[16] Matthew E. Price, *Rethinking Asylum: History, Purpose, Limits* (Cambridge: Cambridge University Press, 2009), p. 71.

(Section 13.1), the distribution of responsibility for refugee protection, assuming full compliance (Section 13.2), and in circumstances of partial compliance (Section 13.3).

13.1 Who is a Refugee?

In this section, I will develop a "political legitimacy" account of refugeehood. I will do so by working through three rival accounts of who should be entitled to refugee status. We can take up this issue by laying out an account that begins from a position somewhat akin to the political legitimacy view being developed in this chapter in focusing on the basic political bond between state and citizens. The starting point here is the 1951 Convention criteria of refugeehood previously cited. This basic legal definition involves the following assumptions:

a) a bond of trust, loyalty, protection, and assistance between citizen and state constitutes the normal basis of political society;

b) in the case of the refugee, this bond has been severed;

c) persecution and alienage are always the physical manifestations of this severed bond;

d) these manifestations are necessary and sufficient conditions for determining refugeehood.[17]

But this definition, it is cogently argued, is inadequate for the following reasons:

1) Persecution is a sufficient but not necessary condition for the severing of the normal political bond—it is one manifestation of a broader phenomenon: the absence of state protection of citizens' basic needs.

2) Alienage is also not a necessary condition, being one subset of the broader category: the physical access of the international community to the unprotected person.[18]

This position, what we may call the "basic needs" view, leads to a definition which is taken to provide a more defensible specification of criteria for refugeehood: "One whose basic needs are unprotected by their country of origin, who has no remaining recourse other than to seek international restitution of their needs, and who are so situated that international assistance is possible."[19] Both elements of this reformulation are controversial. An alternative

---

[17] Andrew E. Shacknove, "Who is a Refugee?" *Ethics* 95:2 (1985), 274–84, p. 275.
[18] See Shacknove, "Who is a Refugee?," p. 277.   [19] Shacknove, "Who is a Refugee?," p. 252.

view, what we may call the "alienage account," adopts the criticism of the necessity of persecution but retains the criterion of alienage:

> ... those people in need of a new state of residence, either temporarily or permanently, because if forced to return home or remain where they are they would—as a result or either the brutality or inadequacy of their state—be persecuted or seriously jeopardise their physical security or vital subsistence needs.[20]

Those who defend the alienage account argue that such a view does not take us far from the actual practices of most liberal democratic states but also insists that

> refugeehood *is*, in one vital respect, conceptually related to migration; what distinguishes the refugee from other foreigners in need is that he or she is in need of the protection afforded by short or long-term asylum (i.e., residence in a new state) because there is no reasonable prospect of that person finding protection any other way.[21]

By contrast, others have rejected both the criticisms of current international law on the basis of a complex mix of normative and empirical arguments in developing what we may call the "surrogate membership" view. For my current purposes, two arguments are particularly relevant. The first argument is predicated on a historical reconstruction of intellectual arguments for asylum as surrogate membership in which it is shown to be conceived as an institution through which a state granting asylum is engaged in expressing its commitment to liberal political values in its condemnation of the persecuting state (a condemnation which marks the first step in a range of actions the liberal state may choose to take and which, if unheeded, may lead all the way to humanitarian intervention). On this view, granting asylum is not a palliative but an expressive act. The second argument points to the normative salience of the distinction between the dispositional and capability dimensions of the norm that a state is responsible to, and for, its own citizens by taking up Rawls' stylized distinction between outlaw states and burdened societies. The point here concerns the distinctiveness of persecution: "Citizens of burdened societies lack protection of their basic rights, but they retain their standing as members. The appropriate stance of outsiders to burdened societies is to lend assistance, not to condemn their failings. Asylum is an inappropriate tool for addressing the needs of those fleeing burdened societies."[22] By contrast, this view claims that asylum as a mode of surrogate membership in another state is the appropriate response for dealing with those of its citizens targeted by outlaw states as states which flout "the requirements of

---

[20] Gibney, *The Ethics and Politics of Asylum*, p. 7.
[21] Gibney, *The Ethics and Politics of Asylum*, p. 8.
[22] Price, *Rethinking Asylum*, p. 73.

international legitimacy by violating basic human rights—such as the per-emptory human rights norms recognized by customary international law" since it provides these persecuted citizens whose very standing as members is being denied with protection "in a manner that also expresses the condemnation that is deserved."[23]

How are we to respond to the debate between the basic needs, alienage, and surrogate membership accounts on refugeehood? We can start by noting that, for all its clarity, the surrogate membership account fails adequately to address its own implicit presuppositions concerning "the requirements of international legitimacy." We can see this by noting that while it is perfectly appropriate to argue that states have a duty to provide assistance to burdened societies in the same way that they have a duty to provide asylum to the persecuted victims of outlaw states, this argument does not lead to the conclusion that refugee status should not be granted to those who flee burdened societies where this is their most practicable option for securing their basic rights. Consider that in cases of environmental disaster or famine or civil war, the capabilities and/or disposition of international society may be such that it is both rational and reasonable for those situated such that they can best secure their basic rights by crossing borders to do so, and it is certainly right that they be granted at least short-term refuge if "there is no reasonable prospect of that person finding protection any other way."[24] It is true that they may well not need *asylum* in the classic sense reconstructed by the surrogate membership view (although this reconstruction is itself controversial). But they do require *refuge*, even if it is temporary in duration, and the principle of non-refoulement, as itself arguably a peremptory norm of customary international law (at least in relation to Convention refugees),[25] is an instrument by means of which the international order of states can effectively bind itself (via a duty on each of its members) to try to ensure that such refuge is provided. Moreover, in providing for such forms of refuge, the institution of refugeehood is still playing an expressive role in the sense that (a) it is a communicative act acknowledging the responsibility of international society to, and for, those subject to its governance and (b) it is a medium of specific communicative acts in which (both blameworthy and no-fault) failures of this regime of governance in relation to the norm of being disposed to, and capable of, assisting burdened societies are acknowledged. In this regard, the distinction between the basic needs and alienage accounts which critics take to offer a merely palliative conception of refugeehood, and the surrogate membership account which sees asylum as a distinctively expressive act, is

---

[23] Price, *Rethinking Asylum*, p. 73.   [24] Gibney, *The Ethics and Politics of Asylum*, p. 8.
[25] See Feller et al., *Refugee Protection in International Law*, Part 2: *Non-refoulement*, for a fuller discussion of this question concerning the peremptory status of non-refoulement.

simply untenable since both positions are reparative and expressive. What the surrogate membership account does do, however, is provide a justification for the claim that the communicative clarity of the institution of refugeehood would be improved if it allowed for a distinction between grants of *asylum* and grants of *refuge* (both of which are necessarily predicated on the principle of non-refoulement).

What of the insistence on a conceptual relationship between refugeehood and migration advanced by the alienage account? Consider two different types of scenario. In the first, a burdened society is incapable of securing basic rights for its citizens in the face of, say, famine or environment degradation and calls for international assistance. In the second, the basic rights of the citizens of a burdened society are violated because the domestic governmental order has broken under conditions of, say, civil war and the international community has constructed "safe havens" within the borders of the state to protect its non-combatant citizens. Both of these scenarios would fit the basic needs account criteria for granting refugeehood, whereas in neither case would citizens who remain within the borders of their state be entitled to refugeehood on the alienage account.[26] On the political legitimacy account that I am developing, however, there is a salient difference between the two scenarios which is not picked up by either the basic needs or the alienage account. One set of cases is that in which the "home" state is acting effectively to secure its citizens basic rights precisely by calling for international assistance in order to supplement its capabilities, and then acts effectively to build its capabilities with such international assistance. Another set of cases is that in which the international community is required to act as a surrogate for the state in order to secure the basic rights of those threatened.[27] In the former cases, the international community *supplements* the state; in the latter cases, the international community *replaces* the state. This distinction points, on the political legitimacy account I am offering, to the crucial distinguishing feature of the refugee being conceptually tied not to migration but to the requirement that acting effectively to secure the basic rights of those threatened entails that the international order of states stand in loco civitatis. Thus, the answer to the question "who is a refugee?" runs thus:

[26] It might be objected here that we have a general duty of assistance to internally displaced persons, but this is distinct from the duty to provide refuge or asylum which does require alienage. However, the case of "safe havens" denotes the international provision of refuge through the construction of legal spaces within the state that do not belong (for the relevant purposes) to the state within whose boundaries they fall but also do not involve alienage in the sense of entering the jurisdiction of another state. I am grateful to Francis Cheneval for pressing me on this point.

[27] I am grateful to Matthew Gibney for pressing me on this issue. It is in response to his criticisms that I have added the emphasis on the need for the home state to act effectively over time to build its capabilities, in order to register the point that perpetual supplementation by the international community without a prospect of the state being able to stand by itself becomes surrogacy by the international community.

one whose basic rights are unprotected by their state and can only be protected through recourse to the international society of states (via a political agency such as another state or international organization) acting in loco civitatis, where it can so act without breaching the constitutive norms of the regime of governance.

Such a view not only presents the institution of refugeehood as playing both reparative and expressive roles but also identifies the central connection between this institution and the political legitimacy of the international order of states. First, this account identifies refugeehood as both a legitimacy-repair mechanism and a governmental technique designed to bring states in conformity with the normative presuppositions of the regime of global governance. Second, it provides a coherent way of specifying who should be entitled to refugeehood such that the institution can effectively play these two roles. Third, it is parsimonious since it only appeals to commitments that are basic to the normative constitution of the international order of states as a regime of global governance.

13.2 Responsibility for Refugees

Let us turn now to the topic of responsibility for refugees. As we have noted, the institution of refugeehood is itself necessarily conceived as a response to a condition of partial compliance to the basic norm of state legitimacy, a response which acknowledges the collective responsibility of the international order of states for acting effectively to secure the basic rights of each and every person subject to the rule of this regime. Moreover, we have already noted the centrality of the principle of non-refoulement for the current refugee regime. One effect of this principle is that the current regime places no restrictions on the numbers of refugees that a state is obligated not to return to their own state or send to another state where they would lack protection for their basic rights. This does not entail that refugees have a right to asylum in the state to which they make application (a possibility advocated, discussed, and rejected in the drafting of both Article 14 of the UNDHR and the 1950 Convention on Refugees). On the contrary, as long as the duty of non-refoulement is not breached, states can come to bilateral, multilateral, or omnilateral arrangements with one another concerning the distributions of refugees and responsibilities for refugees.[28] Even if, in practice, the state of

---

[28] The debate concerning the appropriate institutional form of the international refugee regime has been structured most prominently in recent years around the reform proposals put forward by James C. Hathaway and R. Alexander Neve, "Making International Refugee Law Relevant Again: A Proposal for Collectivized and Solution-Oriented Protection," *Harvard Human Rights Journal* 10 (1997), 155–87, and Peter H. Schuck, "Refugee Burden-Sharing: A Modest Proposal," *Yale Journal of International Law* 22 (1997), 243–97.

application is the default state of asylum, this point has two important implications. First, responsibility for effective refugee protection lies squarely with
the international order of states. Second, this responsibility is specified by the
current regime in a way that is maximally consistent with respect for the norm
of state sovereignty. It is up to states, collectively, to work out terms of
reasonable cooperation for the fair distribution of refugees. If, or to the extent
that, they fail to do so, the duty of non-refoulement serves as a default
condition of regime legitimacy by requiring that the states to whom applications are made provide protection. But what would a fair distribution of
refugees involve?

The first question to address—and one often overlooked—concerns the
distribution of responsibility for the condition of partial compliance. This
question concerns, first of all, whether full compliance is a plausible option
in the sense that (a) all states (supplemented by international assistance where
necessary) have or can plausibly develop the capabilities requisite for conformity with the norm of states' responsibility for their citizens, and (b) all
states (supported by international actions where necessary) can reasonably
be expected to possess or acquire the disposition to act in accordance with
this norm.

Suppose, *ex hypothesi*, that full compliance is a plausible option but that a
few rogue states do not comply and that some (perhaps all) states are still
vulnerable to the actions (or side effects of the actions) of these rogue states or
to environmental or other disasters that have the propensity to be refugee-
producing. How should responsibility for refugees be distributed? In such
circumstances, a reasonable basic rule for generating a norm of fair distribution of burdens would have recourse to the remedial capacities of states, where
the salient capacities may be of diverse kinds which are differentially distributed. There are three key capacities. The first is *proximity*: it is easier to reach
the territories of nearby states, to maintain contact with those left behind, and
to return as and when the conditions are appropriate. The second is *integrative
capacity*: different states have different capacities for integrating refugees into
their societies and providing protection depending on factors such as population density, immigration history, and strength of rights and welfare protection.[29] The third is *wealth*: states are differently situated in terms of their
ability to bear the economic costs of providing refugee protection. Any norm
of fair distribution will have to involve a balanced weighting of these elements
that either integrates them to generate a single proportional system of distribution of refugees or treats the dimensions of presence and finance separately,
and generates distinct systems of proportionality under each aspect. Decisions

---

[29] A superb account of the complexities of "integrative capacity" can be found in Gibney, *The
Ethics and Politics of Asylum*, pp. 213–28.

concerning which of these options to adopt (and furthermore specific features of institutional design) can legitimately encompass issues such as ethnic or linguistic affinity and historical connections between states where these are likely to facilitate the effective functioning of such a refugee regime. (The basic rule should, of course, be qualified in contexts in which particular states bear specific outcome responsibility for the production of refugees in other states. Thus, for example, states that have participated in the recent war in Afghanistan have particular responsibility for refugees produced by this conflict.)

However, since it is barely credible that full compliance in the specified sense is—or is likely to be—a plausible option in respect of either the capability condition or the dispositional condition without significant reform of the economic, financial, legal, and political practices of the current global order, we face a somewhat different set of issues for generating criteria of fair distribution. If we confront, as I believe, a "normal" condition of partial compliance as a product—most plausibly, a side effect—of norms and practices held in place by relations of power and giving rise to positions of advantage and disadvantage, then appropriate inputs for determining a norm of fair distribution are provided by the relevant distributions of power and of advantage. In other words, any reasonable norm of fair distribution will be a product of considering who acts, and with what degree of power, to support the norms and practices that generate a "normal" condition of partial compliance, and who benefits, and to what extent, from the operation of these norms and practices. This is a complex empirical question, but since distributions of power and wealth are likely to enjoy a reasonable degree of correlation, a first approximation might have fair distribution of refugees as tracking the relative GDP per capita of states.

Recall at this point that on the picture that I am presenting, states are collectively responsible for the legitimacy of the global regime of governance that is comprised by the international order of states, and that the institution of refugeehood is both a legitimacy-repair and governmental mechanism within this regime which is structured by the *grundnorm* of sovereignty/non-intervention that orders it. It is precisely because the institution of refugeehood takes this form that the question of the fair distribution of the burdens of refugee protection among states arises. Notice though that there are two further implications of this point. First, under conditions of partial compliance with the basic norm of state sovereignty, the legitimacy of the global regime of governance is dependent on a legitimate and effective international refugee regime since the absence of such legitimate and effective refugee regime entails that the legitimacy-repair work remains, at least partially, undone. Second, while states that do not to comply with the basic norm of state legitimacy, despite having the capabilities to do so, are, thereby, illegitimate and should not enjoy full standing in the international order of states (i.e., their conduct can justifiably be subject to sanctions), states that do not do their fair share of refugee protection also suffer from a legitimacy deficit and similarly, although not to the same extent, should not be treated as members in good standing of the international society of states. In other words, a state which insists that it has done its fair share in relation to the legitimacy of the international society of states simply by ensuring the basic rights of its own citizens and, hence, has no obligations to accept refugees (or has an obligation to accept refugees only when the costs are low, assuming this is less than its fair share) is itself exposed to a second-order legitimacy problem. That remains the case even if it acts in an exemplary way in relation to its own citizens. In addition to the first order legitimacy problems of rogue states and burdened societies, there are the second order legitimacy problems of *selfish states*.

Two additional issues arise at this juncture. The first is what I will call *the political indeterminacy of fair responsibility*, the second is the issue of *limits of responsibility to refugees*.

On the legitimacy view I am developing, states that comply with the basic norm of state legitimacy have a duty to take their fair share of refugees. However, it is also the case that, under the current refugee regime, there is no scheme in place that determines what would count as fair shares and, as many have rightly pointed out, there is considerable scope for reasonable disagreement about what constitutes a "fair share" in these circumstances. The distinctive character of the legitimacy account, however, can be brought out by contrasting it to one prominent response to this condition, what we may call the "liberal sovereignty" account. As one of its most articulate defenders argues, the liberal sovereignty account claims:

> Realistically...states have to be given considerable autonomy to decide how best to respond to particular asylum applications: beside the refugee's own choice, they are entitled to consider the overall number of applications they face, the demands that temporary or long-term accommodation of refugees will place on existing citizens, and whether there exists any special link between the refugee and the host community...The best hope is that over time conventions will emerge that distribute responsibilities in such a way that refugees from particular places become the special responsibility of one state in particular (or a coalition of states). There can be no guarantee, however, that every bona fide refugee will find a state willing to take her in. The final judgment must rest with the members of the receiving state, who may decide that they have already done their fair share of refugee resettlement.[30]

There are, of course, a wide range of considerations concerning the propensity of political agents, including states, to bias with respect to their own interests

---

[30] Miller, *National Responsibility and Global Justice*, pp. 226–7.

even when endeavoring to act rightly, but while very important, these are not fundamental to the theoretical issue at hand so let us set them aside. Rather, to get at the core issue, suppose (a) that all states who comply with the basic legitimacy norm engage in such good faith efforts, but, perhaps because of the different reasonable interpretations of fair shares that they adopt, some refugees are left unprotected and (b) that protecting these remaining refugees would not take any state to the point that the basic rights of their own citizens are not protected. The contrast between the legitimacy account and the liberal sovereignty account is that whereas the latter leads to the conclusion that states have few stringent obligations to the remaining refugees ("there can be no guarantee, however, that every bona fide refugee will find a state willing to take her in," as the claim cited above puts it), the former is more demanding. It argues that while we may accept that these states have done their best to work out their fair shares, they have not been successful in doing so (which is hardly surprising under the circumstances) and have a duty of legitimacy to distribute the remaining refugees among themselves. This is subject only to the qualification that if providing protection to more refugees entails that a state cannot protect the basic rights of its own citizens, it can at that point justifiably refuse to take more.[31] The view that each state has a right to determine, even in good faith, when its responsibilities of justice to refugees are exhausted, has the unfortunate consequence that effectively it makes the question of whether a given refugee is owed protection as a matter of justice into a matter of luck. The dilemma that confronts the liberal sovereignty view is that it wants to make both of the following claims:

1) There is a duty of justice to refugees to provide them with protection of their human rights.

2) All states may have exhausted their duties of justice to refugees and there are still, tragically, unprotected refugees left.

---

[31] Notably, Miller appears at times to adopt a view that may be closer to the position that arises from the legitimacy stance. Thus, for example, he writes:

Recall . . . : the duty we are considering is a duty either to prevent rights violations being inflicted by third parties . . . or to secure the rights of people where others have failed in their responsibility. Such duties are weaker than the negative duty not to violate human rights oneself, and arguably weaker than the positive duty to secure the rights of those we may be specifically responsible for protecting. At the limit, therefore, we may face tragic cases where the human rights of the refugees clash with a legitimate claim by the receiving state that its obligations to admit refugees has already been exhausted (Miller, *National Responsibility and Global Justice*, pp. 226–7).

However, the argument is unclear because the scope of "the rights of those we may be specifically responsible for protecting" is not specified. Miller's position could equally be strongly contrasting to the legitimacy view if the scope of "the rights of those we may be specifically responsible for protecting" extends beyond basic rights, since this would entail that states could privilege nonbasic rights of their citizens over the basic rights of noncitizens.

These claims are incompatible because it is not intelligible to claim that there is a duty of justice to the unprotected refugees but that there is no one who owes a duty of justice to the unprotected refugees since there cannot be a legal duty independent of a legal person (or persons) on whom that duty falls. By contrast, the legitimacy account presents the duty of legitimacy as extending to cover each and every refugee. It acknowledges that while access to protection by states may be a matter of luck in extreme circumstances, precisely because there is a duty of legitimacy to all refugees, this condition represents a legitimacy crisis for the international order of states. This implies that, in the absence of urgent action to redress this condition, the unprotected refugees are not obligated to accept the authority of the normative regime of governance that is the international order of states. Rather they are free to act in ways that breach those norms to the extent that it is necessary for them to do so in order to protect themselves. They would, for example, be justified in ignoring legalities of entry into another state. The contrast with the liberal sovereignty view is stark. Whereas that account collapses into a claim of tragedy and, thereby, elides the question of the responsibility of states for the conditions under which this tragic situation occurs, the political legitimacy account draws attention to that responsibility and to the fact that the claim of this regime of global governance to legitimate authority hangs on its claim to ensure effective protection of the basic rights of human beings. To the extent that this regime fails to meet the basic legitimacy requirements and fails to take effective action to adapt itself in order to meet these requirements, its claim to legitimacy is undermined and the norms through which it governs (such as the right of states to regulate entry to their own borders) cease to have normatively binding force for those subject to them. This, in the first instance, means those whose protection is unaddressed, but the implications extend further—thus, for example, citizens of states who construct or support an "underground railway" or "people-smuggling system" in order to try to ensure protection for the unprotected refugees could reasonably claim that their actions are justified by the legitimacy failure of the regime of global governance.

13.3 Responsibility and Partial Compliance

Let me turn finally to address the issue of what additional obligations, if any, arise for states that comply with their (initial) duties to refugees in contexts in which there is only partial compliance of the relevant states with these duties, that is, if you like, a world in which rogue states and/or burdened societies as well as selfish states are all present. We can start by noting that in the same way that rogue states and burdened societies create a legitimacy problem for the international order of states, so too do selfish states. Hence, addressing this problem generally requires developing effective governmental mechanisms for supporting compliance with the norm of equitable distribution of refugee protection, but it also requires legitimacy-repair mechanisms that address the problem in its immediacy. This entails norm-abiding states (acting individually, as groups, or as a full collective) protecting more refugees than they would be obligated to under conditions of full compliance with the norm of refugee protection.[32]

In the face of this claim, it is not hard to imagine the following objection arising: how can it be justified that norm-abiding states who take their fair share of refugees be required to shoulder extra burdens as a result of some states failing to abide by the norm of refugee protection? Notice though that this objection has just the same form as one we addressed earlier: why should norm-abiding states who care for their own citizens properly be required to shoulder extra burdens (i.e., take in refugees) as a result of some states failing to abide by the norm of state legitimacy? And the answer also has the same form: states are collectively responsible for the legitimacy of the global regime of governance and, consequently, for addressing the legitimacy problems of this regime. Thus, states who do not comply with their first order duty to protect the basic rights of their citizens or their second order duty to protect a fair share of refugees or their third order duty to protect their fair share of "surplus" refugees are not only contributing to legitimacy problems for the international order of states but themselves suffer from first, second, or third order legitimacy deficits. These in turn both affect the normative grounds of their claim to authority and render them liable to (different) sanction regimes. It is, of course, the case that these duties are ordered in terms of their significance; breaching or neglecting the first order duty to secure the basic rights of their own citizens is a more serious legitimacy deficit than failing to protect their fair share of refugees, which is, in turn, more serious than failing to shoulder their surplus share of unprotected refugees. But all three represent legitimacy problems for states and the international order of states.

It is true that, as responses to distinct contexts of partial compliance, both the duty to admit one's fair share of refugees and the duty to admit refugees beyond one's fair share involve distributive unfairness. However, we should note that the forms that this unfairness takes are made possible by the institutional structure and normative ordering of the regime of global

---

[32] The elements of protection—presence and cost—may of course be distributed differently over different states.

governance comprised of the international order of states, most notably the *grundnorm* of state sovereignty/non-intervention. Thus, for example, the establishment of an international organization with enforcement capability for the fair distribution of refugees could resolve the problem of distributive unfairness raised by the duty to admit refugees beyond one's fair share, while a more fundamental reordering of this regime of global governance around a *grundnorm* of basic human rights could plausibly resolve the problem of partial compliance that requires an international refugee regime. To say this is not to advocate either reform, it is simply to draw attention to the point that to the extent that states are the primary agents in the reproduction of the current normative ordering of global governance, it is states that bear collective responsibility for the possibility of these forms of distributive unfairness. This does not, to repeat, mean that states bear equal responsibility since they may be differentially capable of supporting or adjusting the norms of governance in which they are situated. Rather it implies that states that act to reproduce this regime and/or are relatively advantaged by its current normative ordering have primary responsibility for bearing the burdens that arise as recurrent by-products of this structure of governance. Notice that this does not imply that states who act to transform this regime and/or are relatively disadvantaged by the current governmental order are relieved of responsibility, only that it is distributed in ways that acknowledge that they do not bear the same degree of responsibility as those states who powerfully support or benefit from the existing regime of governance.

Put another way, the duty to secure the basic rights of the human population that falls on the international order of states does not lapse where some states fail to comply with their duties. On the contrary, this generates a general duty on the international society of states to develop more effective governance mechanisms as well as specific duties on states which do observe their duties to take up the slack in the meantime, to perform the "legitimation work" left undone by the non-compliance of other states. Reflecting on this point may reasonably raise the worry that our current regime of global governance is insufficiently responsive to issues of compliance and non-compliance, and that the states who comply with their duties are not sufficiently powerful to institute effective compliance mechanisms, to transform our regime of global governance—and this may, in turn, entail that states are not rationally motivated to comply with their duties. If so, this points to a deeper legitimation problem with this regime of global governance which is liable to have application beyond the international refugee regime and raises the question of whether the claim to legitimate authority of this regime and the agents (states) who are authorized to act in various ways by it can be sustained.

13.4 Conclusion

The point of this chapter has been to provide an account of the normative grounds and character of the institution of refugeehood. I have defended a "political legitimacy" account of refugeehood, drawing out the implications of a view that sees the legitimacy of the state as intrinsically related to the legitimacy of the international society of states. Here, states are collectively responsible for acting effectively to ensure the legitimacy of this global regime of governance, and for ensuring that everyone subject to this regime of governance is entitled to the satisfaction of basic rights. I have argued that the institution of refugeehood should be regarded as a legitimacy-repair mechanism and that we should specify the refugee in terms of one who requires that the international community act in loco civitatis. In addressing issues of responsibility for refugees, I have argued that states characterized by first order legitimacy have a second order duty of legitimacy to take their fair share of refugees and the states characterized by second order legitimacy have a third order duty to take their fair share of "surplus" refugees. I have also argued that in the context of unrepaired breakdowns of legitimacy of the international society of states, refugees are no longer politically bound by the norms of this regime of governance and would be, for example, justified in entering illegally into any state where they have grounds for believing this act would better ensure the protection of their basic rights—and citizens of such states would be justified in helping them do so.[33]

References

Benhabib, Seyla, *The Rights of Others: Aliens, Residents and Citizens* (Cambridge: Cambridge University Press, 2004).
Feller, Erika, Volker Türk, and Frances Nicholson (eds.), *Refugee Protection in International Law: UNHCR's Global Consultations on International Protection* (Cambridge: Cambridge University Press, 2003).

---

[33] I am grateful to Chris Armstrong, Matthew Gibney, and Andy Mason for very rapid and helpful responses to a first draft of this chapter. The distant origins of this chapter lie in a presentation at the Department of International Development/Centre for Refugee Studies at the University of Oxford in 2007 (and which was conceived as a partial response to the argument of Matthew Gibney's *The Ethics and Politics of Asylum*, so I am doubly grateful to Matt for providing the initial inspiration and occasion). A range of other important works on refugees have been published since then and I am grateful to Lea and Sarah for providing the incentive and opportunity to work out my own stance towards these current debates on the refugee regime and obligations to refugees, as well as their detailed editorial comments on the first draft of this chapter. I would also like to thank those present at the Cambridge Conference for their comments and feedback. A version of this chapter was also presented to the Politics Department at the University of St. Gallen and I am particularly grateful to Francis Chevenal, Lisa Herzog, and Andrew Walton for their probing questions and suggestions.

Gibney, Matthew, *The Ethics and Politics of Asylum: Liberal Democracy and the Response to Refugees* (Cambridge: Cambridge University Press, 2004).

Goodwin-Gill, Guy S. and Jane McAdam, *The Refugee in International Law* (Oxford: Oxford University Press, 2007).

Haddad, Emma, *The Refugee in International Society: Between Sovereigns* (Cambridge: Cambridge University Press, 2008).

Hathaway, James and R. Alexander Neve, "Making International Refugee Law Relevant Again: A Proposal for Collectivized and Solution-Oriented Protection," *Harvard Human Rights Journal* 10 (1997), 155–87.

Hindess, Barry, "Divide and Rule: the International Character of Modern Citizenship," *European Journal of Social Theory* 1:1 (1998), 57–70.

May, Larry, *Sharing Responsibility* (Chicago: Chicago University Press, 1992).

Miller, David, *National Responsibility and Global Justice* (Oxford: Oxford University Press, 2007).

Price, Matthew E., *Rethinking Asylum: History, Purpose, Limits* (Cambridge: Cambridge University Press, 2009).

Rawls, John, *The Law of Peoples* (Cambridge, MA: Harvard University Press, 2001).

Risse, Thomas, Stephen C. Ropp, and Kathryn Sikkink, *The Power of Human Rights: International Norms and Domestic Change* (Cambridge: Cambridge University Press, 1999).

Schuck, Peter H., "Refugee Burden-Sharing: A Modest Proposal," *Yale Journal of International Law* 22 (1997), 243–97.

Shacknove, Andrew E.,"Who is a Refugee?" *Ethics* 95:2 (1985), 274–84.

Shue, Henry, *Basic Rights: Subsistence, Affluence and US Foreign Policy*, 2nd edn. (New Haven, CT: Princeton University Press, 1996).

Soguk, Nevzat, *States and Strangers: Refugees and the Displacements of Statecraft* (Minnesota: University of Minnesota Press, 1999).

Tuitt, Patricia, *False Images: Law's Construction of the Refugee* (London: Pluto Press, 1996).

Tully, James, *Public Philosophy in a New Key*, Volume 1 (Cambridge: Cambridge University Press, 2008).

Index

Footnotes and table are indicated by an italic *n* and *t* following the page number.

Printed and bound by CPI Group (UK) Ltd, Croydon, CR0 4YY